CRITICAL ROLE

# VOX MACHINA

## ORIGINS

W9-AAB-742

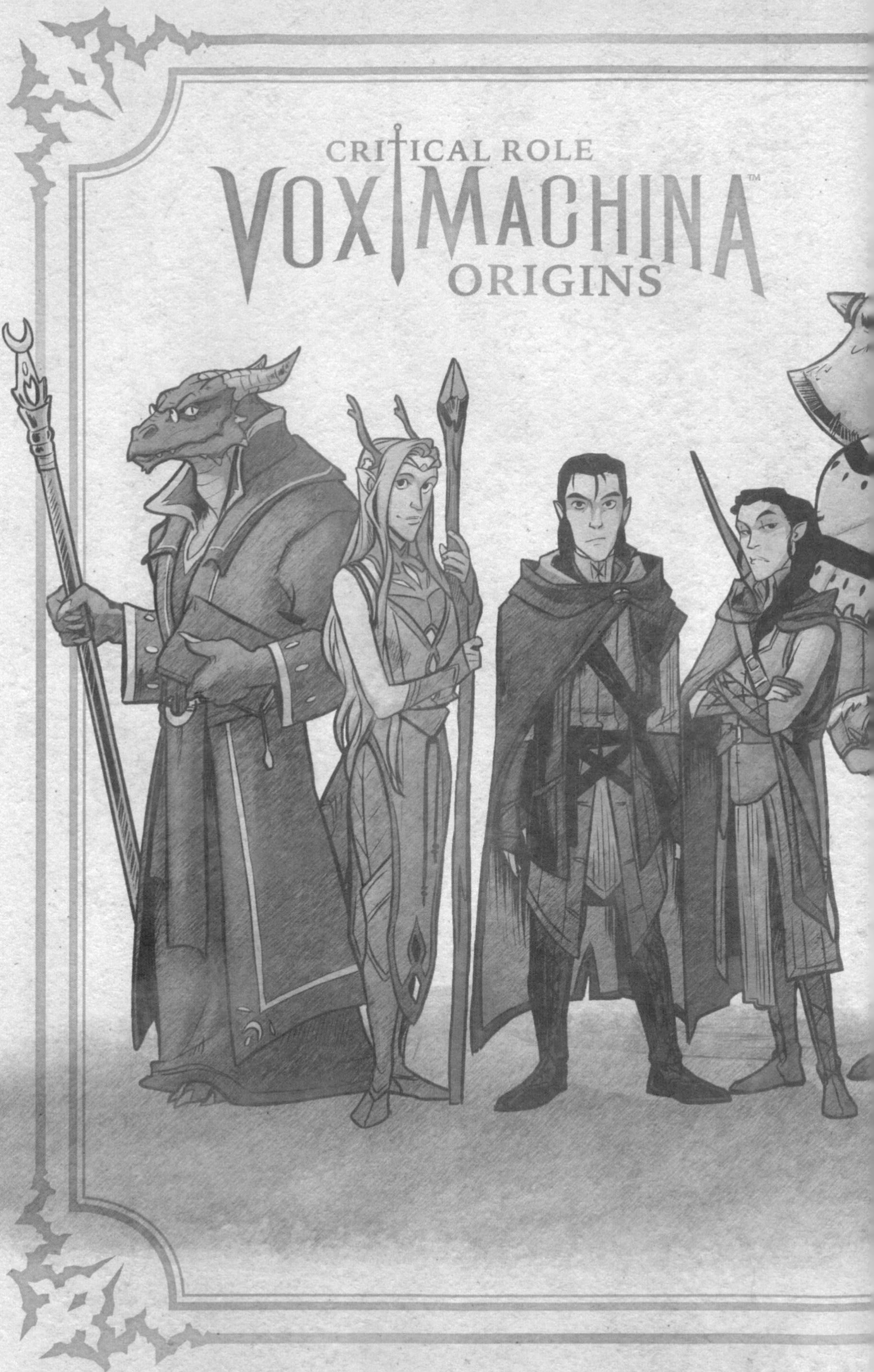
CRITICAL ROLE
VOX MACHINA™
ORIGINS

Critical Role Created by

# MATTHEW MERCER

Characters Created by the Cast of

# CRITICAL ROLE

Story
**MATTHEW COLVILLE &
MATTHEW MERCER**

Script
**MATTHEW COLVILLE**

Art
**OLIVIA SAMSON**

Layouts
**CHRIS KAWAGIWA**

Colors and Lettering
**CHRIS NORTHROP**

Color Assistants
**TRAVIS AMES
CASSIE ANDERSON**

Cover Art
**STJEPAN ŠEJIĆ**

Map of Stilben
**KENDRA WELLS**

# DARK HORSE BOOKS

MAIN LIBRARY
Champaign Public Library
200 West Green Street
Champaign, Illinois 61820-5193

President and Publisher
**MIKE RICHARDSON**

Editors
**F. AVEDON ARCADIO BARRERA II and RACHEL ROBERTS**

Assistant Editor
**JENNY BLENK**

Designers
**ETHAN KIMBERLING and CINDY CACEREZ-SPRAGUE**

Digital Art Technicians
**CHRISTINA McKENZIE, CHRISTIANNE GILLENARDO-GOUDREAU,
and SAMANTHA HUMMER**

⁂

Special thanks to **LAURA BAILEY**, **TALIESIN JAFFE**, **ASHLEY JOHNSON**, **LIAM O'BRIEN**, **MARISHA RAY**, **SAM RIEGEL**, and **TRAVIS WILLINGHAM** at Critical Role and to **KARI YADRO** at Dark Horse Comics.

Facebook.com/DarkHorseComics
Twitter.com/DarkHorseComics

Facebook.com/CriticalRole
Twitter.com/CriticalRole
Twitch.tv/CriticalRole
Youtube.com/CriticalRole

Comicshoplocator.com

CRITICAL ROLE: VOX MACHINA ORIGINS

CRITICAL ROLE © 2019 Critical Role Productions, LLC. All Rights Reserved. Critical Role, its logo, and all characters featured herein and the distinctive likenesses thereof and all related elements are ™ and © Critical Role Productions, LLC. All Rights Reserved. Dark Horse Books® and the Dark Horse logo are trademarks of Dark Horse Comics LLC, registered in various categories and countries. All rights reserved. No portion of this publication may be reproduced or transmitted, in any form or by any means, without the express written permission of Dark Horse Comics LLC. Names, characters, places, and incidents featured in this publication either are the product of the author's imagination or are used fictitiously. Any resemblance to actual persons (living or dead), events, institutions, or locales, without satiric intent, is coincidental.

This volume collects issues #1 through #6 of the Dark Horse comic-book series *Critical Role: Vox Machina Origins*.

Published by Dark Horse Books
A division of Dark Horse Comics LLC
10956 SE Main Street
Milwaukie, OR 97222

DarkHorse.com • CritRole.com
First paperback edition: October 2019
ISBN: 978-1-50671-481-3
Digital ISBN 978-1-50671-482-0

5 7 9 10 8 6 4
Printed in China

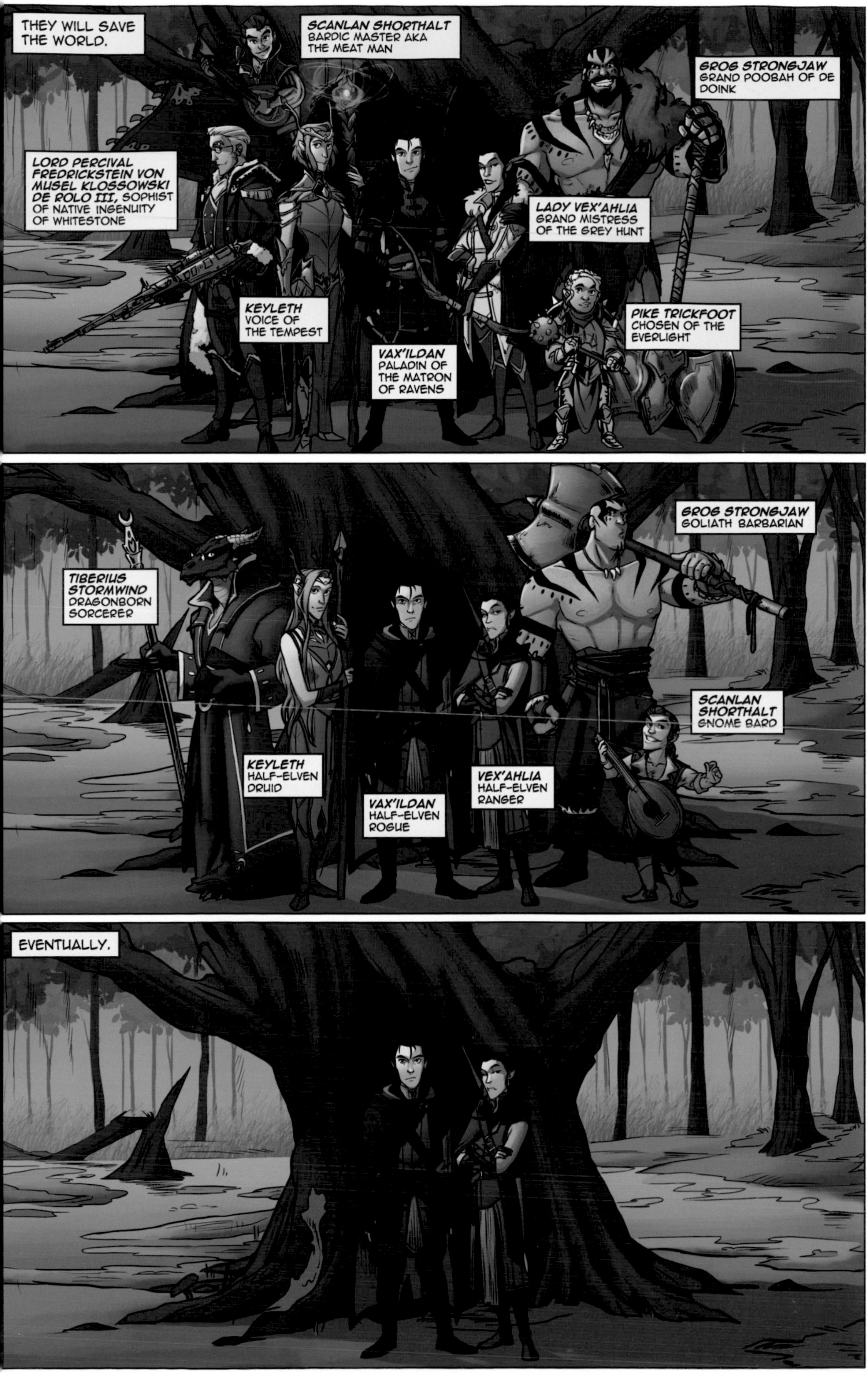
THEY WILL SAVE THE WORLD.
SCANLAN SHORTHALT BARDIC MASTER AKA THE MEAT MAN
GROG STRONGJAW GRAND POOBAH OF DE DOINK
LORD PERCIVAL FREDRICKSTEIN VON MUSEL KLOSSOWSKI DE ROLO III, SOPHIST OF NATIVE INGENUITY OF WHITESTONE
LADY VEX'AHLIA GRAND MISTRESS OF THE GREY HUNT
KEYLETH VOICE OF THE TEMPEST
PIKE TRICKFOOT CHOSEN OF THE EVERLIGHT
VAX'ILDAN PALADIN OF THE MATRON OF RAVENS
GROG STRONGJAW GOLIATH BARBARIAN
TIBERIUS STORMWIND DRAGONBORN SORCERER
SCANLAN SHORTHALT GNOME BARD
KEYLETH HALF-ELVEN DRUID
VEX'AHLIA HALF-ELVEN RANGER
VAX'ILDAN HALF-ELVEN ROGUE
EVENTUALLY.

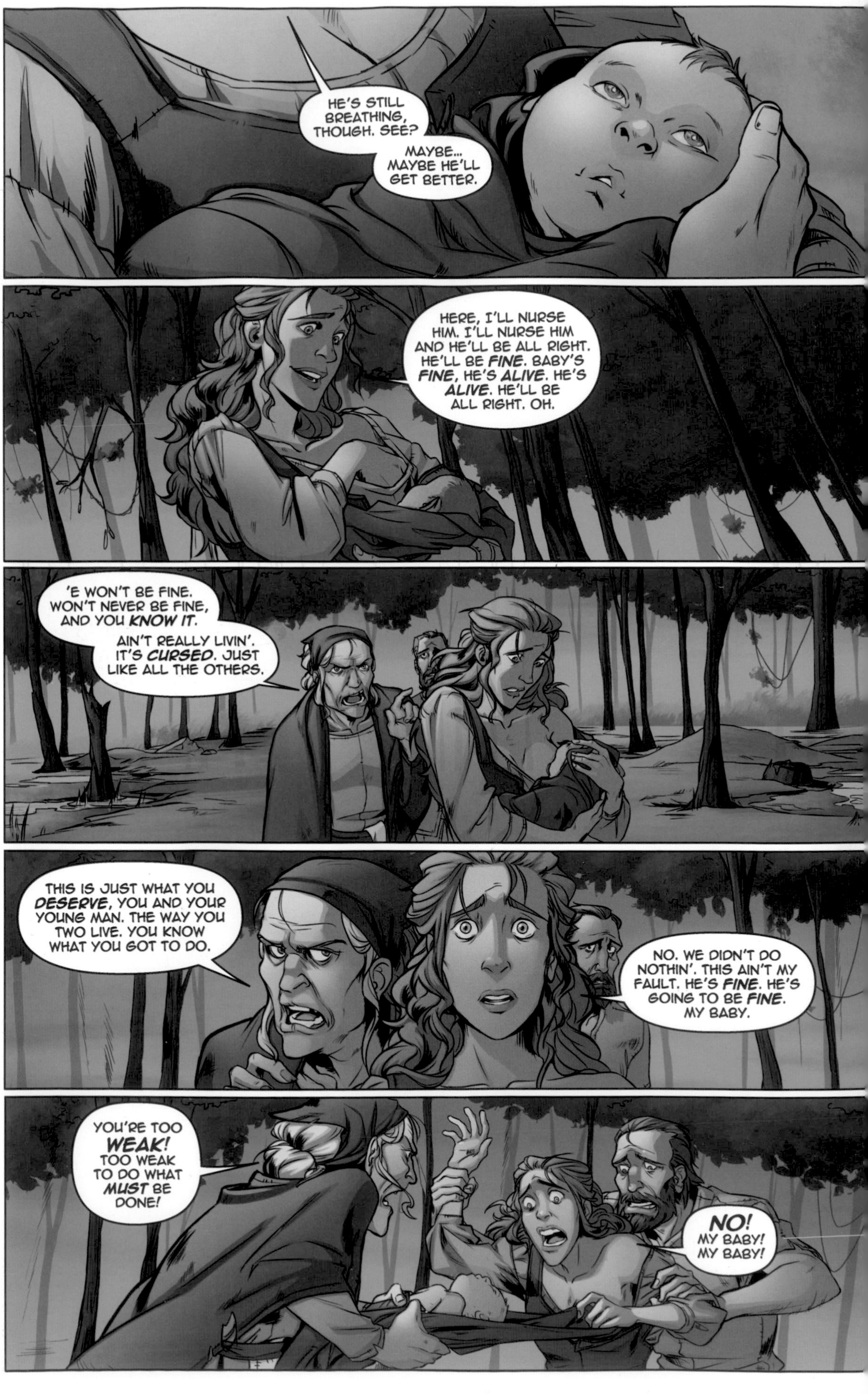
HE'S STILL BREATHING, THOUGH. SEE?
MAYBE... MAYBE HE'LL GET BETTER.
HERE, I'LL NURSE HIM. I'LL NURSE HIM AND HE'LL BE ALL RIGHT. HE'LL BE *FINE*. BABY'S *FINE*, HE'S *ALIVE*. HE'S *ALIVE*. HE'LL BE ALL RIGHT. OH.
'E WON'T BE FINE. WON'T NEVER BE FINE, AND YOU *KNOW IT*.
AIN'T REALLY LIVIN'. IT'S *CURSED*. JUST LIKE ALL THE OTHERS.
THIS IS JUST WHAT YOU *DESERVE*, YOU AND YOUR YOUNG MAN. THE WAY YOU TWO LIVE. YOU KNOW WHAT YOU GOT TO DO.
NO. WE DIDN'T DO NOTHIN'. THIS AIN'T MY FAULT. HE'S *FINE*. HE'S GOING TO BE *FINE*. MY BABY.
YOU'RE TOO *WEAK!* TOO WEAK TO DO WHAT *MUST* BE DONE!
*NO!* MY BABY! MY BABY!

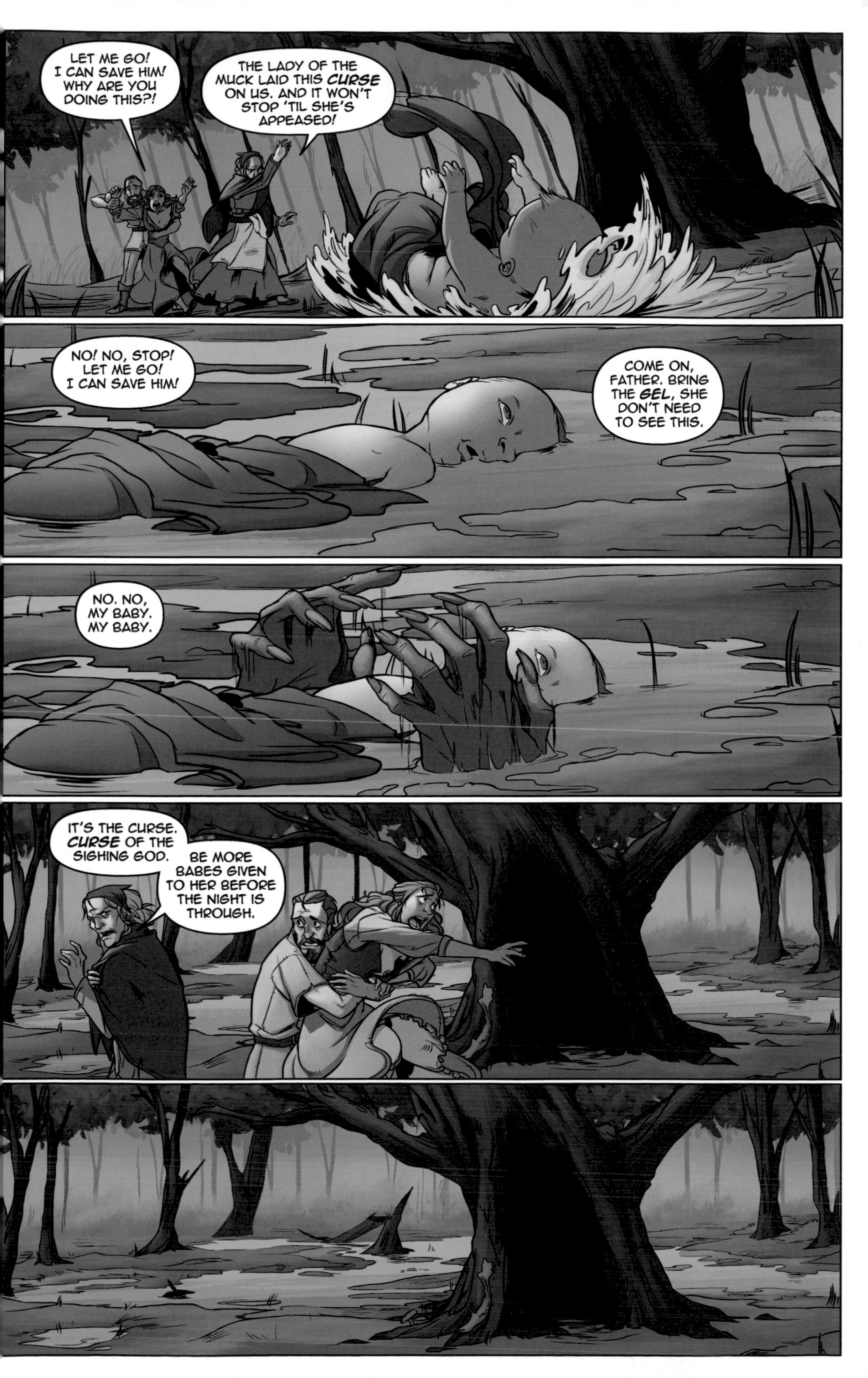
LET ME GO! I CAN SAVE HIM! WHY ARE YOU DOING THIS?!
THE LADY OF THE MUCK LAID THIS CURSE ON US. AND IT WON'T STOP 'TIL SHE'S APPEASED!
NO! NO, STOP! LET ME GO! I CAN SAVE HIM!
COME ON, FATHER. BRING THE GEL, SHE DON'T NEED TO SEE THIS.
NO. NO, MY BABY. MY BABY.
IT'S THE CURSE. CURSE OF THE SIGHING GOD.
BE MORE BABES GIVEN TO HER BEFORE THE NIGHT IS THROUGH.

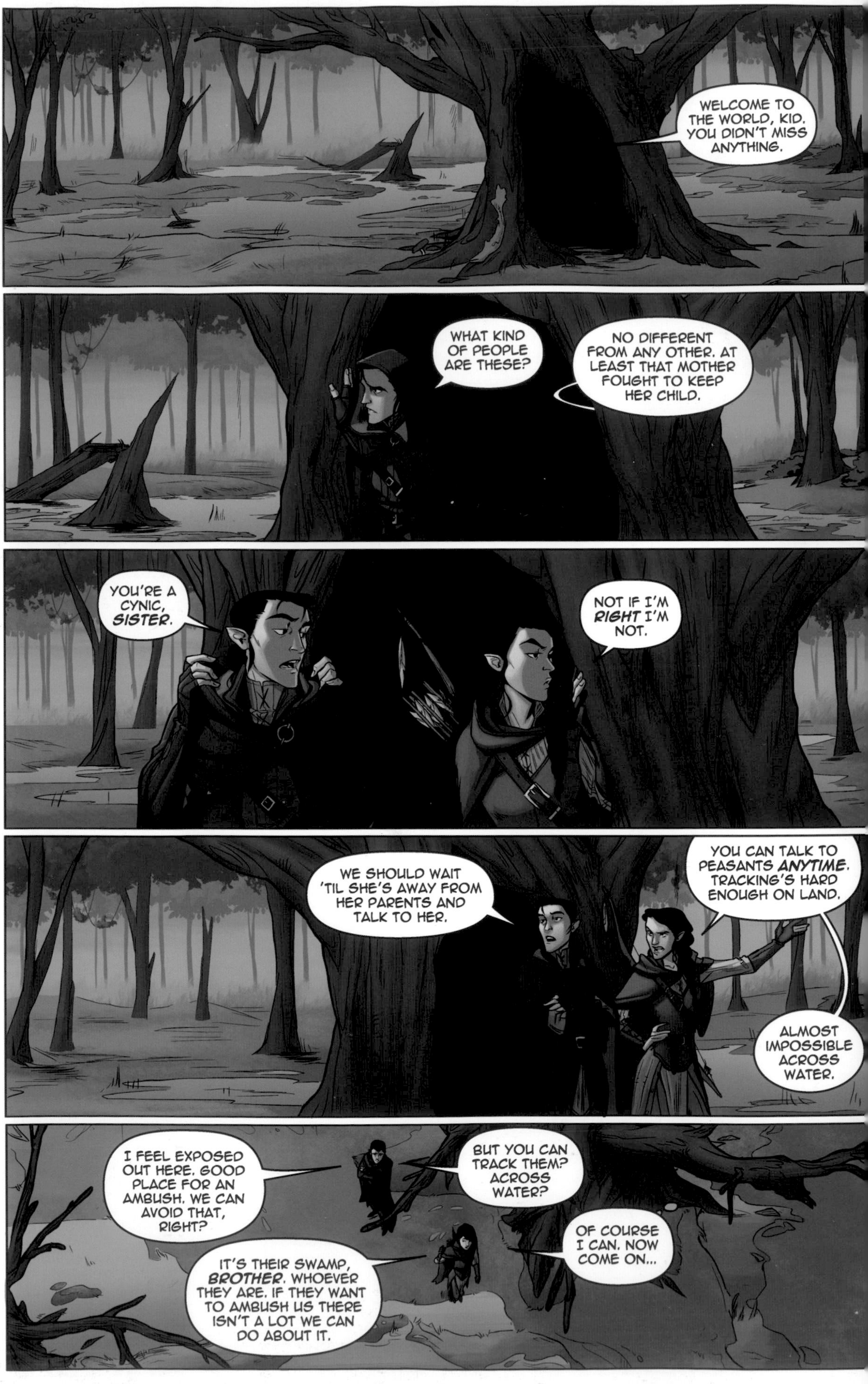
WELCOME TO THE WORLD, KID. YOU DIDN'T MISS ANYTHING.
WHAT KIND OF PEOPLE ARE THESE?
NO DIFFERENT FROM ANY OTHER. AT LEAST THAT MOTHER FOUGHT TO KEEP HER CHILD.
YOU'RE A CYNIC, SISTER.
NOT IF I'M RIGHT I'M NOT.
WE SHOULD WAIT 'TIL SHE'S AWAY FROM HER PARENTS AND TALK TO HER.
YOU CAN TALK TO PEASANTS ANYTIME. TRACKING'S HARD ENOUGH ON LAND.
ALMOST IMPOSSIBLE ACROSS WATER.
I FEEL EXPOSED OUT HERE. GOOD PLACE FOR AN AMBUSH. WE CAN AVOID THAT, RIGHT?
IT'S THEIR SWAMP, BROTHER. WHOEVER THEY ARE. IF THEY WANT TO AMBUSH US THERE ISN'T A LOT WE CAN DO ABOUT IT.
BUT YOU CAN TRACK THEM? ACROSS WATER?
OF COURSE I CAN. NOW COME ON...

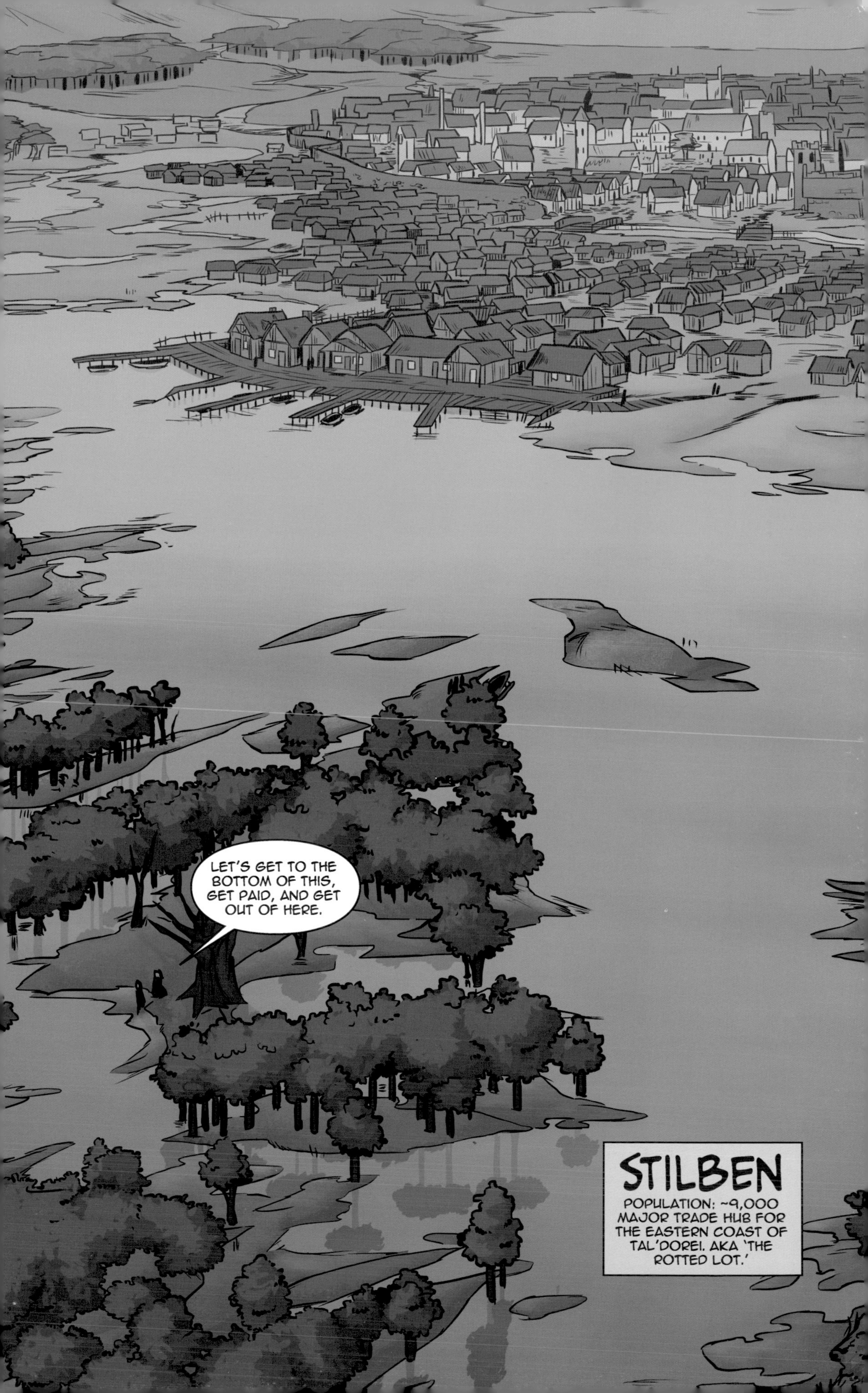
LET'S GET TO THE BOTTOM OF THIS, GET PAID, AND GET OUT OF HERE.
STILBEN
POPULATION: ~9,000 MAJOR TRADE HUB FOR THE EASTERN COAST OF TAL'DOREI. AKA 'THE ROTTED LOT.'

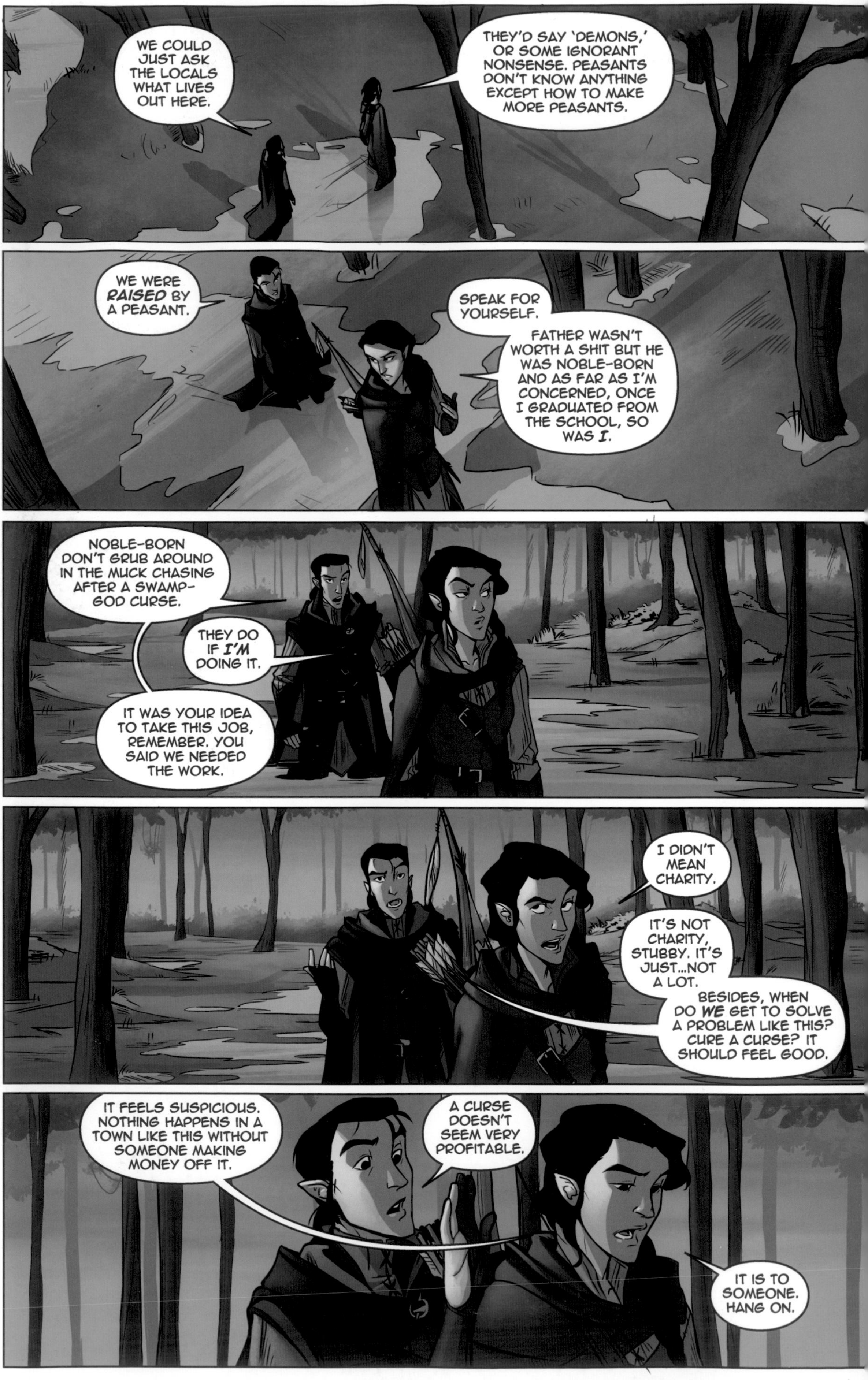
WE COULD JUST ASK THE LOCALS WHAT LIVES OUT HERE.
THEY'D SAY 'DEMONS,' OR SOME IGNORANT NONSENSE. PEASANTS DON'T KNOW ANYTHING EXCEPT HOW TO MAKE MORE PEASANTS.
WE WERE *RAISED* BY A PEASANT.
SPEAK FOR YOURSELF.
FATHER WASN'T WORTH A SHIT BUT HE WAS NOBLE-BORN AND AS FAR AS I'M CONCERNED, ONCE I GRADUATED FROM THE SCHOOL, SO WAS *I*.
NOBLE-BORN DON'T GRUB AROUND IN THE MUCK CHASING AFTER A SWAMP-GOD CURSE.
THEY DO IF *I'M* DOING IT.
IT WAS YOUR IDEA TO TAKE THIS JOB, REMEMBER. YOU SAID WE NEEDED THE WORK.
I DIDN'T MEAN CHARITY.
IT'S NOT CHARITY, STUBBY. IT'S JUST...NOT A LOT.
BESIDES, WHEN DO *WE* GET TO SOLVE A PROBLEM LIKE THIS? CURE A CURSE? IT SHOULD FEEL GOOD.
IT FEELS SUSPICIOUS. NOTHING HAPPENS IN A TOWN LIKE THIS WITHOUT SOMEONE MAKING MONEY OFF IT.
A CURSE DOESN'T SEEM VERY PROFITABLE.
IT IS TO SOMEONE. HANG ON.

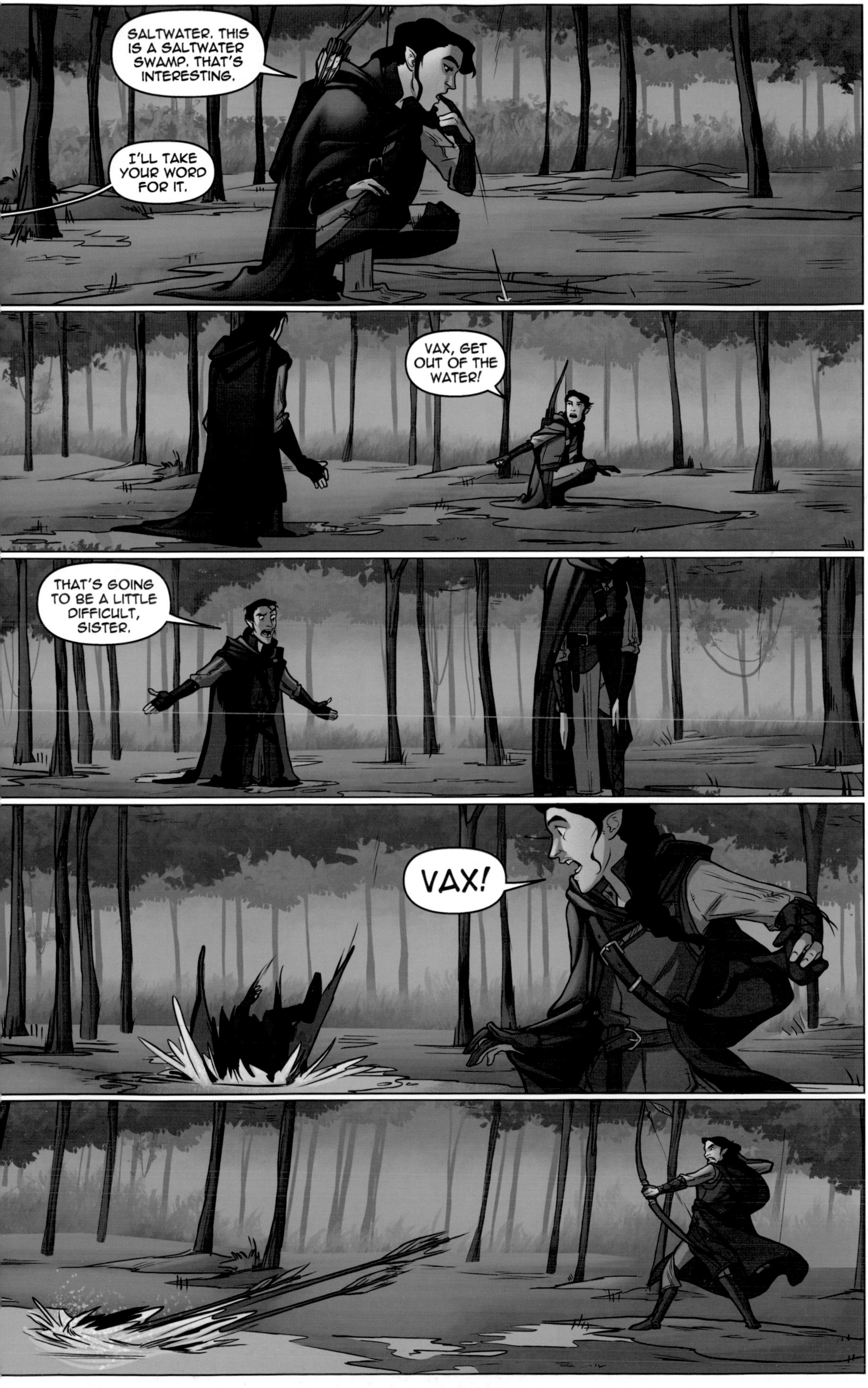
SALTWATER. THIS IS A SALTWATER SWAMP. THAT'S INTERESTING.
I'LL TAKE YOUR WORD FOR IT.
VAX, GET OUT OF THE WATER!
THAT'S GOING TO BE A LITTLE DIFFICULT, SISTER.
VAX!

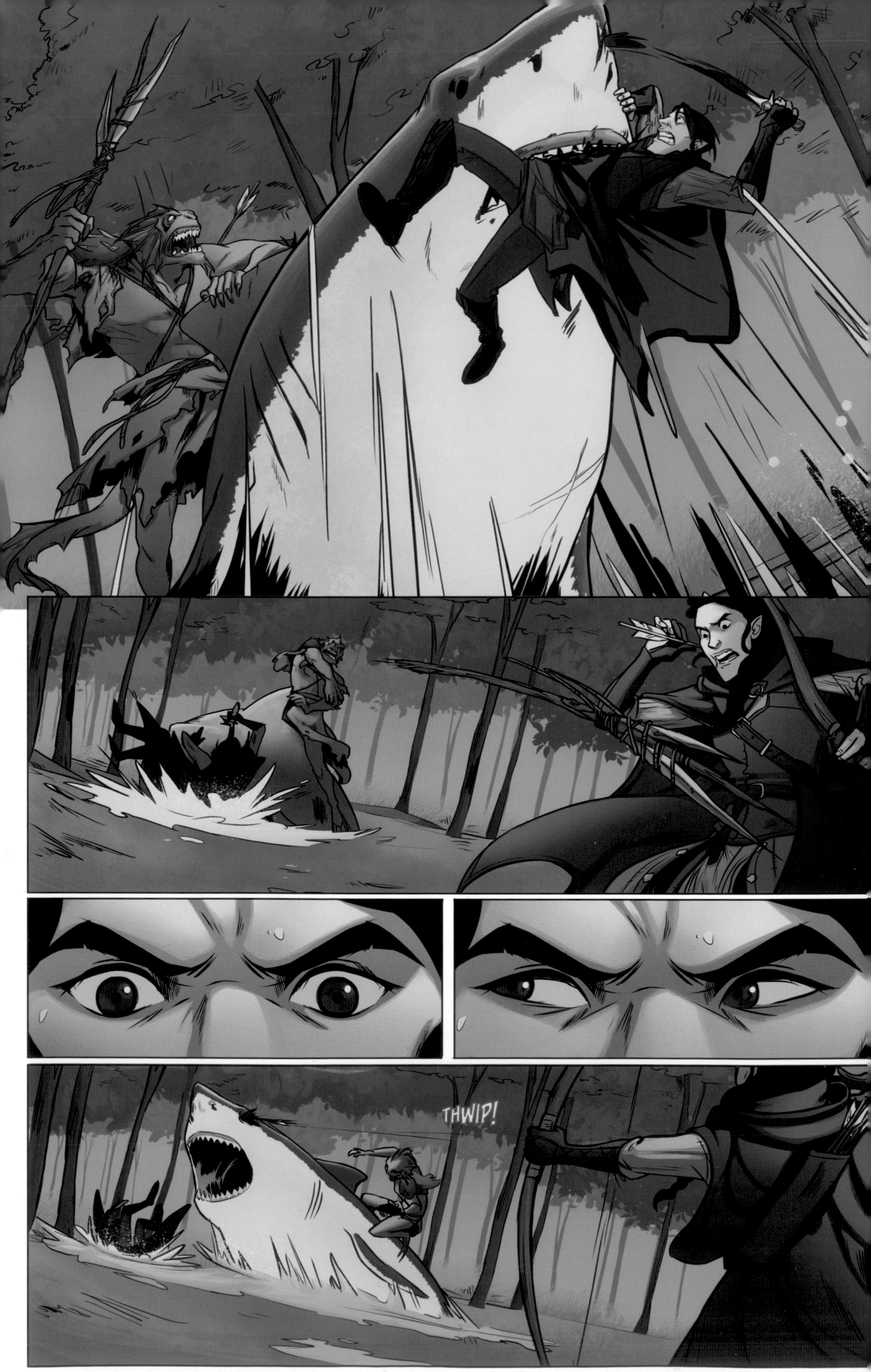
THWIP!

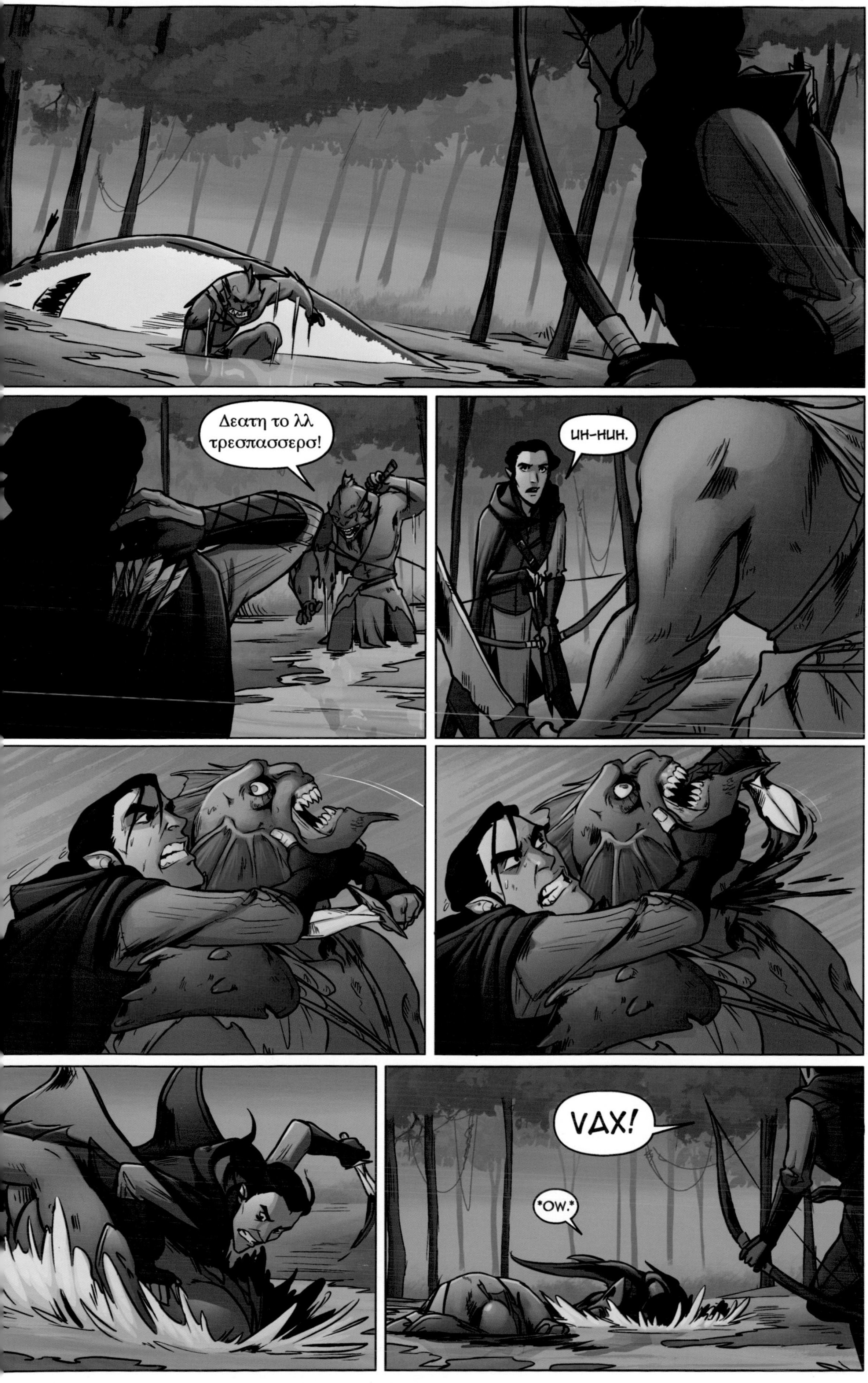
Δεατη το λλ τρεσπασσερσ!
ин-нин.
VAX!
*OW.*

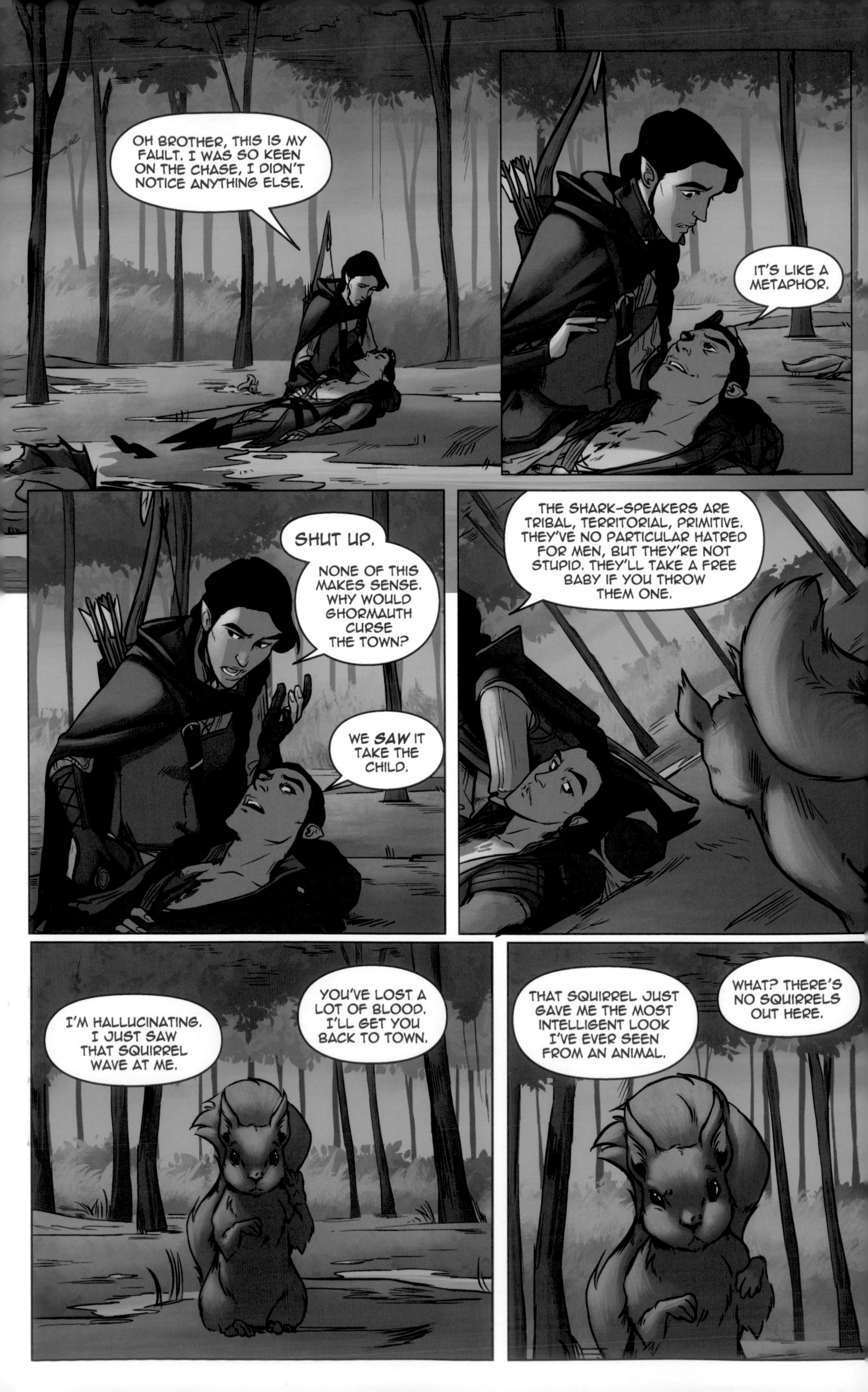
OH BROTHER, THIS IS MY FAULT. I WAS SO KEEN ON THE CHASE, I DIDN'T NOTICE ANYTHING ELSE.
IT'S LIKE A METAPHOR.
SHUT UP.
NONE OF THIS MAKES SENSE. WHY WOULD GHORMAUTH CURSE THE TOWN?
WE SAW IT TAKE THE CHILD.
THE SHARK-SPEAKERS ARE TRIBAL, TERRITORIAL, PRIMITIVE. THEY'VE NO PARTICULAR HATRED FOR MEN, BUT THEY'RE NOT STUPID. THEY'LL TAKE A FREE BABY IF YOU THROW THEM ONE.
I'M HALLUCINATING. I JUST SAW THAT SQUIRREL WAVE AT ME.
YOU'VE LOST A LOT OF BLOOD. I'LL GET YOU BACK TO TOWN.
THAT SQUIRREL JUST GAVE ME THE MOST INTELLIGENT LOOK I'VE EVER SEEN FROM AN ANIMAL.
WHAT? THERE'S NO SQUIRRELS OUT HERE.

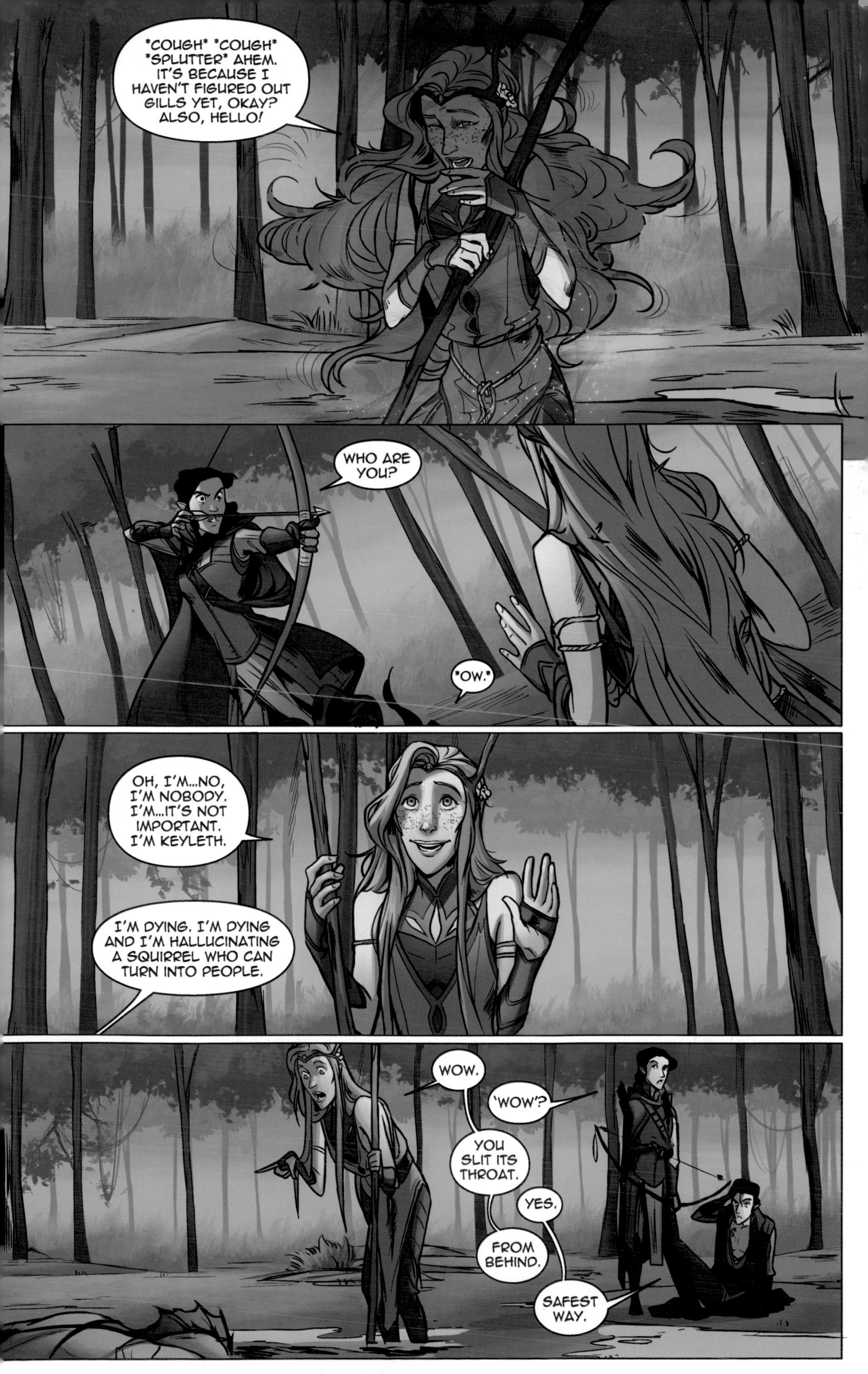
*COUGH* *COUGH* *SPLUTTER* AHEM. IT'S BECAUSE I HAVEN'T FIGURED OUT GILLS YET, OKAY? ALSO, HELLO!
WHO ARE YOU?
*OW.*
OH, I'M...NO, I'M NOBODY. I'M...IT'S NOT IMPORTANT. I'M KEYLETH.
I'M DYING. I'M DYING AND I'M HALLUCINATING A SQUIRREL WHO CAN TURN INTO PEOPLE.
WOW.
'WOW'?
YOU SLIT ITS THROAT.
YES.
FROM BEHIND.
SAFEST WAY.

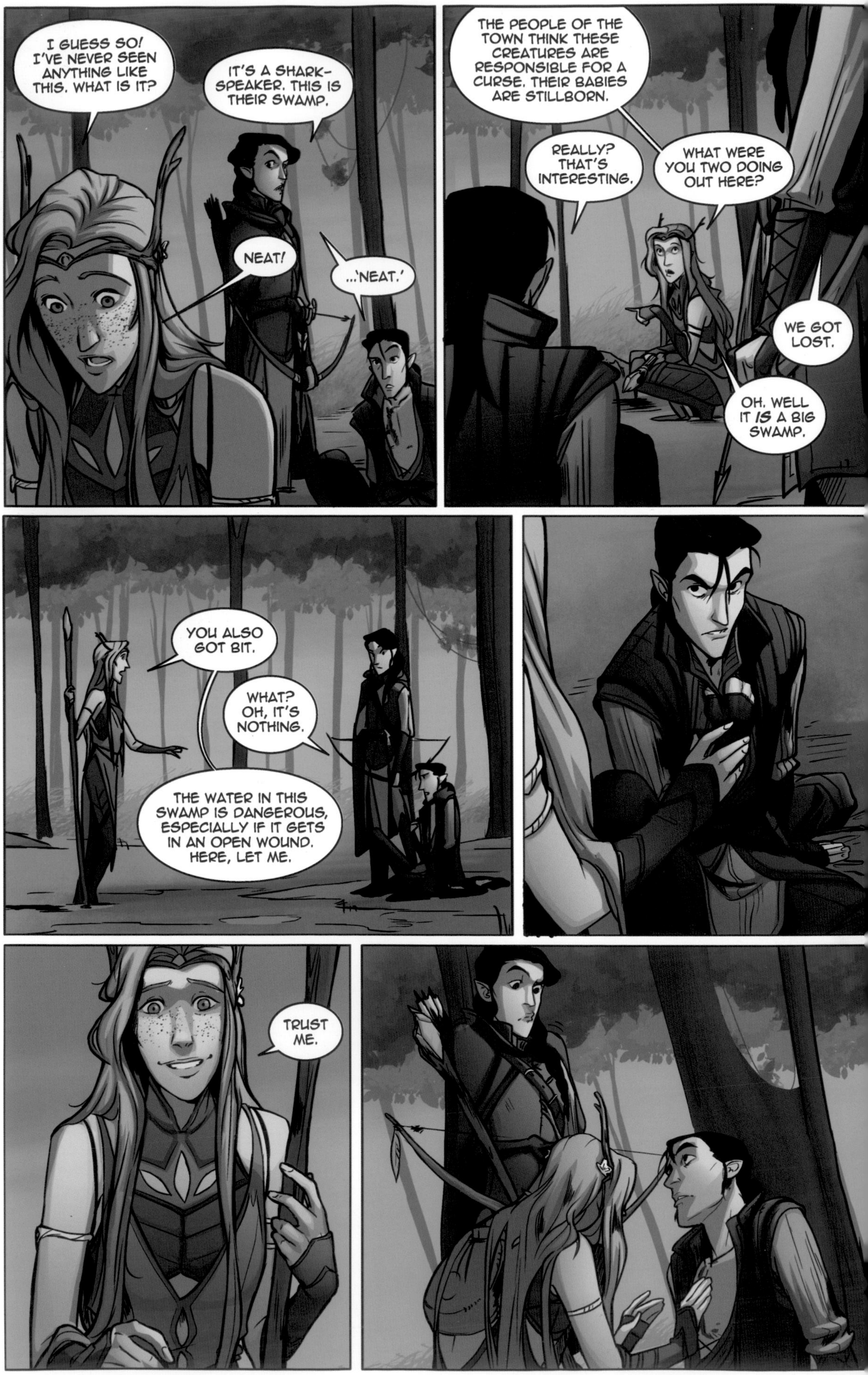
I GUESS SO! I'VE NEVER SEEN ANYTHING LIKE THIS. WHAT IS IT?
IT'S A SHARK-SPEAKER. THIS IS THEIR SWAMP.
NEAT!
...'NEAT.'
THE PEOPLE OF THE TOWN THINK THESE CREATURES ARE RESPONSIBLE FOR A CURSE. THEIR BABIES ARE STILLBORN.
REALLY? THAT'S INTERESTING.
WHAT WERE YOU TWO DOING OUT HERE?
WE GOT LOST.
OH. WELL IT *IS* A BIG SWAMP.
YOU ALSO GOT BIT.
WHAT? OH, IT'S NOTHING.
THE WATER IN THIS SWAMP IS DANGEROUS, ESPECIALLY IF IT GETS IN AN OPEN WOUND. HERE, LET ME.
TRUST ME.

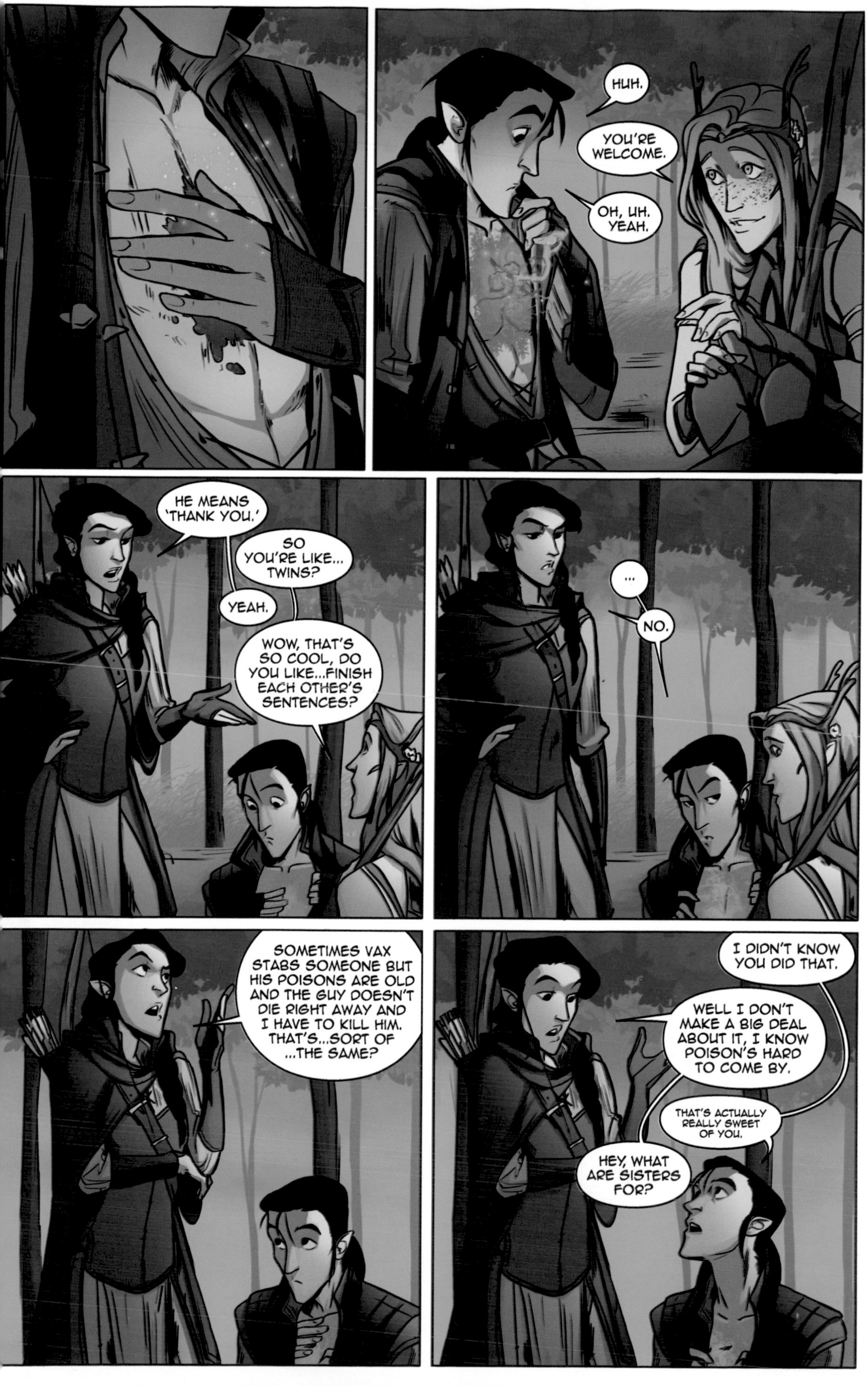
HUH.
YOU'RE WELCOME.
OH, UH. YEAH.
HE MEANS 'THANK YOU.'
SO YOU'RE LIKE... TWINS?
YEAH.
WOW, THAT'S SO COOL, DO YOU LIKE...FINISH EACH OTHER'S SENTENCES?
...
NO.
SOMETIMES VAX STABS SOMEONE BUT HIS POISONS ARE OLD AND THE GUY DOESN'T DIE RIGHT AWAY AND I HAVE TO KILL HIM. THAT'S...SORT OF ...THE SAME?
I DIDN'T KNOW YOU DID THAT.
WELL I DON'T MAKE A BIG DEAL ABOUT IT, I KNOW POISON'S HARD TO COME BY.
THAT'S ACTUALLY REALLY SWEET OF YOU.
HEY, WHAT ARE SISTERS FOR?

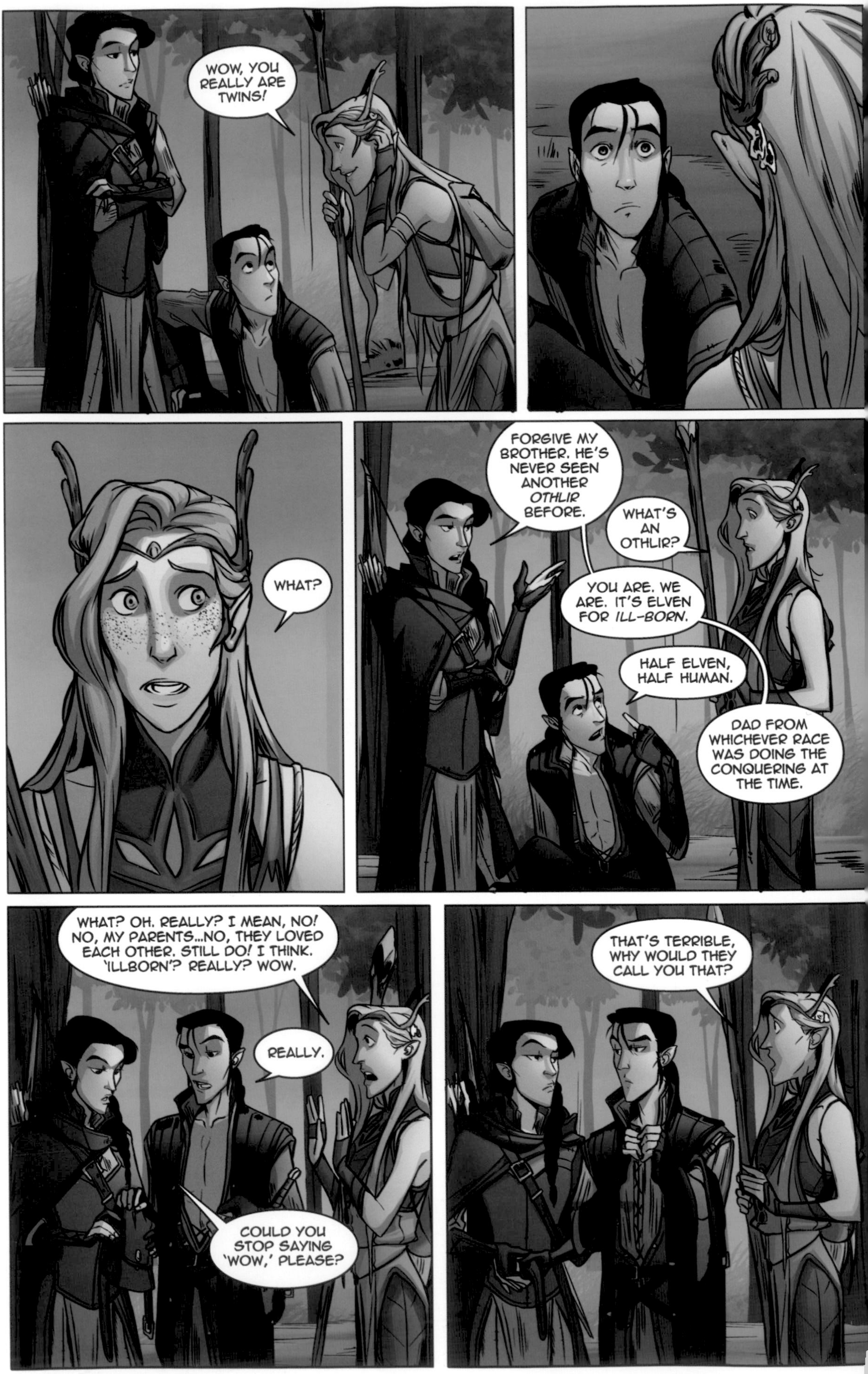
WOW, YOU REALLY ARE TWINS!
WHAT?
FORGIVE MY BROTHER. HE'S NEVER SEEN ANOTHER *OTHLIR* BEFORE.
WHAT'S AN OTHLIR?
YOU ARE. WE ARE. IT'S ELVEN FOR *ILL-BORN*.
HALF ELVEN, HALF HUMAN.
DAD FROM WHICHEVER RACE WAS DOING THE CONQUERING AT THE TIME.
WHAT? OH. REALLY? I MEAN, NO! NO, MY PARENTS...NO, THEY LOVED EACH OTHER. STILL DO! I THINK. 'ILLBORN'? REALLY? WOW.
REALLY.
COULD YOU STOP SAYING 'WOW,' PLEASE?
THAT'S TERRIBLE, WHY WOULD THEY CALL YOU THAT?

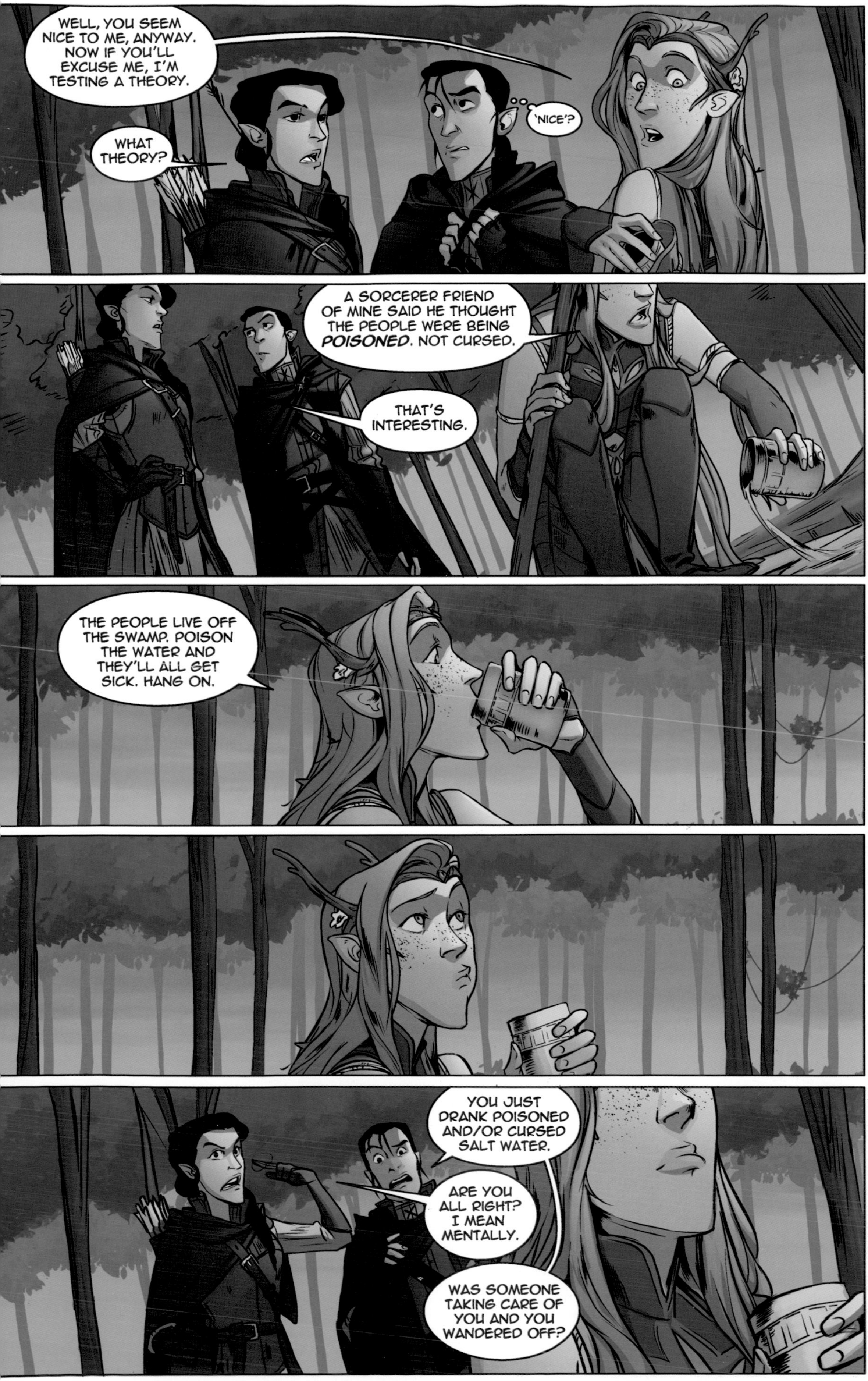
WELL, YOU SEEM NICE TO ME, ANYWAY. NOW IF YOU'LL EXCUSE ME, I'M TESTING A THEORY.
'NICE'?
WHAT THEORY?
A SORCERER FRIEND OF MINE SAID HE THOUGHT THE PEOPLE WERE BEING *POISONED*. NOT CURSED.
THAT'S INTERESTING.
THE PEOPLE LIVE OFF THE SWAMP. POISON THE WATER AND THEY'LL ALL GET SICK. HANG ON.
YOU JUST DRANK POISONED AND/OR CURSED SALT WATER.
ARE YOU ALL RIGHT? I MEAN MENTALLY.
WAS SOMEONE TAKING CARE OF YOU AND YOU WANDERED OFF?

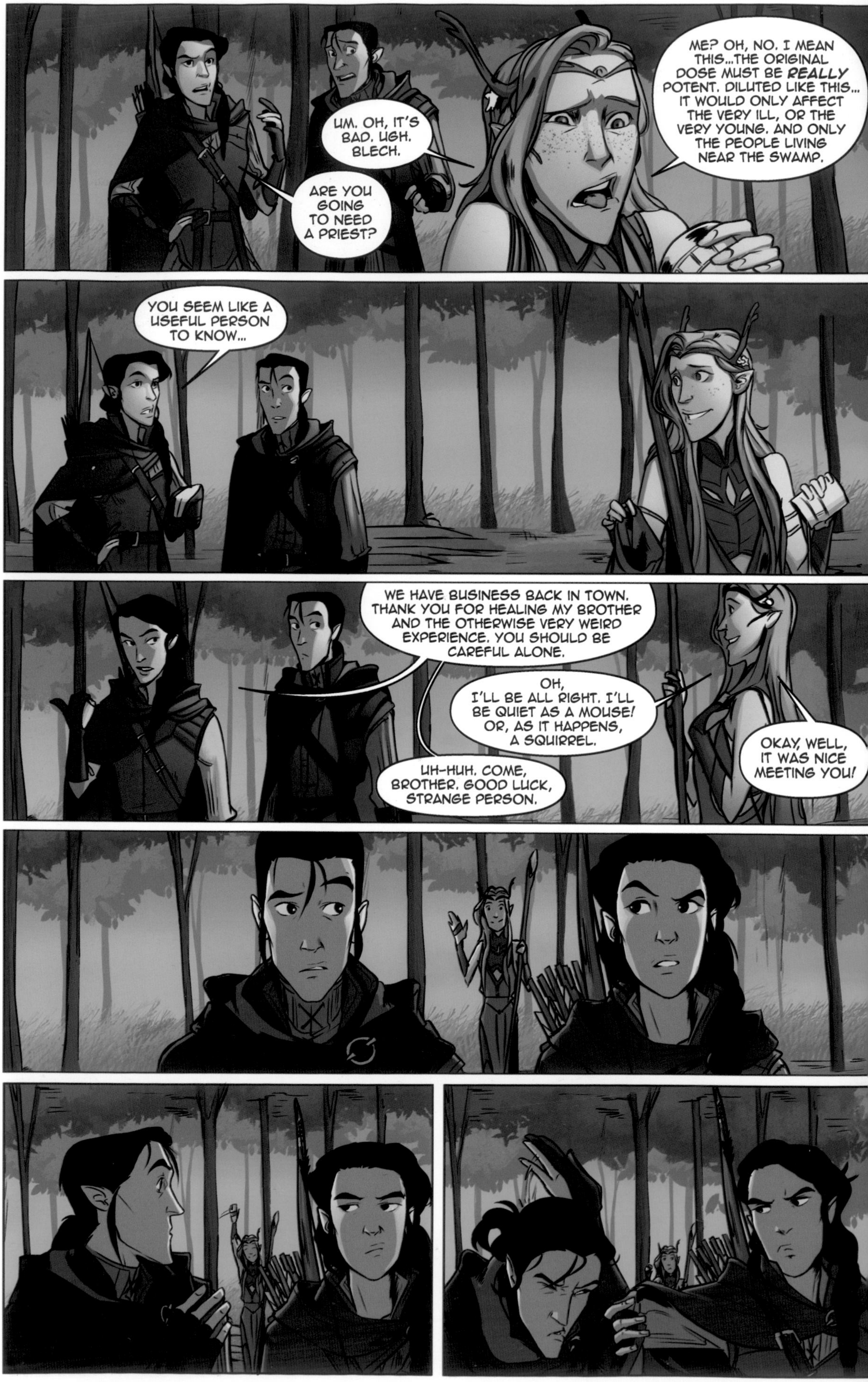
ARE YOU GOING TO NEED A PRIEST?
UM. OH, IT'S BAD. UGH. BLECH.
ME? OH, NO. I MEAN THIS...THE ORIGINAL DOSE MUST BE *REALLY* POTENT. DILUTED LIKE THIS... IT WOULD ONLY AFFECT THE VERY ILL, OR THE VERY YOUNG. AND ONLY THE PEOPLE LIVING NEAR THE SWAMP.
YOU SEEM LIKE A USEFUL PERSON TO KNOW...
WE HAVE BUSINESS BACK IN TOWN. THANK YOU FOR HEALING MY BROTHER AND THE OTHERWISE VERY WEIRD EXPERIENCE. YOU SHOULD BE CAREFUL ALONE.
OH, I'LL BE ALL RIGHT. I'LL BE QUIET AS A MOUSE! OR, AS IT HAPPENS, A SQUIRREL.
UH-HUH. COME, BROTHER. GOOD LUCK, STRANGE PERSON.
OKAY, WELL, IT WAS NICE MEETING YOU!

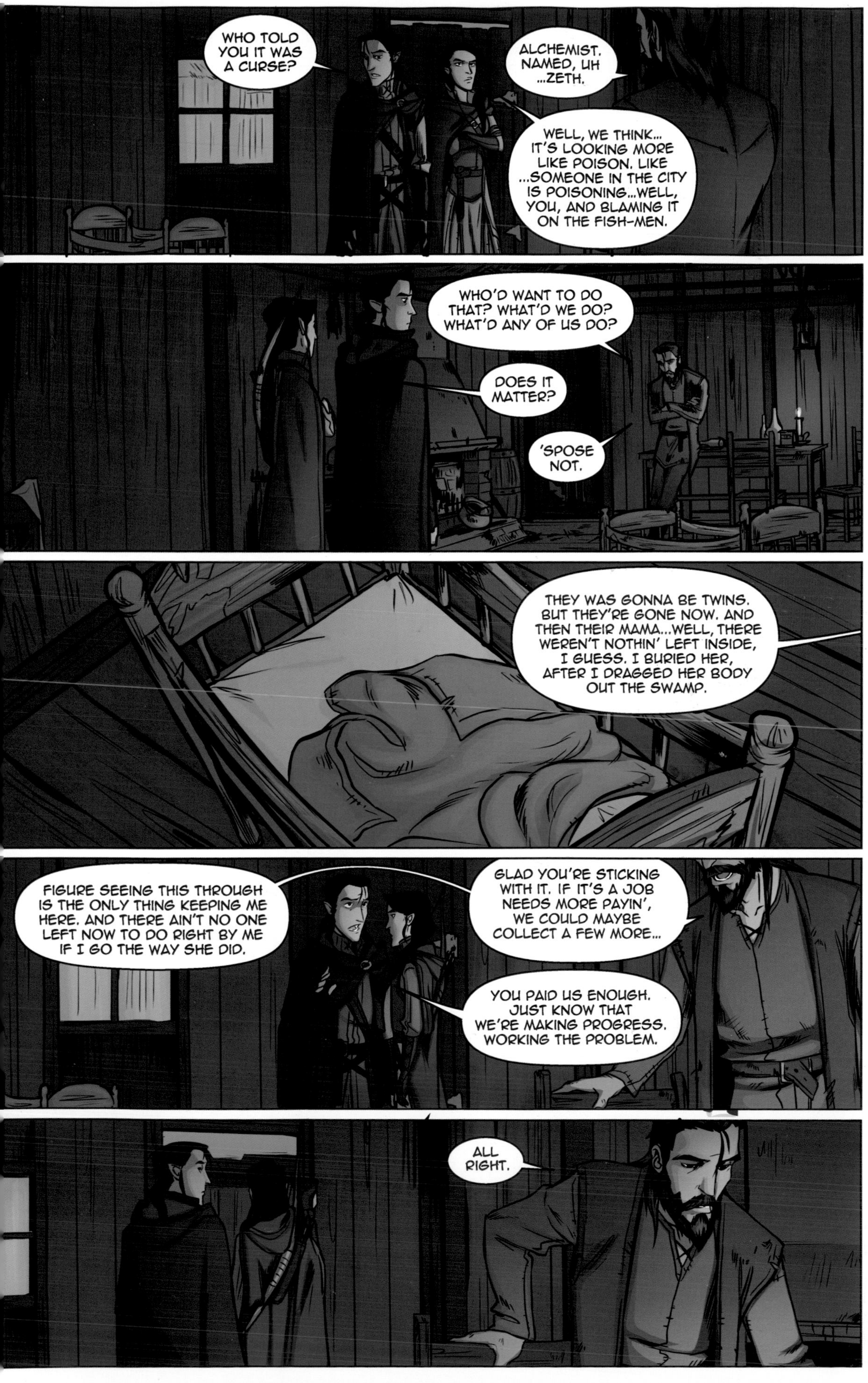
WHO TOLD YOU IT WAS A CURSE?
ALCHEMIST. NAMED, UH ...ZETH.
WELL, WE THINK... IT'S LOOKING MORE LIKE POISON. LIKE ...SOMEONE IN THE CITY IS POISONING...WELL, YOU, AND BLAMING IT ON THE FISH-MEN.
WHO'D WANT TO DO THAT? WHAT'D WE DO? WHAT'D ANY OF US DO?
DOES IT MATTER?
'SPOSE NOT.
THEY WAS GONNA BE TWINS. BUT THEY'RE GONE NOW. AND THEN THEIR MAMA...WELL, THERE WEREN'T NOTHIN' LEFT INSIDE, I GUESS. I BURIED HER, AFTER I DRAGGED HER BODY OUT THE SWAMP.
FIGURE SEEING THIS THROUGH IS THE ONLY THING KEEPING ME HERE. AND THERE AIN'T NO ONE LEFT NOW TO DO RIGHT BY ME IF I GO THE WAY SHE DID.
GLAD YOU'RE STICKING WITH IT. IF IT'S A JOB NEEDS MORE PAYIN', WE COULD MAYBE COLLECT A FEW MORE...
YOU PAID US ENOUGH. JUST KNOW THAT WE'RE MAKING PROGRESS. WORKING THE PROBLEM.
ALL RIGHT.

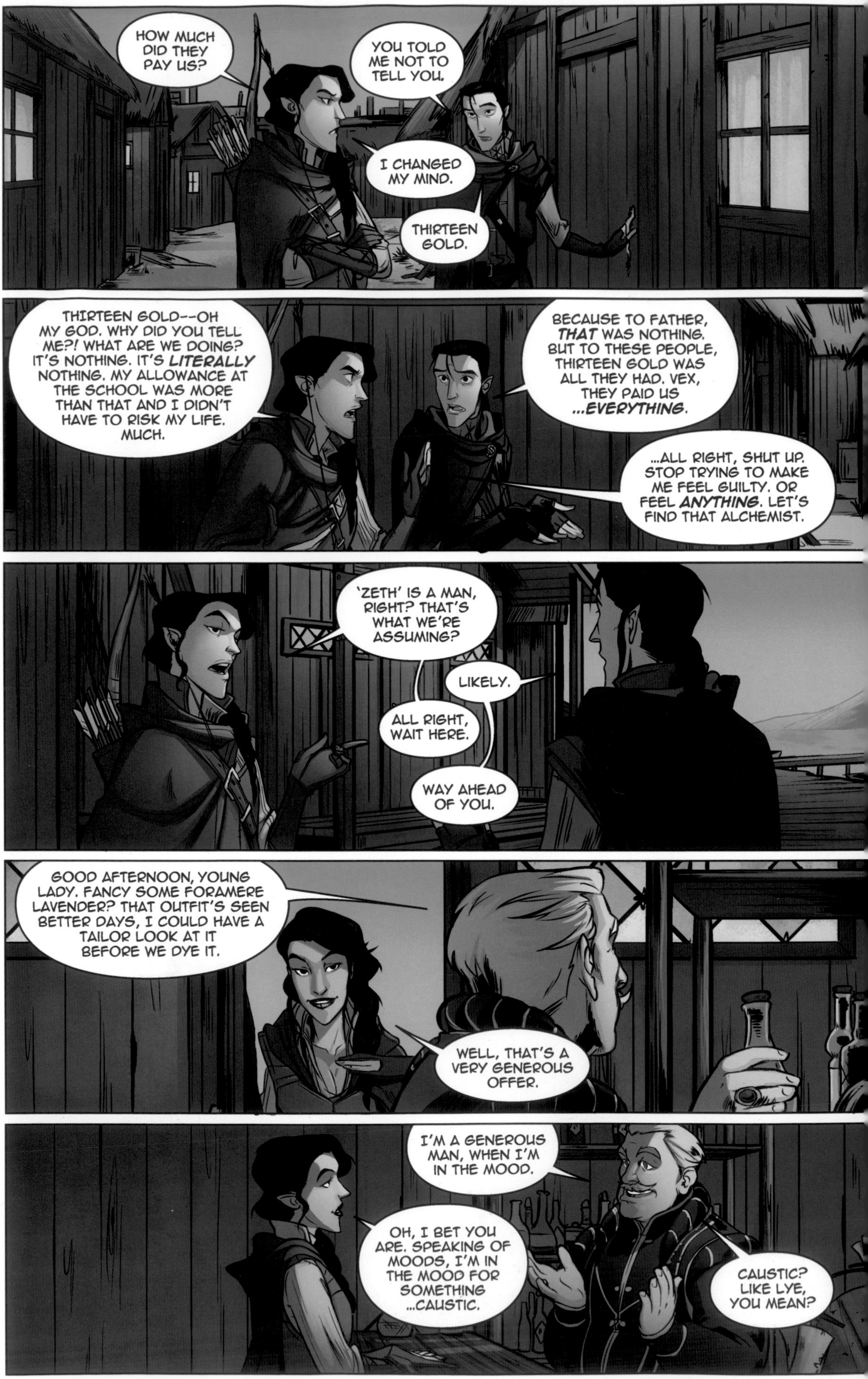
HOW MUCH DID THEY PAY US?
YOU TOLD ME NOT TO TELL YOU.
I CHANGED MY MIND.
THIRTEEN GOLD.
THIRTEEN GOLD--OH MY GOD. WHY DID YOU TELL ME?! WHAT ARE WE DOING? IT'S NOTHING. IT'S LITERALLY NOTHING. MY ALLOWANCE AT THE SCHOOL WAS MORE THAN THAT AND I DIDN'T HAVE TO RISK MY LIFE. MUCH.
BECAUSE TO FATHER, THAT WAS NOTHING. BUT TO THESE PEOPLE, THIRTEEN GOLD WAS ALL THEY HAD. VEX, THEY PAID US ...EVERYTHING.
...ALL RIGHT, SHUT UP. STOP TRYING TO MAKE ME FEEL GUILTY. OR FEEL ANYTHING. LET'S FIND THAT ALCHEMIST.
'ZETH' IS A MAN, RIGHT? THAT'S WHAT WE'RE ASSUMING?
LIKELY.
ALL RIGHT, WAIT HERE.
WAY AHEAD OF YOU.
GOOD AFTERNOON, YOUNG LADY. FANCY SOME FORAMERE LAVENDER? THAT OUTFIT'S SEEN BETTER DAYS, I COULD HAVE A TAILOR LOOK AT IT BEFORE WE DYE IT.
WELL, THAT'S A VERY GENEROUS OFFER.
I'M A GENEROUS MAN, WHEN I'M IN THE MOOD.
OH, I BET YOU ARE. SPEAKING OF MOODS, I'M IN THE MOOD FOR SOMETHING ...CAUSTIC.
CAUSTIC? LIKE LYE, YOU MEAN?

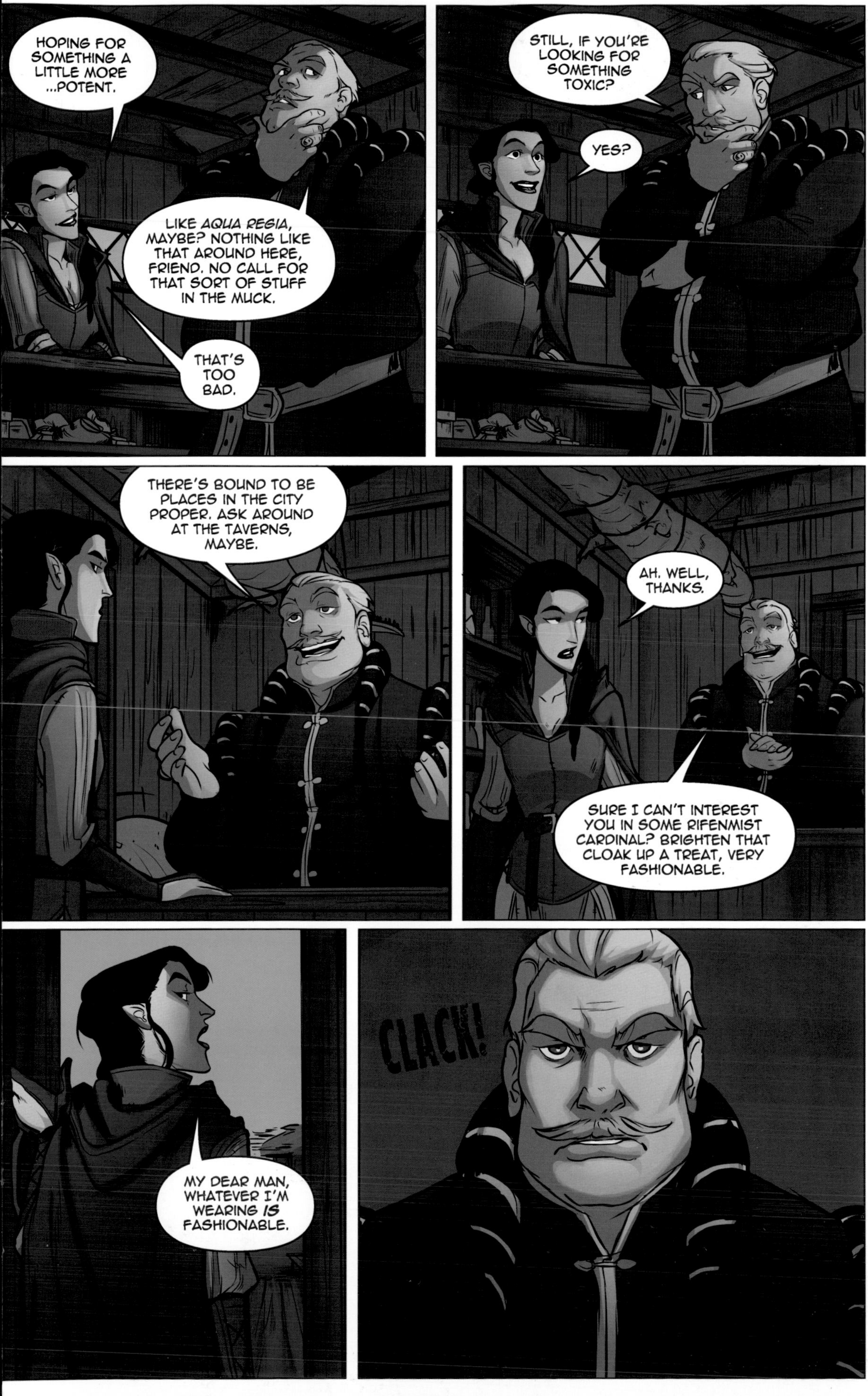
HOPING FOR SOMETHING A LITTLE MORE ...POTENT.
LIKE AQUA REGIA, MAYBE? NOTHING LIKE THAT AROUND HERE, FRIEND. NO CALL FOR THAT SORT OF STUFF IN THE MUCK.
THAT'S TOO BAD.
STILL, IF YOU'RE LOOKING FOR SOMETHING TOXIC?
YES?
THERE'S BOUND TO BE PLACES IN THE CITY PROPER. ASK AROUND AT THE TAVERNS, MAYBE.
AH. WELL, THANKS.
SURE I CAN'T INTEREST YOU IN SOME RIFENMIST CARDINAL? BRIGHTEN THAT CLOAK UP A TREAT, VERY FASHIONABLE.
MY DEAR MAN, WHATEVER I'M WEARING IS FASHIONABLE.
CLACK!

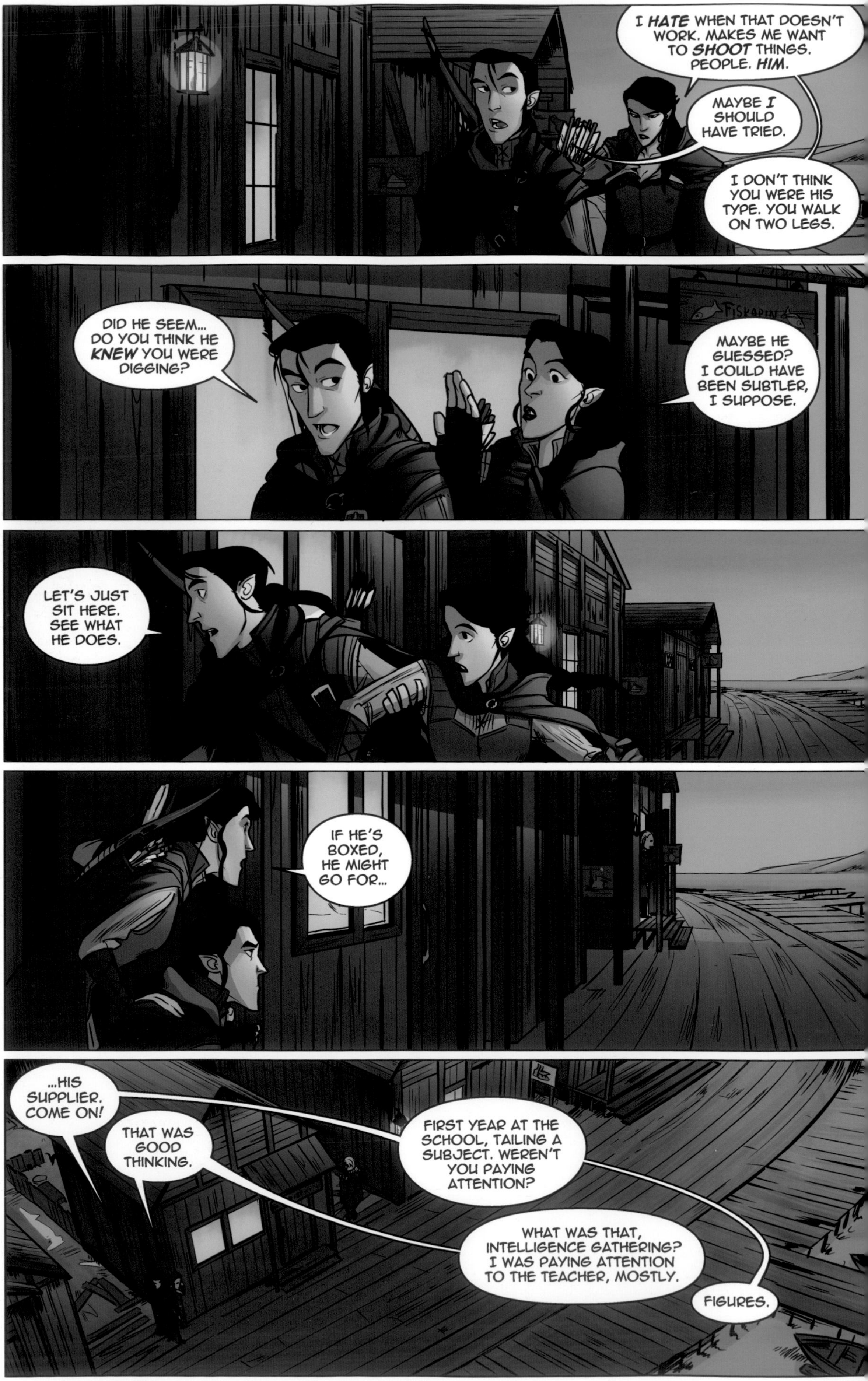
I *HATE* WHEN THAT DOESN'T WORK. MAKES ME WANT TO *SHOOT* THINGS. PEOPLE. *HIM*.
MAYBE *I* SHOULD HAVE TRIED.
I DON'T THINK YOU WERE HIS TYPE. YOU WALK ON TWO LEGS.
DID HE SEEM... DO YOU THINK HE *KNEW* YOU WERE DIGGING?
MAYBE HE GUESSED? I COULD HAVE BEEN SUBTLER, I SUPPOSE.
LET'S JUST SIT HERE. SEE WHAT HE DOES.
IF HE'S BOXED, HE MIGHT GO FOR...
...HIS SUPPLIER. COME ON!
THAT WAS GOOD THINKING.
FIRST YEAR AT THE SCHOOL, TAILING A SUBJECT. WEREN'T YOU PAYING ATTENTION?
WHAT WAS THAT, INTELLIGENCE GATHERING? I WAS PAYING ATTENTION TO THE TEACHER, MOSTLY.
FIGURES.

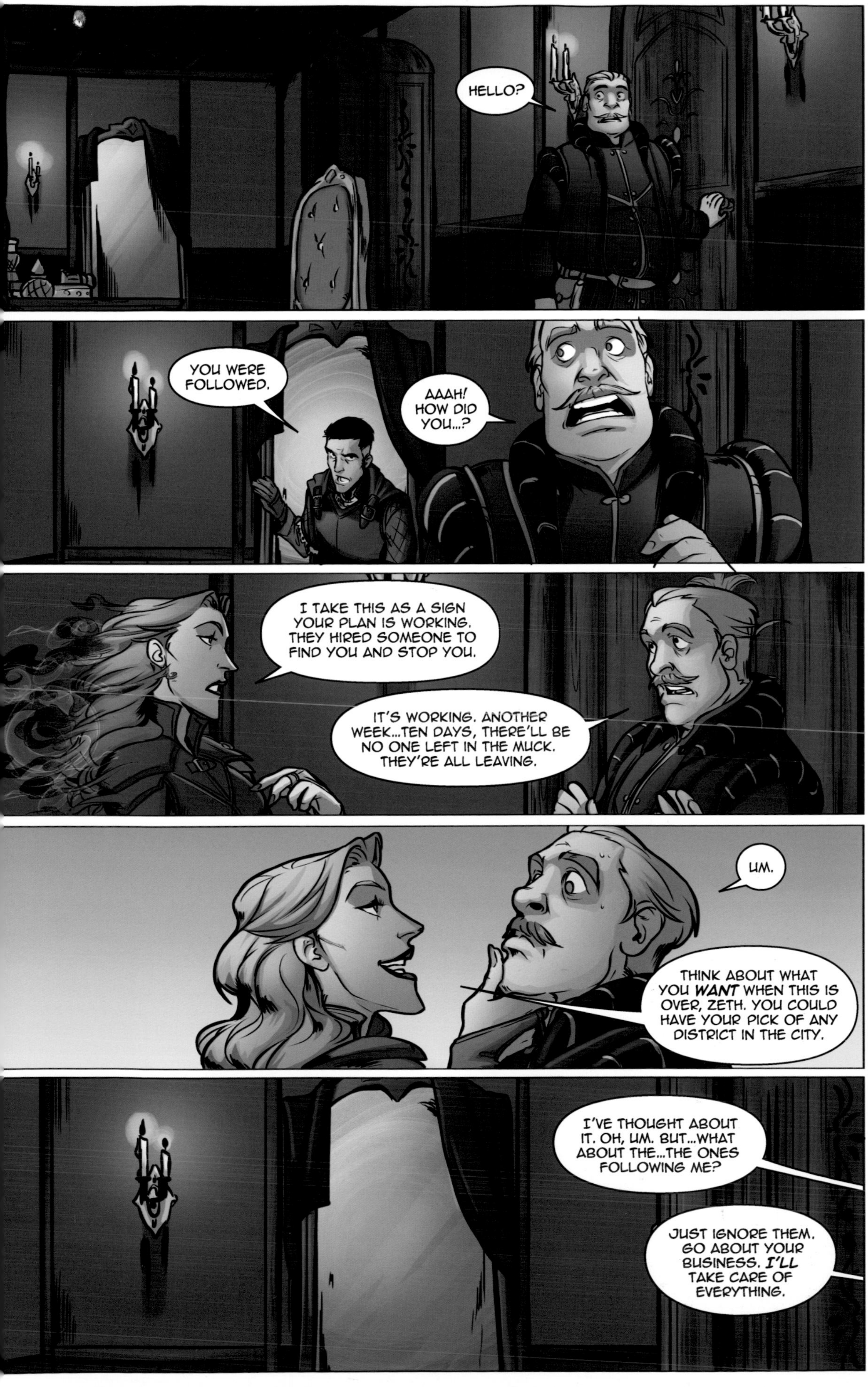

HELLO?
YOU WERE FOLLOWED.
AAAH! HOW DID YOU...?
I TAKE THIS AS A SIGN YOUR PLAN IS WORKING. THEY HIRED SOMEONE TO FIND YOU AND STOP YOU.
IT'S WORKING. ANOTHER WEEK...TEN DAYS, THERE'LL BE NO ONE LEFT IN THE MUCK. THEY'RE ALL LEAVING.
UM.
THINK ABOUT WHAT YOU *WANT* WHEN THIS IS OVER, ZETH. YOU COULD HAVE YOUR PICK OF ANY DISTRICT IN THE CITY.
I'VE THOUGHT ABOUT IT. OH, UM. BUT...WHAT ABOUT THE...THE ONES FOLLOWING ME?
JUST IGNORE THEM. GO ABOUT YOUR BUSINESS. *I'LL* TAKE CARE OF EVERYTHING.

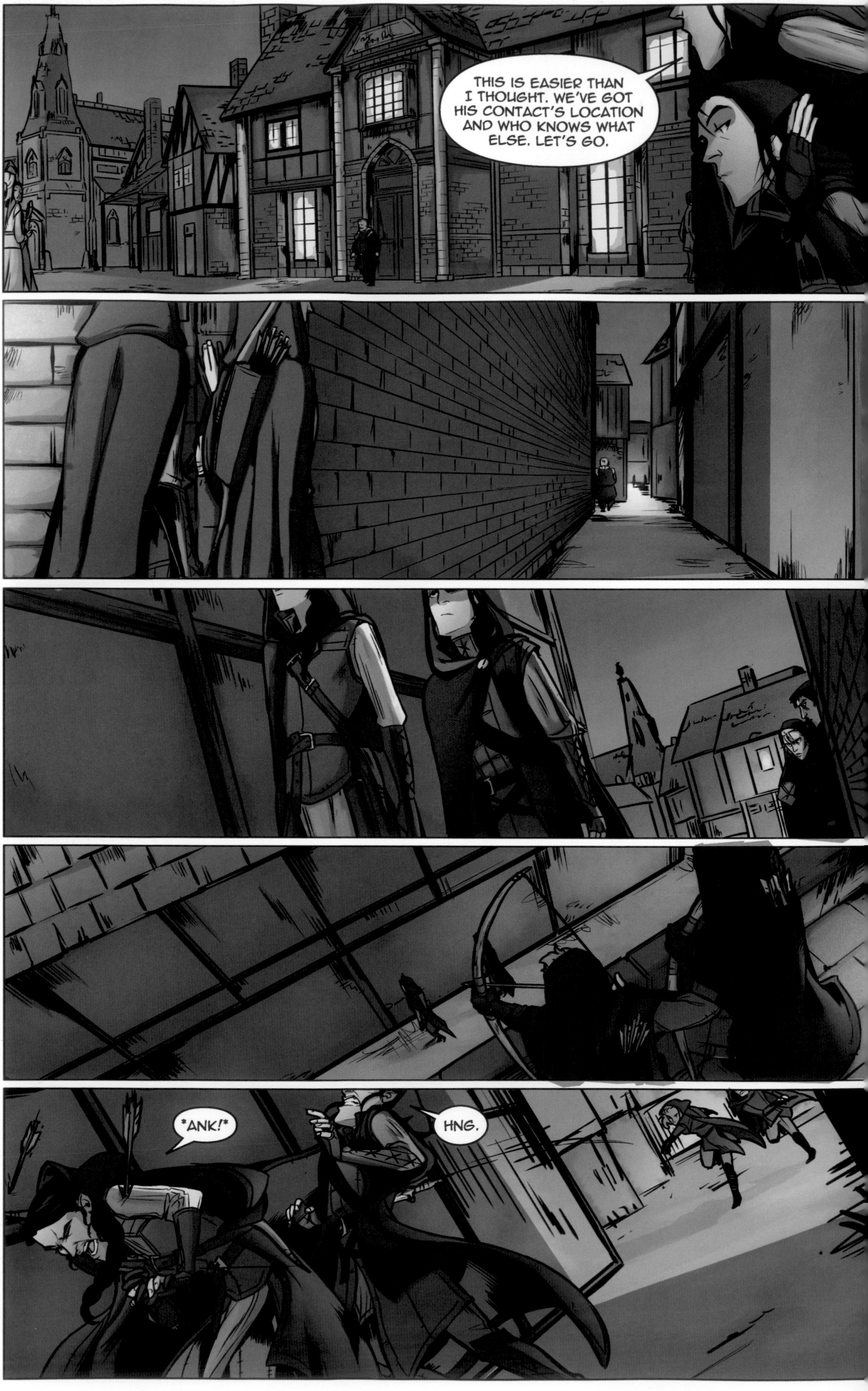

THIS IS EASIER THAN I THOUGHT. WE'VE GOT HIS CONTACT'S LOCATION AND WHO KNOWS WHAT ELSE. LET'S GO.
*ANK!*
HNG.

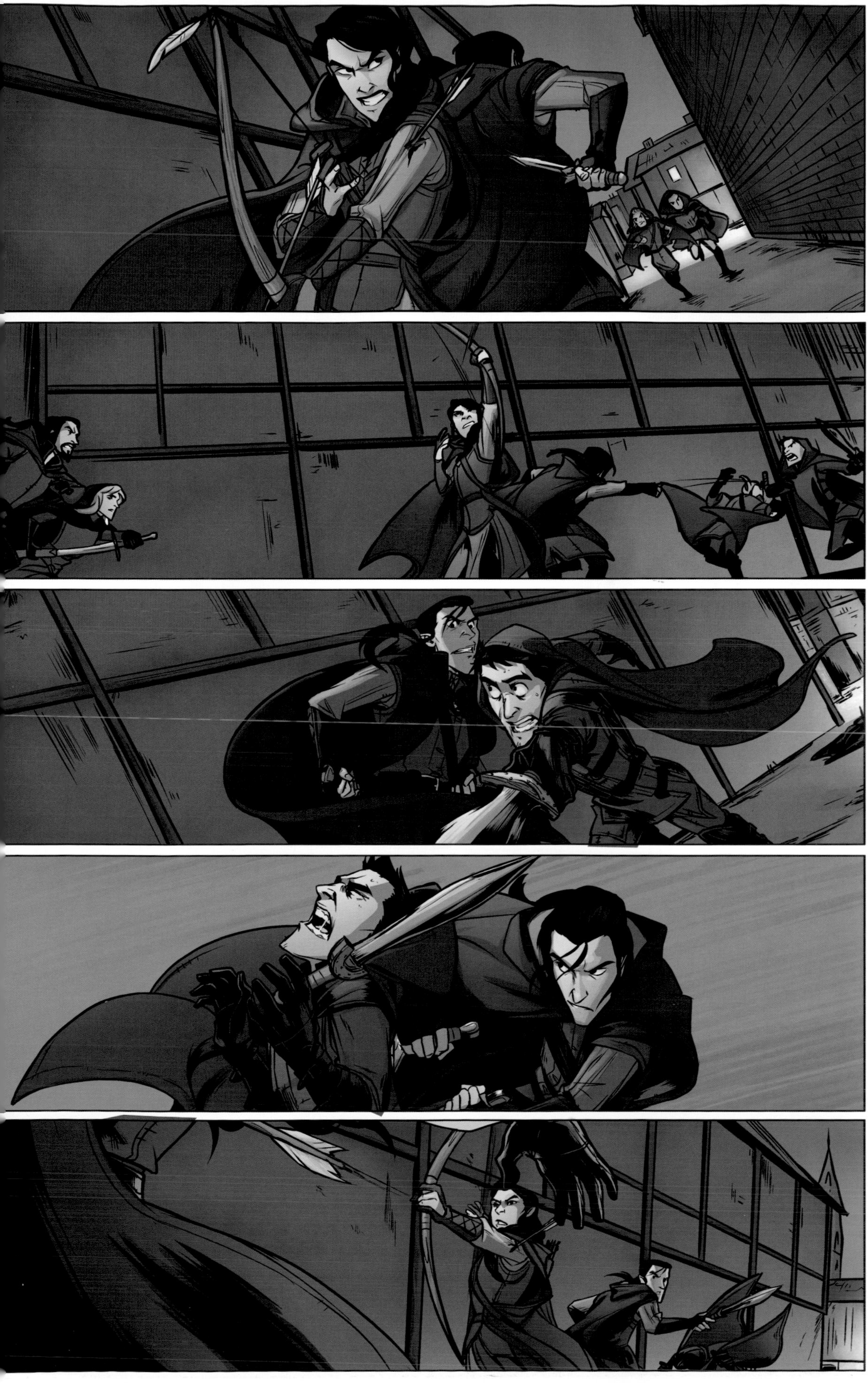

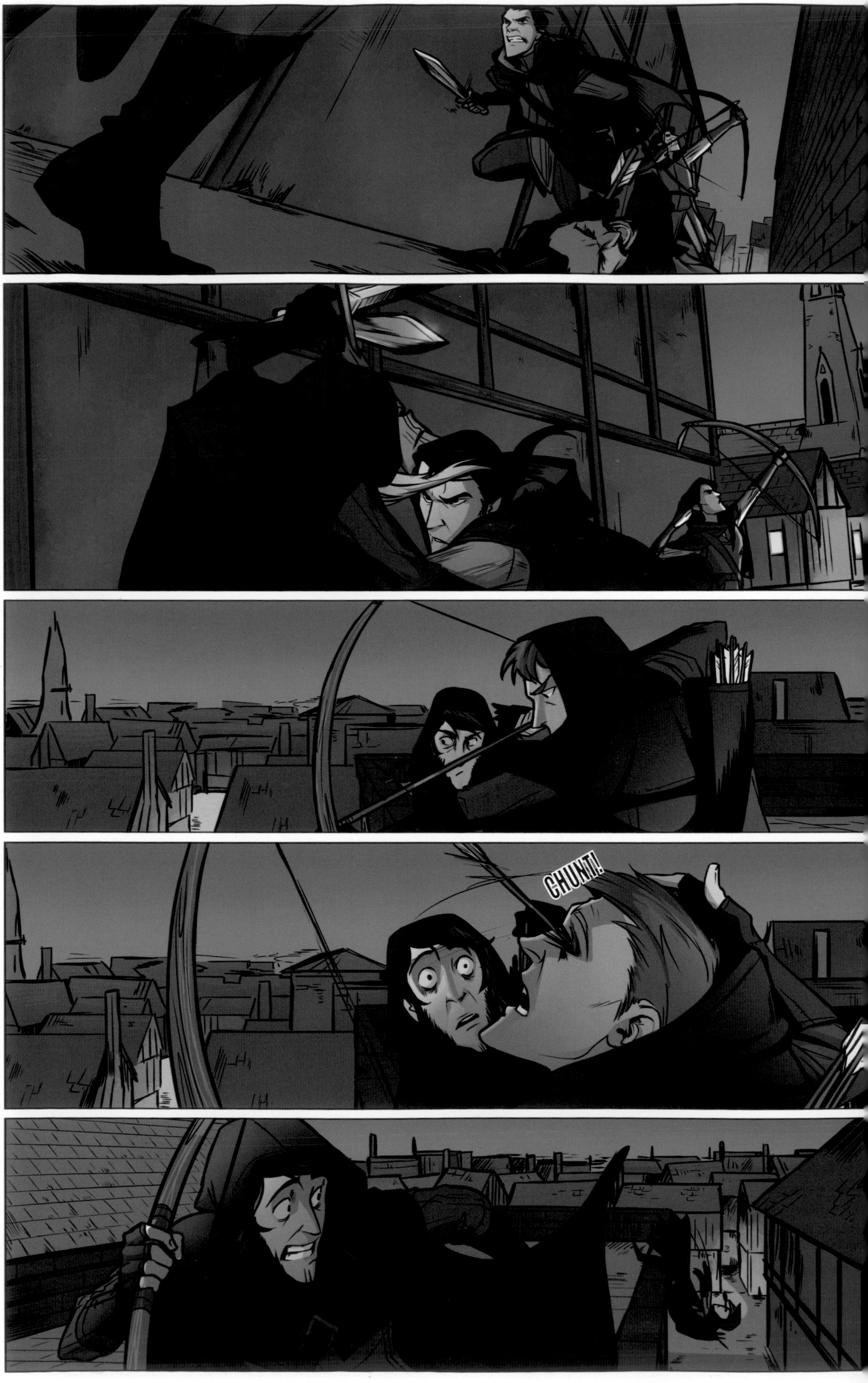
CHUNT!

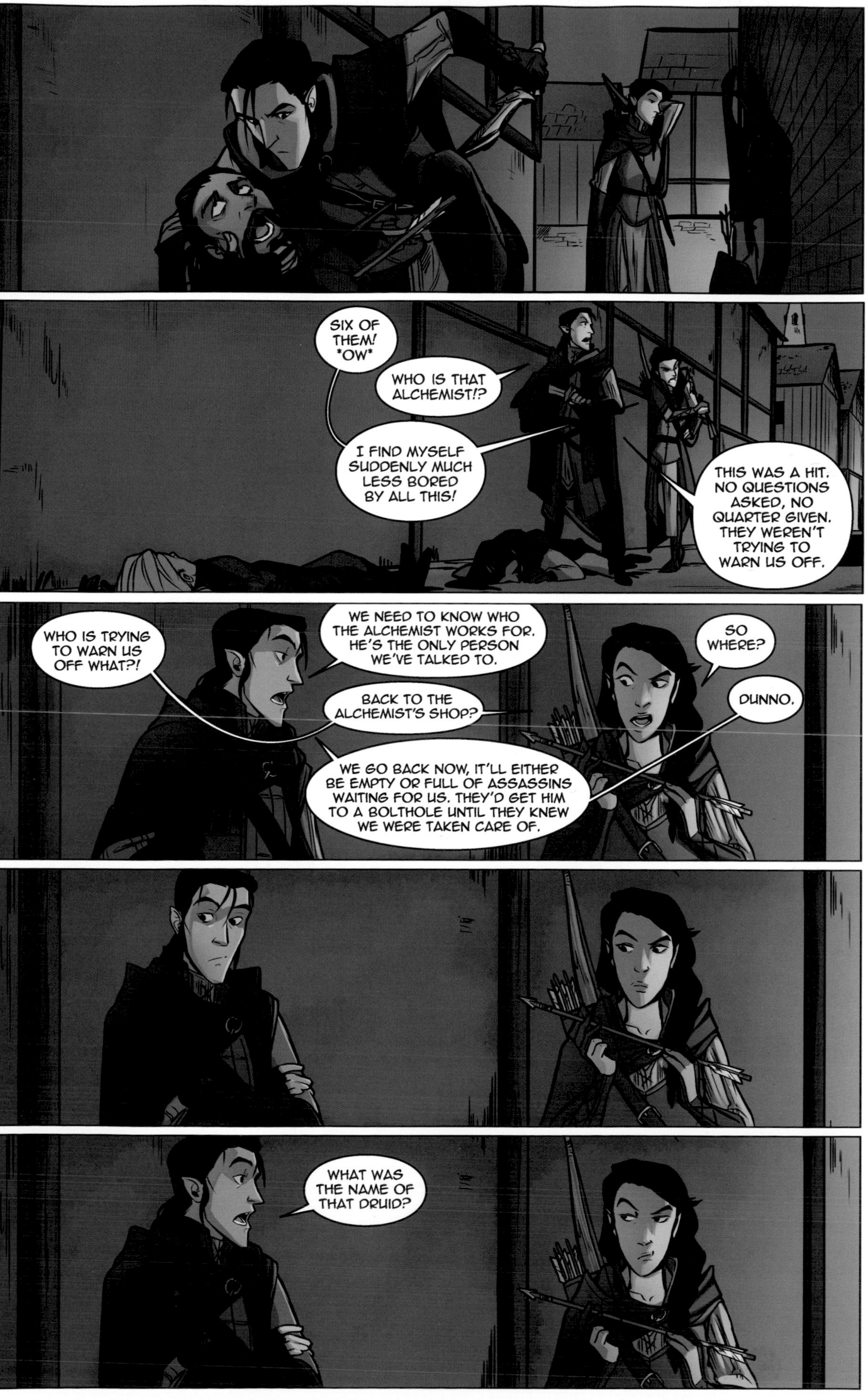
SIX OF THEM! *OW*
WHO IS THAT ALCHEMIST!?
I FIND MYSELF SUDDENLY MUCH LESS BORED BY ALL THIS!
THIS WAS A HIT. NO QUESTIONS ASKED, NO QUARTER GIVEN. THEY WEREN'T TRYING TO WARN US OFF.
WHO IS TRYING TO WARN US OFF WHAT?!
WE NEED TO KNOW WHO THE ALCHEMIST WORKS FOR. HE'S THE ONLY PERSON WE'VE TALKED TO.
SO WHERE?
BACK TO THE ALCHEMIST'S SHOP?
DUNNO.
WE GO BACK NOW, IT'LL EITHER BE EMPTY OR FULL OF ASSASSINS WAITING FOR US. THEY'D GET HIM TO A BOLTHOLE UNTIL THEY KNEW WE WERE TAKEN CARE OF.
WHAT WAS THE NAME OF THAT DRUID?

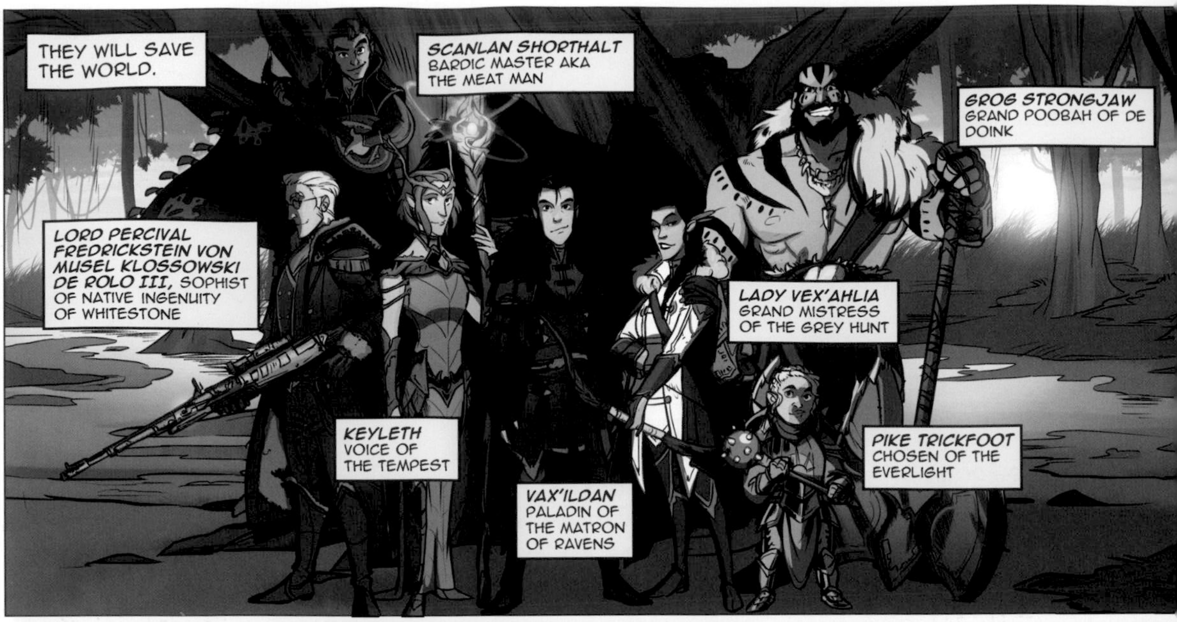
THEY WILL SAVE THE WORLD.
SCANLAN SHORTHALT BARDIC MASTER AKA THE MEAT MAN
GROG STRONGJAW GRAND POOBAH OF DE DOINK
LORD PERCIVAL FREDRICKSTEIN VON MUSEL KLOSSOWSKI DE ROLO III, SOPHIST OF NATIVE INGENUITY OF WHITESTONE
LADY VEX'AHLIA GRAND MISTRESS OF THE GREY HUNT
KEYLETH VOICE OF THE TEMPEST
PIKE TRICKFOOT CHOSEN OF THE EVERLIGHT
VAX'ILDAN PALADIN OF THE MATRON OF RAVENS

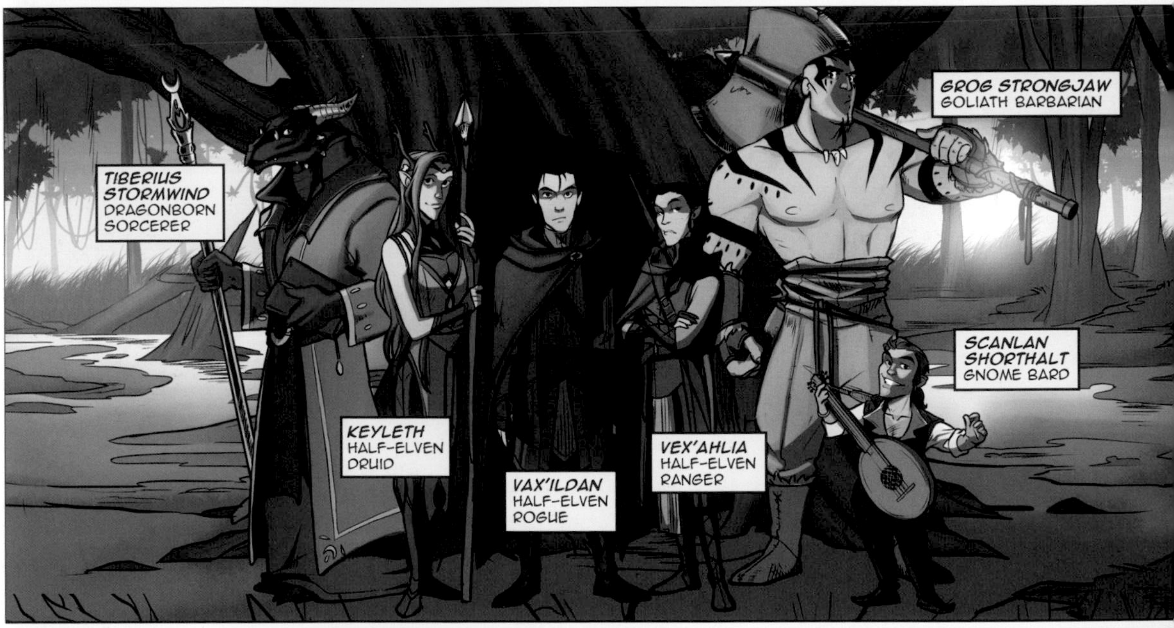
GROG STRONGJAW GOLIATH BARBARIAN
TIBERIUS STORMWIND DRAGONBORN SORCERER
SCANLAN SHORTHALT GNOME BARD
KEYLETH HALF-ELVEN DRUID
VEX'AHLIA HALF-ELVEN RANGER
VAX'ILDAN HALF-ELVEN ROGUE

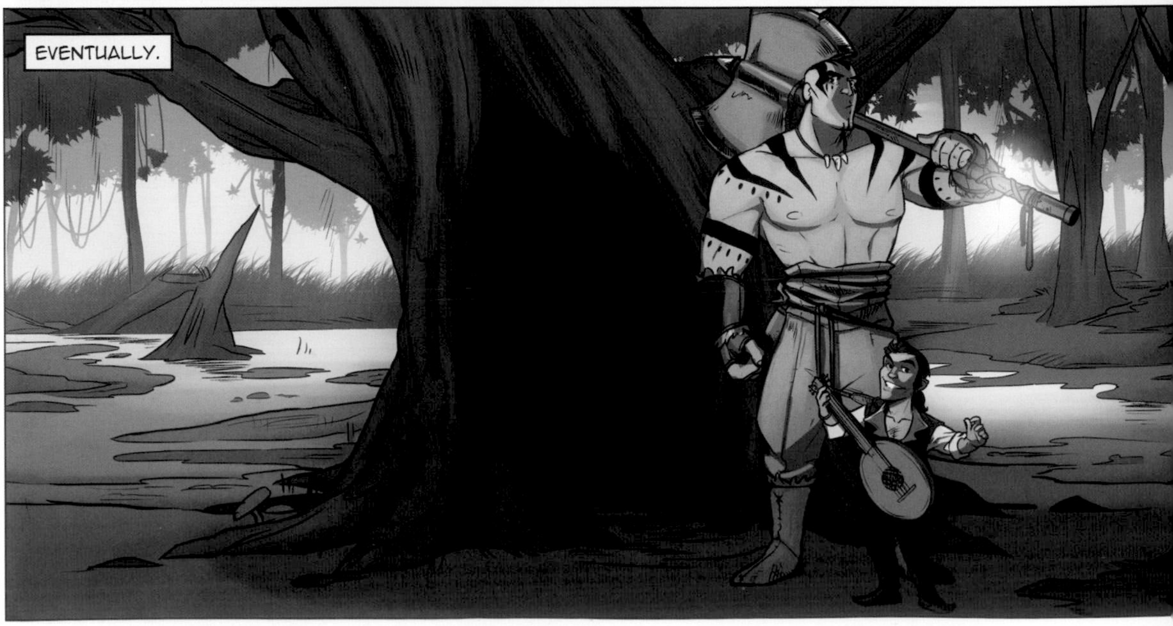
EVENTUALLY.

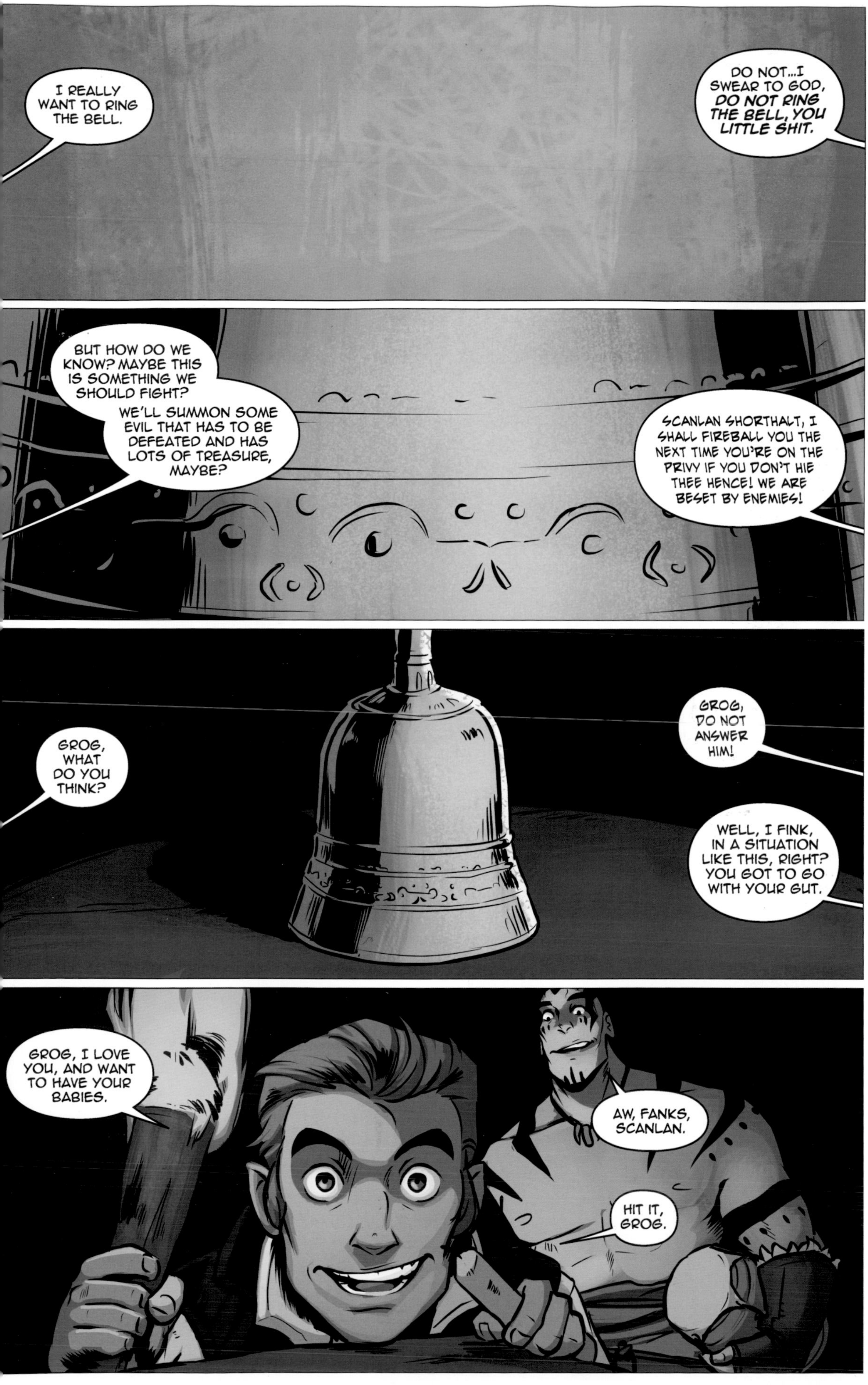

I REALLY WANT TO RING THE BELL.
DO NOT...I SWEAR TO GOD, DO NOT RING THE BELL, YOU LITTLE SHIT.
BUT HOW DO WE KNOW? MAYBE THIS IS SOMETHING WE SHOULD FIGHT?
WE'LL SUMMON SOME EVIL THAT HAS TO BE DEFEATED AND HAS LOTS OF TREASURE, MAYBE?
SCANLAN SHORTHALT, I SHALL FIREBALL YOU THE NEXT TIME YOU'RE ON THE PRIVY IF YOU DON'T HIE THEE HENCE! WE ARE BESET BY ENEMIES!
GROG, WHAT DO YOU THINK?
GROG, DO NOT ANSWER HIM!
WELL, I FINK, IN A SITUATION LIKE THIS, RIGHT? YOU GOT TO GO WITH YOUR GUT.
GROG, I LOVE YOU, AND WANT TO HAVE YOUR BABIES.
AW, FANKS, SCANLAN.
HIT IT, GROG.

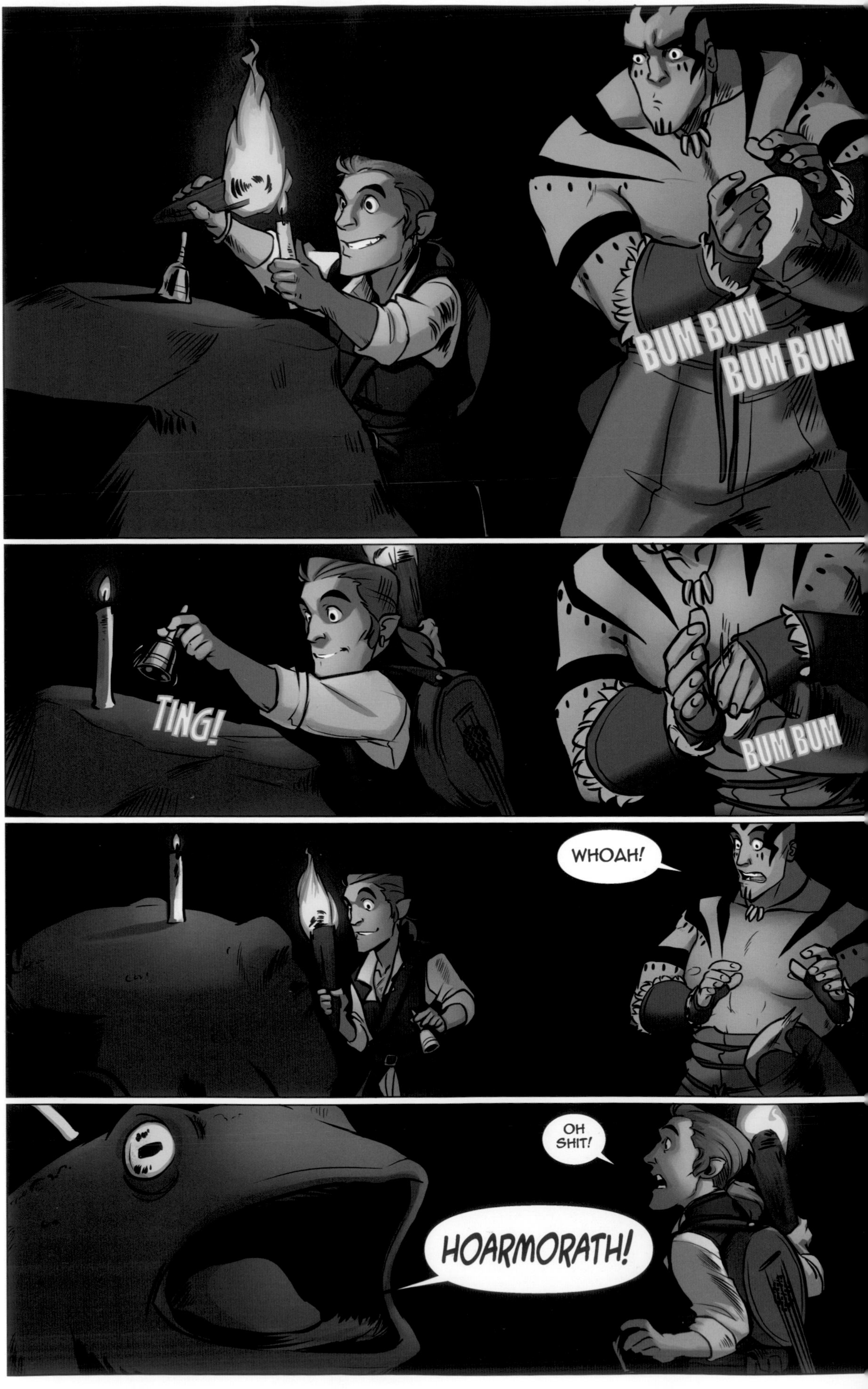
BUM BUM
BUM BUM
TING!
BUM BUM
WHOAH!
OH SHIT!
HOARMORATH!

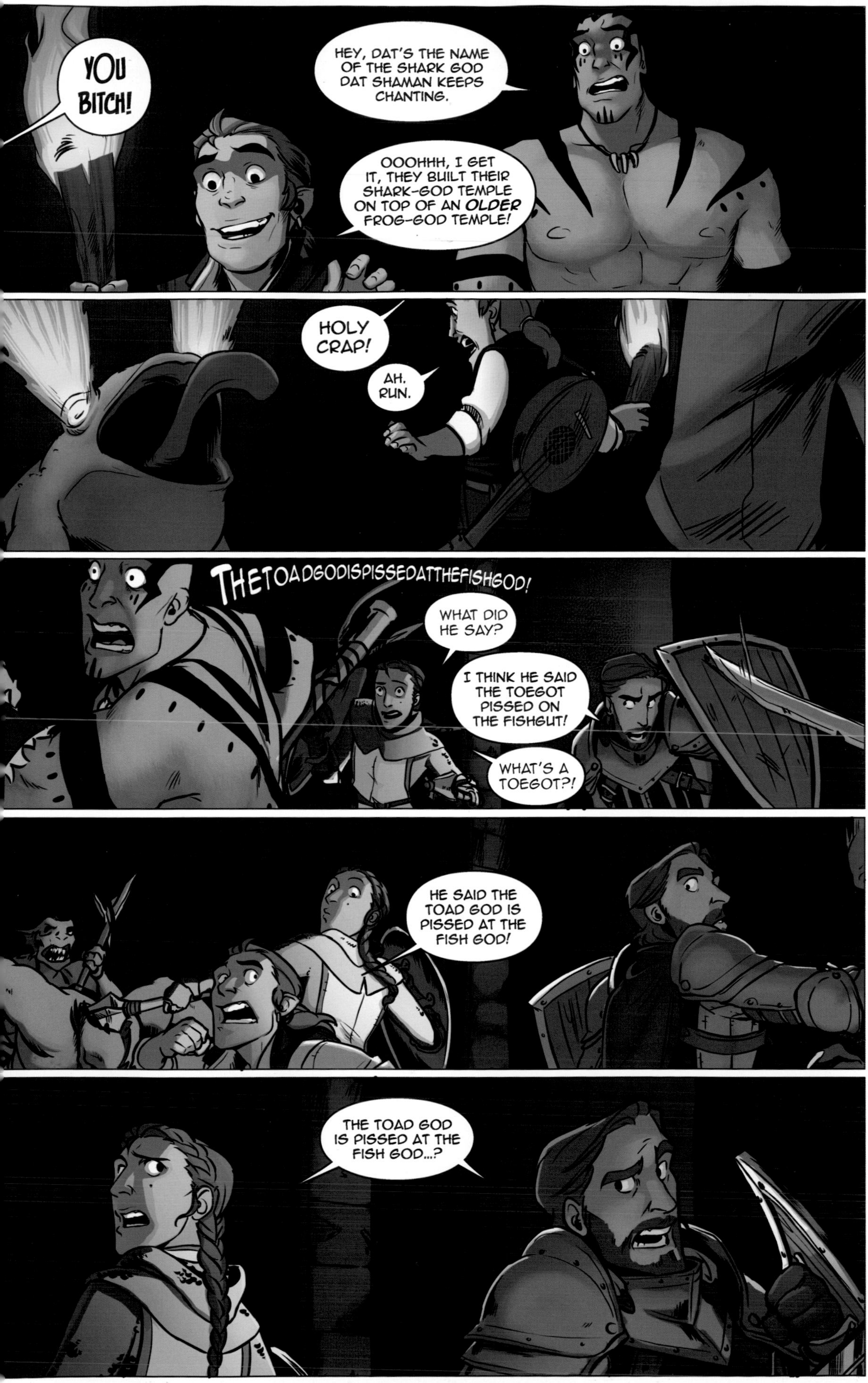
YOU BITCH!
HEY, DAT'S THE NAME OF THE SHARK GOD DAT SHAMAN KEEPS CHANTING.
OOOHHH, I GET IT, THEY BUILT THEIR SHARK-GOD TEMPLE ON TOP OF AN *OLDER* FROG-GOD TEMPLE!
HOLY CRAP!
AH. RUN.
THETOADGODISPISSEDATTHEFISHGOD!
WHAT DID HE SAY?
I THINK HE SAID THE TOEGOT PISSED ON THE FISHGUT!
WHAT'S A TOEGOT?!
HE SAID THE TOAD GOD IS PISSED AT THE FISH GOD!
THE TOAD GOD IS PISSED AT THE FISH GOD...?

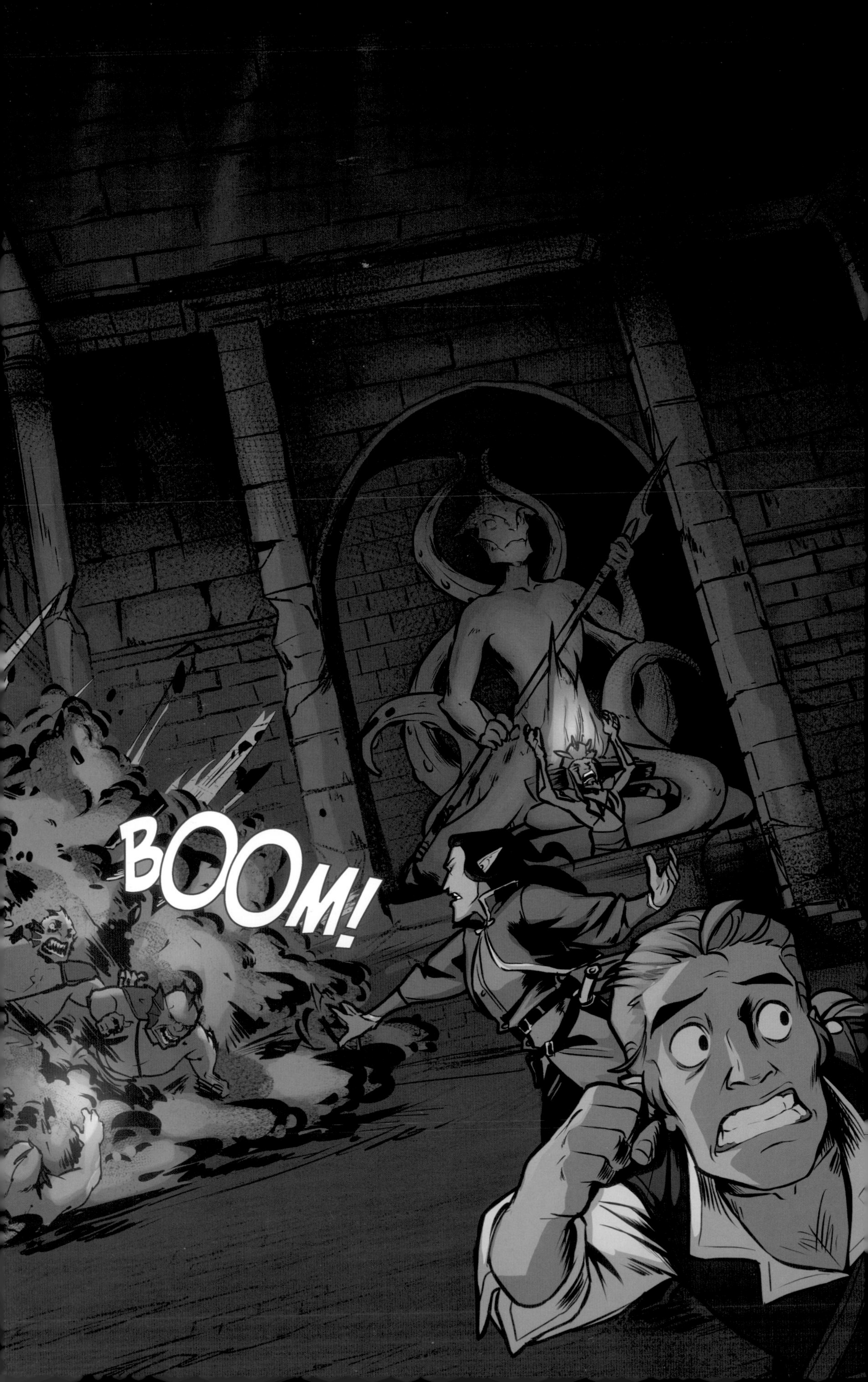
BOOM!

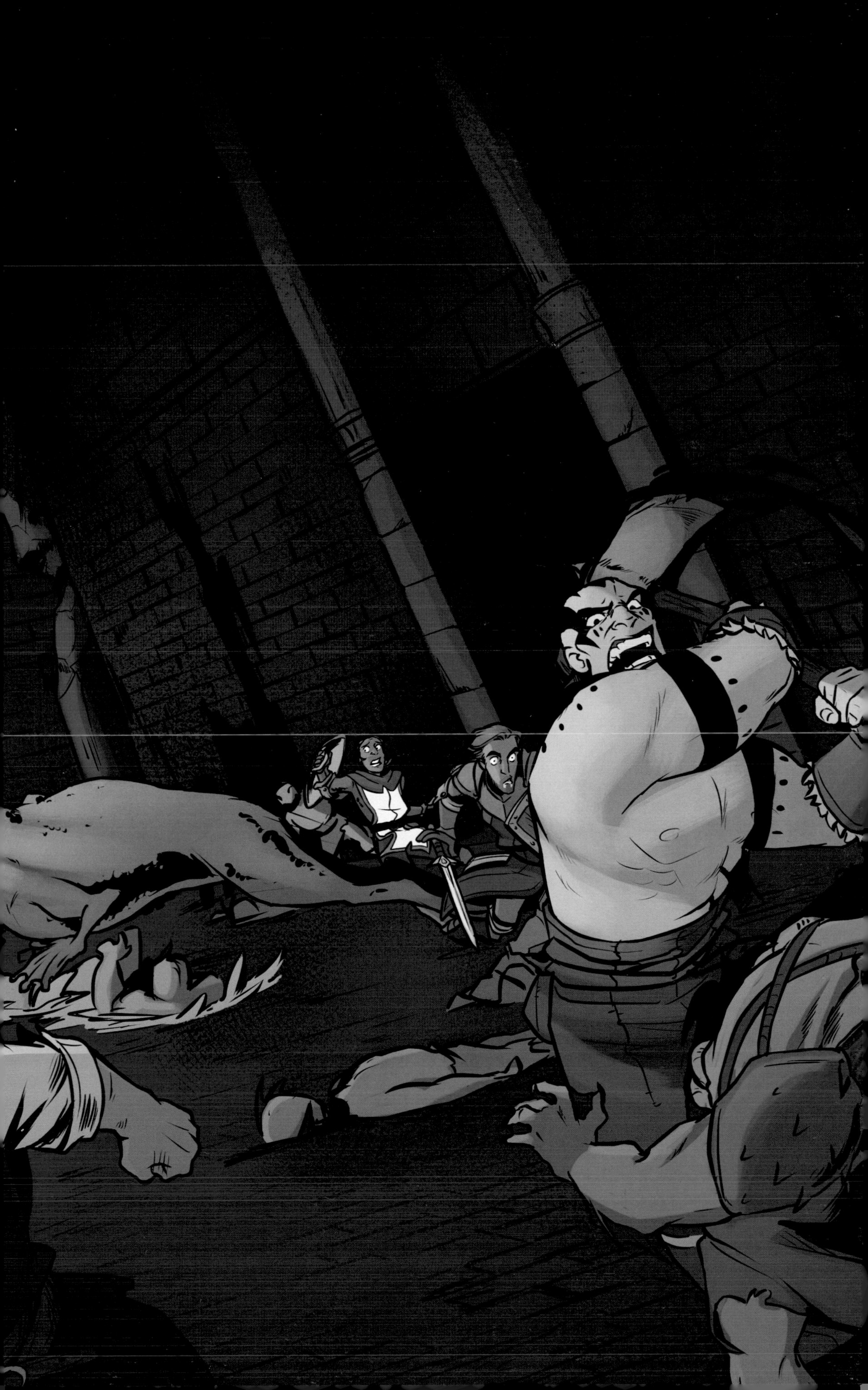

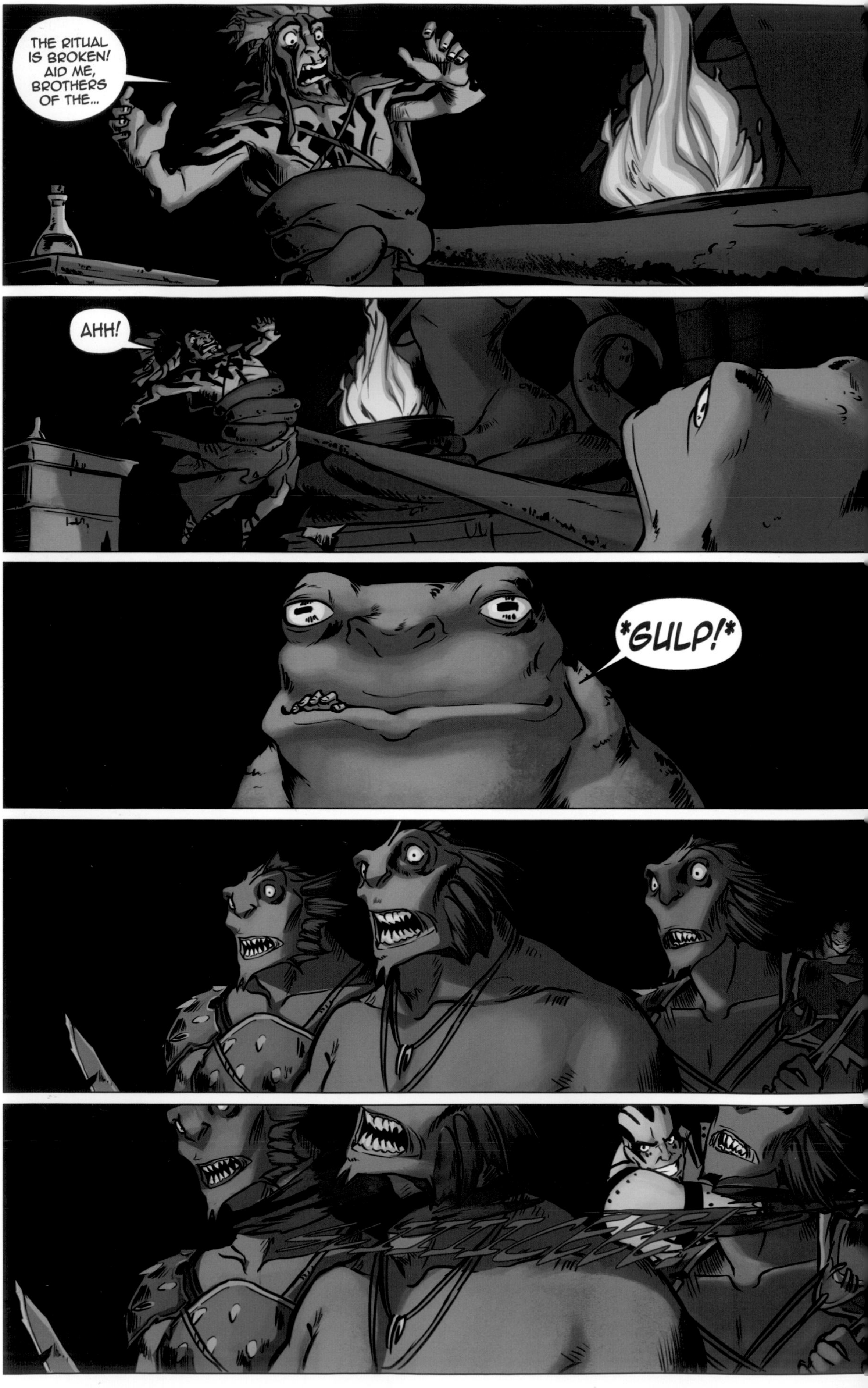
THE RITUAL IS BROKEN! AID ME, BROTHERS OF THE...
AHH!
*GULP!*

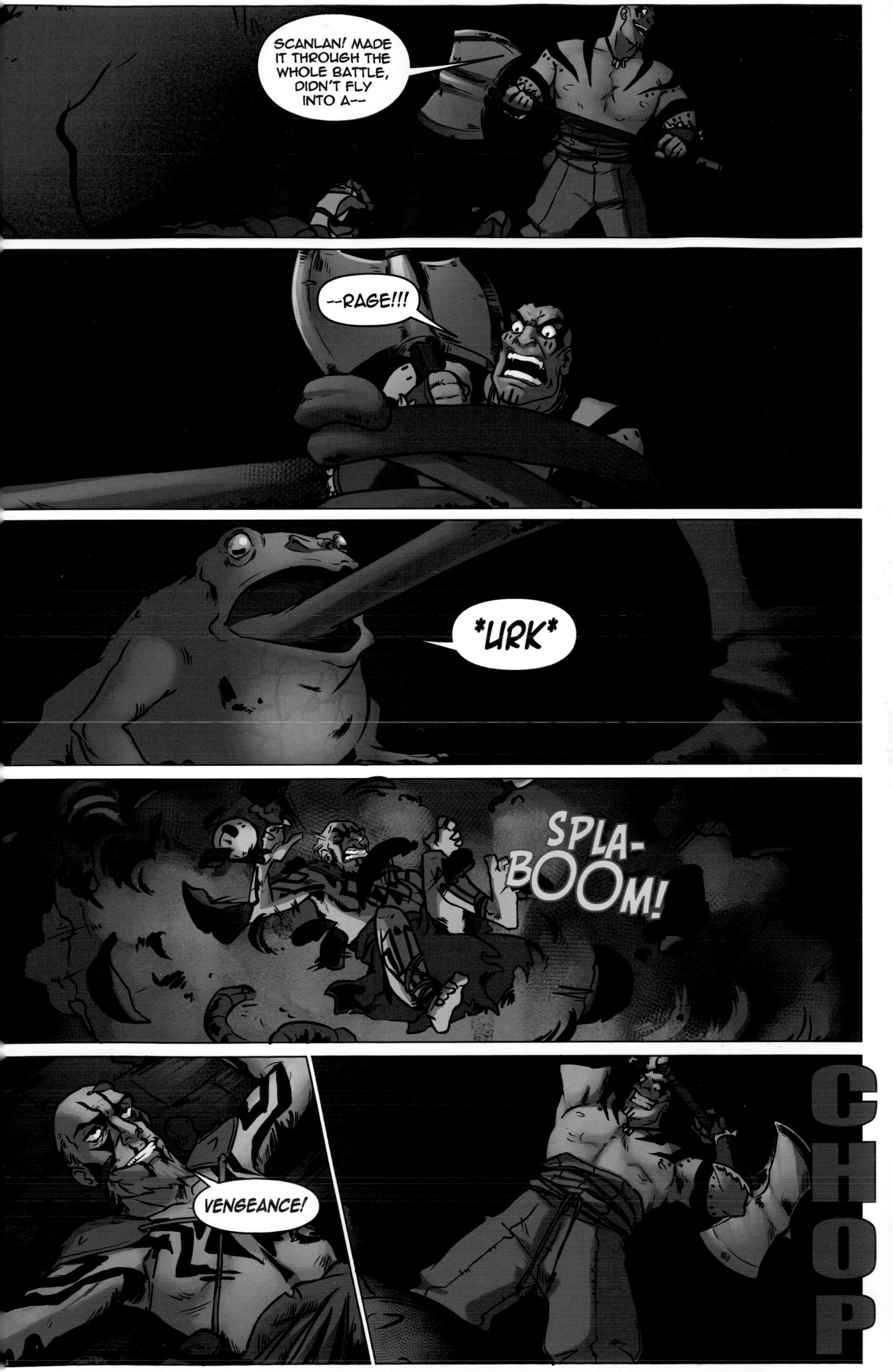
SCANLAN! MADE IT THROUGH THE WHOLE BATTLE, DIDN'T FLY INTO A--
--RAGE!!!
*URK*
SPLA-BOOM!
VENGEANCE!
CHOP

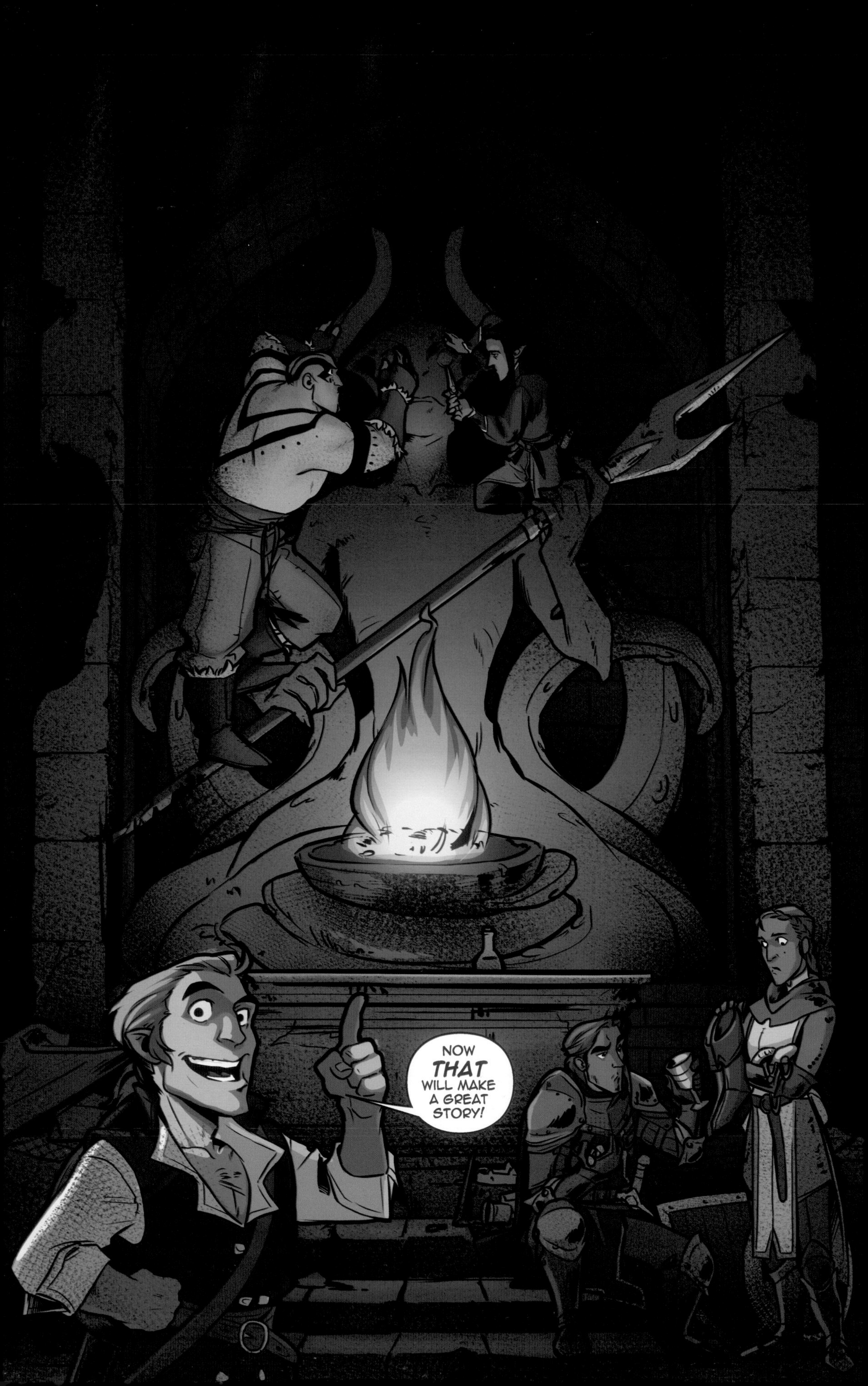
NOW *THAT* WILL MAKE A GREAT STORY!

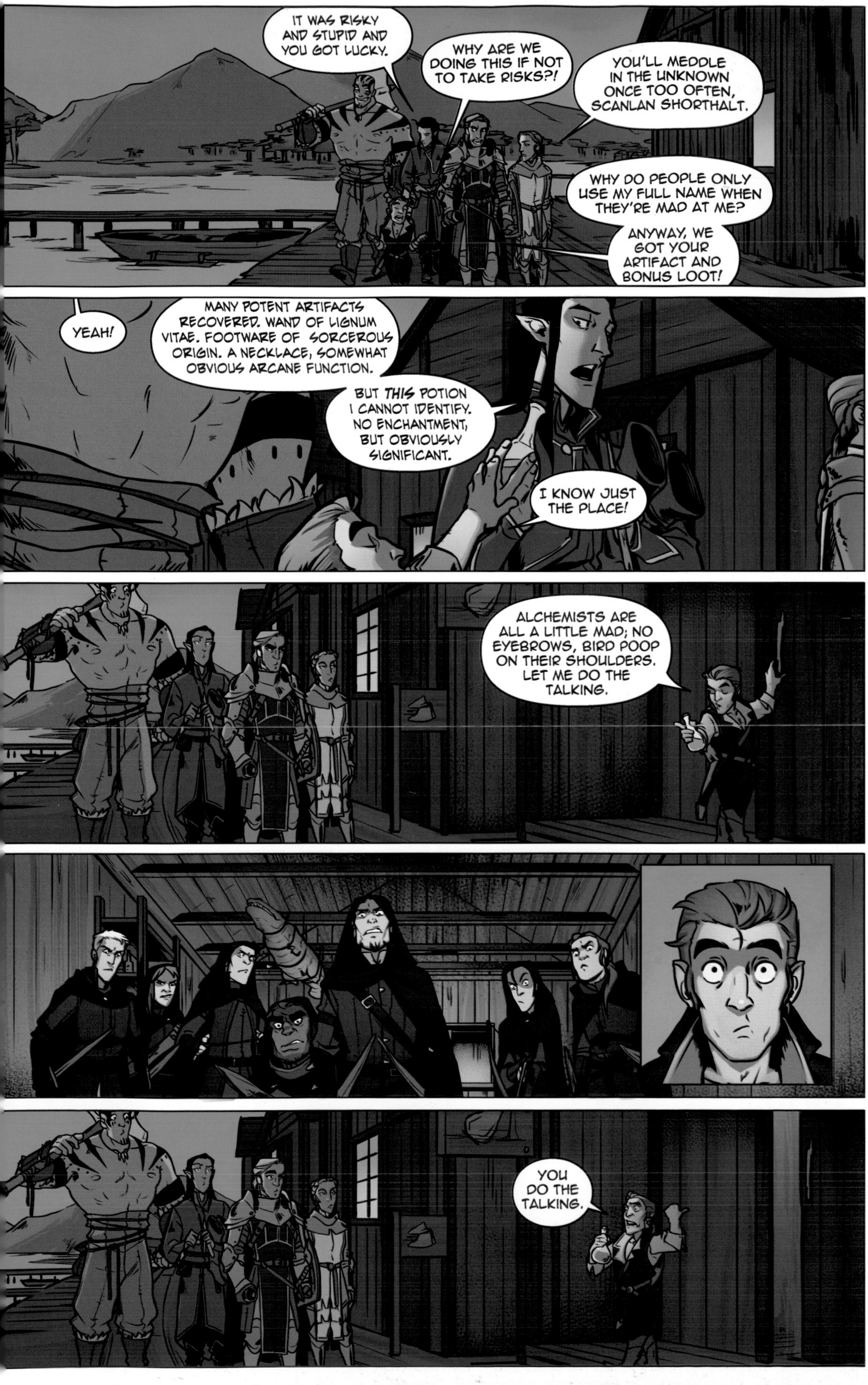
IT WAS RISKY AND STUPID AND YOU GOT LUCKY.
WHY ARE WE DOING THIS IF NOT TO TAKE RISKS?!
YOU'LL MEDDLE IN THE UNKNOWN ONCE TOO OFTEN, SCANLAN SHORTHALT.
WHY DO PEOPLE ONLY USE MY FULL NAME WHEN THEY'RE MAD AT ME?
ANYWAY, WE GOT YOUR ARTIFACT AND BONUS LOOT!
YEAH!
MANY POTENT ARTIFACTS RECOVERED. WAND OF LIGNUM VITAE. FOOTWARE OF SORCEROUS ORIGIN. A NECKLACE, SOMEWHAT OBVIOUS ARCANE FUNCTION.
BUT THIS POTION I CANNOT IDENTIFY. NO ENCHANTMENT, BUT OBVIOUSLY SIGNIFICANT.
I KNOW JUST THE PLACE!
ALCHEMISTS ARE ALL A LITTLE MAD; NO EYEBROWS, BIRD POOP ON THEIR SHOULDERS. LET ME DO THE TALKING.
YOU DO THE TALKING.

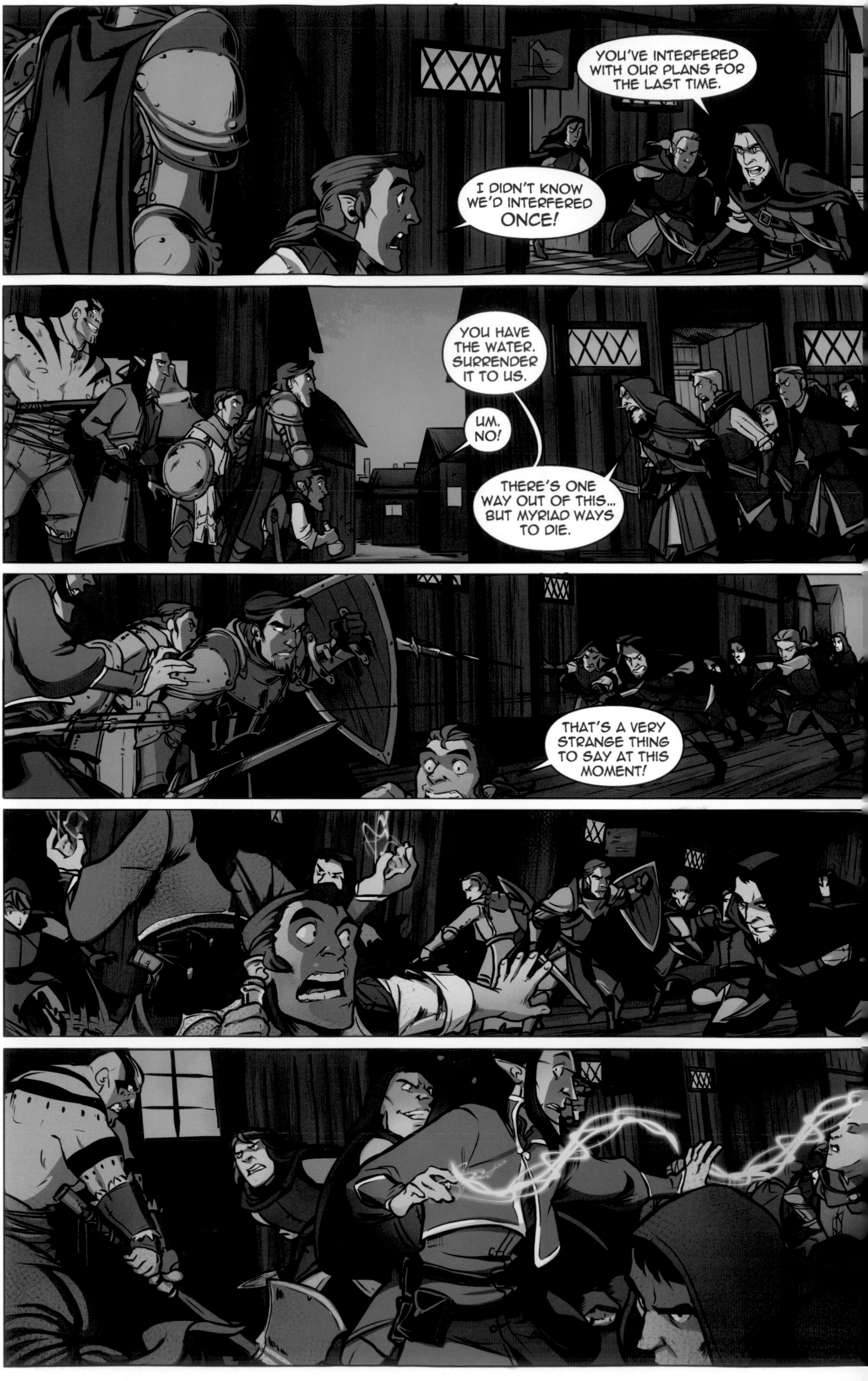
YOU'VE INTERFERED WITH OUR PLANS FOR THE LAST TIME.
I DIDN'T KNOW WE'D INTERFERED ONCE!
YOU HAVE THE WATER. SURRENDER IT TO US.
UM. NO!
THERE'S ONE WAY OUT OF THIS... BUT MYRIAD WAYS TO DIE.
THAT'S A VERY STRANGE THING TO SAY AT THIS MOMENT!

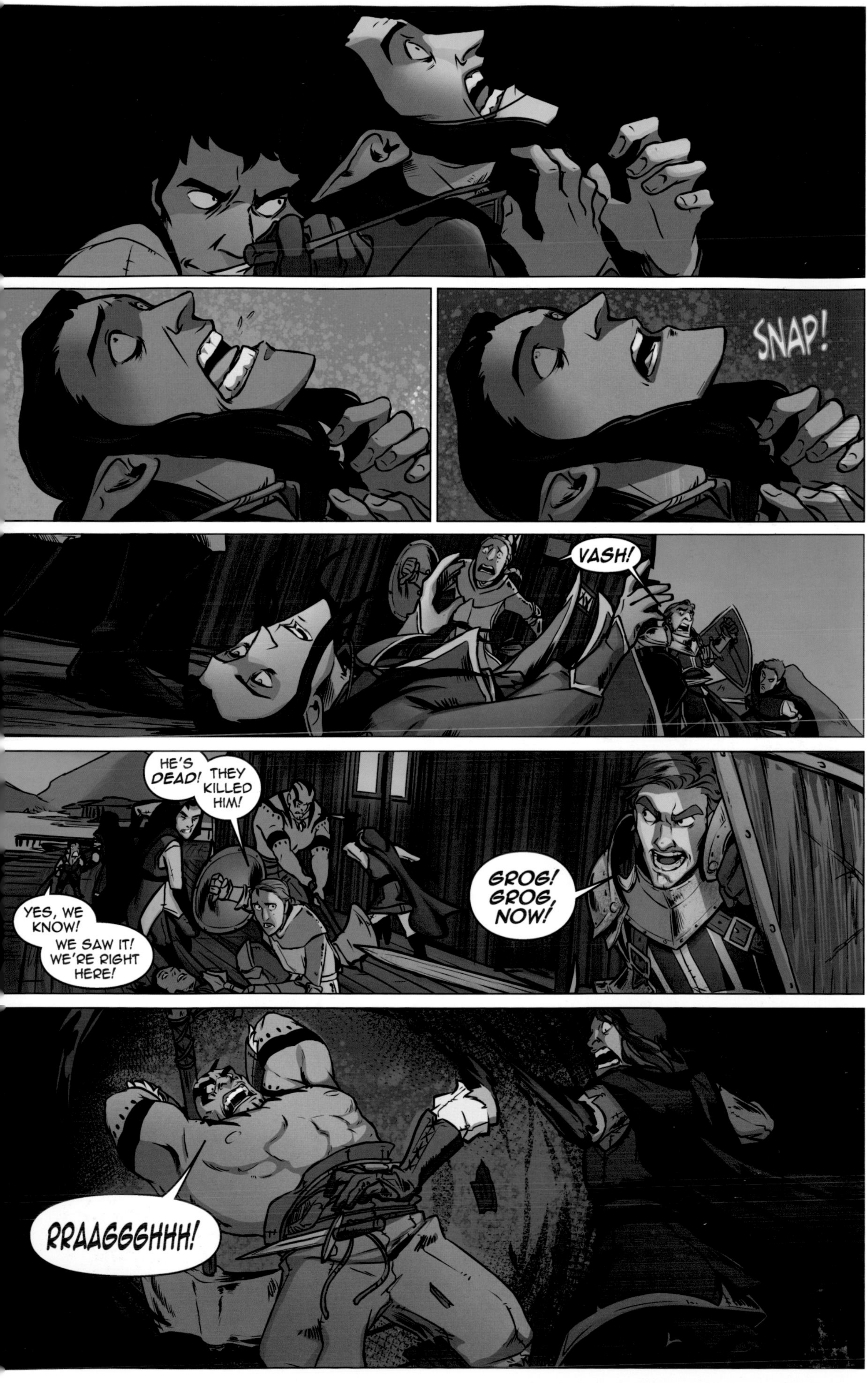
SNAP!
VASH!
HE'S DEAD!
THEY KILLED HIM!
YES, WE KNOW! WE SAW IT! WE'RE RIGHT HERE!
GROG! GROG, NOW!
RRAAGGGHHH!

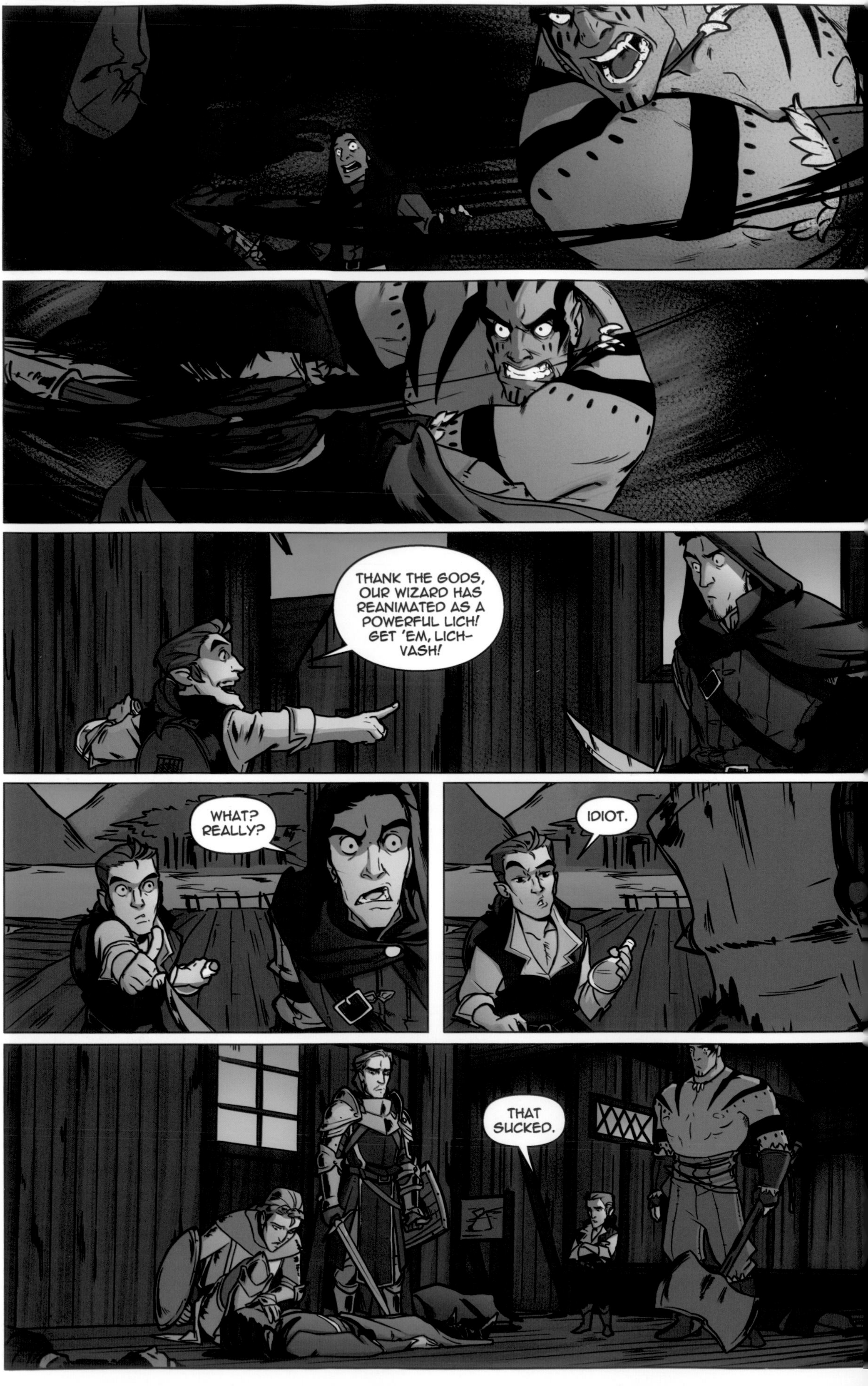
THANK THE GODS, OUR WIZARD HAS REANIMATED AS A POWERFUL LICH! GET 'EM, LICH-VASH!
WHAT? REALLY?
IDIOT.
THAT SUCKED.

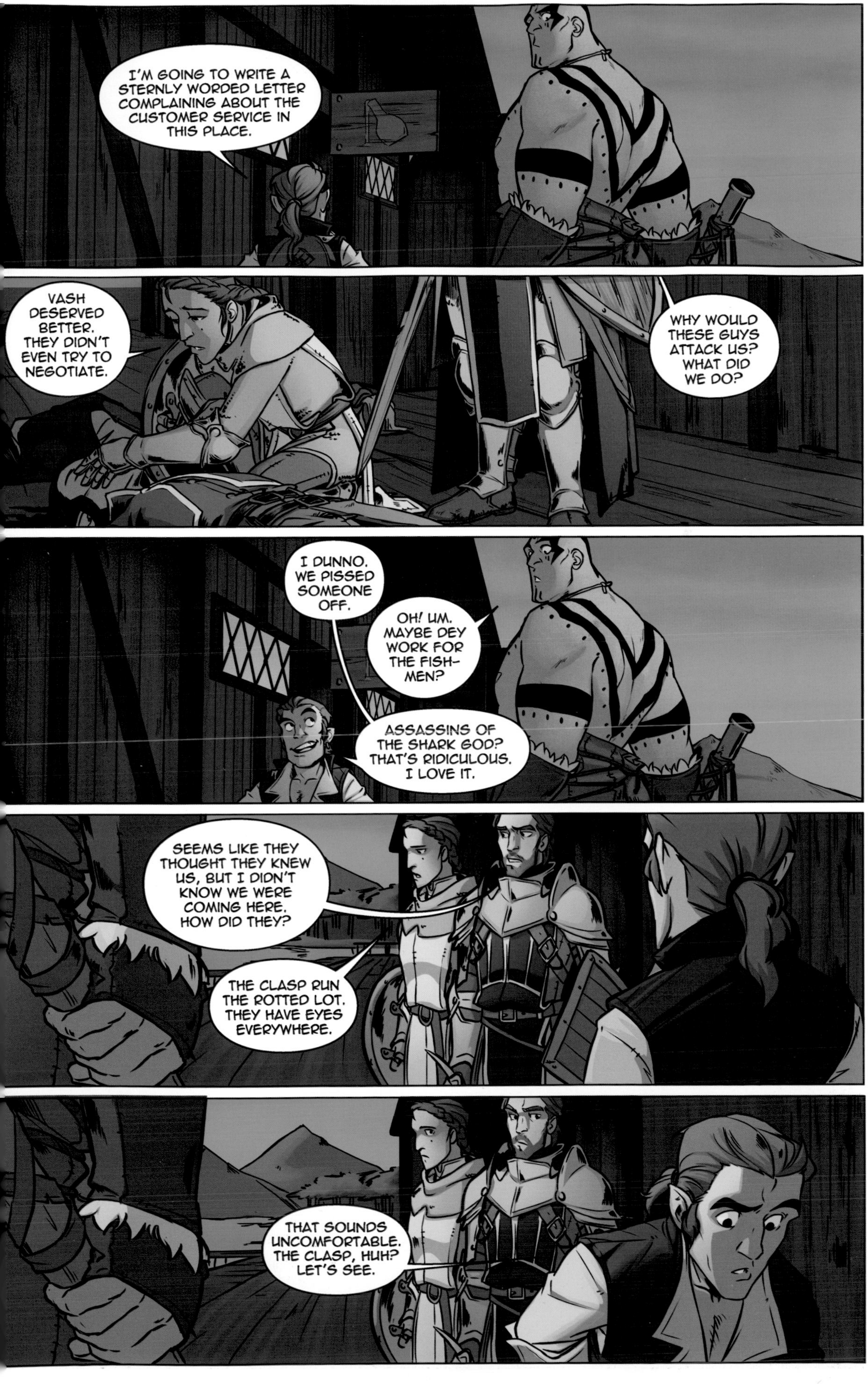
I'M GOING TO WRITE A STERNLY WORDED LETTER COMPLAINING ABOUT THE CUSTOMER SERVICE IN THIS PLACE.
VASH DESERVED BETTER. THEY DIDN'T EVEN TRY TO NEGOTIATE.
WHY WOULD THESE GUYS ATTACK US? WHAT DID WE DO?
I DUNNO. WE PISSED SOMEONE OFF.
OH! UM. MAYBE DEY WORK FOR THE FISH-MEN?
ASSASSINS OF THE SHARK GOD? THAT'S RIDICULOUS. I LOVE IT.
SEEMS LIKE THEY THOUGHT THEY KNEW US, BUT I DIDN'T KNOW WE WERE COMING HERE. HOW DID THEY?
THE CLASP RUN THE ROTTED LOT. THEY HAVE EYES EVERYWHERE.
THAT SOUNDS UNCOMFORTABLE. THE CLASP, HUH? LET'S SEE.

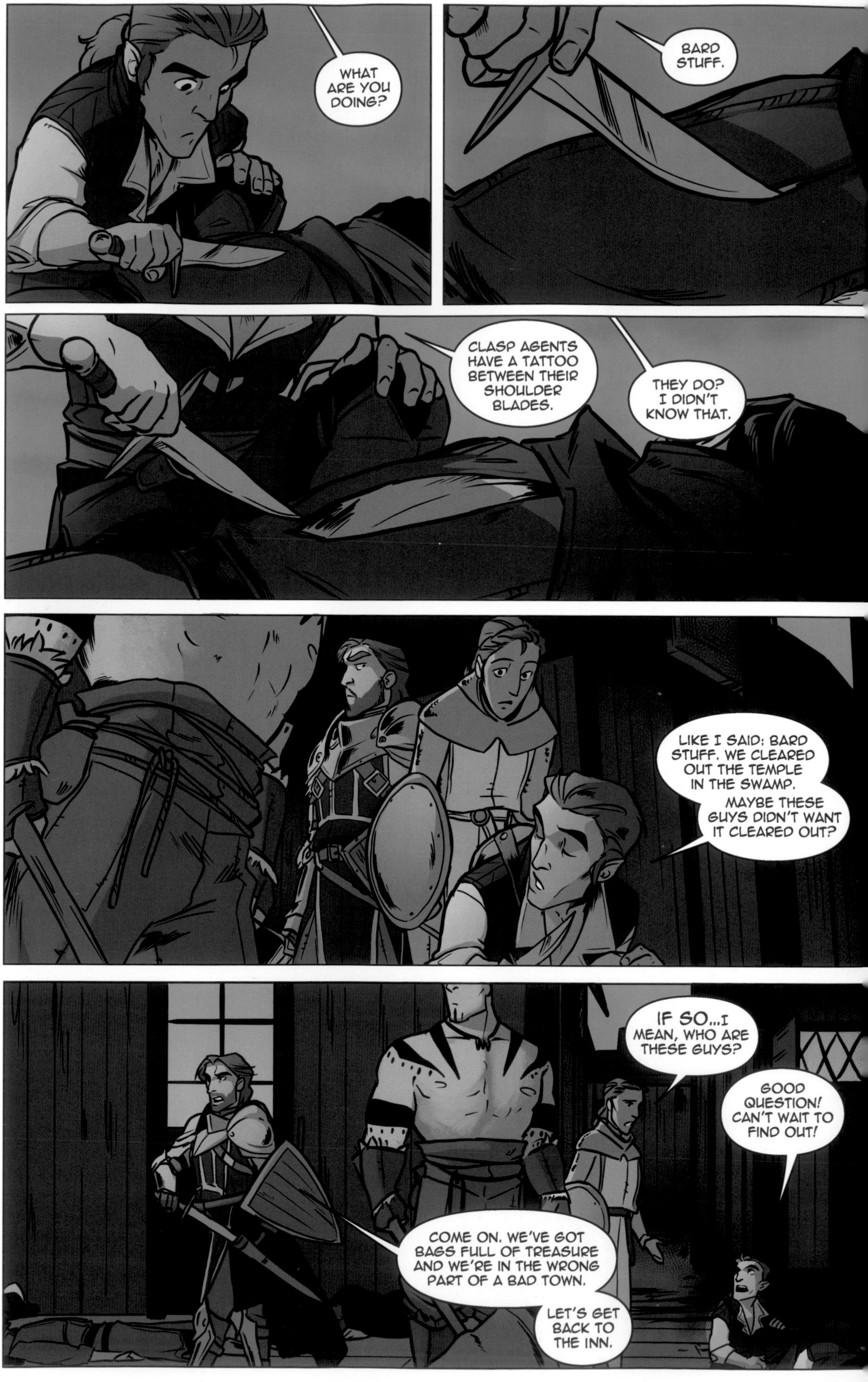
WHAT ARE YOU DOING?
BARD STUFF.
CLASP AGENTS HAVE A TATTOO BETWEEN THEIR SHOULDER BLADES.
THEY DO? I DIDN'T KNOW THAT.
LIKE I SAID: BARD STUFF. WE CLEARED OUT THE TEMPLE IN THE SWAMP.
MAYBE THESE GUYS DIDN'T WANT IT CLEARED OUT?
IF SO...I MEAN, WHO ARE THESE GUYS?
GOOD QUESTION! CAN'T WAIT TO FIND OUT!
COME ON. WE'VE GOT BAGS FULL OF TREASURE AND WE'RE IN THE WRONG PART OF A BAD TOWN.
LET'S GET BACK TO THE INN.

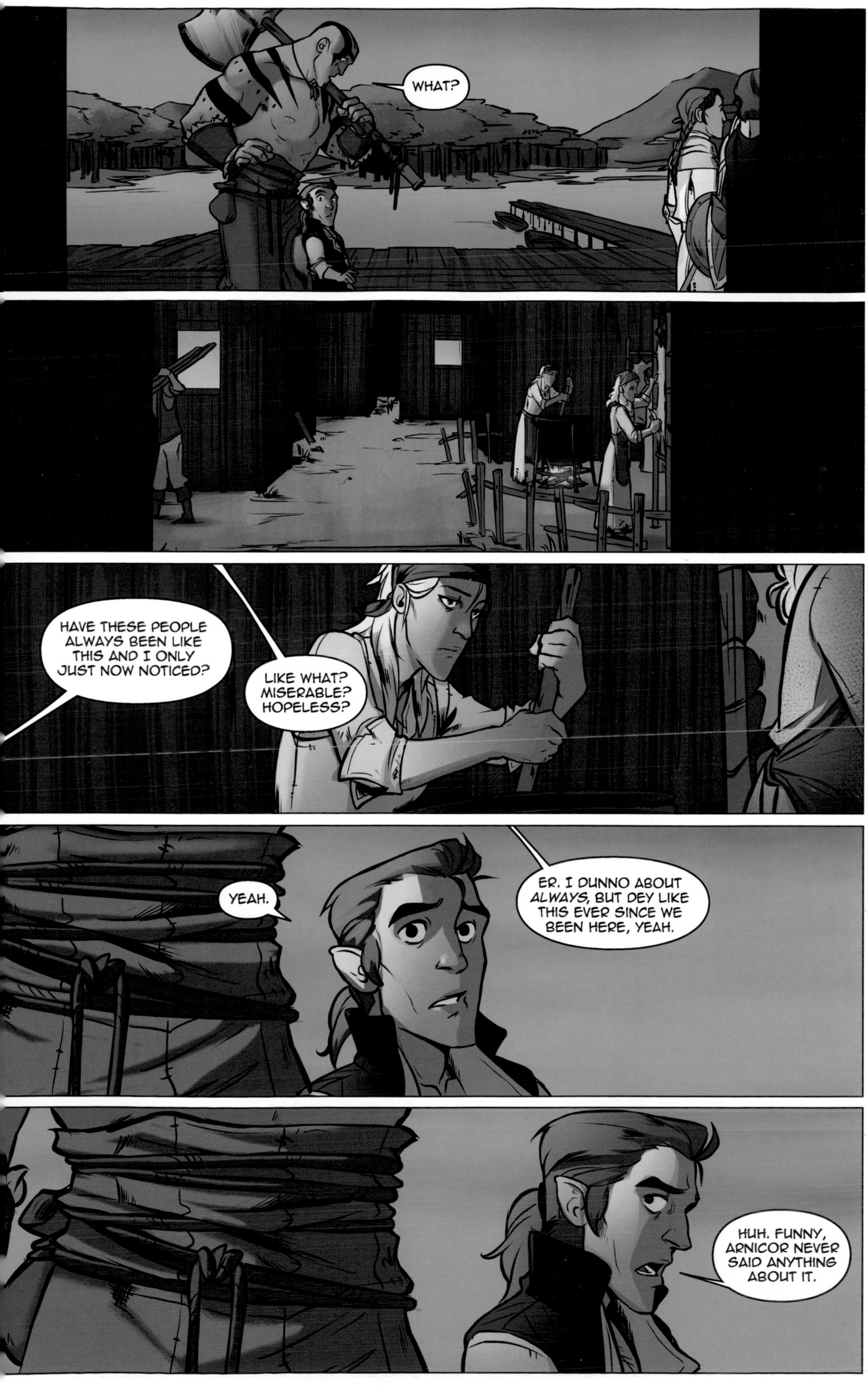
WHAT?
HAVE THESE PEOPLE ALWAYS BEEN LIKE THIS AND I ONLY JUST NOW NOTICED?
LIKE WHAT? MISERABLE? HOPELESS?
YEAH.
ER. I DUNNO ABOUT *ALWAYS*, BUT DEY LIKE THIS EVER SINCE WE BEEN HERE, YEAH.
HUH. FUNNY, ARNICOR NEVER SAID ANYTHING ABOUT IT.

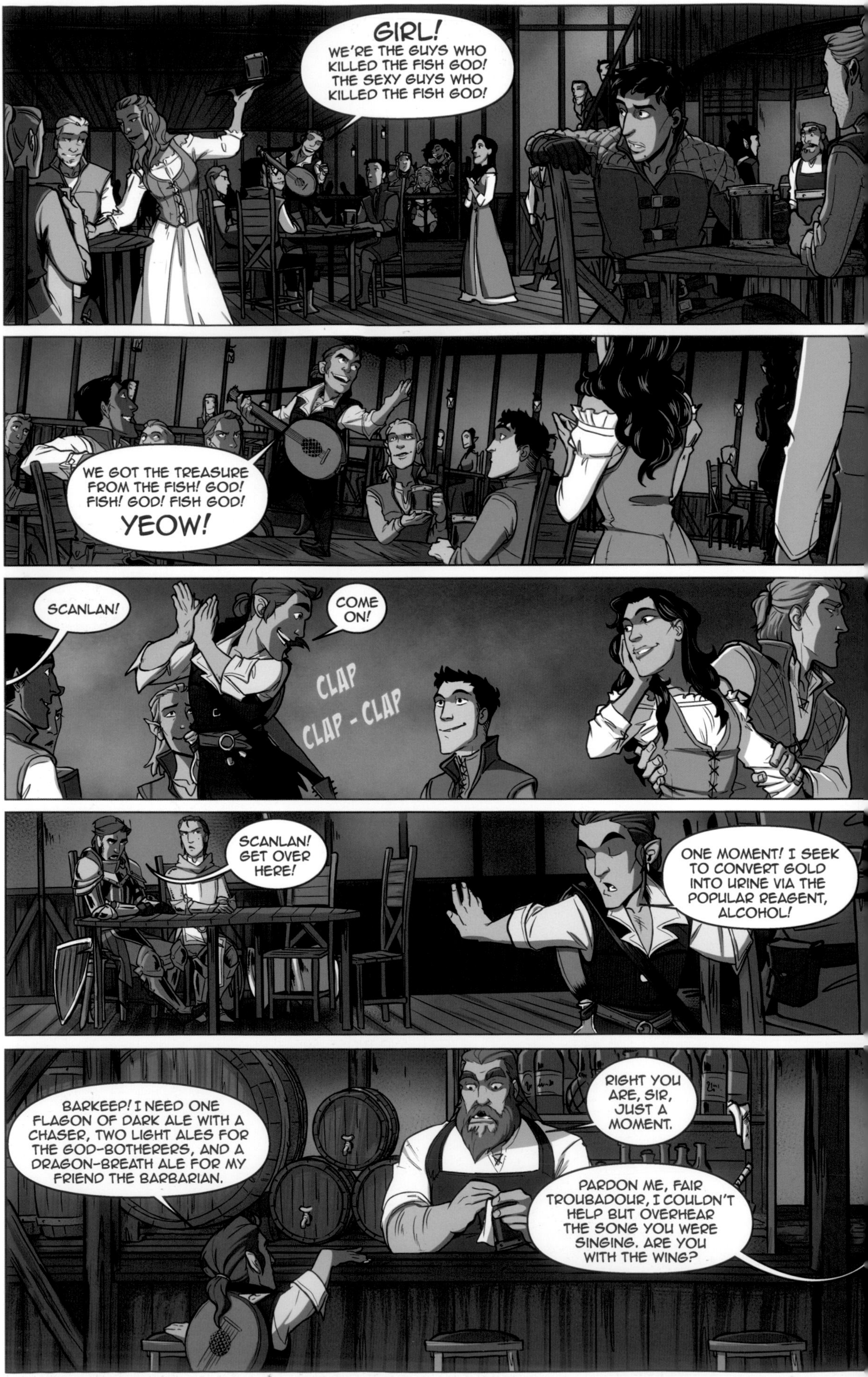
GIRL! WE'RE THE GUYS WHO KILLED THE FISH GOD! THE SEXY GUYS WHO KILLED THE FISH GOD!
WE GOT THE TREASURE FROM THE FISH! GOD! FISH! GOD! FISH GOD! YEOW!
SCANLAN!
COME ON!
CLAP CLAP - CLAP
SCANLAN! GET OVER HERE!
ONE MOMENT! I SEEK TO CONVERT GOLD INTO URINE VIA THE POPULAR REAGENT, ALCOHOL!
BARKEEP! I NEED ONE FLAGON OF DARK ALE WITH A CHASER, TWO LIGHT ALES FOR THE GOD-BOTHERERS, AND A DRAGON-BREATH ALE FOR MY FRIEND THE BARBARIAN.
RIGHT YOU ARE, SIR, JUST A MOMENT.
PARDON ME, FAIR TROUBADOUR, I COULDN'T HELP BUT OVERHEAR THE SONG YOU WERE SINGING. ARE YOU WITH THE WING?

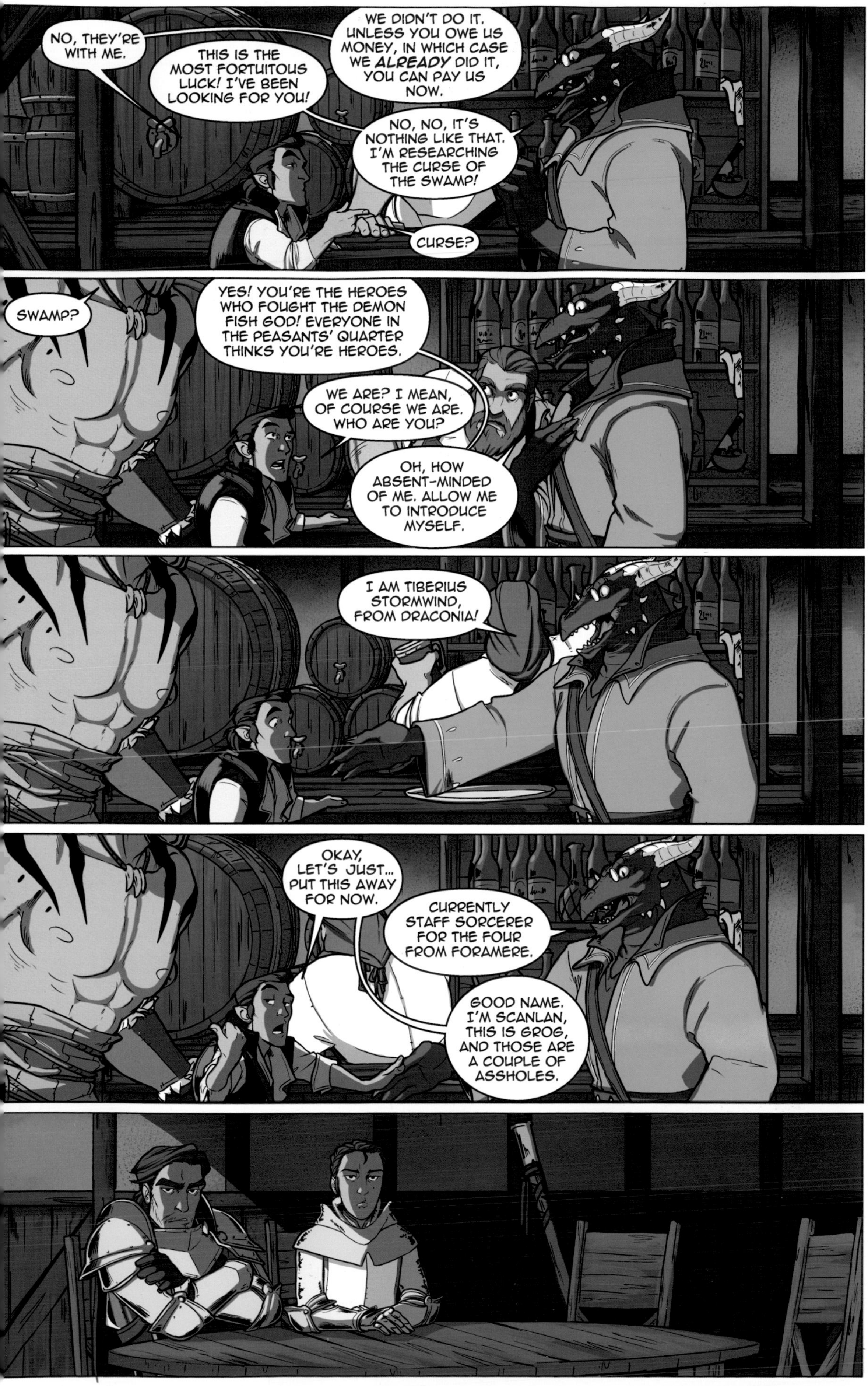
NO, THEY'RE WITH ME.
WE DIDN'T DO IT. UNLESS YOU OWE US MONEY, IN WHICH CASE WE *ALREADY* DID IT, YOU CAN PAY US NOW.
THIS IS THE MOST FORTUITOUS LUCK! I'VE BEEN LOOKING FOR YOU!
NO, NO, IT'S NOTHING LIKE THAT. I'M RESEARCHING THE CURSE OF THE SWAMP!
CURSE?
SWAMP?
YES! YOU'RE THE HEROES WHO FOUGHT THE DEMON FISH GOD! EVERYONE IN THE PEASANTS' QUARTER THINKS YOU'RE HEROES.
WE ARE? I MEAN, OF COURSE WE ARE. WHO ARE YOU?
OH, HOW ABSENT-MINDED OF ME. ALLOW ME TO INTRODUCE MYSELF.
I AM TIBERIUS STORMWIND, FROM DRACONIA!
OKAY, LET'S JUST... PUT THIS AWAY FOR NOW.
CURRENTLY STAFF SORCERER FOR THE FOUR FROM FORAMERE.
GOOD NAME. I'M SCANLAN, THIS IS GROG, AND THOSE ARE A COUPLE OF ASSHOLES.

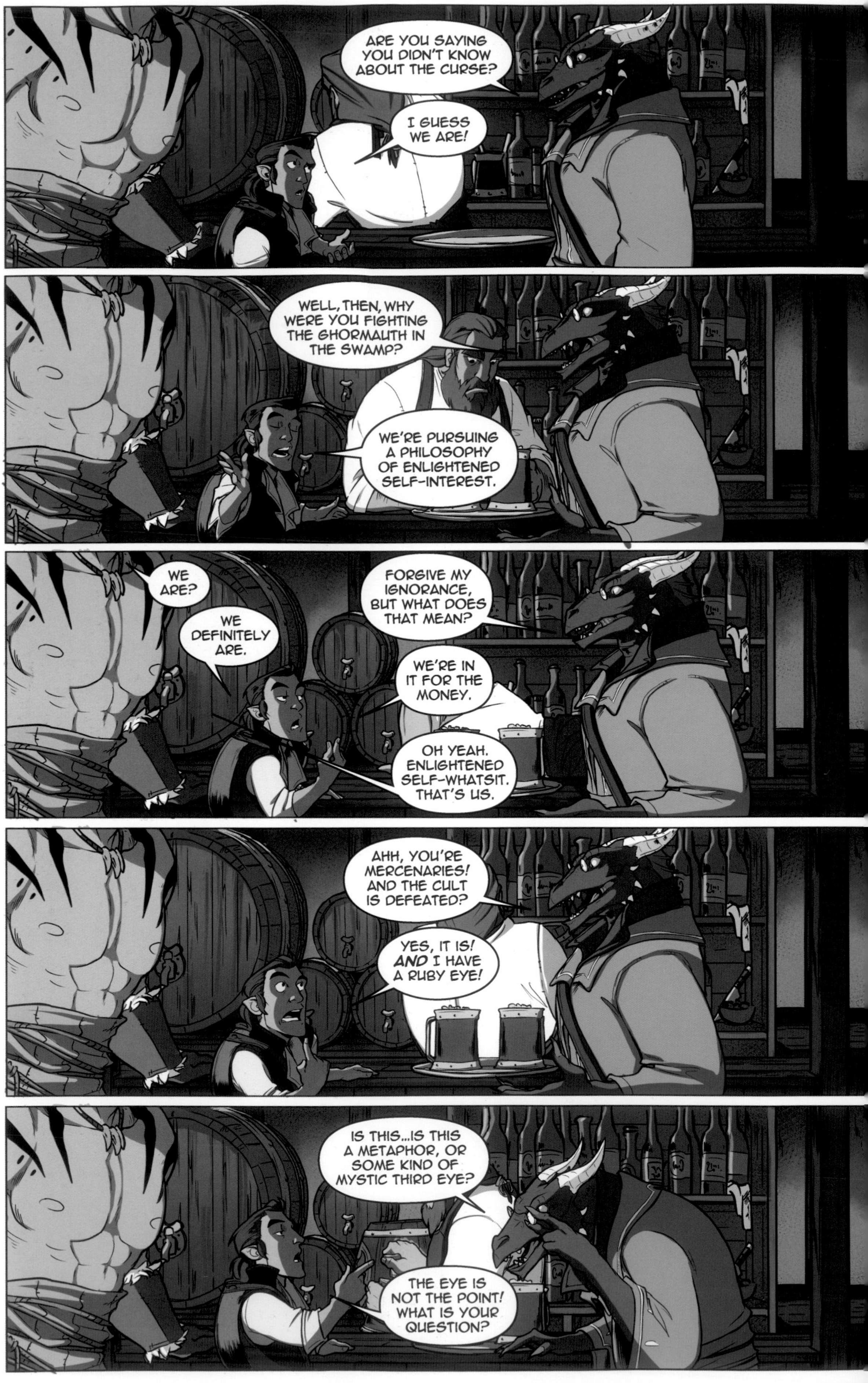
ARE YOU SAYING YOU DIDN'T KNOW ABOUT THE CURSE?
I GUESS WE ARE!
WELL, THEN, WHY WERE YOU FIGHTING THE GHORMAUTH IN THE SWAMP?
WE'RE PURSUING A PHILOSOPHY OF ENLIGHTENED SELF-INTEREST.
WE ARE?
WE DEFINITELY ARE.
FORGIVE MY IGNORANCE, BUT WHAT DOES THAT MEAN?
WE'RE IN IT FOR THE MONEY.
OH YEAH. ENLIGHTENED SELF-WHATSIT. THAT'S US.
AHH, YOU'RE MERCENARIES! AND THE CULT IS DEFEATED?
YES, IT IS! ***AND*** I HAVE A RUBY EYE!
IS THIS...IS THIS A METAPHOR, OR SOME KIND OF MYSTIC THIRD EYE?
THE EYE IS NOT THE POINT! WHAT IS YOUR QUESTION?

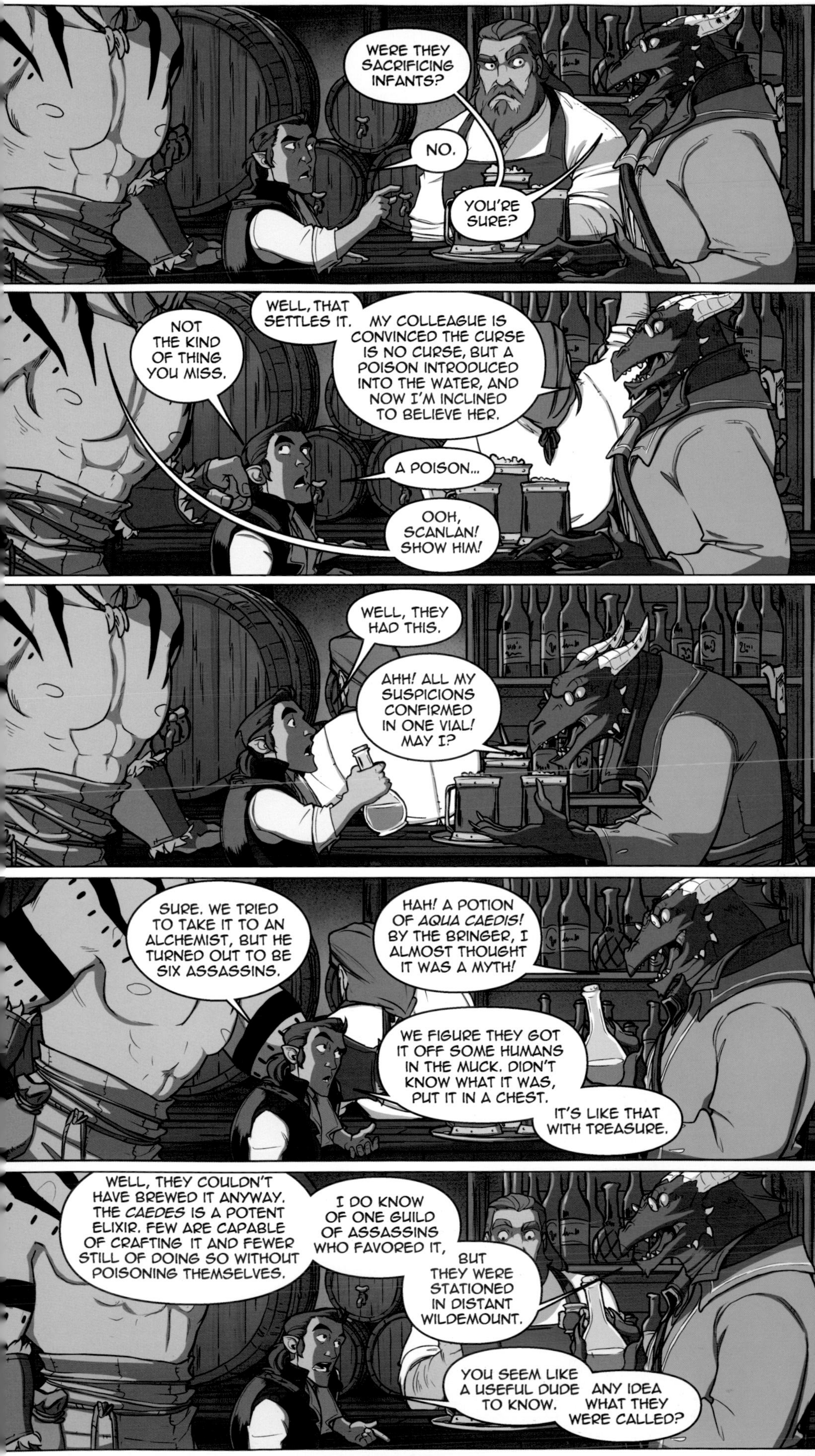
WERE THEY SACRIFICING INFANTS?
NO.
YOU'RE SURE?
NOT THE KIND OF THING YOU MISS.
WELL, THAT SETTLES IT.
MY COLLEAGUE IS CONVINCED THE CURSE IS NO CURSE, BUT A POISON INTRODUCED INTO THE WATER, AND NOW I'M INCLINED TO BELIEVE HER.
A POISON...
OOH, SCANLAN! SHOW HIM!
WELL, THEY HAD THIS.
AHH! ALL MY SUSPICIONS CONFIRMED IN ONE VIAL! MAY I?
SURE. WE TRIED TO TAKE IT TO AN ALCHEMIST, BUT HE TURNED OUT TO BE SIX ASSASSINS.
HAH! A POTION OF *AQUA CAEDIS*! BY THE BRINGER, I ALMOST THOUGHT IT WAS A MYTH!
WE FIGURE THEY GOT IT OFF SOME HUMANS IN THE MUCK. DIDN'T KNOW WHAT IT WAS, PUT IT IN A CHEST.
IT'S LIKE THAT WITH TREASURE.
WELL, THEY COULDN'T HAVE BREWED IT ANYWAY. THE *CAEDES* IS A POTENT ELIXIR. FEW ARE CAPABLE OF CRAFTING IT AND FEWER STILL OF DOING SO WITHOUT POISONING THEMSELVES.
I DO KNOW OF ONE GUILD OF ASSASSINS WHO FAVORED IT,
BUT THEY WERE STATIONED IN DISTANT WILDEMOUNT.
YOU SEEM LIKE A USEFUL DUDE TO KNOW.
ANY IDEA WHAT THEY WERE CALLED?

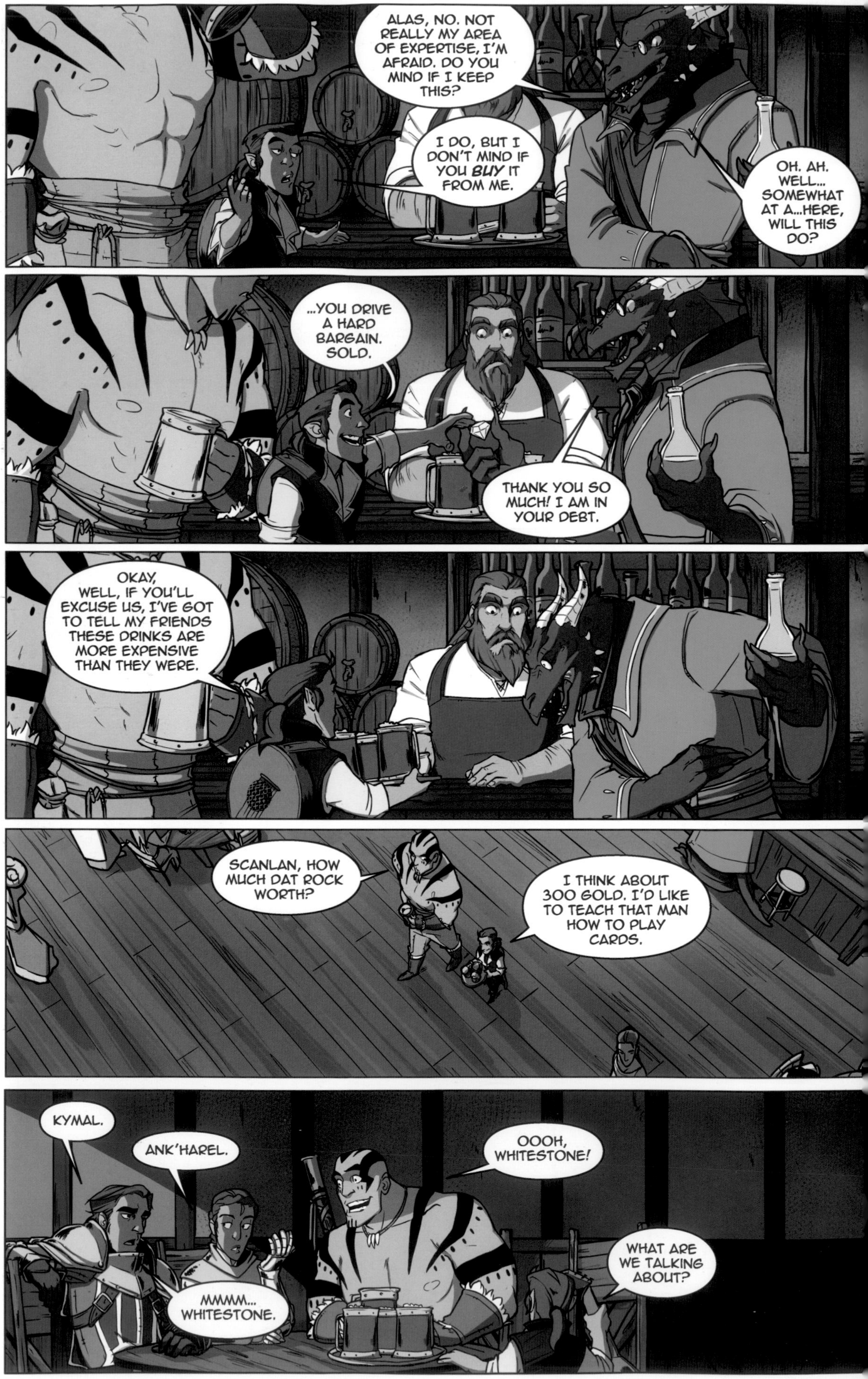
ALAS, NO. NOT REALLY MY AREA OF EXPERTISE, I'M AFRAID. DO YOU MIND IF I KEEP THIS?
I DO, BUT I DON'T MIND IF YOU **BUY** IT FROM ME.
OH. AH. WELL... SOMEWHAT AT A...HERE, WILL THIS DO?
...YOU DRIVE A HARD BARGAIN. SOLD.
THANK YOU SO MUCH! I AM IN YOUR DEBT.
OKAY, WELL, IF YOU'LL EXCUSE US, I'VE GOT TO TELL MY FRIENDS THESE DRINKS ARE MORE EXPENSIVE THAN THEY WERE.
SCANLAN, HOW MUCH DAT ROCK WORTH?
I THINK ABOUT 300 GOLD. I'D LIKE TO TEACH THAT MAN HOW TO PLAY CARDS.
KYMAL.
ANK'HAREL.
OOOH, WHITESTONE!
MMMM... WHITESTONE.
WHAT ARE WE TALKING ABOUT?

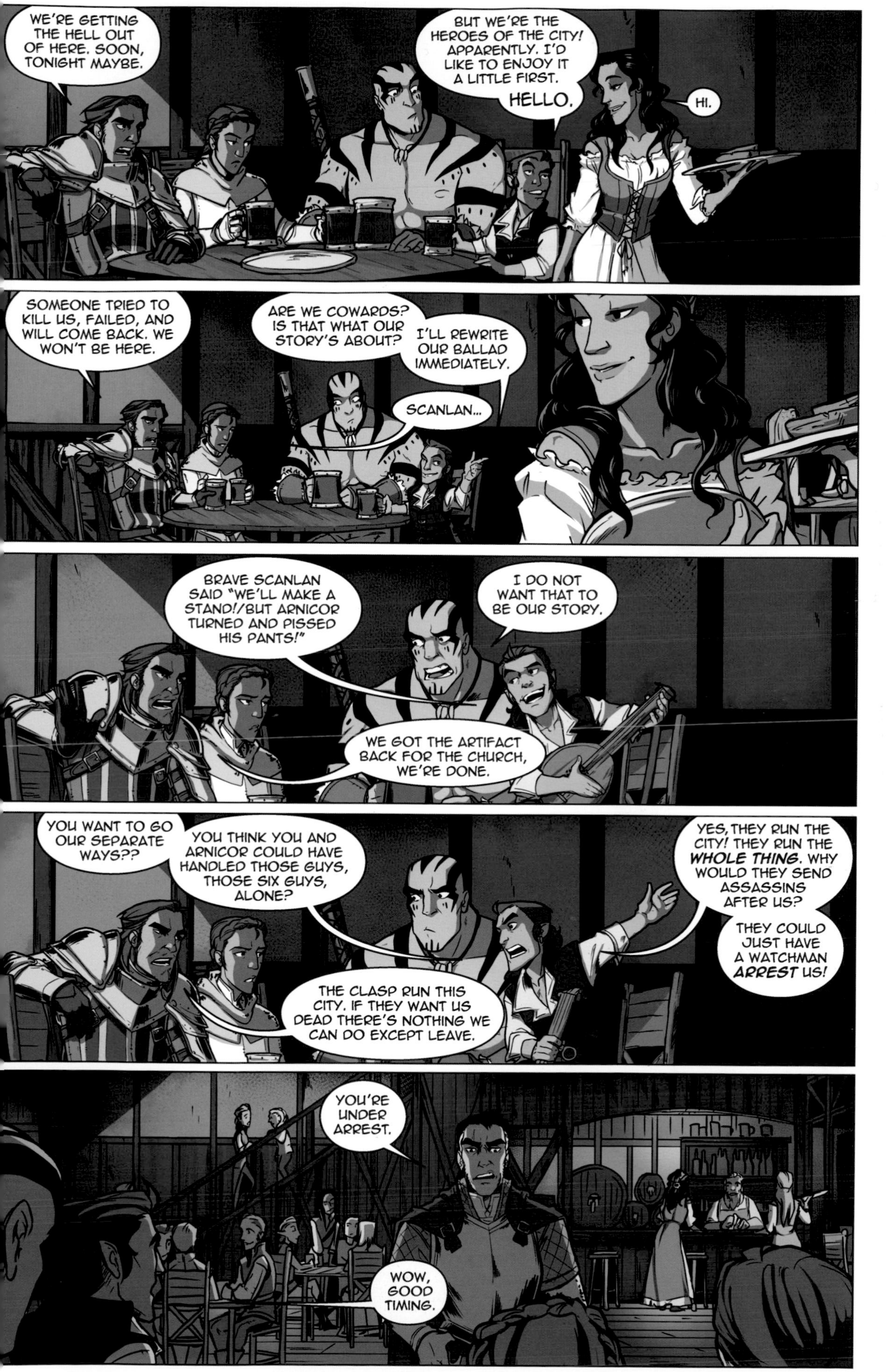
WE'RE GETTING THE HELL OUT OF HERE. SOON, TONIGHT MAYBE.
BUT WE'RE THE HEROES OF THE CITY! APPARENTLY. I'D LIKE TO ENJOY IT A LITTLE FIRST.
HELLO.
HI.
SOMEONE TRIED TO KILL US, FAILED, AND WILL COME BACK. WE WON'T BE HERE.
ARE WE COWARDS? IS THAT WHAT OUR STORY'S ABOUT?
I'LL REWRITE OUR BALLAD IMMEDIATELY.
SCANLAN...
BRAVE SCANLAN SAID "WE'LL MAKE A STAND!/BUT ARNICOR TURNED AND PISSED HIS PANTS!"
I DO NOT WANT THAT TO BE OUR STORY.
WE GOT THE ARTIFACT BACK FOR THE CHURCH, WE'RE DONE.
YOU WANT TO GO OUR SEPARATE WAYS??
YOU THINK YOU AND ARNICOR COULD HAVE HANDLED THOSE GUYS, THOSE SIX GUYS, ALONE?
YES, THEY RUN THE CITY! THEY RUN THE WHOLE THING. WHY WOULD THEY SEND ASSASSINS AFTER US?
THEY COULD JUST HAVE A WATCHMAN ARREST US!
THE CLASP RUN THIS CITY. IF THEY WANT US DEAD THERE'S NOTHING WE CAN DO EXCEPT LEAVE.
YOU'RE UNDER ARREST.
WOW, GOOD TIMING.

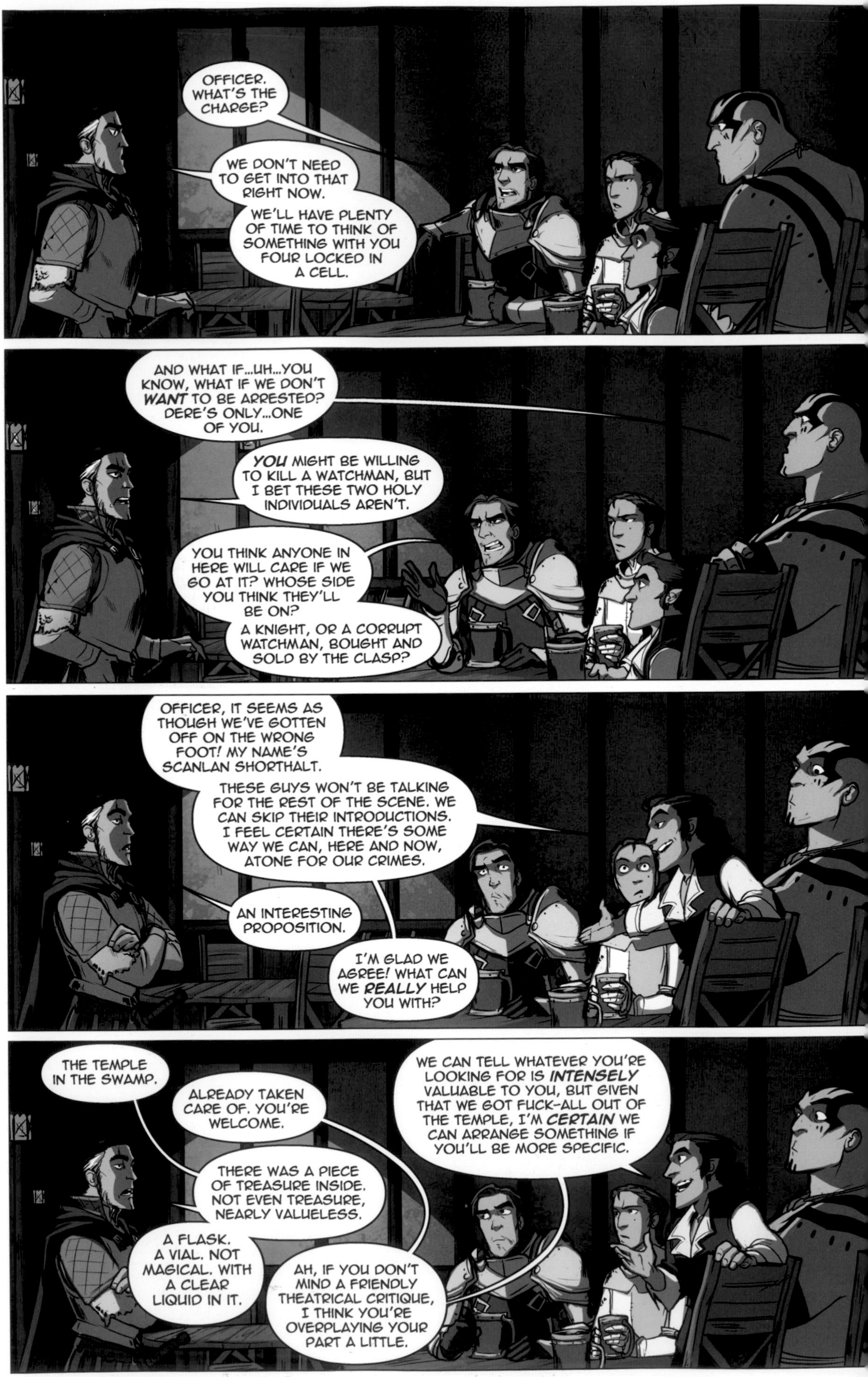
OFFICER. WHAT'S THE CHARGE?
WE DON'T NEED TO GET INTO THAT RIGHT NOW.
WE'LL HAVE PLENTY OF TIME TO THINK OF SOMETHING WITH YOU FOUR LOCKED IN A CELL.
AND WHAT IF...UH...YOU KNOW, WHAT IF WE DON'T *WANT* TO BE ARRESTED? DERE'S ONLY...ONE OF YOU.
*YOU* MIGHT BE WILLING TO KILL A WATCHMAN, BUT I BET THESE TWO HOLY INDIVIDUALS AREN'T.
YOU THINK ANYONE IN HERE WILL CARE IF WE GO AT IT? WHOSE SIDE YOU THINK THEY'LL BE ON?
A KNIGHT, OR A CORRUPT WATCHMAN, BOUGHT AND SOLD BY THE CLASP?
OFFICER, IT SEEMS AS THOUGH WE'VE GOTTEN OFF ON THE WRONG FOOT! MY NAME'S SCANLAN SHORTHALT.
THESE GUYS WON'T BE TALKING FOR THE REST OF THE SCENE. WE CAN SKIP THEIR INTRODUCTIONS. I FEEL CERTAIN THERE'S SOME WAY WE CAN, HERE AND NOW, ATONE FOR OUR CRIMES.
AN INTERESTING PROPOSITION.
I'M GLAD WE AGREE! WHAT CAN WE *REALLY* HELP YOU WITH?
THE TEMPLE IN THE SWAMP.
ALREADY TAKEN CARE OF. YOU'RE WELCOME.
THERE WAS A PIECE OF TREASURE INSIDE. NOT EVEN TREASURE, NEARLY VALUELESS.
A FLASK. A VIAL. NOT MAGICAL. WITH A CLEAR LIQUID IN IT.
AH, IF YOU DON'T MIND A FRIENDLY THEATRICAL CRITIQUE, I THINK YOU'RE OVERPLAYING YOUR PART A LITTLE.
WE CAN TELL WHATEVER YOU'RE LOOKING FOR IS *INTENSELY* VALUABLE TO YOU, BUT GIVEN THAT WE GOT FUCK-ALL OUT OF THE TEMPLE, I'M *CERTAIN* WE CAN ARRANGE SOMETHING IF YOU'LL BE MORE SPECIFIC.

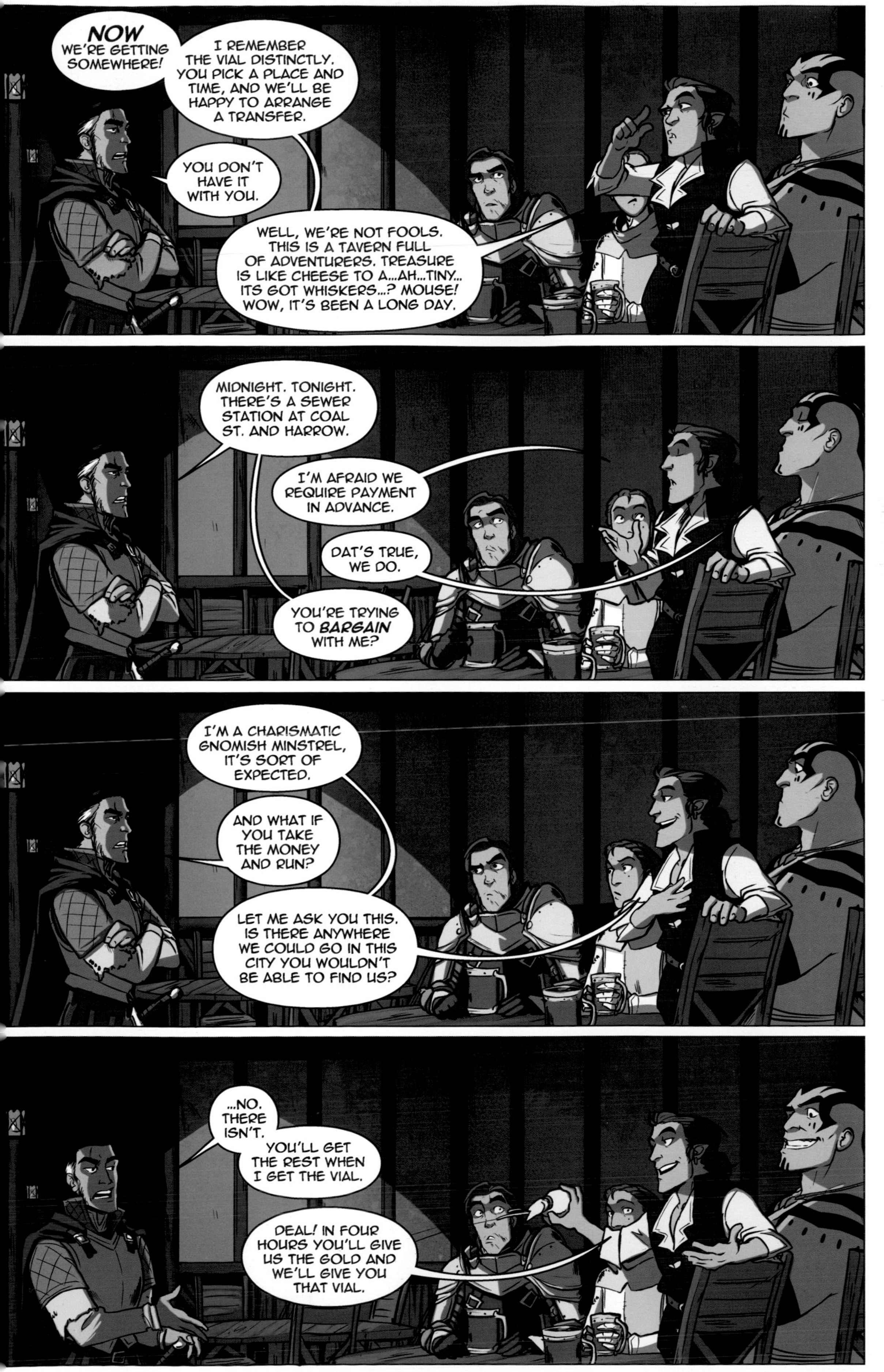
NOW WE'RE GETTING SOMEWHERE!
I REMEMBER THE VIAL DISTINCTLY. YOU PICK A PLACE AND TIME, AND WE'LL BE HAPPY TO ARRANGE A TRANSFER.
YOU DON'T HAVE IT WITH YOU.
WELL, WE'RE NOT FOOLS. THIS IS A TAVERN FULL OF ADVENTURERS. TREASURE IS LIKE CHEESE TO A...AH...TINY... ITS GOT WHISKERS...? MOUSE! WOW, IT'S BEEN A LONG DAY.
MIDNIGHT. TONIGHT. THERE'S A SEWER STATION AT COAL ST. AND HARROW.
I'M AFRAID WE REQUIRE PAYMENT IN ADVANCE.
DAT'S TRUE, WE DO.
YOU'RE TRYING TO BARGAIN WITH ME?
I'M A CHARISMATIC GNOMISH MINSTREL, IT'S SORT OF EXPECTED.
AND WHAT IF YOU TAKE THE MONEY AND RUN?
LET ME ASK YOU THIS. IS THERE ANYWHERE WE COULD GO IN THIS CITY YOU WOULDN'T BE ABLE TO FIND US?
...NO. THERE ISN'T.
YOU'LL GET THE REST WHEN I GET THE VIAL.
DEAL! IN FOUR HOURS YOU'LL GIVE US THE GOLD AND WE'LL GIVE YOU THAT VIAL.

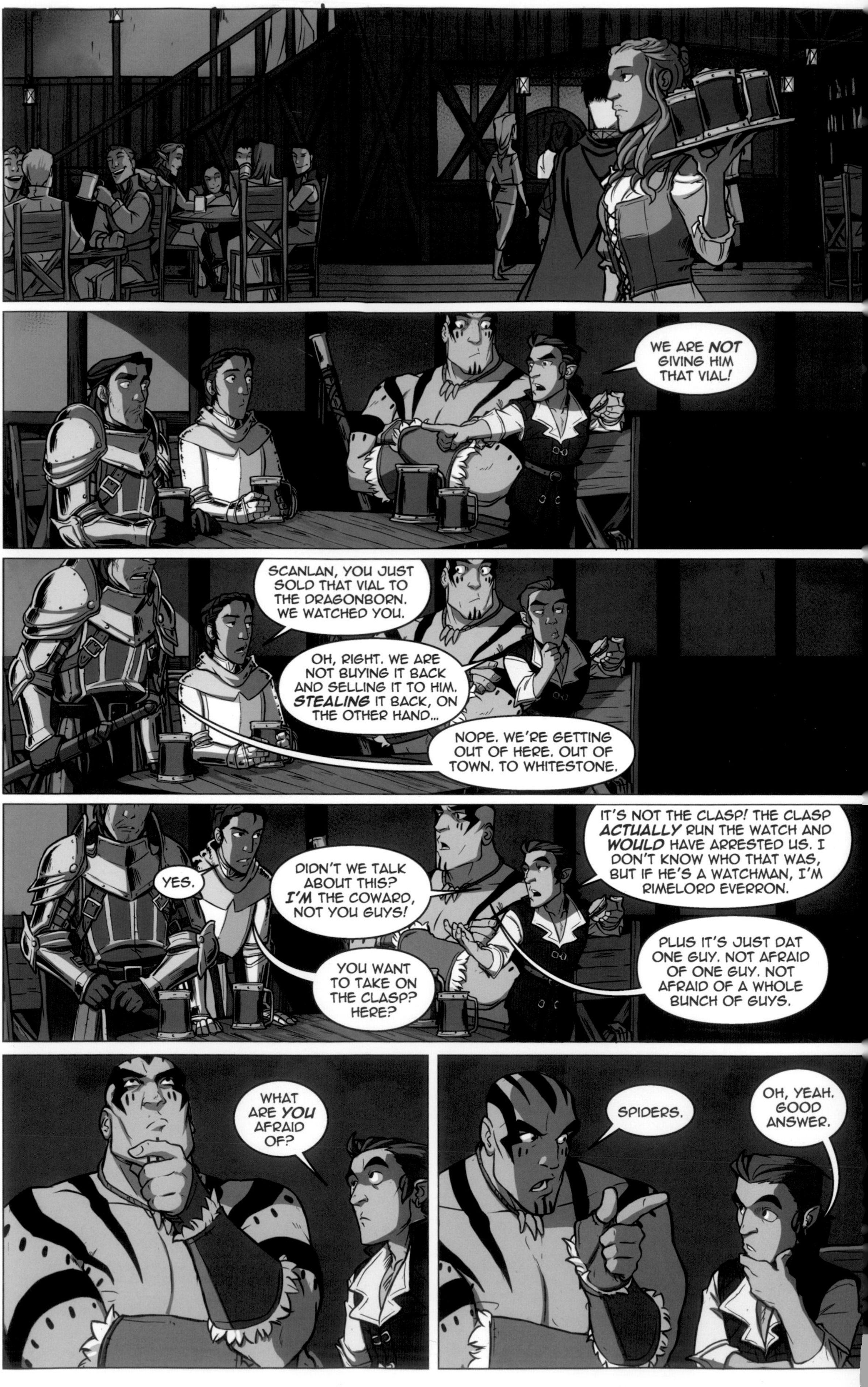
WE ARE **NOT** GIVING HIM THAT VIAL!
SCANLAN, YOU JUST SOLD THAT VIAL TO THE DRAGONBORN. WE WATCHED YOU.
OH, RIGHT. WE ARE NOT BUYING IT BACK AND SELLING IT TO HIM. ***STEALING*** IT BACK, ON THE OTHER HAND...
NOPE. WE'RE GETTING OUT OF HERE. OUT OF TOWN. TO WHITESTONE.
YES.
DIDN'T WE TALK ABOUT THIS? ***I'M*** THE COWARD, NOT YOU GUYS!
YOU WANT TO TAKE ON THE CLASP? HERE?
IT'S NOT THE CLASP! THE CLASP ***ACTUALLY*** RUN THE WATCH AND ***WOULD*** HAVE ARRESTED US. I DON'T KNOW WHO THAT WAS, BUT IF HE'S A WATCHMAN, I'M RIMELORD EVERRON.
PLUS IT'S JUST DAT ONE GUY. NOT AFRAID OF ONE GUY. NOT AFRAID OF A WHOLE BUNCH OF GUYS.
WHAT ARE ***YOU*** AFRAID OF?
SPIDERS.
OH, YEAH. GOOD ANSWER.

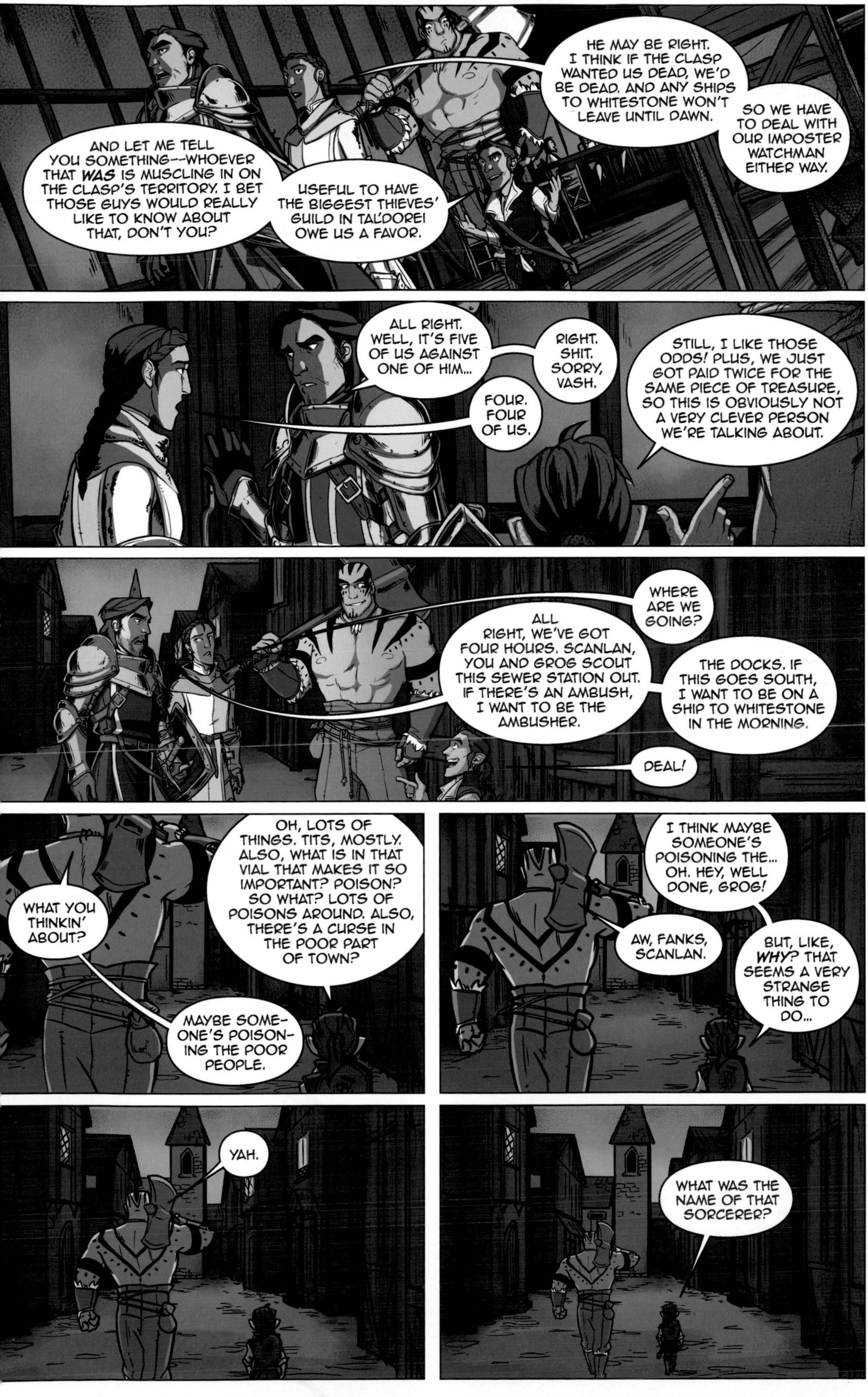
AND LET ME TELL YOU SOMETHING--WHOEVER THAT WAS IS MUSCLING IN ON THE CLASP'S TERRITORY. I BET THOSE GUYS WOULD REALLY LIKE TO KNOW ABOUT THAT, DON'T YOU?
USEFUL TO HAVE THE BIGGEST THIEVES' GUILD IN TAL'DOREI OWE US A FAVOR.
HE MAY BE RIGHT. I THINK IF THE CLASP WANTED US DEAD, WE'D BE DEAD. AND ANY SHIPS TO WHITESTONE WON'T LEAVE UNTIL DAWN.
SO WE HAVE TO DEAL WITH OUR IMPOSTER WATCHMAN EITHER WAY.
ALL RIGHT. WELL, IT'S FIVE OF US AGAINST ONE OF HIM...
FOUR. FOUR OF US.
RIGHT. SHIT. SORRY, VASH.
STILL, I LIKE THOSE ODDS! PLUS, WE JUST GOT PAID TWICE FOR THE SAME PIECE OF TREASURE, SO THIS IS OBVIOUSLY NOT A VERY CLEVER PERSON WE'RE TALKING ABOUT.
ALL RIGHT, WE'VE GOT FOUR HOURS. SCANLAN, YOU AND GROG SCOUT THIS SEWER STATION OUT. IF THERE'S AN AMBUSH, I WANT TO BE THE AMBUSHER.
WHERE ARE WE GOING?
THE DOCKS. IF THIS GOES SOUTH, I WANT TO BE ON A SHIP TO WHITESTONE IN THE MORNING.
DEAL!
WHAT YOU THINKIN' ABOUT?
OH, LOTS OF THINGS. TITS, MOSTLY. ALSO, WHAT IS IN THAT VIAL THAT MAKES IT SO IMPORTANT? POISON? SO WHAT? LOTS OF POISONS AROUND. ALSO, THERE'S A CURSE IN THE POOR PART OF TOWN?
MAYBE SOME-ONE'S POISON-ING THE POOR PEOPLE.
I THINK MAYBE SOMEONE'S POISONING THE... OH. HEY, WELL DONE, GROG!
AW, FANKS, SCANLAN.
BUT, LIKE, WHY? THAT SEEMS A VERY STRANGE THING TO DO...
YAH.
WHAT WAS THE NAME OF THAT SORCERER?

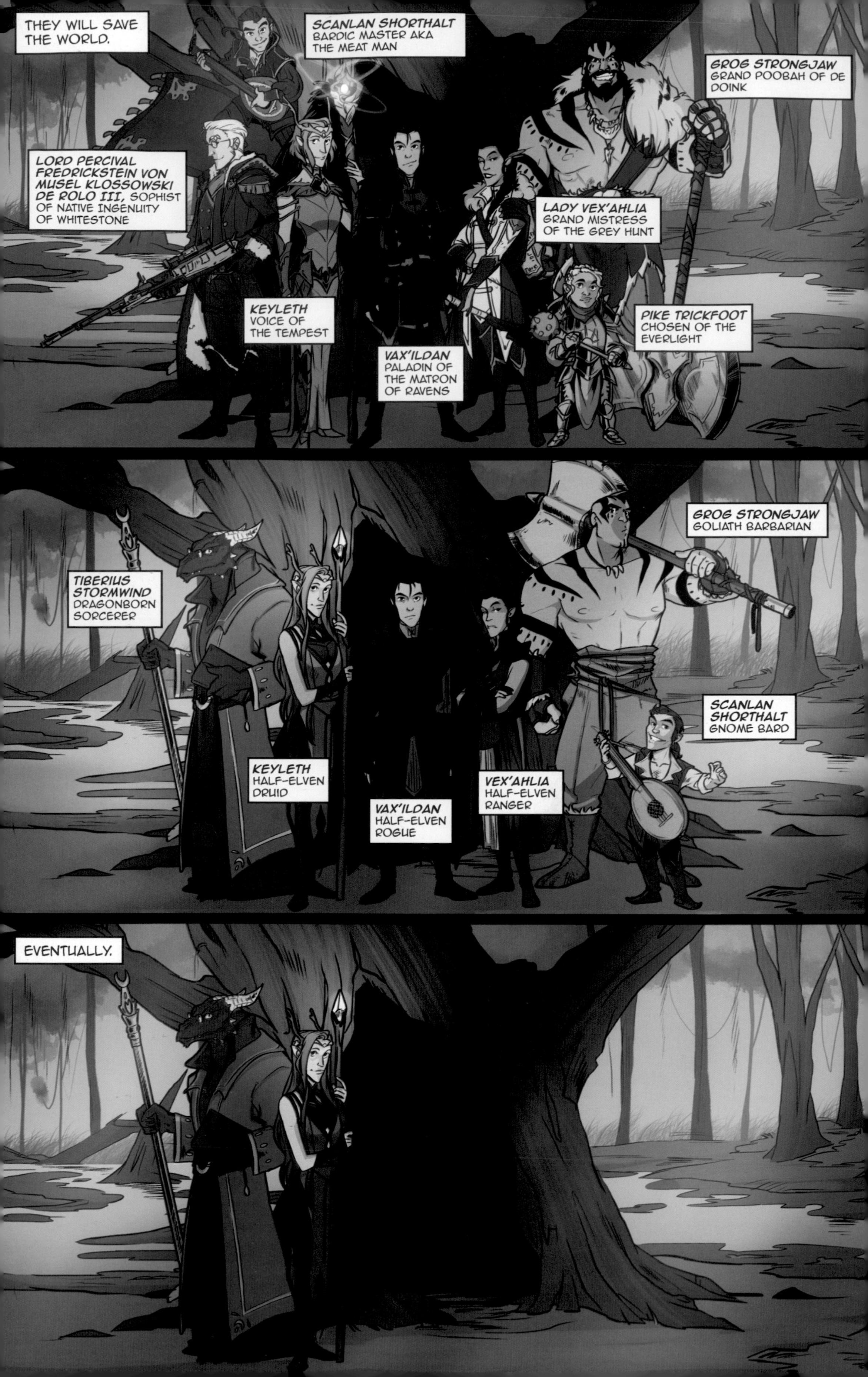
THEY WILL SAVE THE WORLD.
SCANLAN SHORTHALT BARDIC MASTER AKA THE MEAT MAN
GROG STRONGJAW GRAND POOBAH OF DE DOINK
LORD PERCIVAL FREDRICKSTEIN VON MUSEL KLOSSOWSKI DE ROLO III, SOPHIST OF NATIVE INGENUITY OF WHITESTONE
LADY VEX'AHLIA GRAND MISTRESS OF THE GREY HUNT
KEYLETH VOICE OF THE TEMPEST
PIKE TRICKFOOT CHOSEN OF THE EVERLIGHT
VAX'ILDAN PALADIN OF THE MATRON OF RAVENS
GROG STRONGJAW GOLIATH BARBARIAN
TIBERIUS STORMWIND DRAGONBORN SORCERER
SCANLAN SHORTHALT GNOME BARD
KEYLETH HALF-ELVEN DRUID
VEX'AHLIA HALF-ELVEN RANGER
VAX'ILDAN HALF-ELVEN ROGUE
EVENTUALLY.

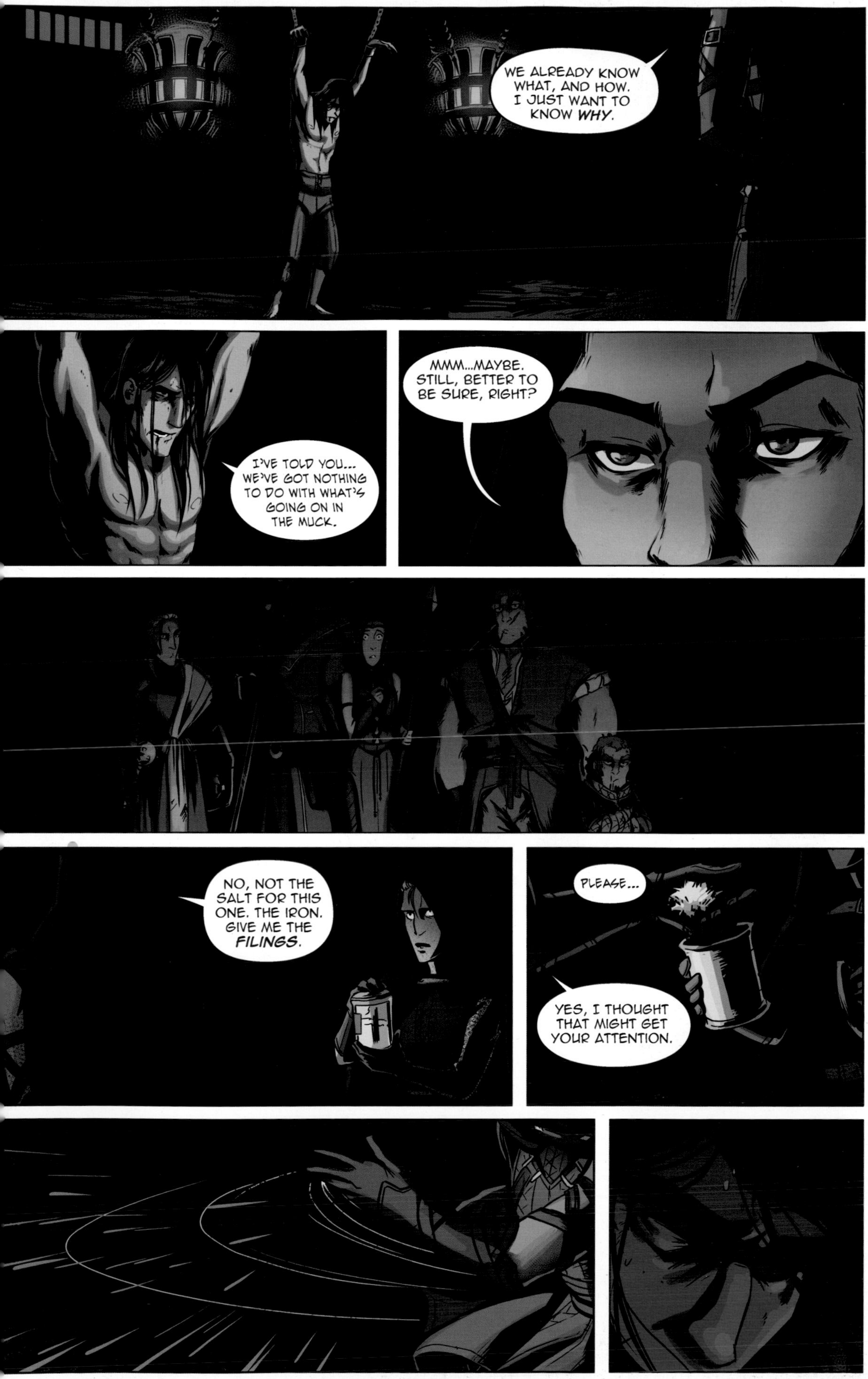
WE ALREADY KNOW WHAT, AND HOW. I JUST WANT TO KNOW *WHY*.
I'VE TOLD YOU... WE'VE GOT NOTHING TO DO WITH WHAT'S GOING ON IN THE MUCK.
MMM...MAYBE. STILL, BETTER TO BE SURE, RIGHT?
NO, NOT THE SALT FOR THIS ONE. THE IRON. GIVE ME THE *FILINGS*.
PLEASE...
YES, I THOUGHT THAT MIGHT GET YOUR ATTENTION.

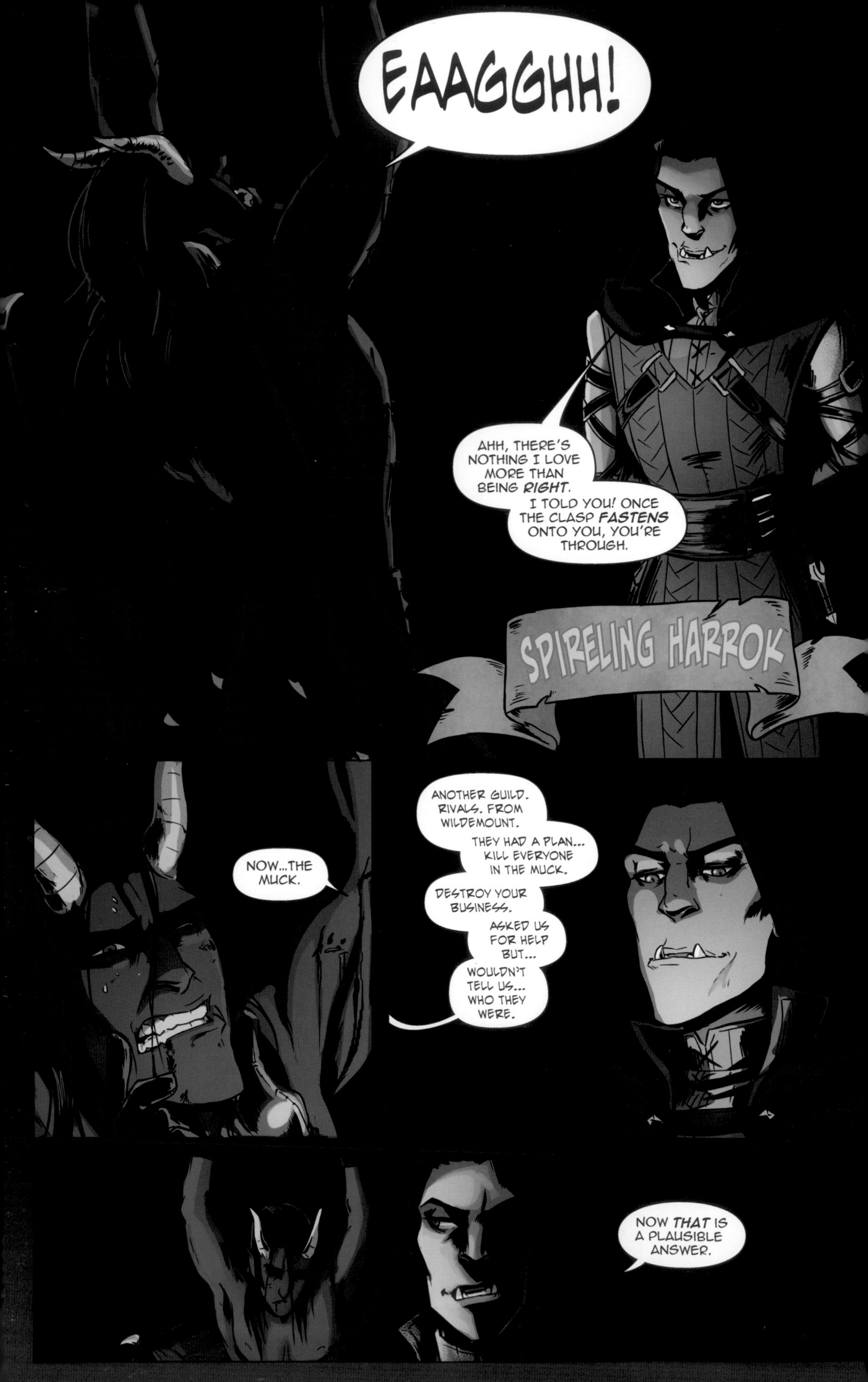
EAAGGHH!
AHH, THERE'S NOTHING I LOVE MORE THAN BEING RIGHT.
I TOLD YOU! ONCE THE CLASP FASTENS ONTO YOU, YOU'RE THROUGH.
SPIRELING HARROK
NOW...THE MUCK.
ANOTHER GUILD. RIVALS. FROM WILDEMOUNT.
THEY HAD A PLAN... KILL EVERYONE IN THE MUCK.
DESTROY YOUR BUSINESS.
ASKED US FOR HELP BUT...
WOULDN'T TELL US... WHO THEY WERE.
NOW THAT IS A PLAUSIBLE ANSWER.

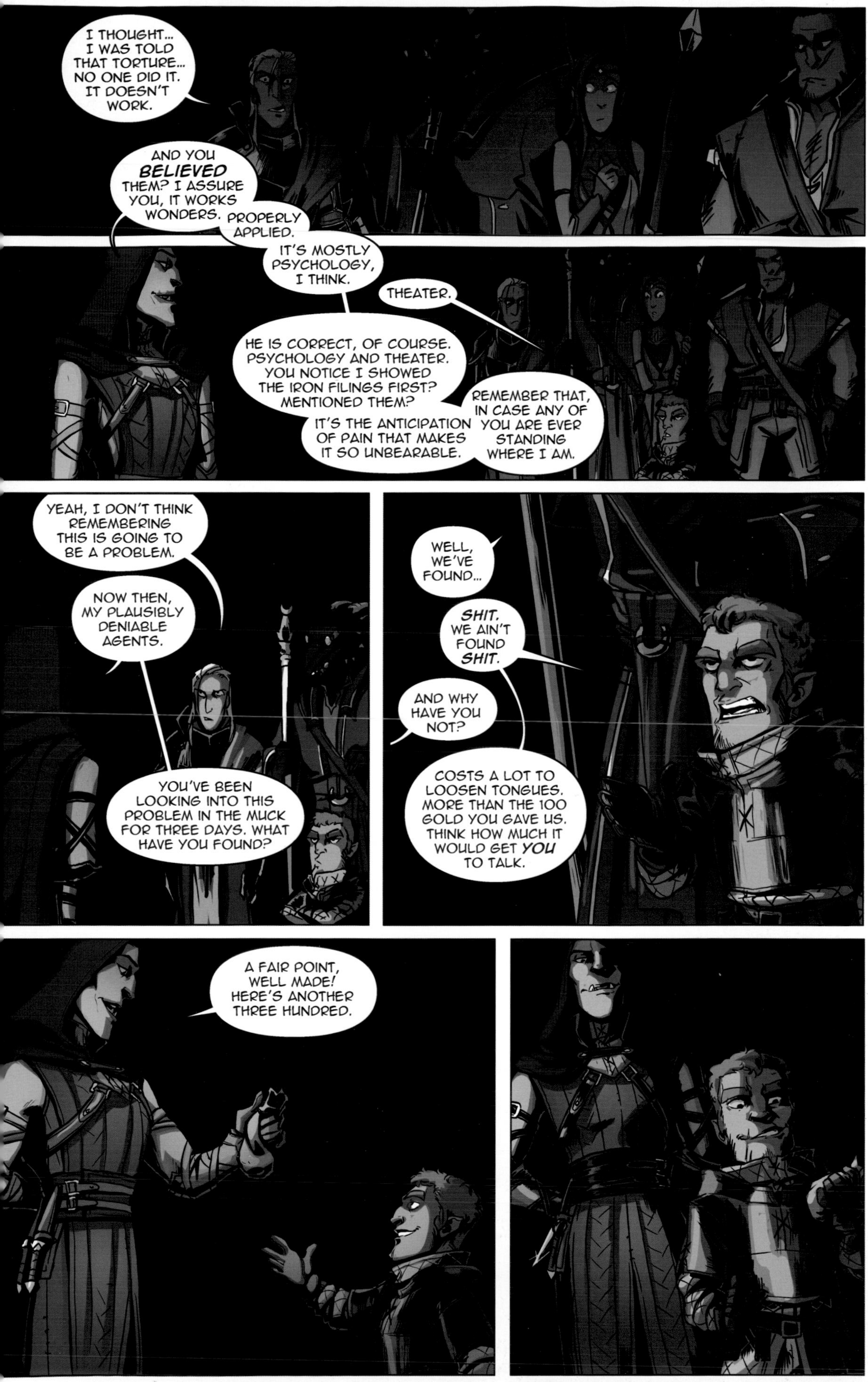
I THOUGHT... I WAS TOLD THAT TORTURE... NO ONE DID IT. IT DOESN'T WORK.
AND YOU **BELIEVED** THEM? I ASSURE YOU, IT WORKS WONDERS.
PROPERLY APPLIED.
IT'S MOSTLY PSYCHOLOGY, I THINK.
THEATER.
HE IS CORRECT, OF COURSE. PSYCHOLOGY AND THEATER. YOU NOTICE I SHOWED THE IRON FILINGS FIRST? MENTIONED THEM?
IT'S THE ANTICIPATION OF PAIN THAT MAKES IT SO UNBEARABLE.
REMEMBER THAT, IN CASE ANY OF YOU ARE EVER STANDING WHERE I AM.
YEAH, I DON'T THINK REMEMBERING THIS IS GOING TO BE A PROBLEM.
NOW THEN, MY PLAUSIBLY DENIABLE AGENTS.
YOU'VE BEEN LOOKING INTO THIS PROBLEM IN THE MUCK FOR THREE DAYS. WHAT HAVE YOU FOUND?
WELL, WE'VE FOUND...
*SHIT.* WE AIN'T FOUND *SHIT*.
AND WHY HAVE YOU NOT?
COSTS A LOT TO LOOSEN TONGUES. MORE THAN THE 100 GOLD YOU GAVE US. THINK HOW MUCH IT WOULD GET *YOU* TO TALK.
A FAIR POINT, WELL MADE! HERE'S ANOTHER THREE HUNDRED.

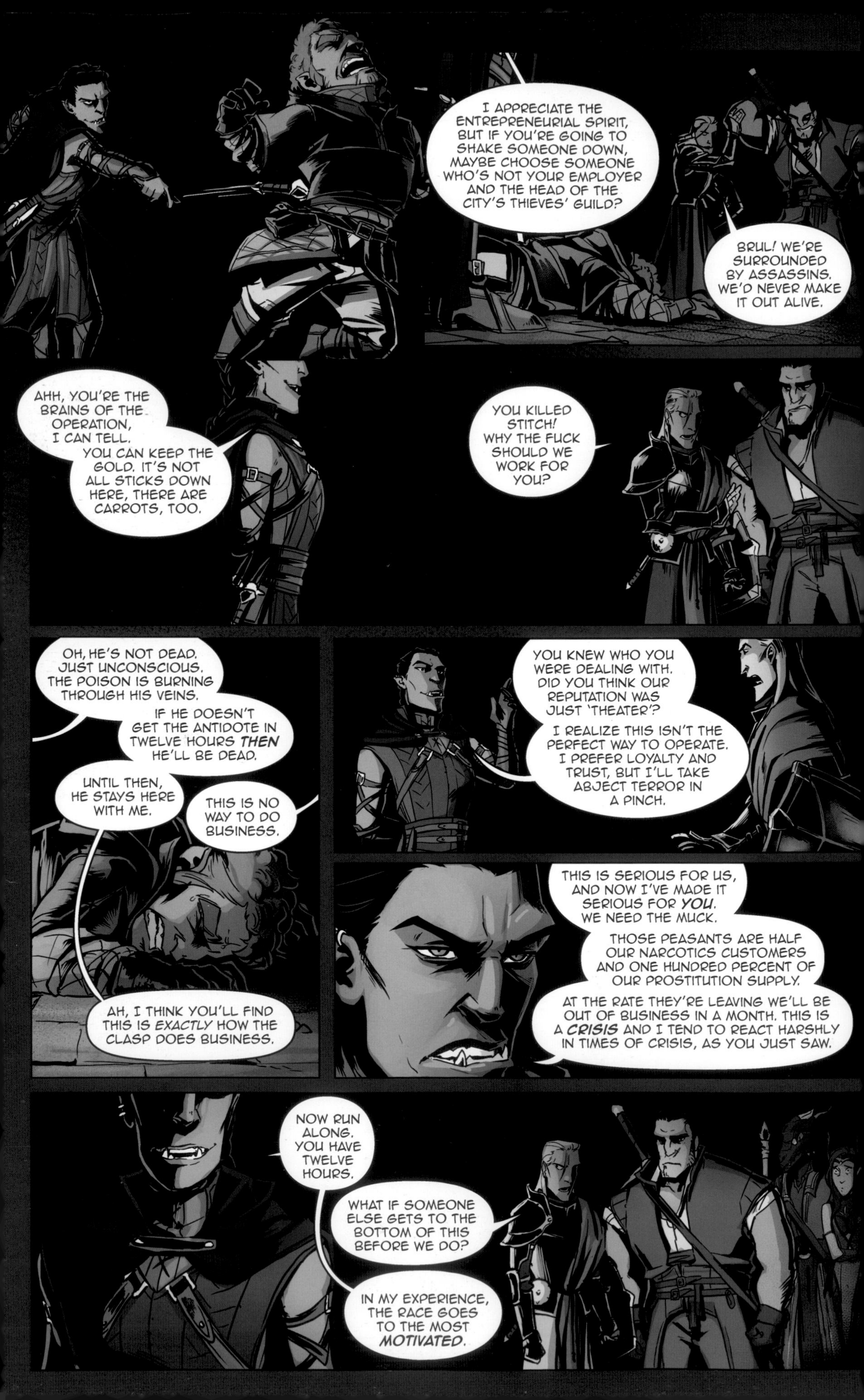

I APPRECIATE THE ENTREPRENEURIAL SPIRIT, BUT IF YOU'RE GOING TO SHAKE SOMEONE DOWN, MAYBE CHOOSE SOMEONE WHO'S NOT YOUR EMPLOYER AND THE HEAD OF THE CITY'S THIEVES' GUILD?
BRUL! WE'RE SURROUNDED BY ASSASSINS. WE'D NEVER MAKE IT OUT ALIVE.
AHH, YOU'RE THE BRAINS OF THE OPERATION, I CAN TELL.
YOU CAN KEEP THE GOLD. IT'S NOT ALL STICKS DOWN HERE, THERE ARE CARROTS, TOO.
YOU KILLED STITCH! WHY THE FUCK SHOULD WE WORK FOR YOU?
OH, HE'S NOT DEAD. JUST UNCONSCIOUS. THE POISON IS BURNING THROUGH HIS VEINS.
IF HE DOESN'T GET THE ANTIDOTE IN TWELVE HOURS *THEN* HE'LL BE DEAD.
UNTIL THEN, HE STAYS HERE WITH ME.
THIS IS NO WAY TO DO BUSINESS.
AH, I THINK YOU'LL FIND THIS IS *EXACTLY* HOW THE CLASP DOES BUSINESS.
YOU KNEW WHO YOU WERE DEALING WITH. DID YOU THINK OUR REPUTATION WAS JUST 'THEATER'?
I REALIZE THIS ISN'T THE PERFECT WAY TO OPERATE. I PREFER LOYALTY AND TRUST, BUT I'LL TAKE ABJECT TERROR IN A PINCH.
THIS IS SERIOUS FOR US, AND NOW I'VE MADE IT SERIOUS FOR *YOU*. WE NEED THE MUCK.
THOSE PEASANTS ARE HALF OUR NARCOTICS CUSTOMERS AND ONE HUNDRED PERCENT OF OUR PROSTITUTION SUPPLY.
AT THE RATE THEY'RE LEAVING WE'LL BE OUT OF BUSINESS IN A MONTH. THIS IS A ***CRISIS*** AND I TEND TO REACT HARSHLY IN TIMES OF CRISIS, AS YOU JUST SAW.
NOW RUN ALONG. YOU HAVE TWELVE HOURS.
WHAT IF SOMEONE ELSE GETS TO THE BOTTOM OF THIS BEFORE WE DO?
IN MY EXPERIENCE, THE RACE GOES TO THE MOST ***MOTIVATED***.

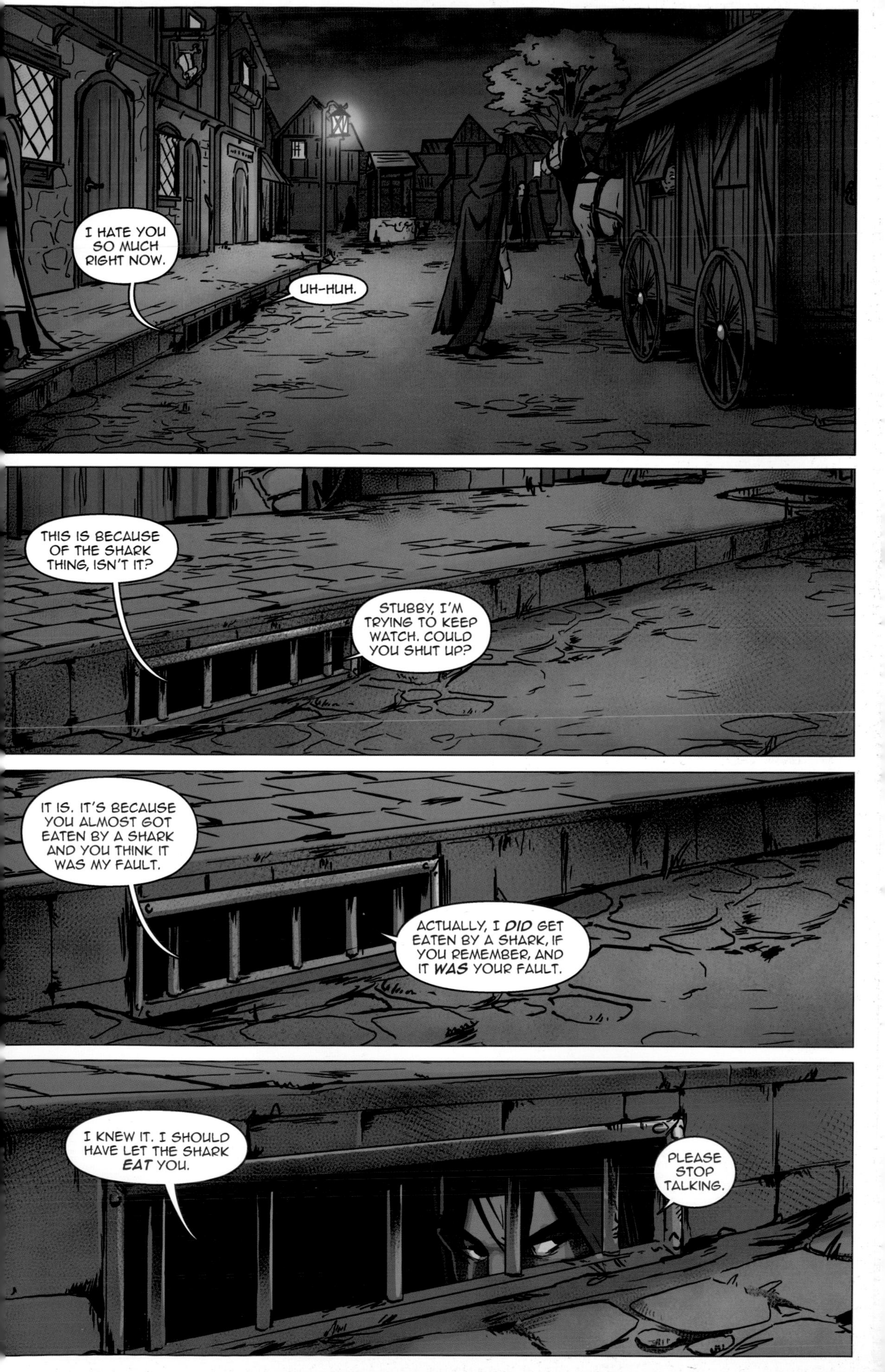
I HATE YOU SO MUCH RIGHT NOW.
UH-HUH.
THIS IS BECAUSE OF THE SHARK THING, ISN'T IT?
STUBBY, I'M TRYING TO KEEP WATCH. COULD YOU SHUT UP?
IT IS. IT'S BECAUSE YOU ALMOST GOT EATEN BY A SHARK AND YOU THINK IT WAS MY FAULT.
ACTUALLY, I *DID* GET EATEN BY A SHARK, IF YOU REMEMBER, AND IT *WAS* YOUR FAULT.
I KNEW IT. I SHOULD HAVE LET THE SHARK *EAT* YOU.
PLEASE STOP TALKING.

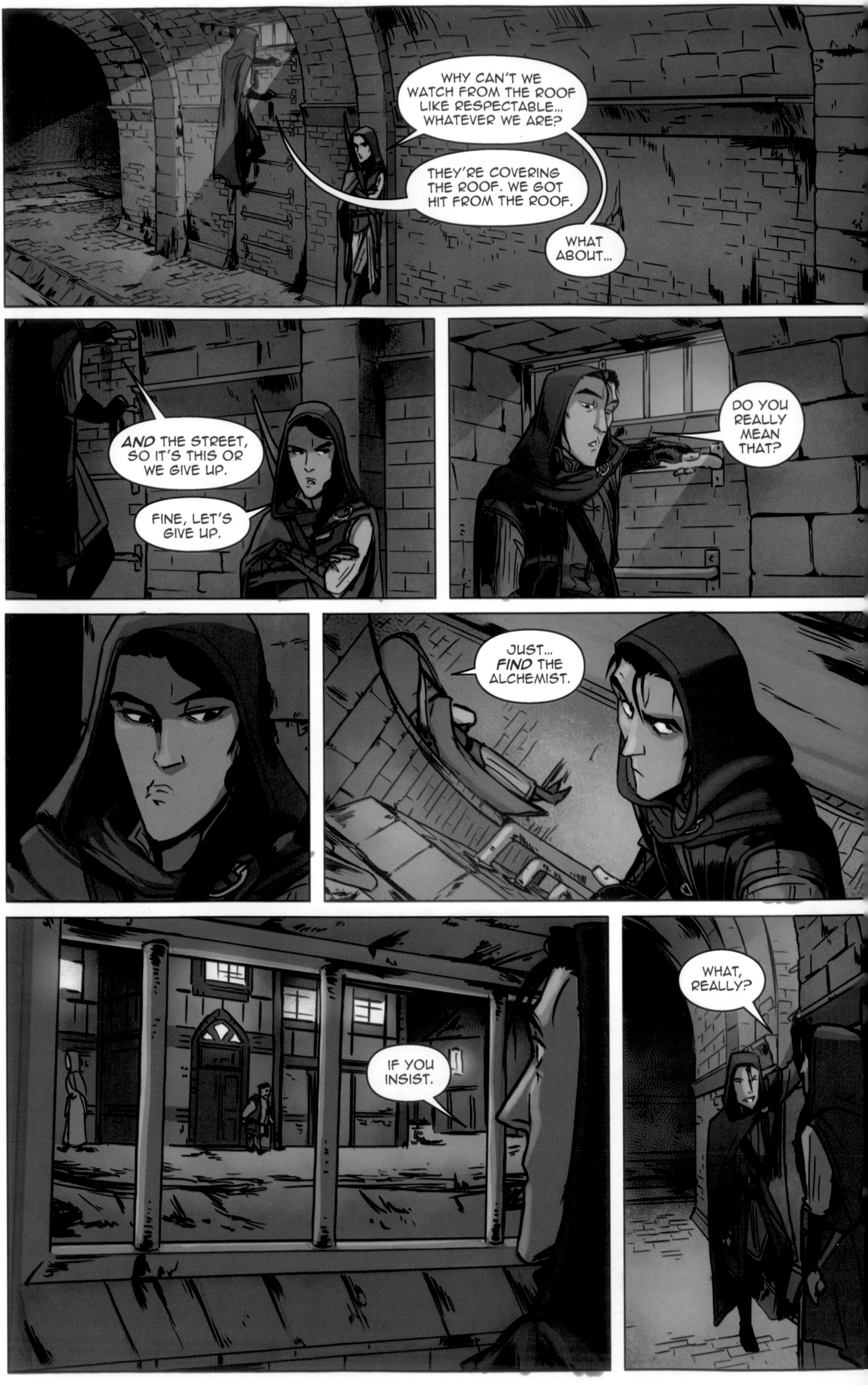
WHY CAN'T WE WATCH FROM THE ROOF LIKE RESPECTABLE... WHATEVER WE ARE?
THEY'RE COVERING THE ROOF. WE GOT HIT FROM THE ROOF.
WHAT ABOUT...
AND THE STREET, SO IT'S THIS OR WE GIVE UP.
FINE, LET'S GIVE UP.
DO YOU REALLY MEAN THAT?
JUST... FIND THE ALCHEMIST.
IF YOU INSIST.
WHAT, REALLY?

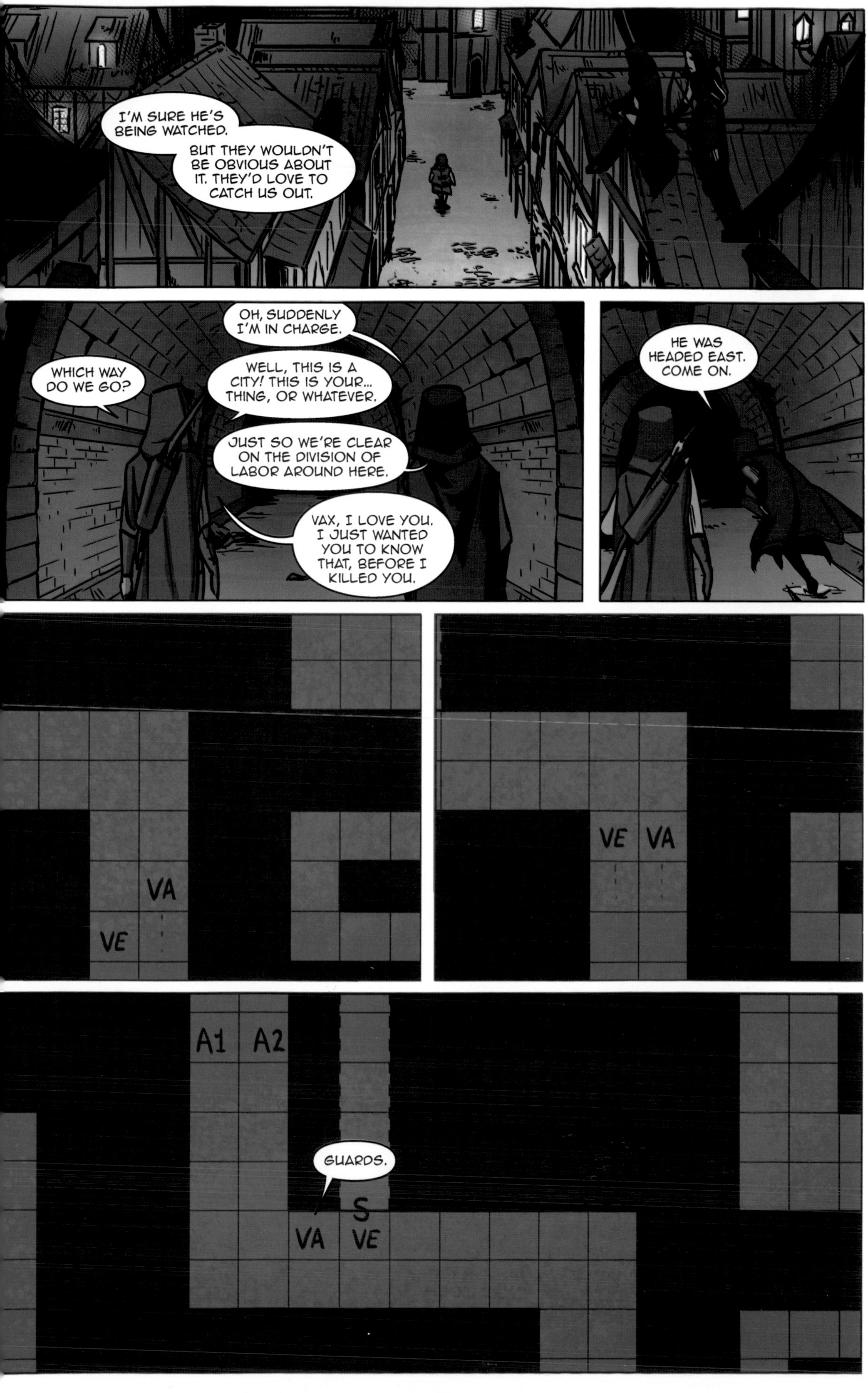
I'M SURE HE'S BEING WATCHED.
BUT THEY WOULDN'T BE OBVIOUS ABOUT IT. THEY'D LOVE TO CATCH US OUT.
WHICH WAY DO WE GO?
OH, SUDDENLY I'M IN CHARGE.
WELL, THIS IS A CITY! THIS IS YOUR... THING, OR WHATEVER.
JUST SO WE'RE CLEAR ON THE DIVISION OF LABOR AROUND HERE.
VAX, I LOVE YOU. I JUST WANTED YOU TO KNOW THAT, BEFORE I KILLED YOU.
HE WAS HEADED EAST. COME ON.
VA
VE
VE
VA
A1
A2
GUARDS.
S
VA
VE

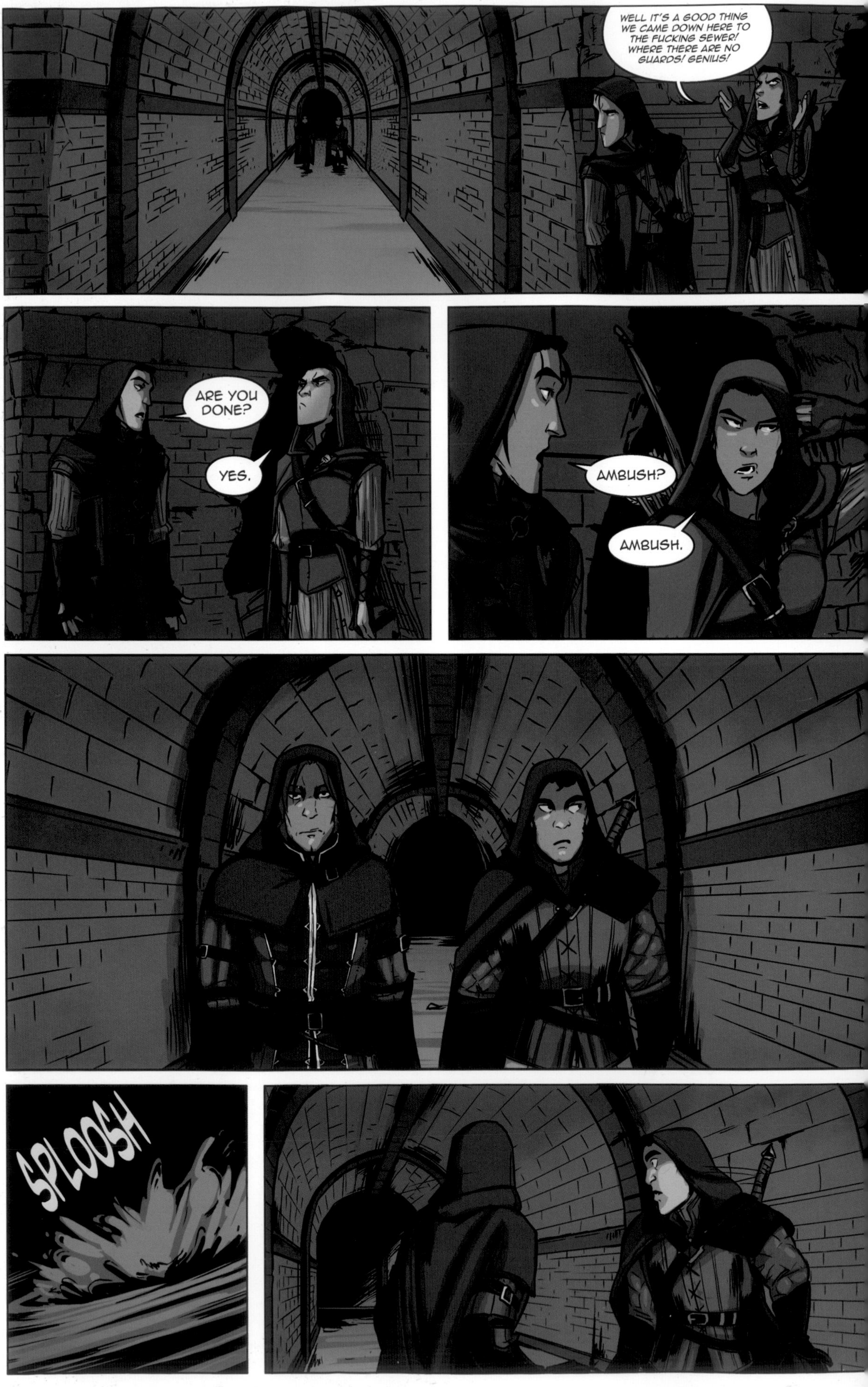
WELL IT'S A GOOD THING WE CAME DOWN HERE TO THE FUCKING SEWER! WHERE THERE ARE NO GUARDS! GENIUS!
ARE YOU DONE?
YES.
AMBUSH?
AMBUSH.
SPLOOSH

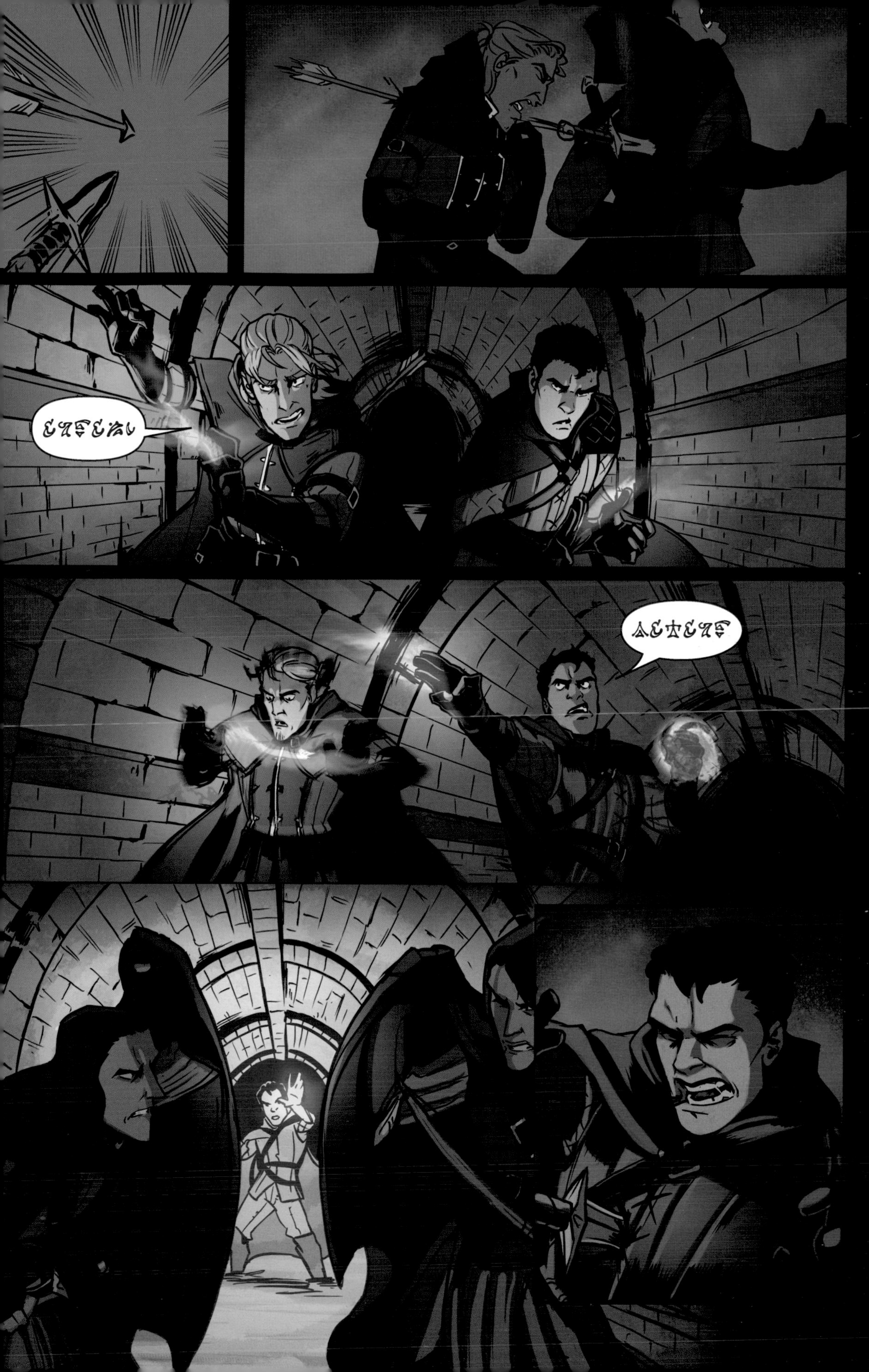

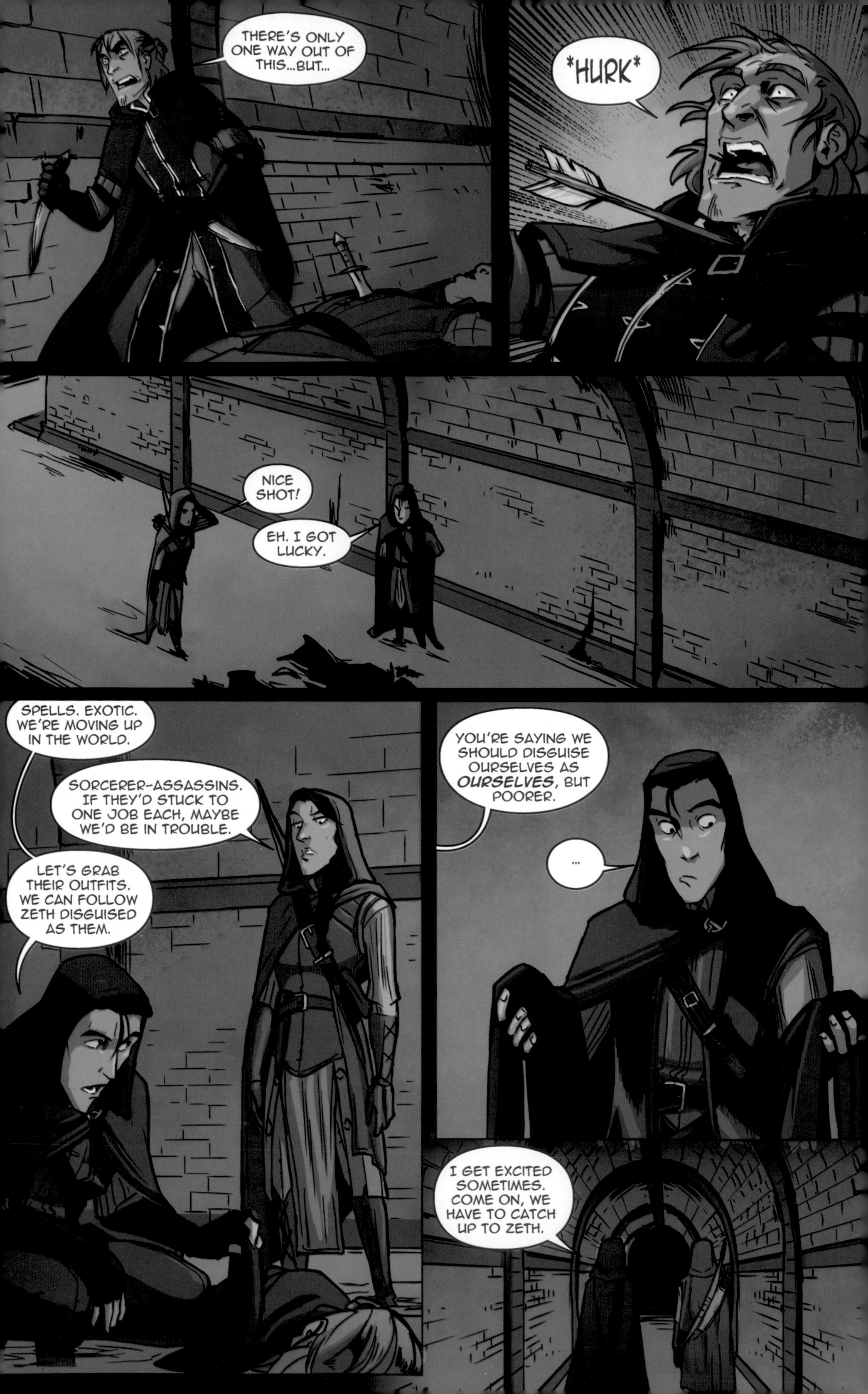

THERE'S ONLY ONE WAY OUT OF THIS...BUT...
*HURK*
NICE SHOT!
EH. I GOT LUCKY.
SPELLS. EXOTIC. WE'RE MOVING UP IN THE WORLD.
SORCERER-ASSASSINS. IF THEY'D STUCK TO ONE JOB EACH, MAYBE WE'D BE IN TROUBLE.
LET'S GRAB THEIR OUTFITS. WE CAN FOLLOW ZETH DISGUISED AS THEM.
YOU'RE SAYING WE SHOULD DISGUISE OURSELVES AS *OURSELVES*, BUT POORER.
...
I GET EXCITED SOMETIMES. COME ON, WE HAVE TO CATCH UP TO ZETH.

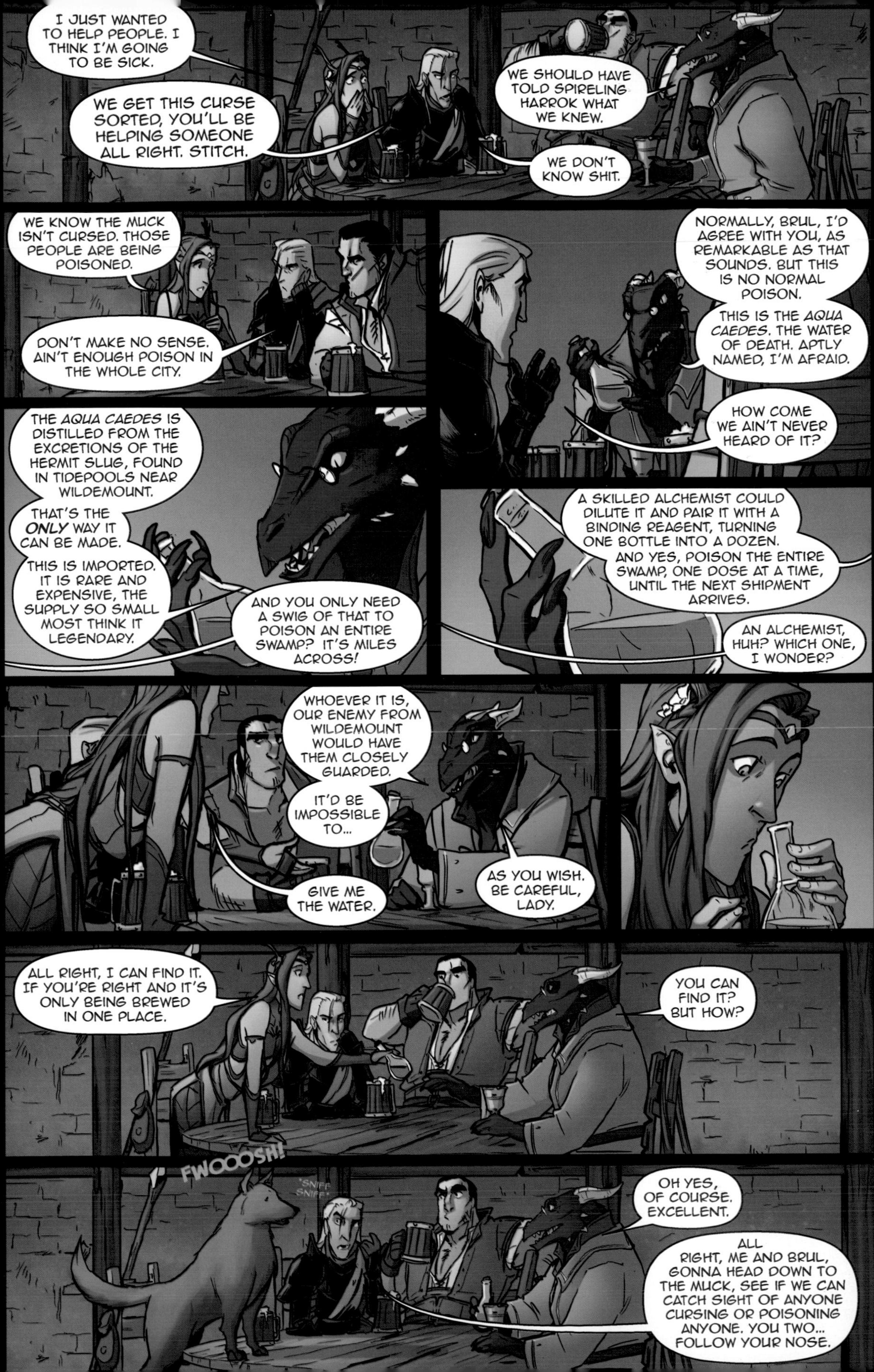
I JUST WANTED TO HELP PEOPLE. I THINK I'M GOING TO BE SICK.
WE GET THIS CURSE SORTED, YOU'LL BE HELPING SOMEONE ALL RIGHT. STITCH.
WE SHOULD HAVE TOLD SPIRELING HARROK WHAT WE KNEW.
WE DON'T KNOW SHIT.
WE KNOW THE MUCK ISN'T CURSED. THOSE PEOPLE ARE BEING POISONED.
DON'T MAKE NO SENSE. AIN'T ENOUGH POISON IN THE WHOLE CITY.
NORMALLY, BRUL, I'D AGREE WITH YOU, AS REMARKABLE AS THAT SOUNDS. BUT THIS IS NO NORMAL POISON.
THIS IS THE *AQUA CAEDES*. THE WATER OF DEATH. APTLY NAMED, I'M AFRAID.
HOW COME WE AIN'T NEVER HEARD OF IT?
THE *AQUA CAEDES* IS DISTILLED FROM THE EXCRETIONS OF THE HERMIT SLUG, FOUND IN TIDEPOOLS NEAR WILDEMOUNT.
THAT'S THE ***ONLY*** WAY IT CAN BE MADE.
THIS IS IMPORTED. IT IS RARE AND EXPENSIVE, THE SUPPLY SO SMALL MOST THINK IT LEGENDARY.
AND YOU ONLY NEED A SWIG OF THAT TO POISON AN ENTIRE SWAMP? IT'S MILES ACROSS!
A SKILLED ALCHEMIST COULD DILUTE IT AND PAIR IT WITH A BINDING REAGENT, TURNING ONE BOTTLE INTO A DOZEN.
AND YES, POISON THE ENTIRE SWAMP, ONE DOSE AT A TIME, UNTIL THE NEXT SHIPMENT ARRIVES.
AN ALCHEMIST, HUH? WHICH ONE, I WONDER?
WHOEVER IT IS, OUR ENEMY FROM WILDEMOUNT WOULD HAVE THEM CLOSELY GUARDED.
IT'D BE IMPOSSIBLE TO...
GIVE ME THE WATER.
AS YOU WISH. BE CAREFUL, LADY.
ALL RIGHT, I CAN FIND IT. IF YOU'RE RIGHT AND IT'S ONLY BEING BREWED IN ONE PLACE.
YOU CAN FIND IT? BUT HOW?
FWOOOSH!
*SNIFF SNIFF*
OH YES, OF COURSE. EXCELLENT.
ALL RIGHT, ME AND BRUL, GONNA HEAD DOWN TO THE MUCK, SEE IF WE CAN CATCH SIGHT OF ANYONE CURSING OR POISONING ANYONE. YOU TWO... FOLLOW YOUR NOSE.

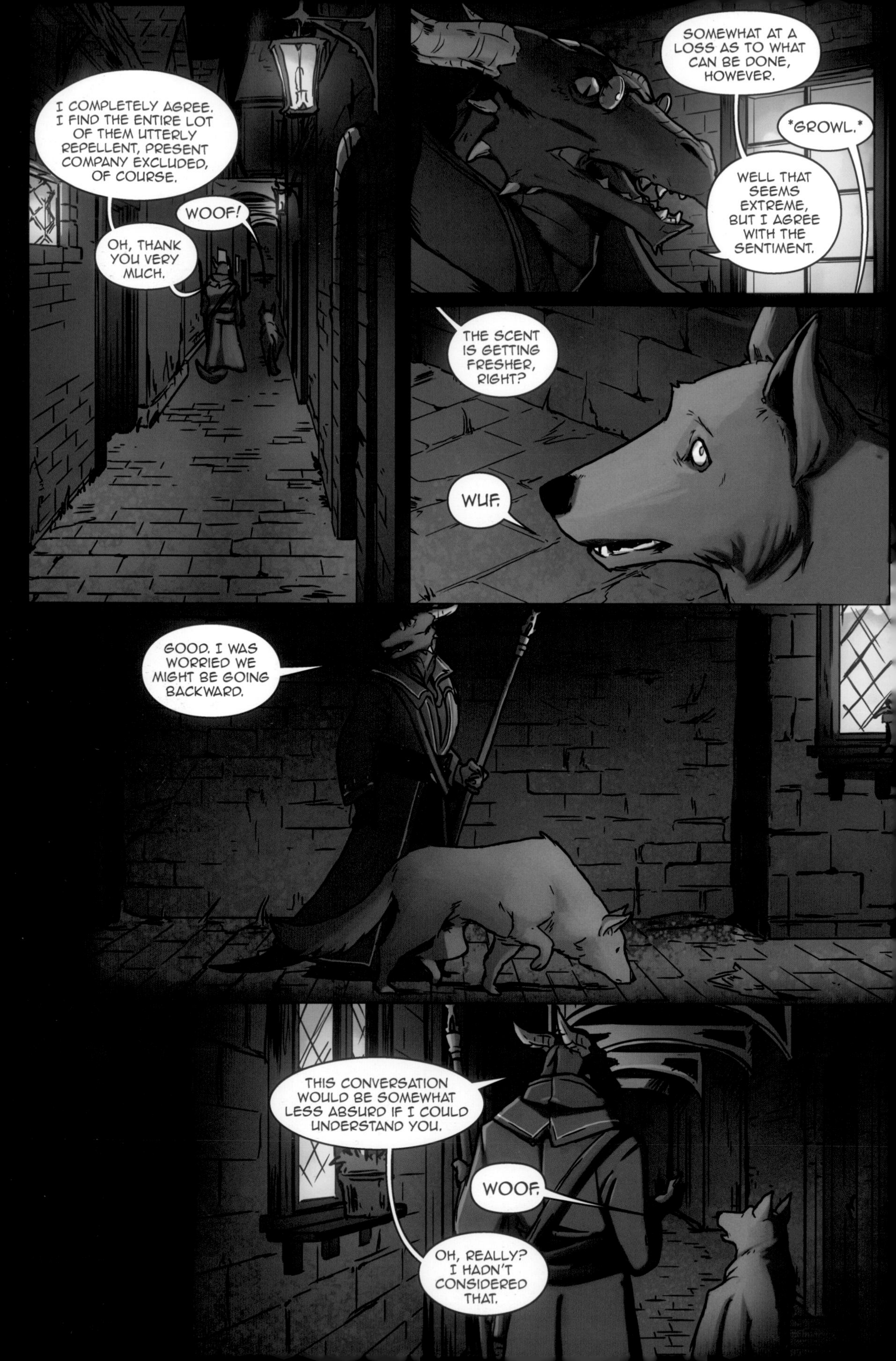
I COMPLETELY AGREE. I FIND THE ENTIRE LOT OF THEM UTTERLY REPELLENT, PRESENT COMPANY EXCLUDED, OF COURSE.
WOOF!
OH, THANK YOU VERY MUCH.
SOMEWHAT AT A LOSS AS TO WHAT CAN BE DONE, HOWEVER.
*GROWL.*
WELL THAT SEEMS EXTREME, BUT I AGREE WITH THE SENTIMENT.
THE SCENT IS GETTING FRESHER, RIGHT?
WUF.
GOOD. I WAS WORRIED WE MIGHT BE GOING BACKWARD.
THIS CONVERSATION WOULD BE SOMEWHAT LESS ABSURD IF I COULD UNDERSTAND YOU.
WOOF.
OH, REALLY? I HADN'T CONSIDERED THAT.

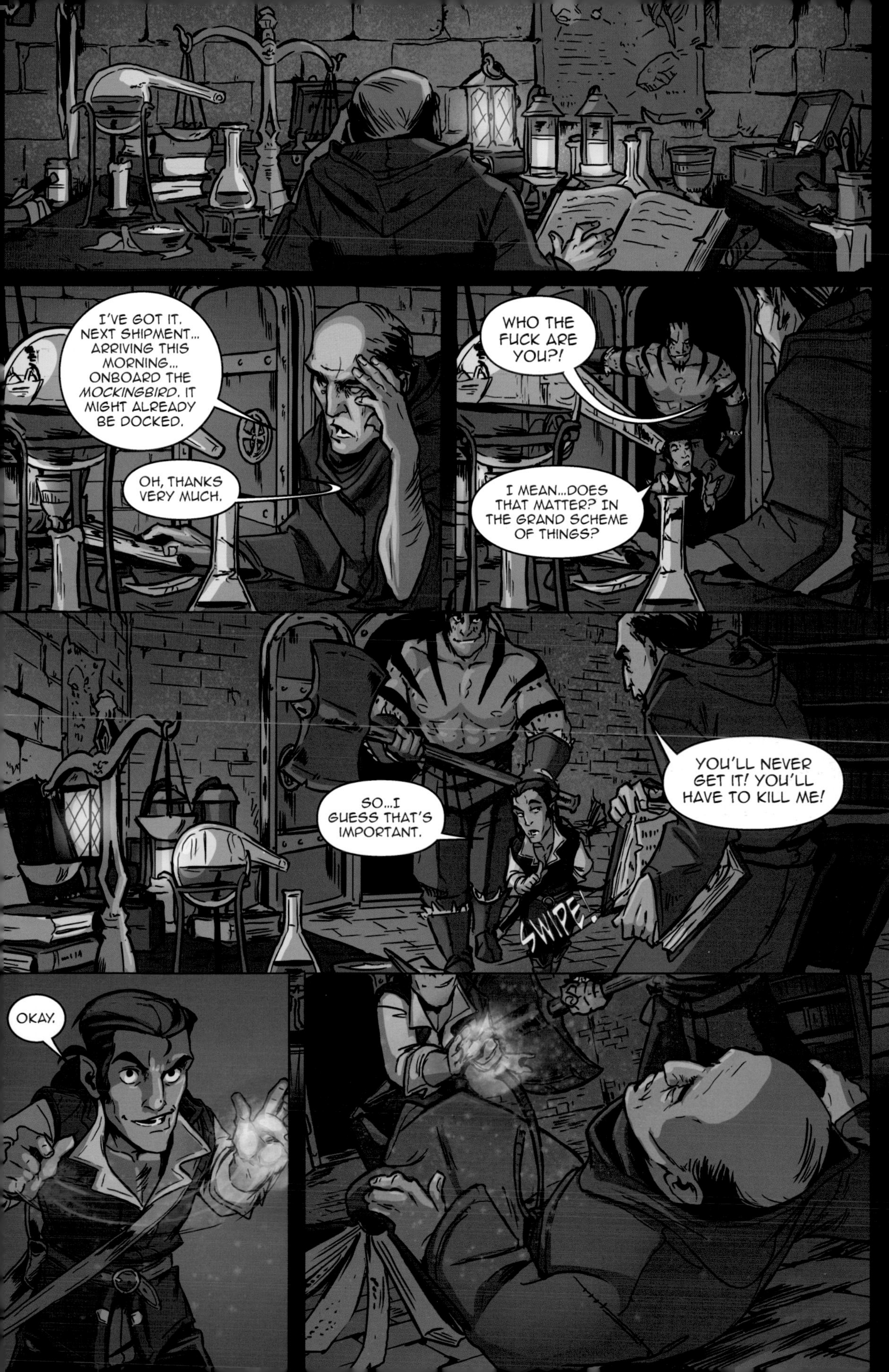
I'VE GOT IT. NEXT SHIPMENT... ARRIVING THIS MORNING... ONBOARD THE *MOCKINGBIRD*. IT MIGHT ALREADY BE DOCKED.
OH, THANKS VERY MUCH.
WHO THE FUCK ARE YOU?!
I MEAN...DOES THAT MATTER? IN THE GRAND SCHEME OF THINGS?
YOU'LL NEVER GET IT! YOU'LL HAVE TO KILL ME!
SO...I GUESS THAT'S IMPORTANT.
SWIPE!
OKAY.

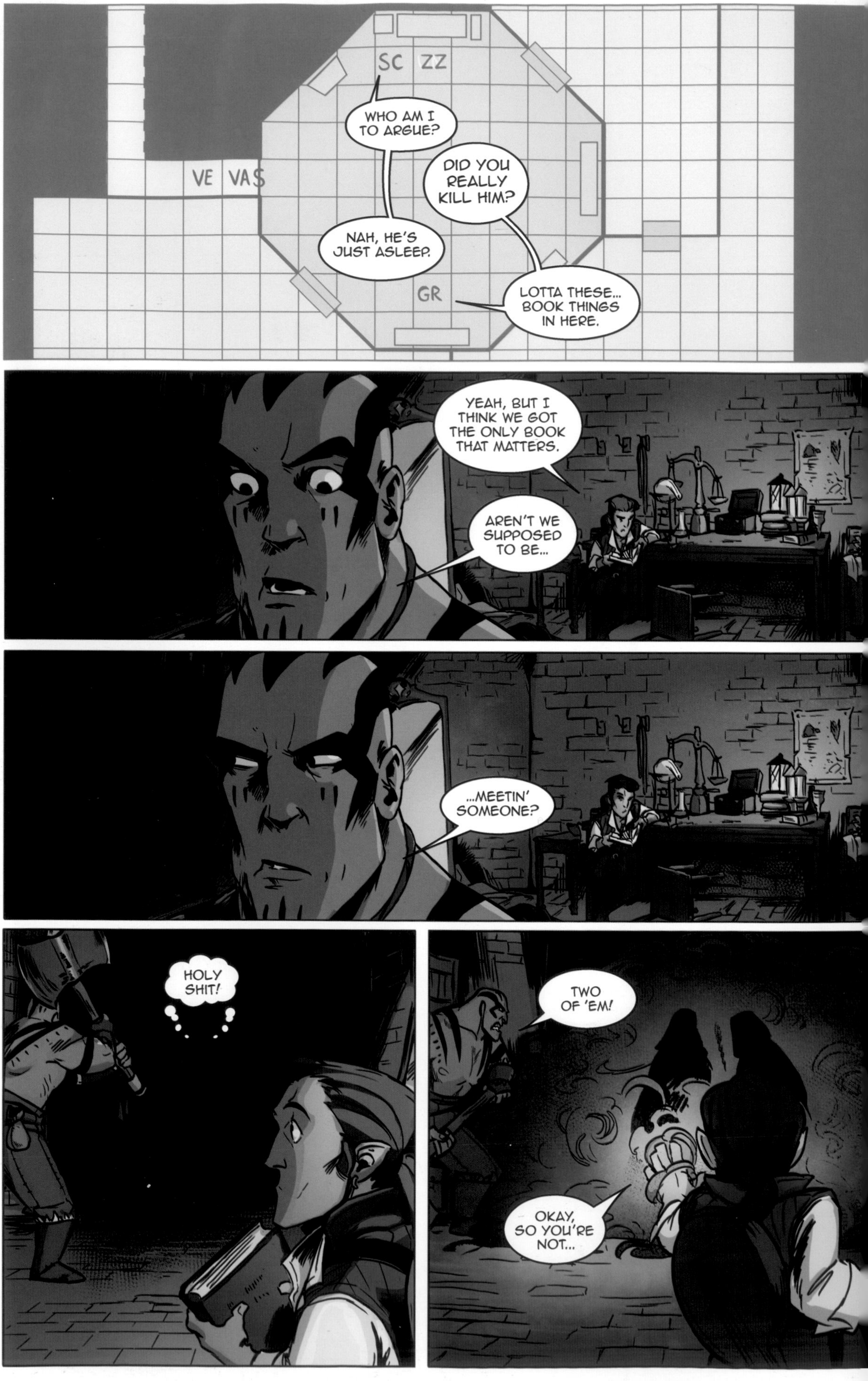
SC ZZ
VE VAS
GR
WHO AM I TO ARGUE?
DID YOU REALLY KILL HIM?
NAH, HE'S JUST ASLEEP.
LOTTA THESE... BOOK THINGS IN HERE.
YEAH, BUT I THINK WE GOT THE ONLY BOOK THAT MATTERS.
AREN'T WE SUPPOSED TO BE...
...MEETIN' SOMEONE?
HOLY SHIT!
TWO OF 'EM!
OKAY, SO YOU'RE NOT...

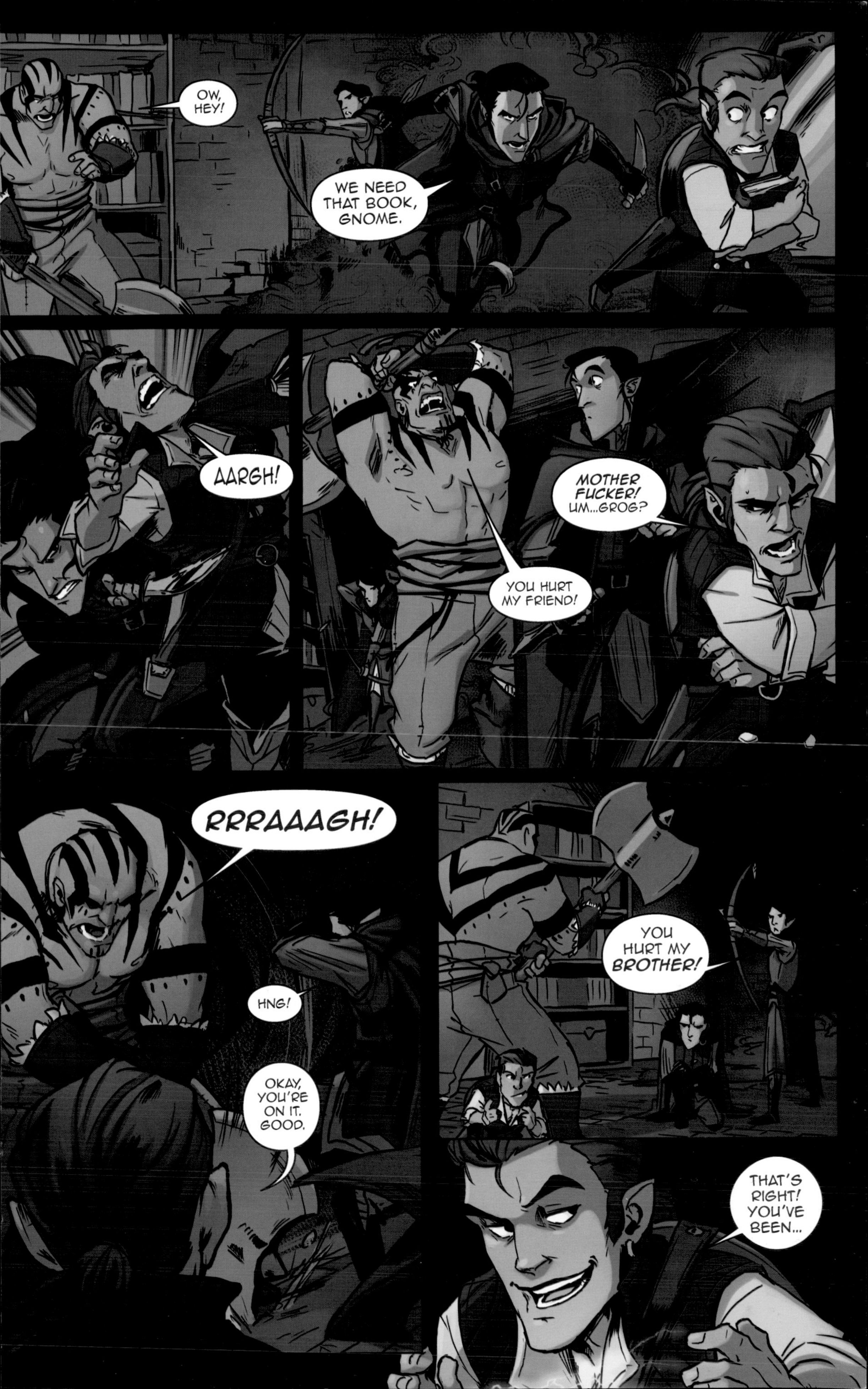
OW, HEY!
WE NEED THAT BOOK, GNOME.
AARGH!
MOTHER FUCKER! UM...GROG?
YOU HURT MY FRIEND!
RRRAAAGH!
HNG!
OKAY, YOU'RE ON IT. GOOD.
YOU HURT MY BROTHER!
THAT'S RIGHT! YOU'VE BEEN...

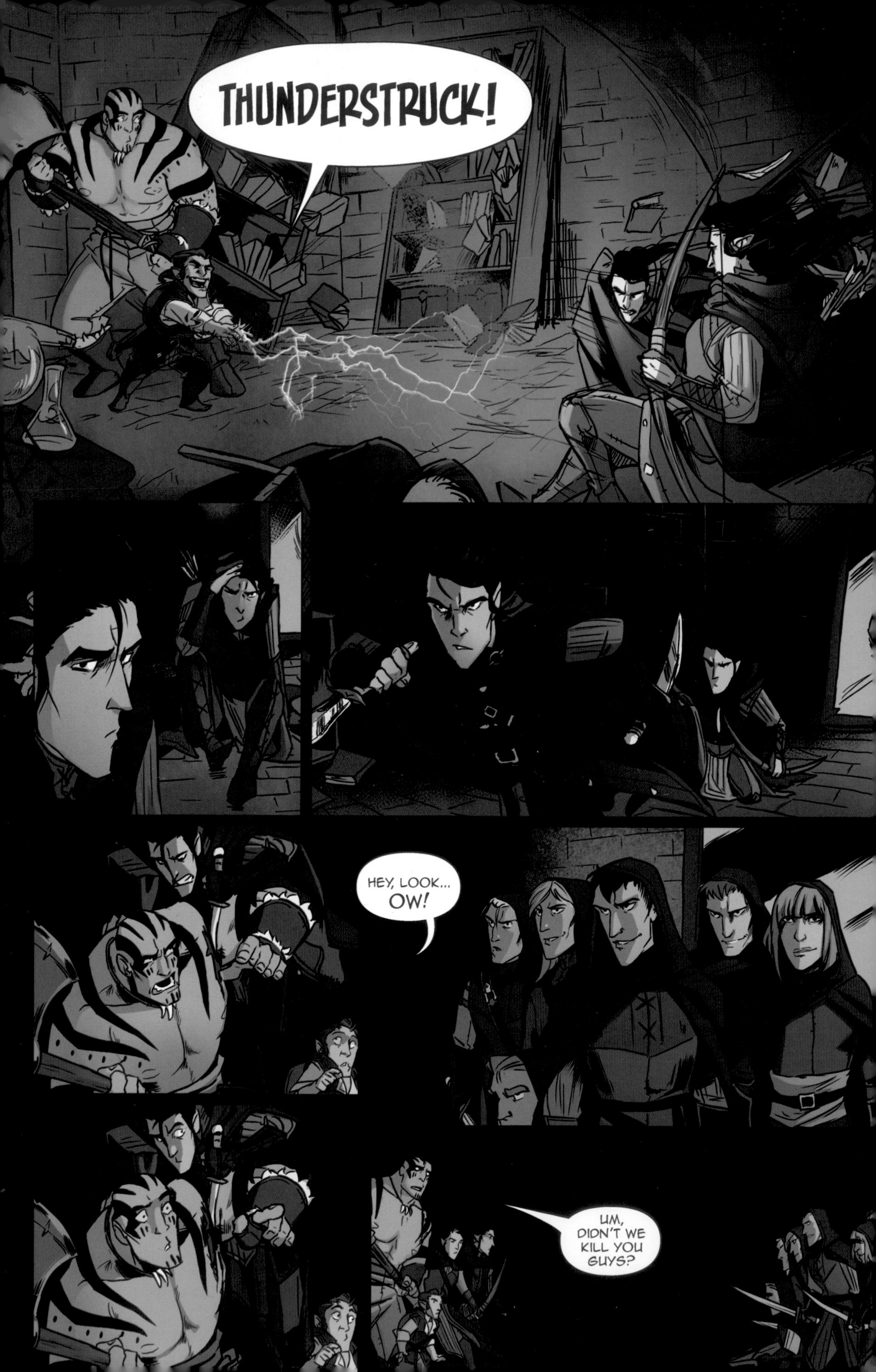
THUNDERSTRUCK!
HEY, LOOK... OW!
UM, DIDN'T WE KILL YOU GUYS?

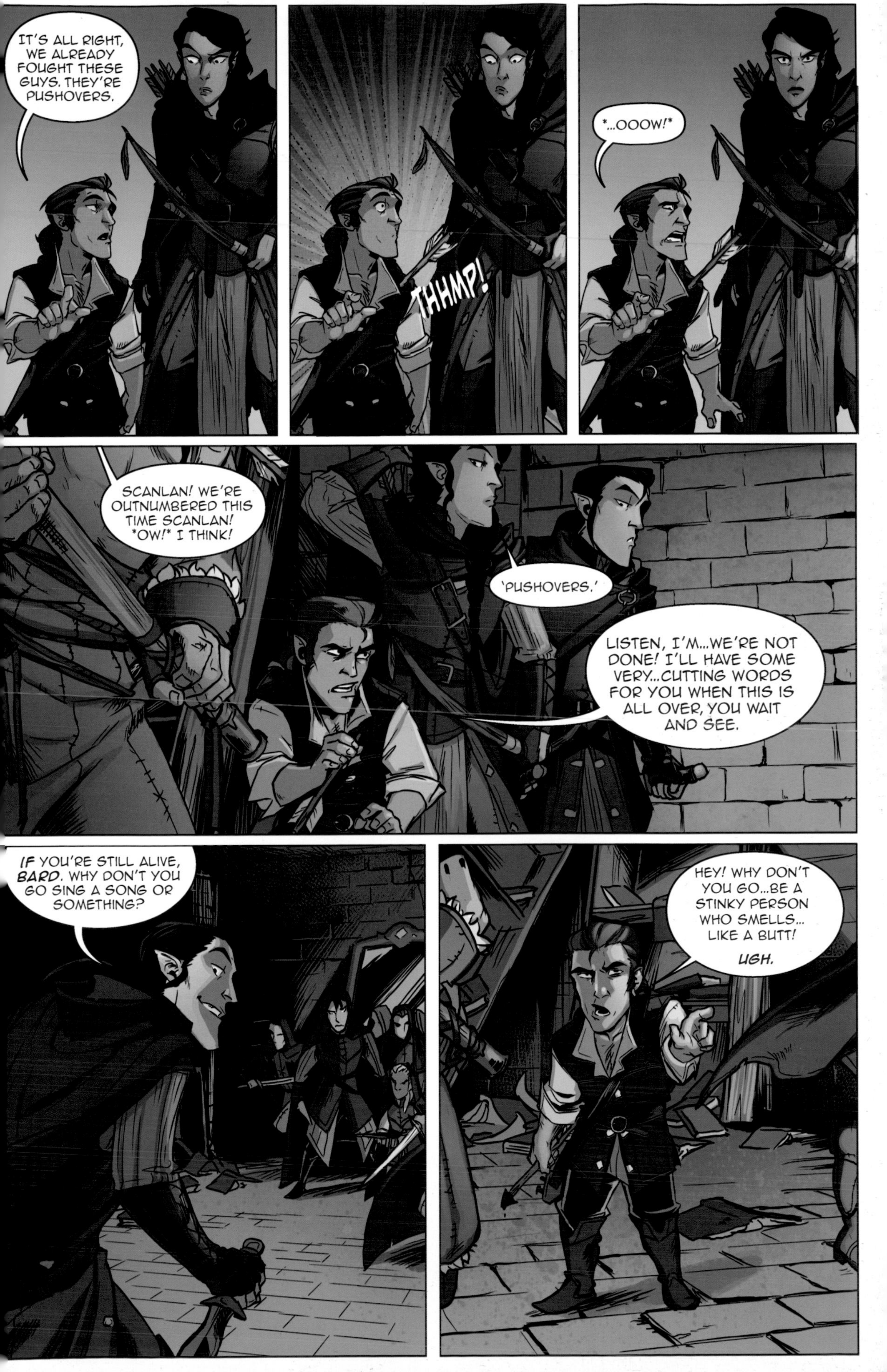
IT'S ALL RIGHT, WE ALREADY FOUGHT THESE GUYS. THEY'RE PUSHOVERS.
THHMP!
*...OOOW!*
SCANLAN! WE'RE OUTNUMBERED THIS TIME SCANLAN! *OW!* I THINK!
'PUSHOVERS.'
LISTEN, I'M...WE'RE NOT DONE! I'LL HAVE SOME VERY...CUTTING WORDS FOR YOU WHEN THIS IS ALL OVER, YOU WAIT AND SEE.
IF YOU'RE STILL ALIVE, BARD. WHY DON'T YOU GO SING A SONG OR SOMETHING?
HEY! WHY DON'T YOU GO...BE A STINKY PERSON WHO SMELLS... LIKE A BUTT!
UGH.

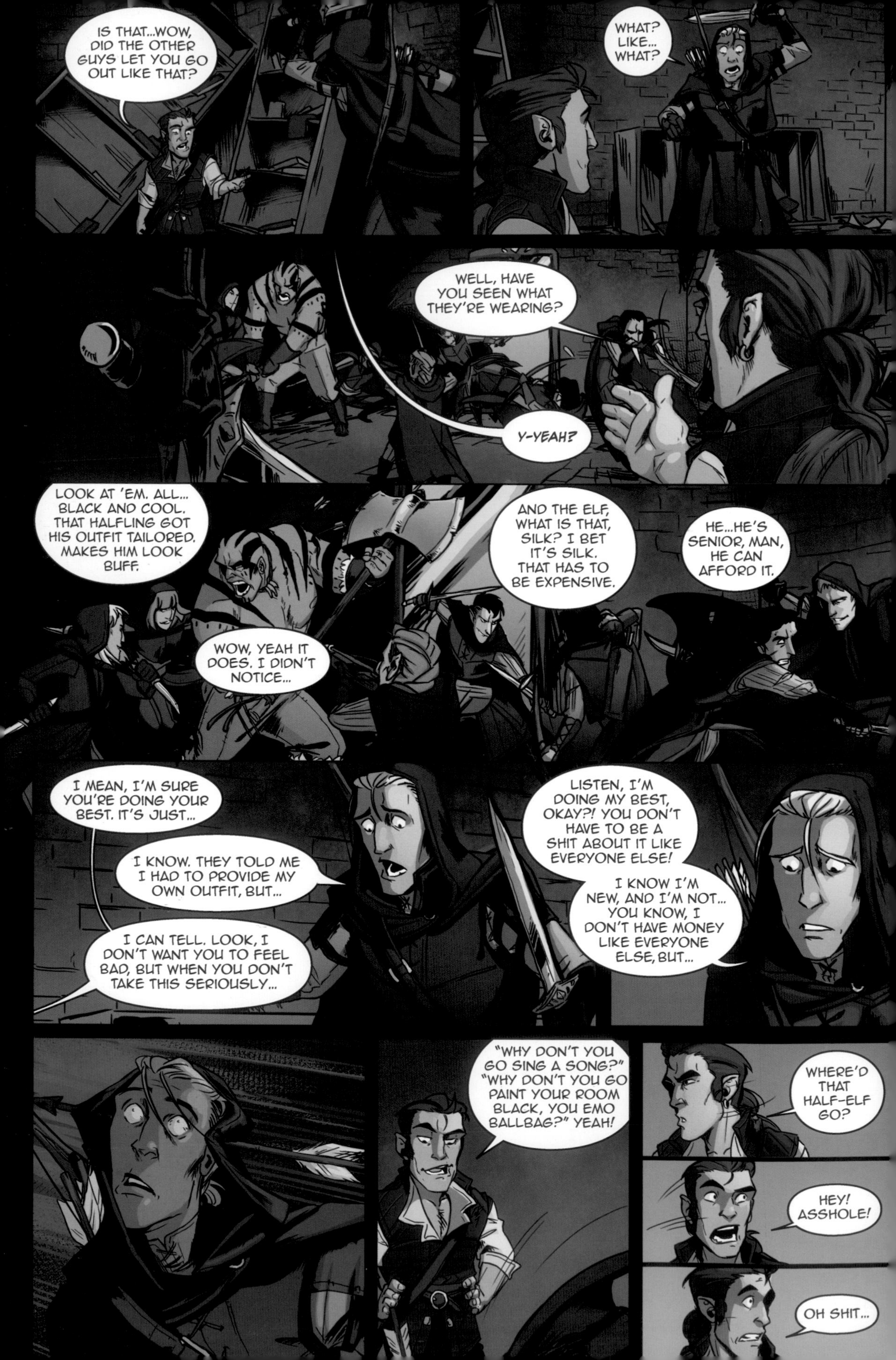
IS THAT...WOW, DID THE OTHER GUYS LET YOU GO OUT LIKE THAT?
WHAT? LIKE... WHAT?
WELL, HAVE YOU SEEN WHAT THEY'RE WEARING?
Y-YEAH?
LOOK AT 'EM. ALL... BLACK AND COOL. THAT HALFLING GOT HIS OUTFIT TAILORED. MAKES HIM LOOK BUFF.
WOW, YEAH IT DOES. I DIDN'T NOTICE...
AND THE ELF, WHAT IS THAT, SILK? I BET IT'S SILK. THAT HAS TO BE EXPENSIVE.
HE...HE'S SENIOR, MAN, HE CAN AFFORD IT.
I MEAN, I'M SURE YOU'RE DOING YOUR BEST. IT'S JUST...
I KNOW. THEY TOLD ME I HAD TO PROVIDE MY OWN OUTFIT, BUT...
I CAN TELL. LOOK, I DON'T WANT YOU TO FEEL BAD, BUT WHEN YOU DON'T TAKE THIS SERIOUSLY...
LISTEN, I'M DOING MY BEST, OKAY?! YOU DON'T HAVE TO BE A SHIT ABOUT IT LIKE EVERYONE ELSE!
I KNOW I'M NEW, AND I'M NOT... YOU KNOW, I DON'T HAVE MONEY LIKE EVERYONE ELSE, BUT...
"WHY DON'T YOU GO SING A SONG?" "WHY DON'T YOU GO PAINT YOUR ROOM BLACK, YOU EMO BALLBAG?" YEAH!
WHERE'D THAT HALF-ELF GO?
HEY! ASSHOLE!
OH SHIT...

...WE'RE LOSING.

HEY!

I WANT YOU TO REMEMBER THAT NEXT TIME YOU'RE TRYING TO KILL ME!

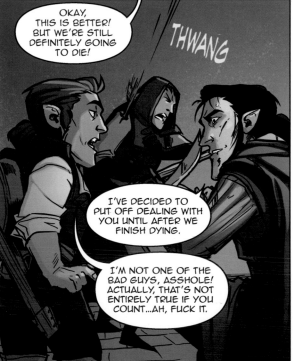

OKAY, THIS IS BETTER! BUT WE'RE STILL DEFINITELY GOING TO DIE!

THWANG

I'VE DECIDED TO PUT OFF DEALING WITH YOU UNTIL AFTER WE FINISH DYING.

I'M NOT ONE OF THE BAD GUYS, ASSHOLE! ACTUALLY, THAT'S NOT ENTIRELY TRUE IF YOU COUNT...AH, FUCK IT.

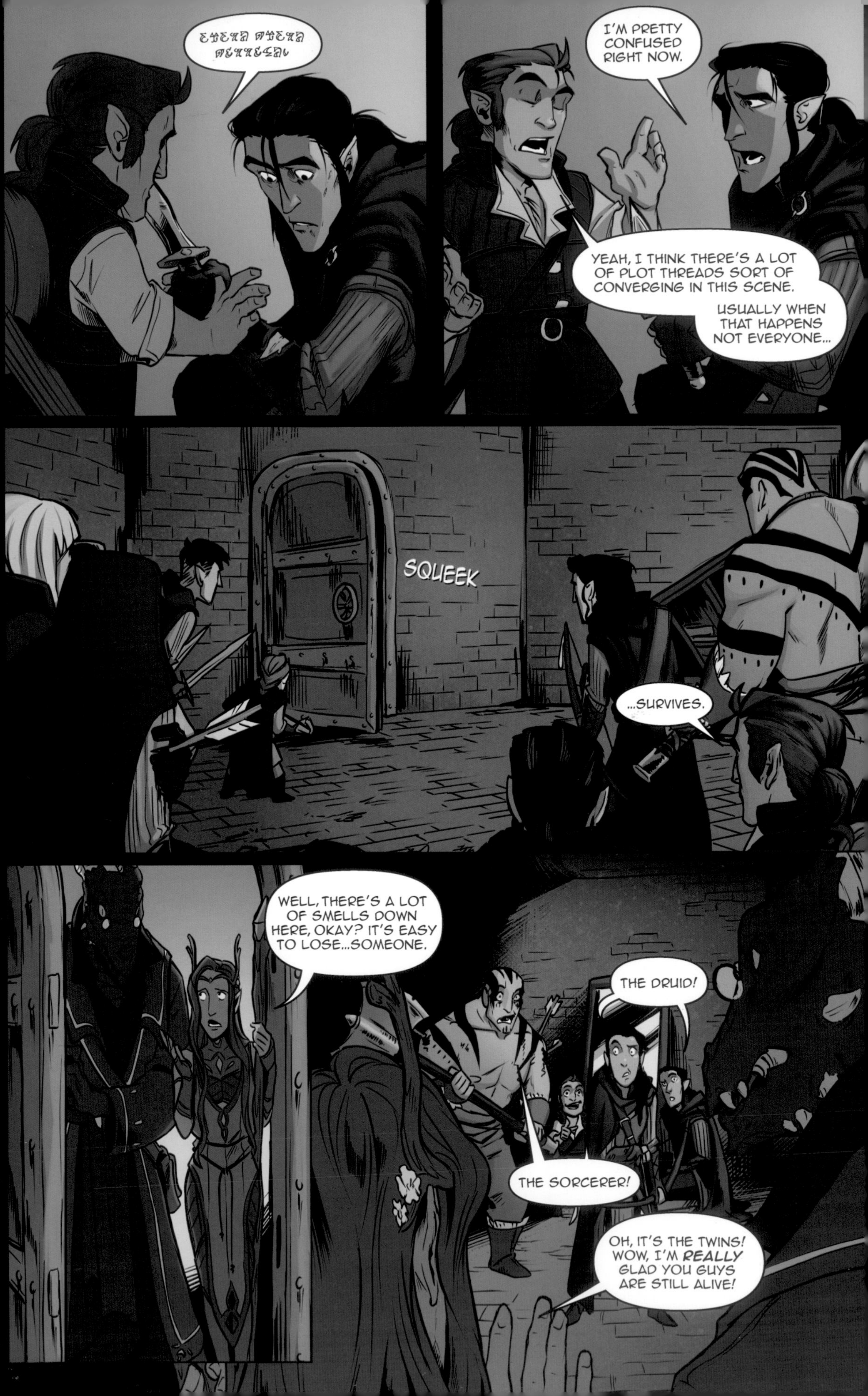
I'M PRETTY CONFUSED RIGHT NOW.
YEAH, I THINK THERE'S A LOT OF PLOT THREADS SORT OF CONVERGING IN THIS SCENE.
USUALLY WHEN THAT HAPPENS NOT EVERYONE...
SQUEEK
...SURVIVES.
WELL, THERE'S A LOT OF SMELLS DOWN HERE, OKAY? IT'S EASY TO LOSE...SOMEONE.
THE DRUID!
THE SORCERER!
OH, IT'S THE TWINS! WOW, I'M ***REALLY*** GLAD YOU GUYS ARE STILL ALIVE!

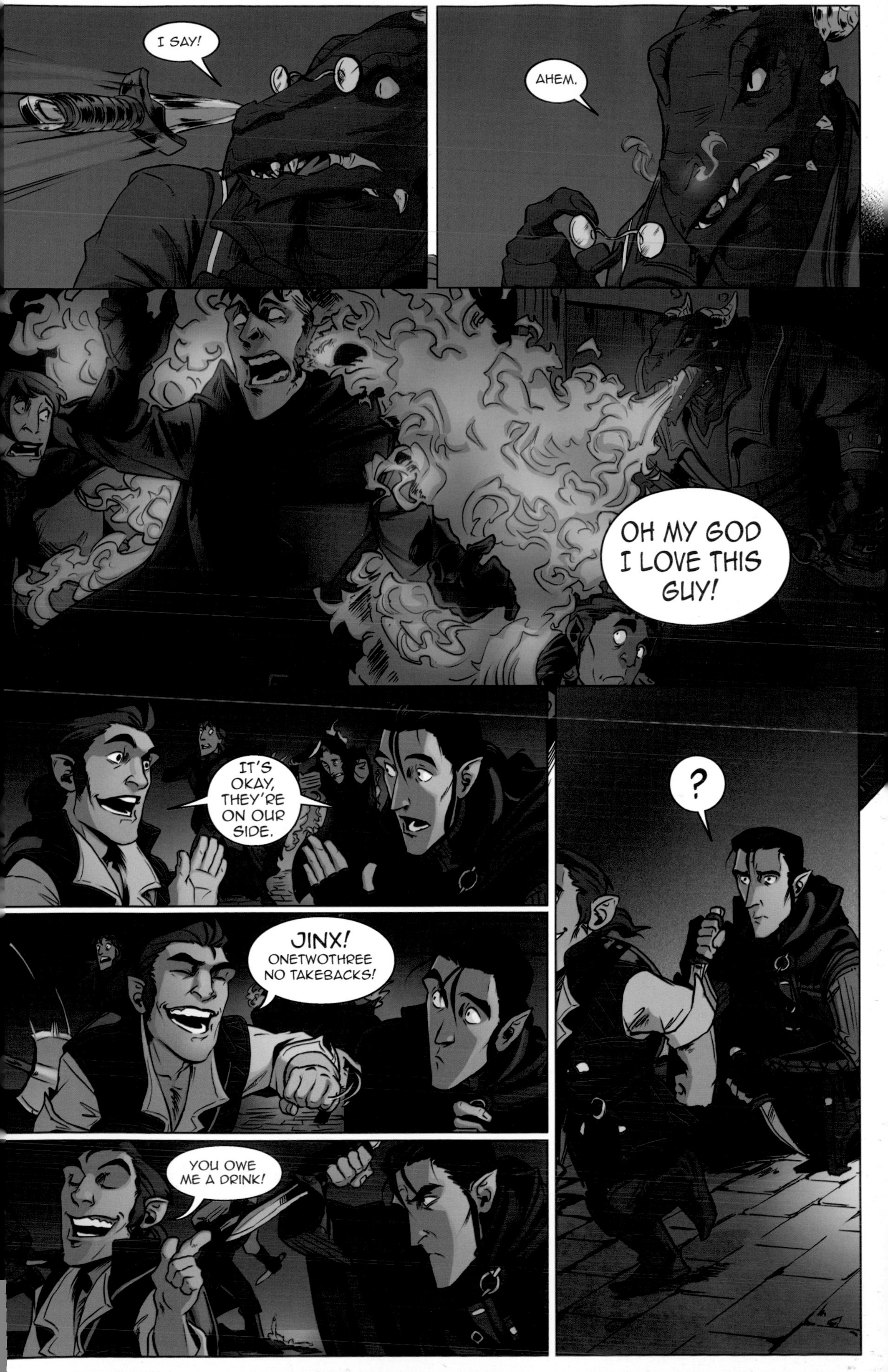
I SAY!
AHEM.
OH MY GOD I LOVE THIS GUY!
IT'S OKAY, THEY'RE ON OUR SIDE.
?
JINX! ONETWOTHREE NO TAKEBACKS!
YOU OWE ME A DRINK!

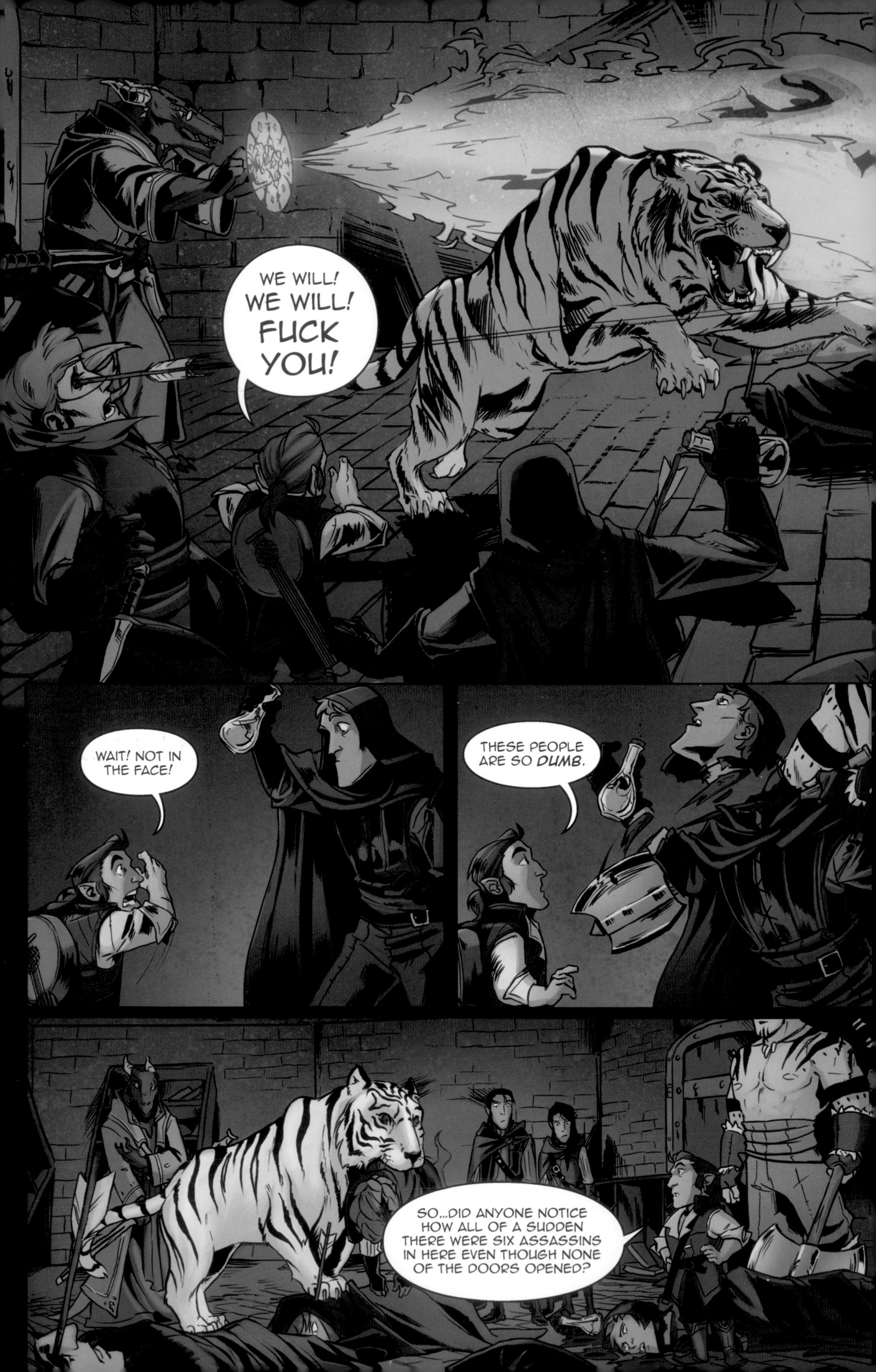
WE WILL! WE WILL! FUCK YOU!
WAIT! NOT IN THE FACE!
THESE PEOPLE ARE SO *DUMB*.
SO...DID ANYONE NOTICE HOW ALL OF A SUDDEN THERE WERE SIX ASSASSINS IN HERE EVEN THOUGH NONE OF THE DOORS OPENED?

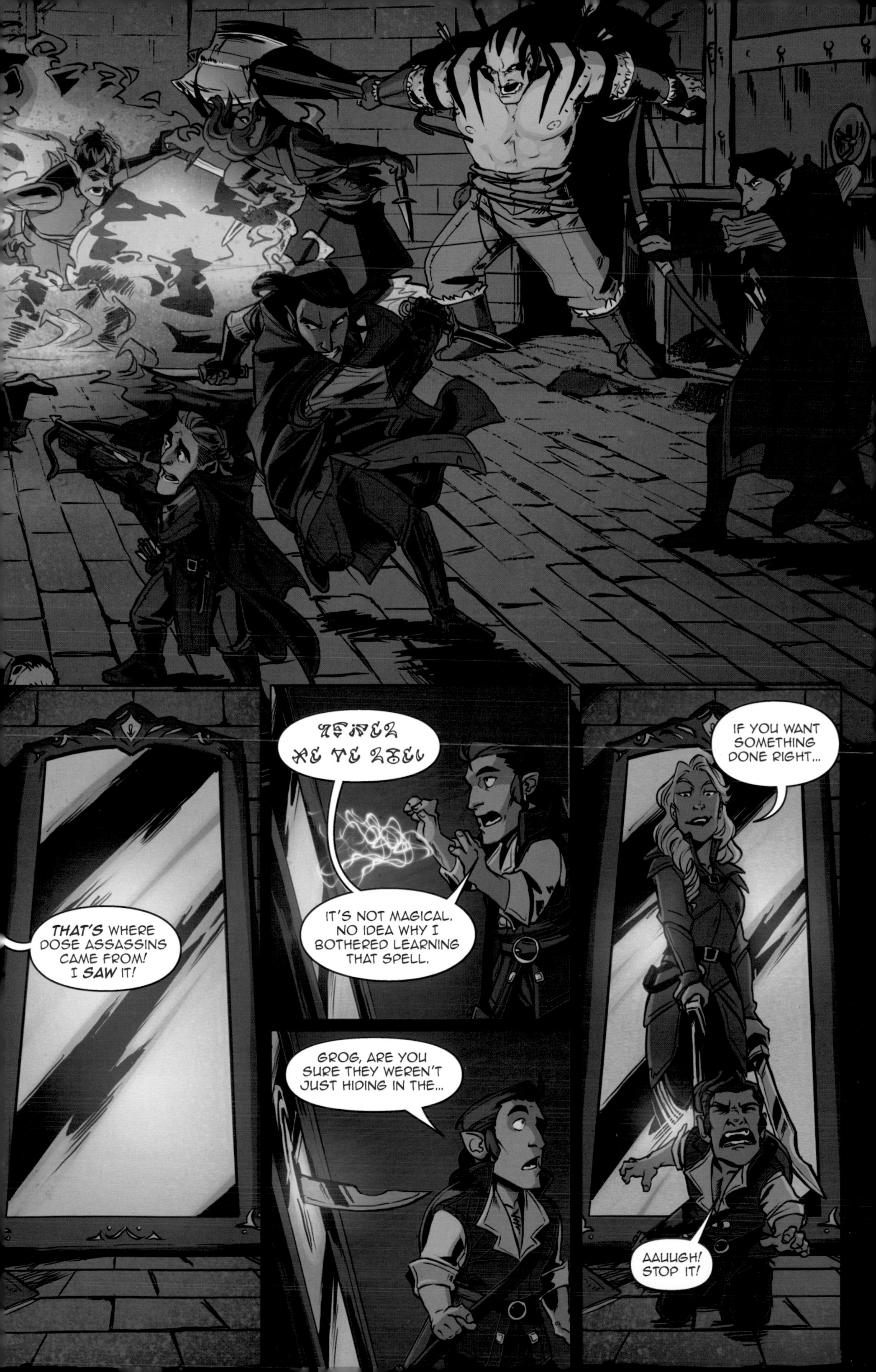
THAT'S WHERE DOSE ASSASSINS CAME FROM! I SAW IT!
IT'S NOT MAGICAL. NO IDEA WHY I BOTHERED LEARNING THAT SPELL.
GROG, ARE YOU SURE THEY WEREN'T JUST HIDING IN THE...
IF YOU WANT SOMETHING DONE RIGHT...
AAUUGH! STOP IT!

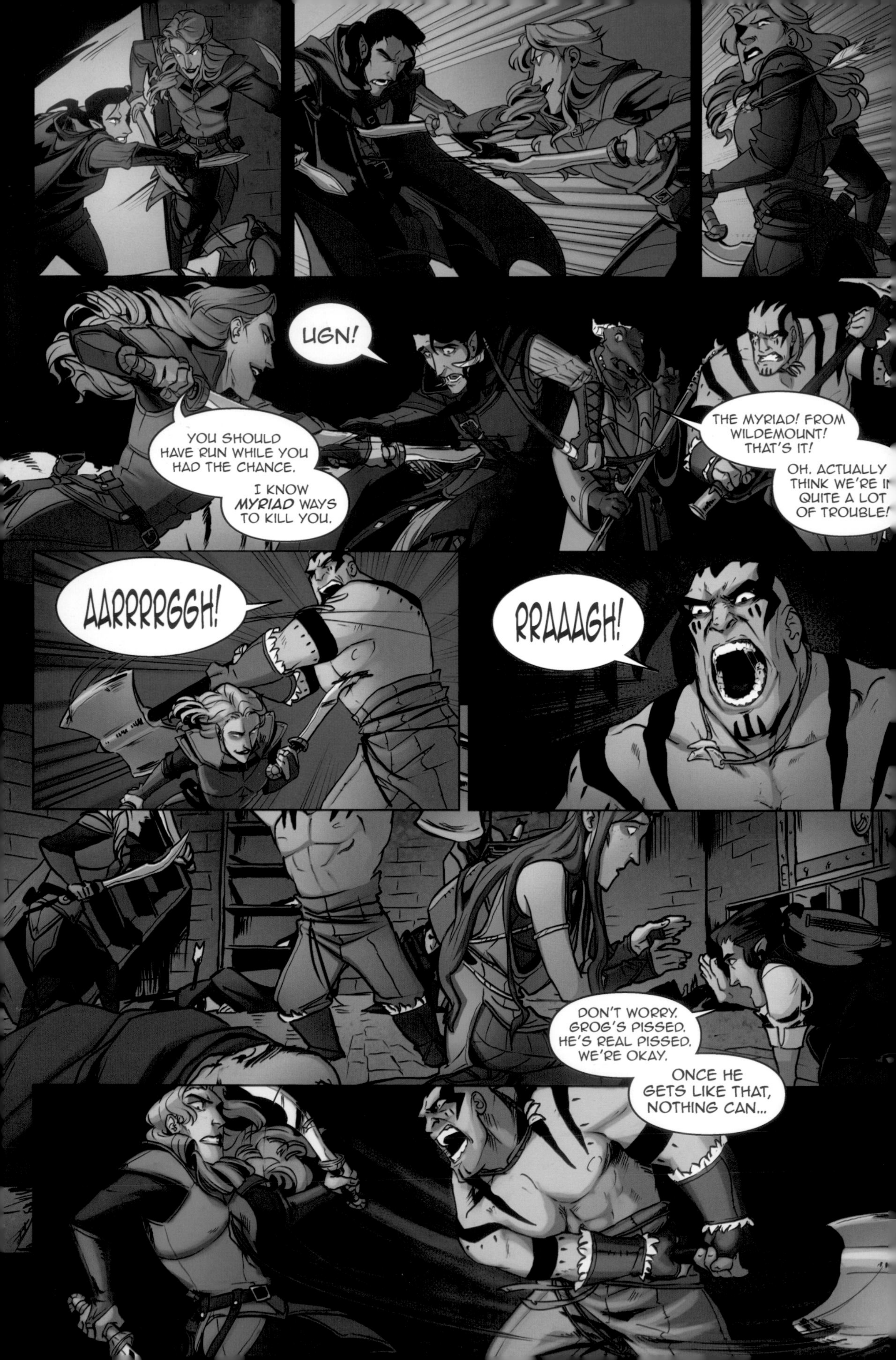
UGN!
YOU SHOULD HAVE RUN WHILE YOU HAD THE CHANCE.
I KNOW *MYRIAD* WAYS TO KILL YOU.
THE MYRIAD! FROM WILDEMOUNT! THAT'S IT!
OH. ACTUALLY THINK WE'RE I QUITE A LOT OF TROUBLE!
AARRRRGGH!
RRAAAGH!
DON'T WORRY. GROG'S PISSED. HE'S REAL PISSED. WE'RE OKAY.
ONCE HE GETS LIKE THAT, NOTHING CAN...

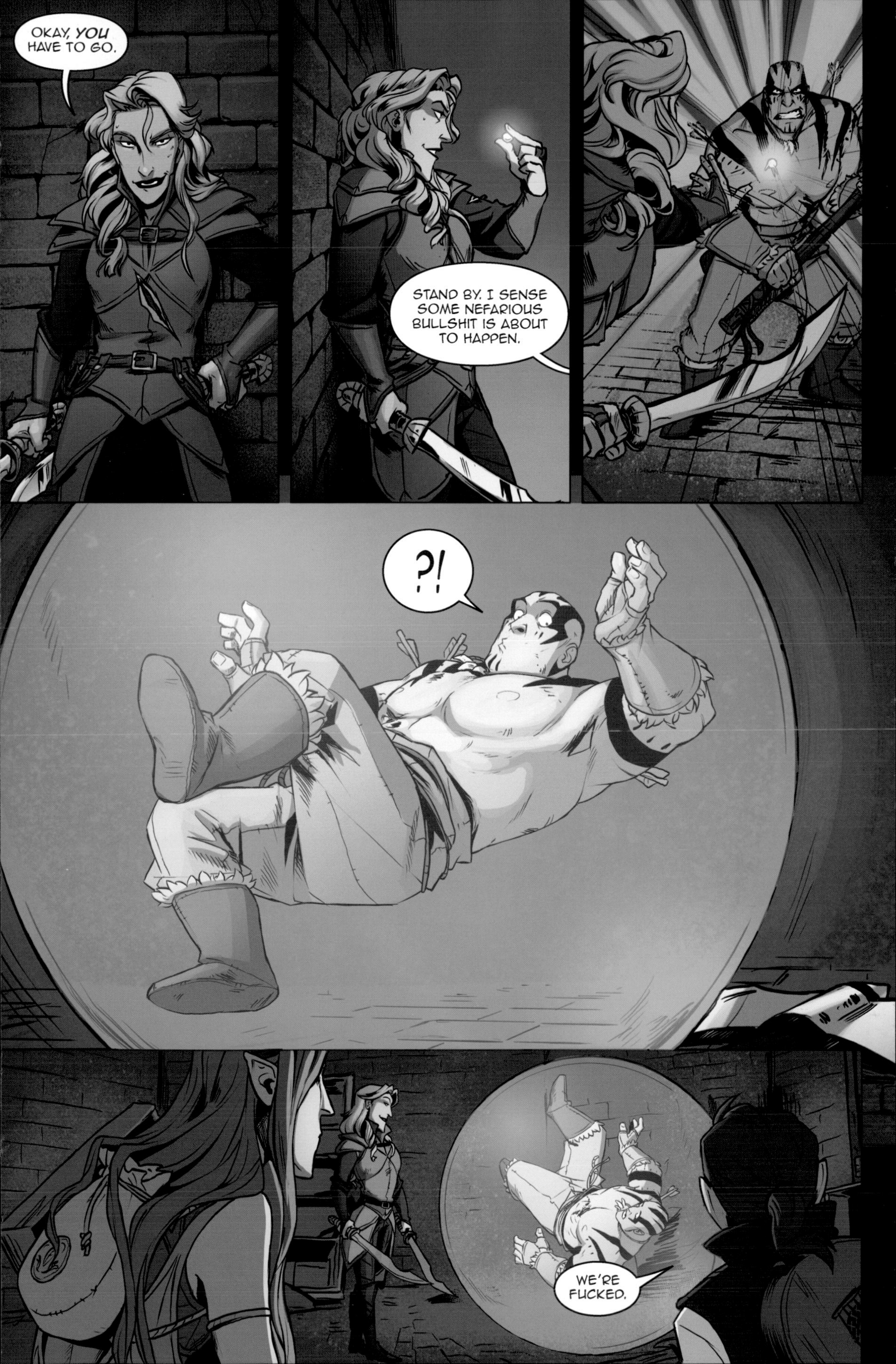
OKAY, YOU HAVE TO GO.
STAND BY. I SENSE SOME NEFARIOUS BULLSHIT IS ABOUT TO HAPPEN.
?!
WE'RE FUCKED.

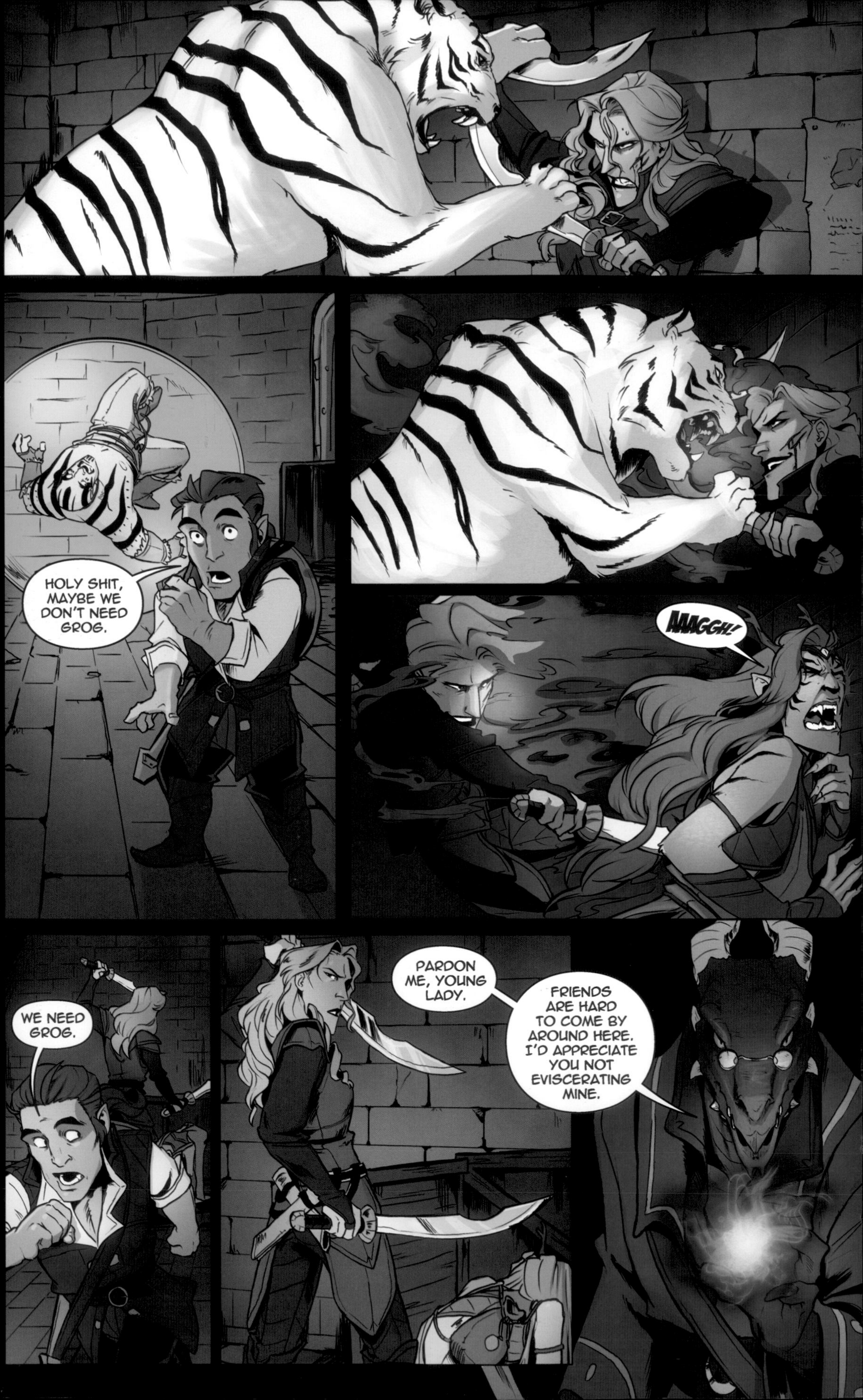
HOLY SHIT, MAYBE WE DON'T NEED GROG.
AAAGGH!
WE NEED GROG.
PARDON ME, YOUNG LADY.
FRIENDS ARE HARD TO COME BY AROUND HERE. I'D APPRECIATE YOU NOT EVISCERATING MINE.

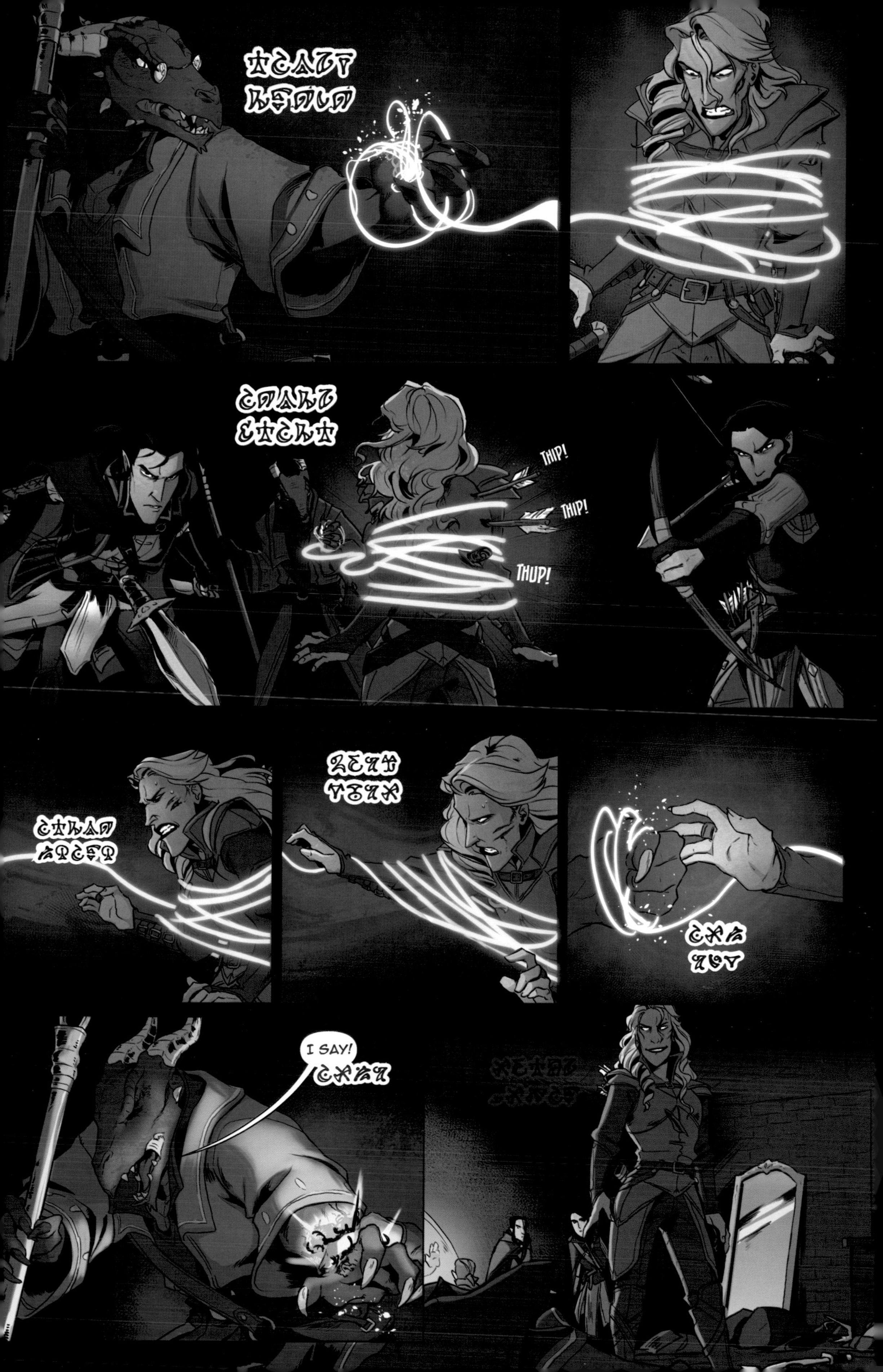
THIP!
THIP!
THUP!
I SAY!

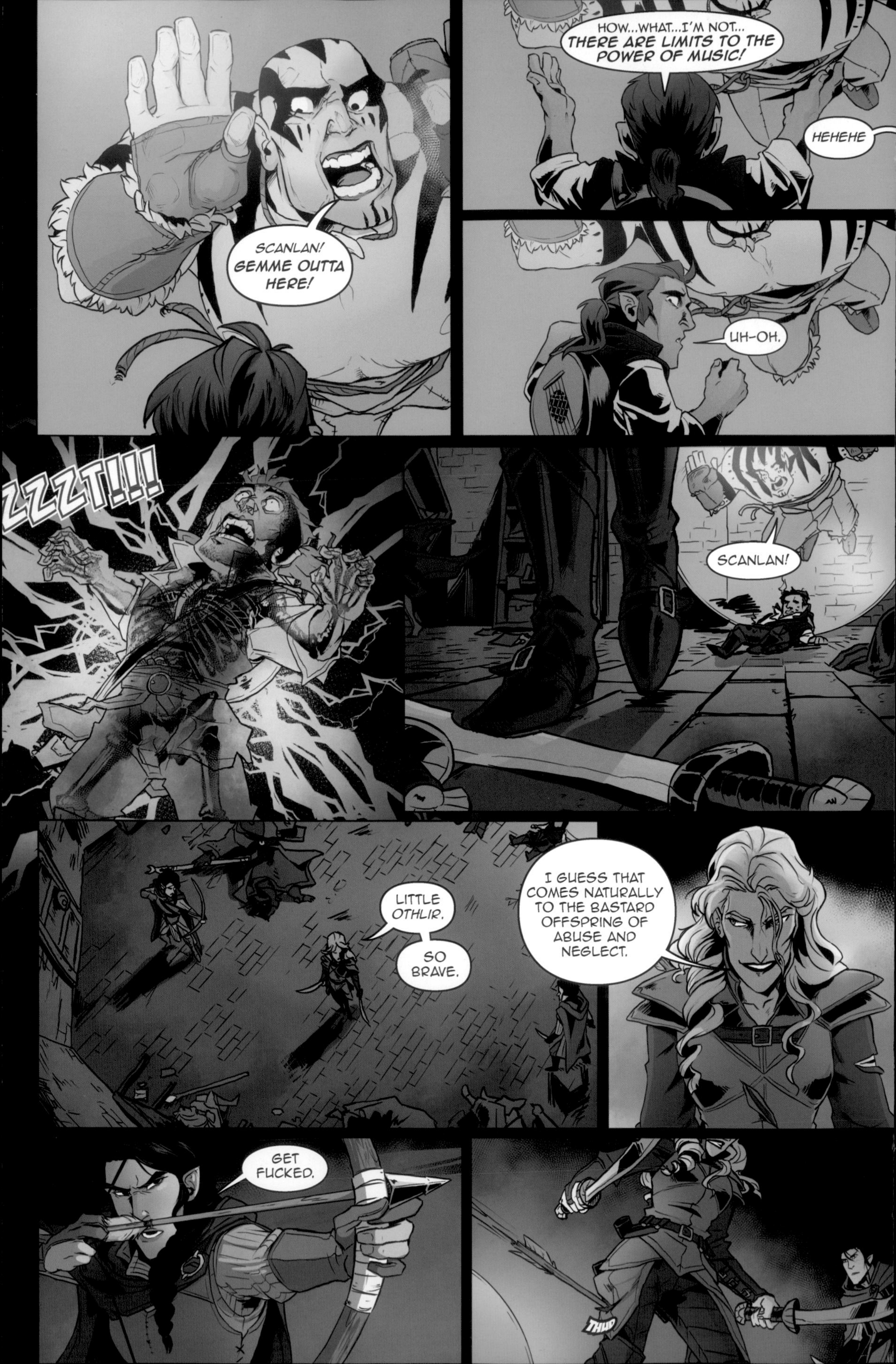
SCANLAN! GEMME OUTTA HERE!
HOW...WHAT...I'M NOT... THERE ARE LIMITS TO THE POWER OF MUSIC!
HEHEHE
UH-OH.
ZZZZT!!!
SCANLAN!
LITTLE OTHLIR.
SO BRAVE.
I GUESS THAT COMES NATURALLY TO THE BASTARD OFFSPRING OF ABUSE AND NEGLECT.
GET FUCKED.
THUD

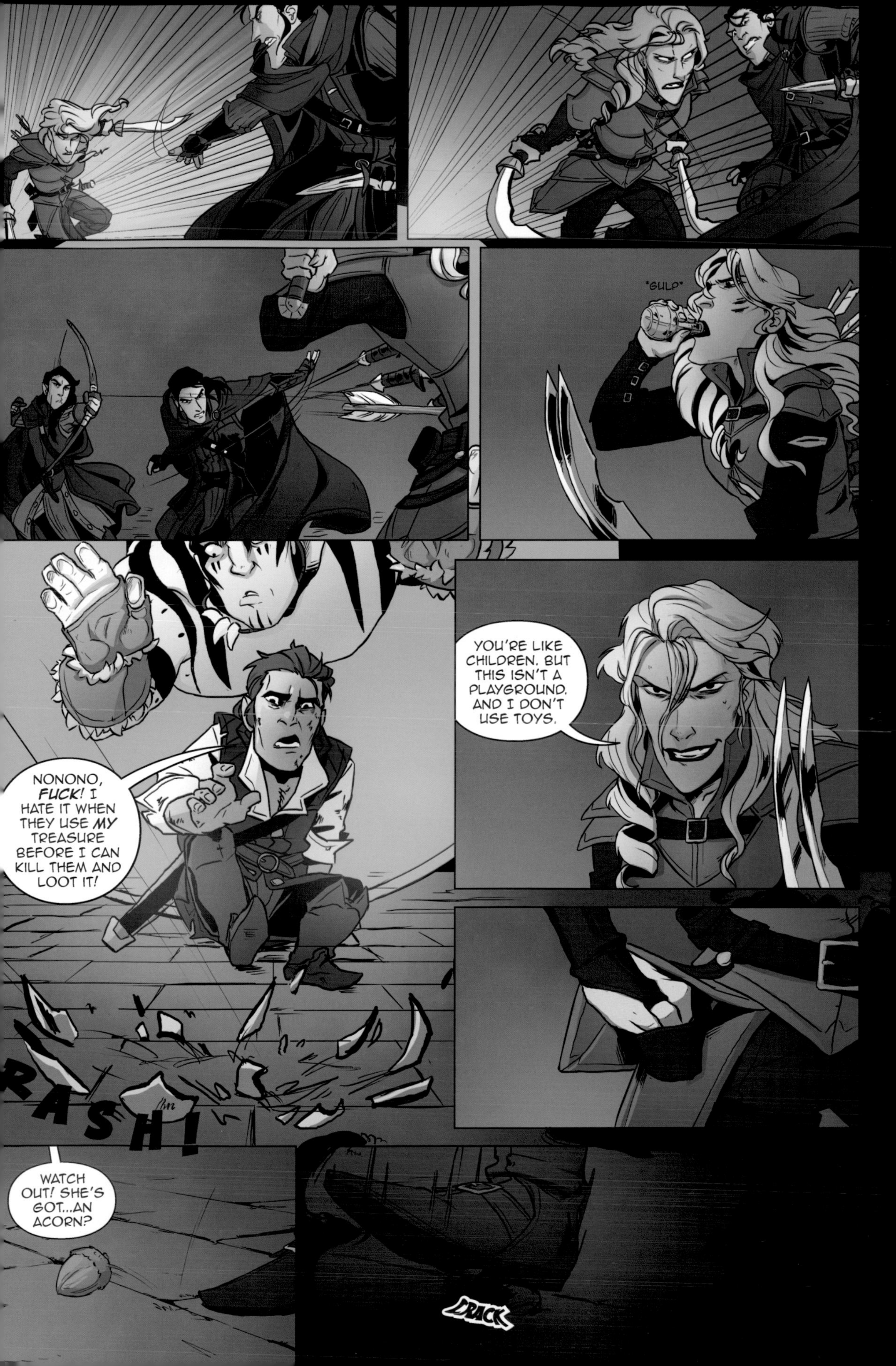

*GULP*
NONONO, ***FUCK***! I HATE IT WHEN THEY USE ***MY*** TREASURE BEFORE I CAN KILL THEM AND LOOT IT!
YOU'RE LIKE CHILDREN. BUT THIS ISN'T A PLAYGROUND. AND I DON'T USE TOYS.
RASH!
WATCH OUT! SHE'S GOT...AN ACORN?
CRACK

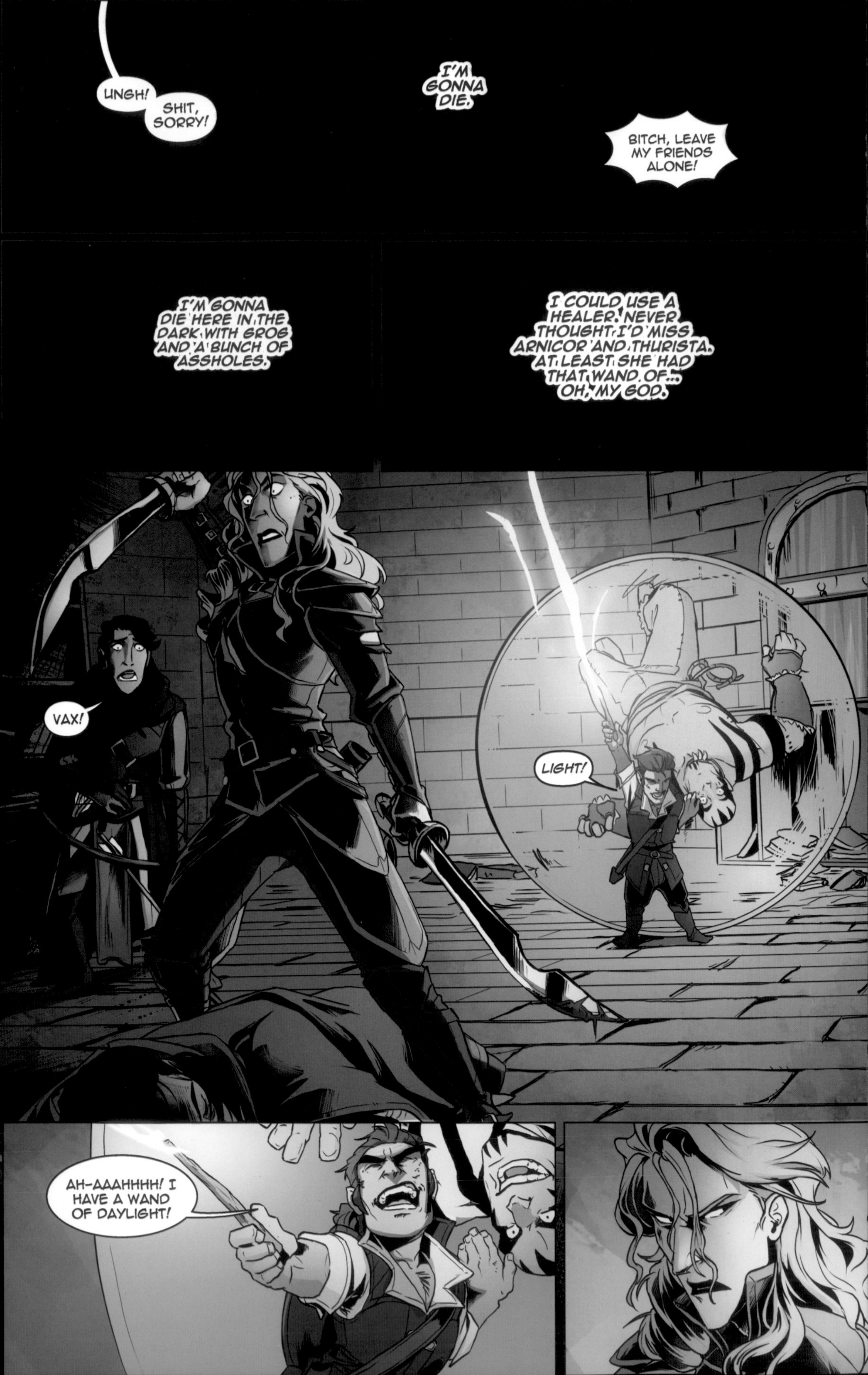
UNGH!
SHIT, SORRY!
I'M GONNA DIE.
BITCH, LEAVE MY FRIENDS ALONE!
I'M GONNA DIE HERE IN THE DARK WITH GROG AND A BUNCH OF ASSHOLES.
I COULD USE A HEALER. NEVER THOUGHT I'D MISS ARNICOR AND THURISTA. AT LEAST SHE HAD THAT WAND OF... OH, MY GOD.
VAX!
LIGHT!
AH-AAAHHHH! I HAVE A WAND OF DAYLIGHT!

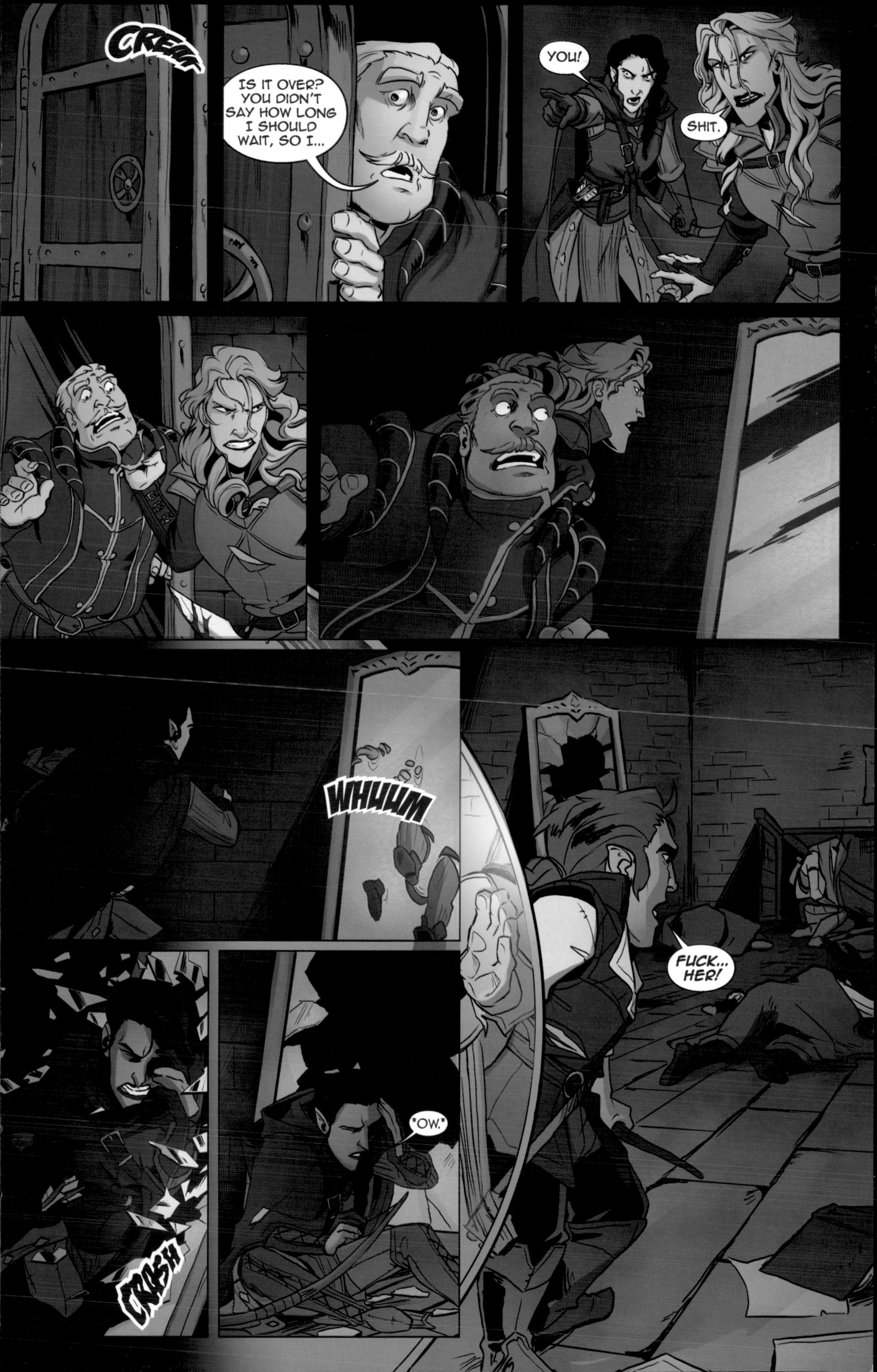
CREAK
IS IT OVER? YOU DIDN'T SAY HOW LONG I SHOULD WAIT, SO I...
YOU!
SHIT.
WHUUM
FUCK... HER!
CRASH
*OW.*

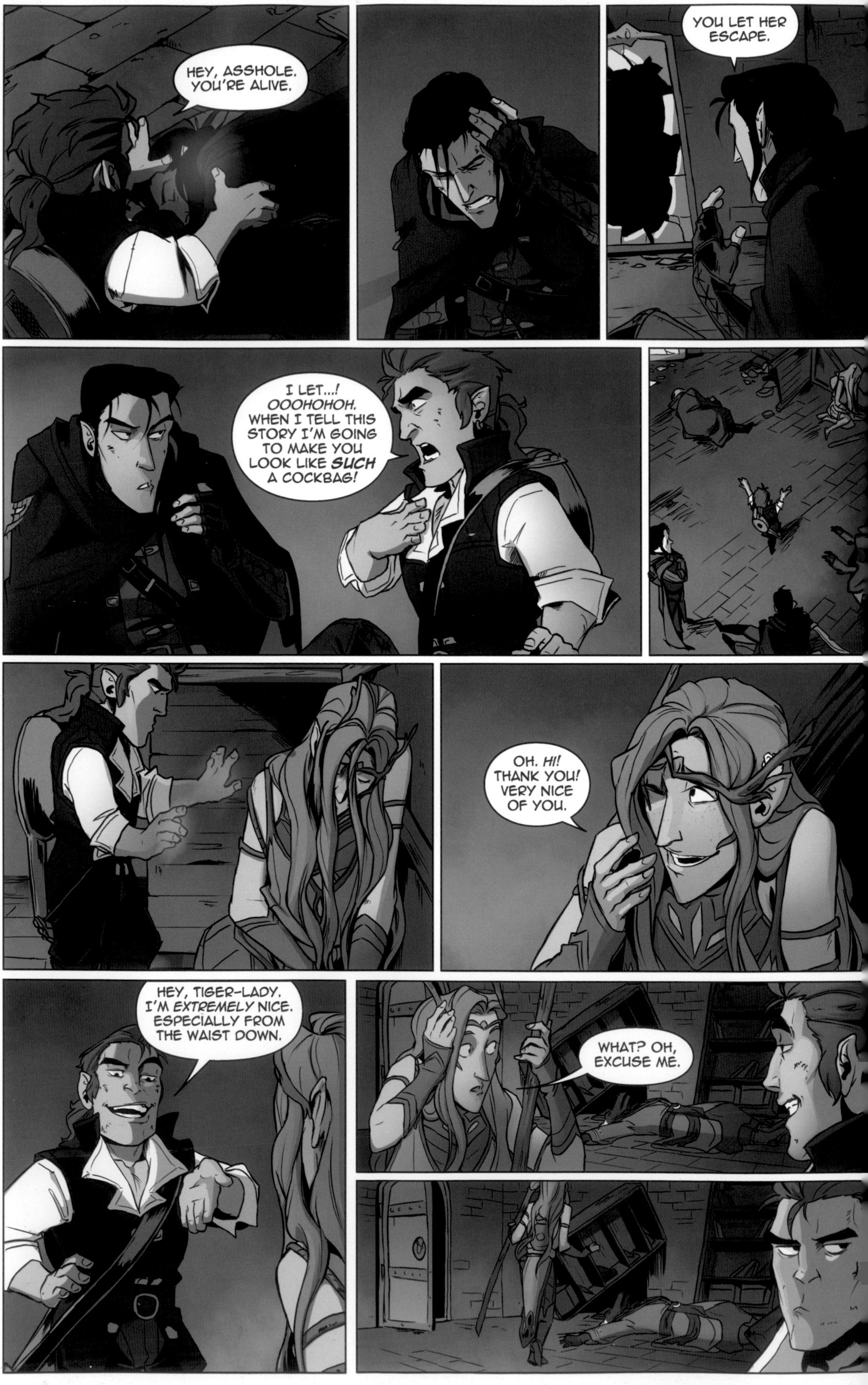
HEY, ASSHOLE. YOU'RE ALIVE.
YOU LET HER ESCAPE.
I LET...! OOOHOHOH. WHEN I TELL THIS STORY I'M GOING TO MAKE YOU LOOK LIKE SUCH A COCKBAG!
OH. HI! THANK YOU! VERY NICE OF YOU.
HEY, TIGER-LADY. I'M EXTREMELY NICE. ESPECIALLY FROM THE WAIST DOWN.
WHAT? OH, EXCUSE ME.

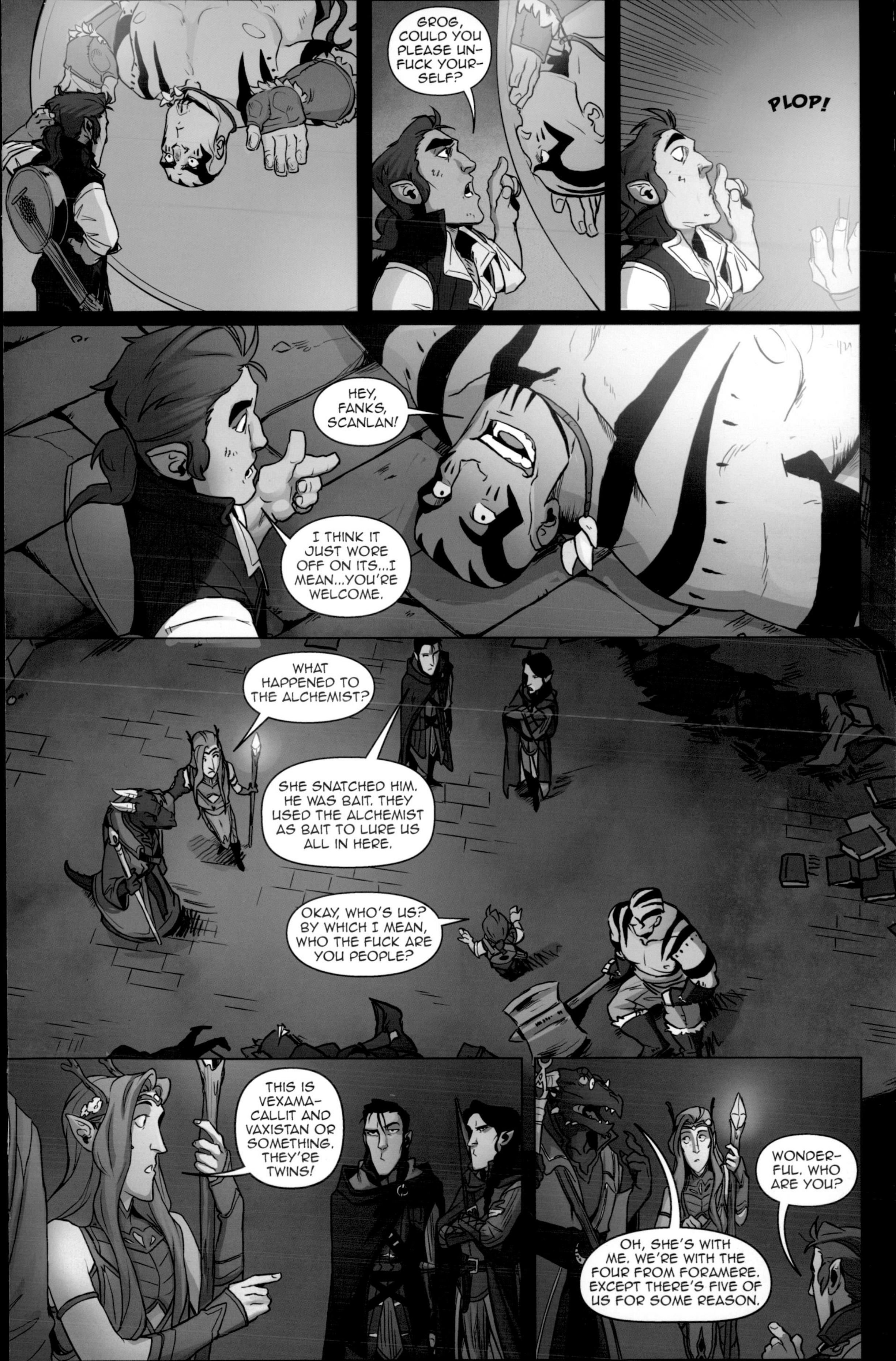
GROG, COULD YOU PLEASE UN-FUCK YOUR-SELF?
PLOP!
HEY, FANKS, SCANLAN!
I THINK IT JUST WORE OFF ON ITS...I MEAN...YOU'RE WELCOME.
WHAT HAPPENED TO THE ALCHEMIST?
SHE SNATCHED HIM. HE WAS BAIT. THEY USED THE ALCHEMIST AS BAIT TO LURE US ALL IN HERE.
OKAY, WHO'S US? BY WHICH I MEAN, WHO THE FUCK ARE YOU PEOPLE?
THIS IS VEXAMA-CALLIT AND VAXISTAN OR SOMETHING. THEY'RE TWINS!
WONDER-FUL. WHO ARE YOU?
OH, SHE'S WITH ME. WE'RE WITH THE FOUR FROM FORAMERE. EXCEPT THERE'S FIVE OF US FOR SOME REASON.

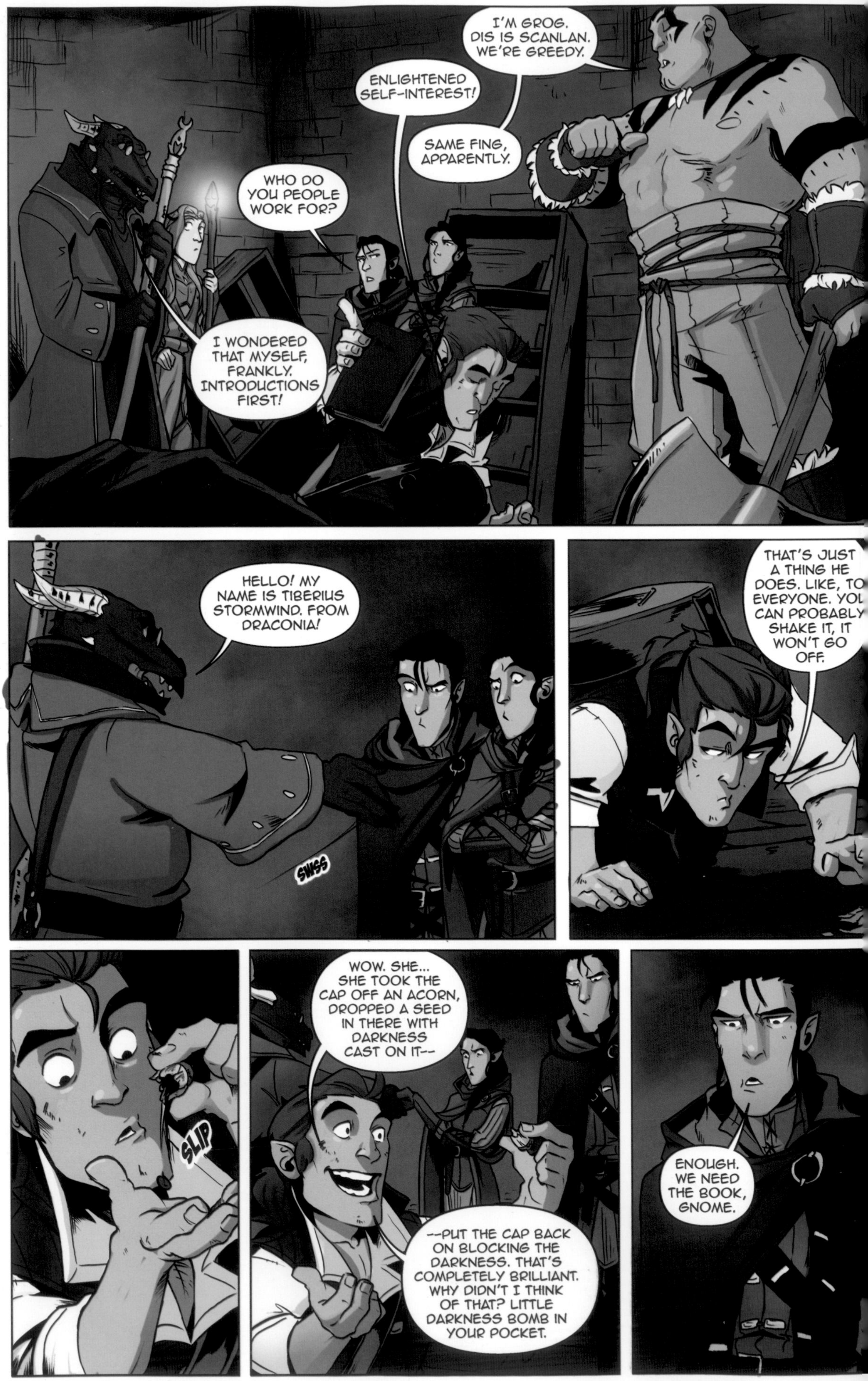
WHO DO YOU PEOPLE WORK FOR?
I WONDERED THAT MYSELF, FRANKLY. INTRODUCTIONS FIRST!
ENLIGHTENED SELF-INTEREST!
I'M GROG. DIS IS SCANLAN. WE'RE GREEDY.
SAME FING, APPARENTLY.
HELLO! MY NAME IS TIBERIUS STORMWIND. FROM DRACONIA!
SWISS
THAT'S JUST A THING HE DOES. LIKE, TO EVERYONE. YOU CAN PROBABLY SHAKE IT, IT WON'T GO OFF.
SLIP
WOW. SHE... SHE TOOK THE CAP OFF AN ACORN, DROPPED A SEED IN THERE WITH DARKNESS CAST ON IT--
--PUT THE CAP BACK ON BLOCKING THE DARKNESS. THAT'S COMPLETELY BRILLIANT. WHY DIDN'T I THINK OF THAT? LITTLE DARKNESS BOMB IN YOUR POCKET.
ENOUGH. WE NEED THE BOOK, GNOME.

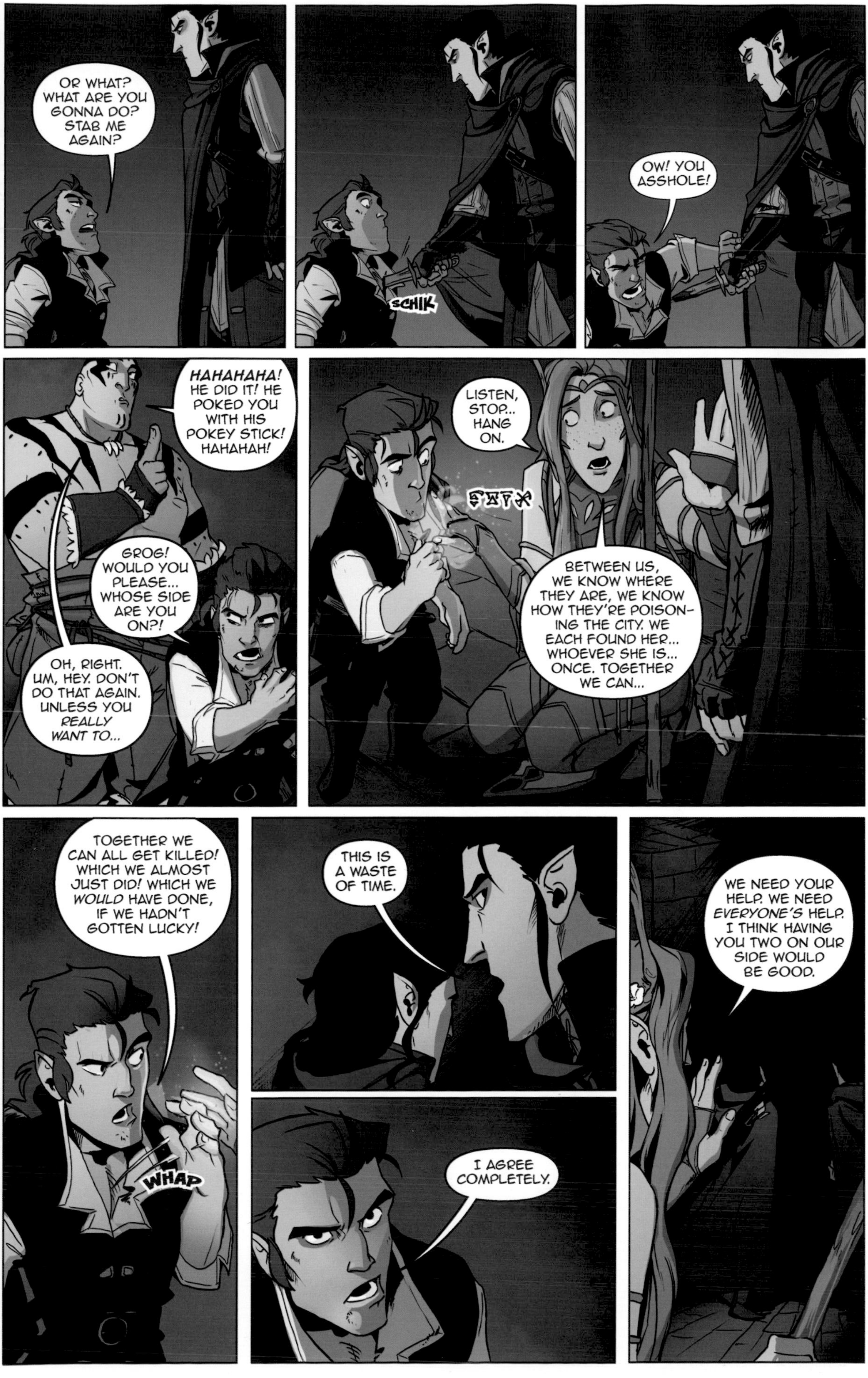
OR WHAT? WHAT ARE YOU GONNA DO? STAB ME AGAIN?
SCHIK
OW! YOU ASSHOLE!
HAHAHAHA! HE DID IT! HE POKED YOU WITH HIS POKEY STICK! HAHAHAH!
GROG! WOULD YOU PLEASE... WHOSE SIDE ARE YOU ON?!
OH, RIGHT. UM, HEY. DON'T DO THAT AGAIN. UNLESS YOU REALLY WANT TO...
LISTEN, STOP... HANG ON.
BETWEEN US, WE KNOW WHERE THEY ARE, WE KNOW HOW THEY'RE POISONING THE CITY. WE EACH FOUND HER... WHOEVER SHE IS... ONCE. TOGETHER WE CAN...
TOGETHER WE CAN ALL GET KILLED! WHICH WE ALMOST JUST DID! WHICH WE WOULD HAVE DONE, IF WE HADN'T GOTTEN LUCKY!
WHAP
THIS IS A WASTE OF TIME.
I AGREE COMPLETELY.
WE NEED YOUR HELP. WE NEED EVERYONE'S HELP. I THINK HAVING YOU TWO ON OUR SIDE WOULD BE GOOD.

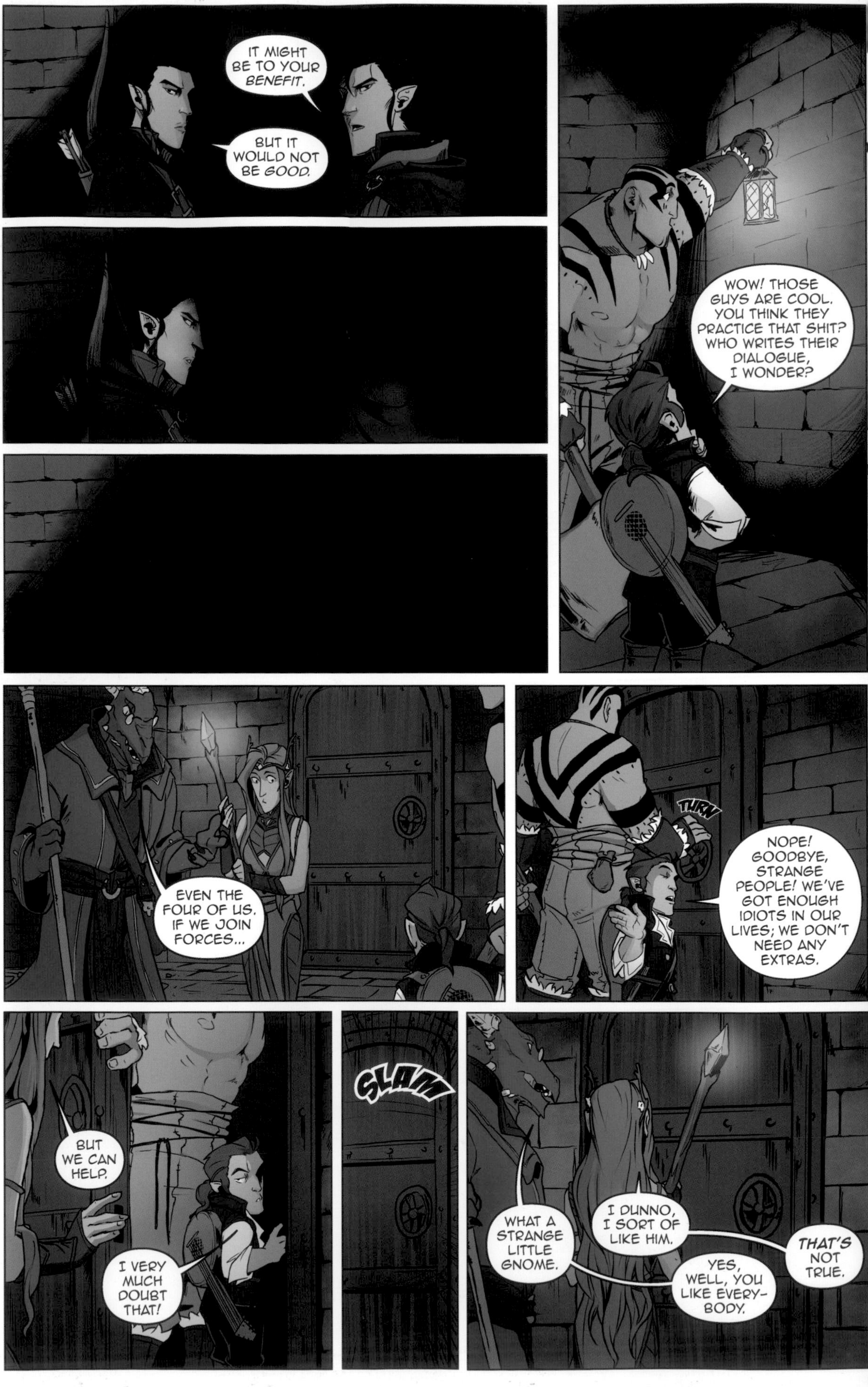

IT MIGHT BE TO YOUR *BENEFIT*.
BUT IT WOULD NOT BE *GOOD*.
WOW! THOSE GUYS ARE COOL. YOU THINK THEY PRACTICE THAT SHIT? WHO WRITES THEIR DIALOGUE, I WONDER?
EVEN THE FOUR OF US. IF WE JOIN FORCES...
TURN
NOPE! GOODBYE, STRANGE PEOPLE! WE'VE GOT ENOUGH IDIOTS IN OUR LIVES; WE DON'T NEED ANY EXTRAS.
BUT WE CAN HELP.
I VERY MUCH DOUBT THAT!
SLAM
WHAT A STRANGE LITTLE GNOME.
I DUNNO, I SORT OF LIKE HIM.
YES, WELL, YOU LIKE EVERY-BODY.
*THAT'S* NOT TRUE.

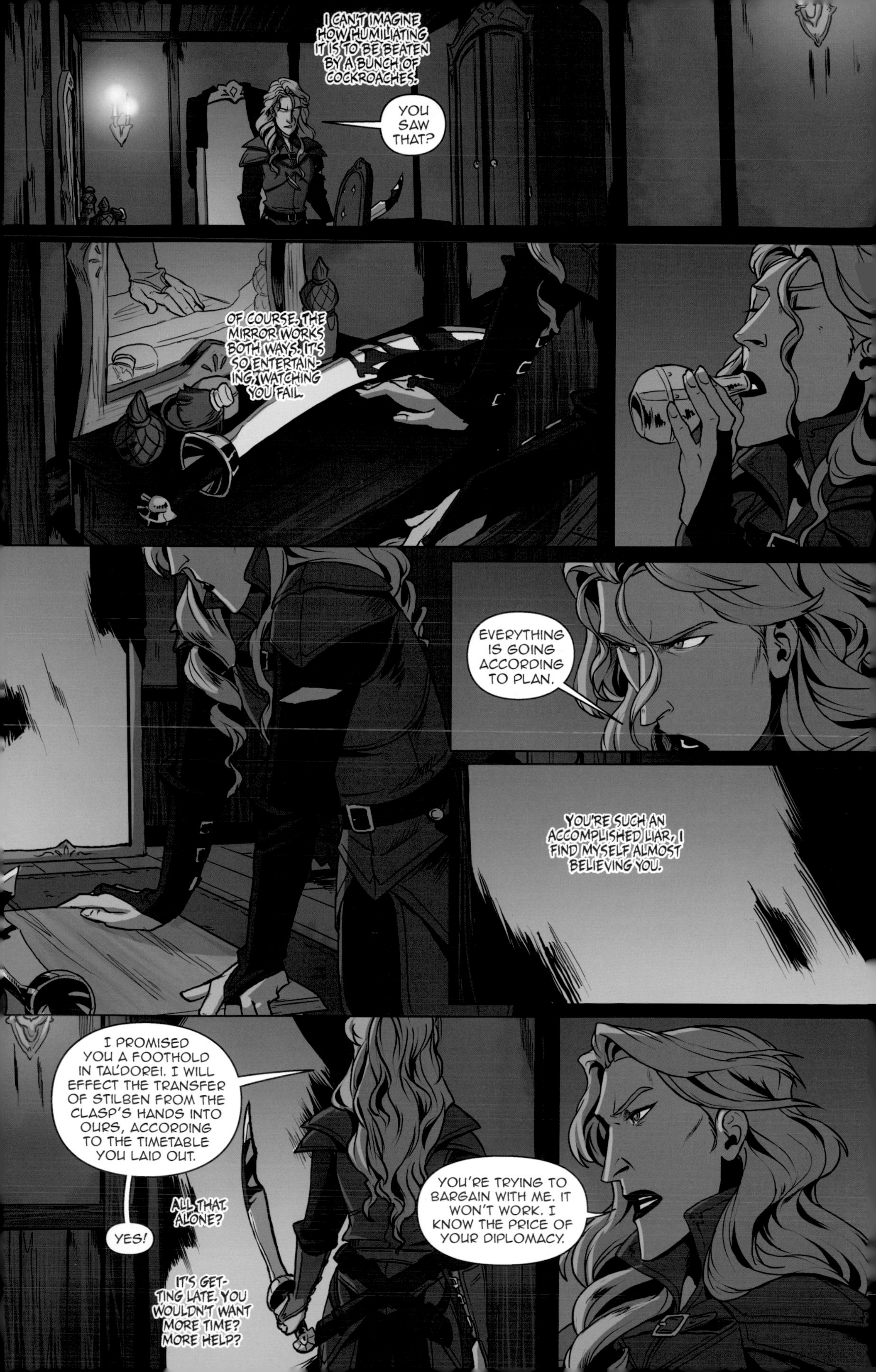
I CAN'T IMAGINE HOW HUMILIATING IT IS TO BE BEATEN BY A BUNCH OF COCKROACHES.
YOU SAW THAT?
OF COURSE. THE MIRROR WORKS BOTH WAYS. IT'S SO ENTERTAINING, WATCHING YOU FAIL.
EVERYTHING IS GOING ACCORDING TO PLAN.
YOU'RE SUCH AN ACCOMPLISHED LIAR, I FIND MYSELF ALMOST BELIEVING YOU.
I PROMISED YOU A FOOTHOLD IN TAL'DOREI. I WILL EFFECT THE TRANSFER OF STILBEN FROM THE CLASP'S HANDS INTO OURS, ACCORDING TO THE TIMETABLE YOU LAID OUT.
ALL THAT. ALONE?
YES!
IT'S GETTING LATE. YOU WOULDN'T WANT MORE TIME? MORE HELP?
YOU'RE TRYING TO BARGAIN WITH ME. IT WON'T WORK. I KNOW THE PRICE OF YOUR DIPLOMACY.

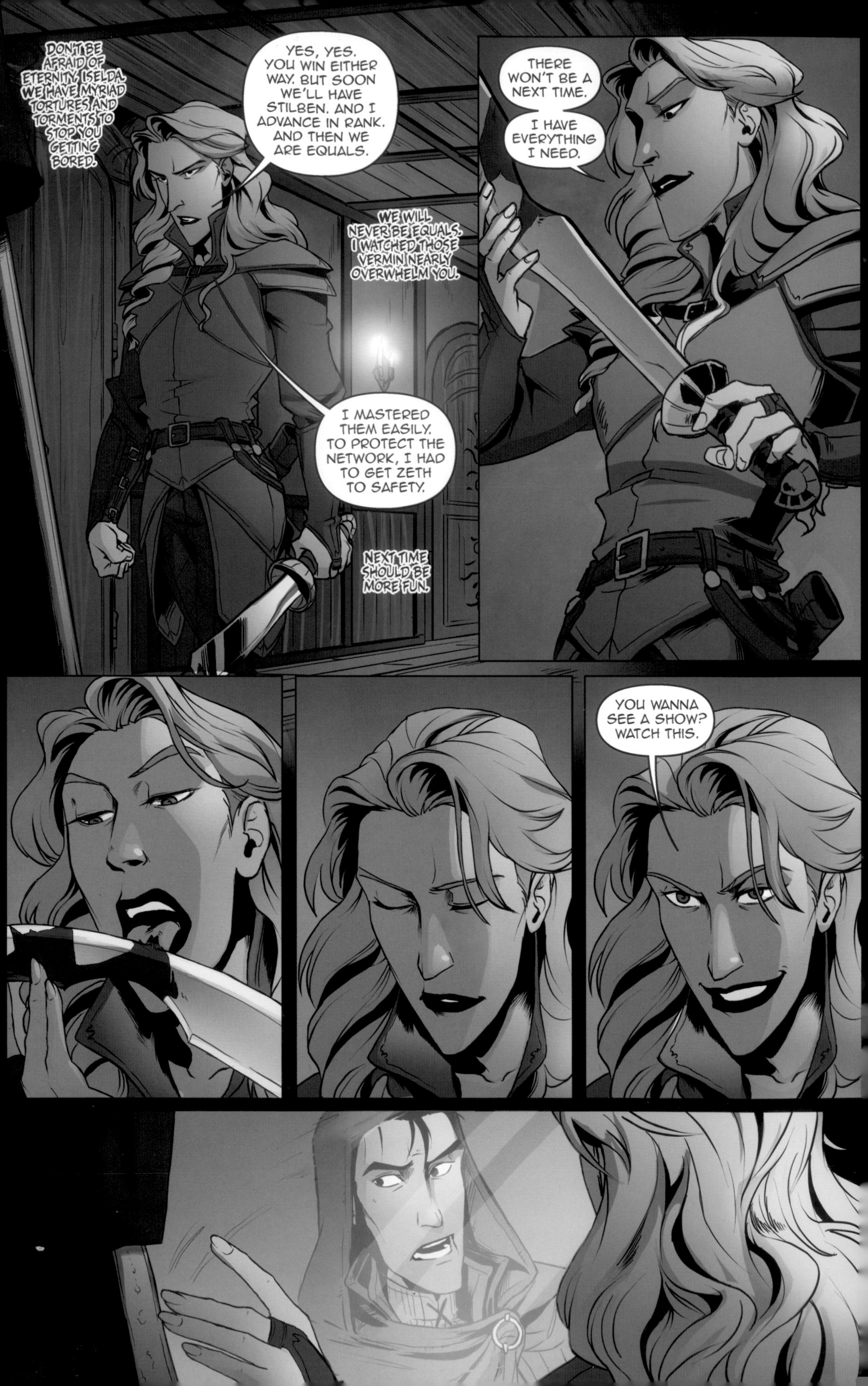
DON'T BE AFRAID OF ETERNITY, ISELDA. WE HAVE MYRIAD TORTURES AND TORMENTS TO STOP YOU GETTING BORED.
YES, YES. YOU WIN EITHER WAY. BUT SOON WE'LL HAVE STILBEN. AND I ADVANCE IN RANK. AND THEN WE ARE EQUALS.
WE WILL NEVER BE EQUALS. I WATCHED THOSE VERMIN NEARLY OVERWHELM YOU.
I MASTERED THEM EASILY. TO PROTECT THE NETWORK, I HAD TO GET ZETH TO SAFETY.
NEXT TIME SHOULD BE MORE FUN.
THERE WON'T BE A NEXT TIME.
I HAVE EVERYTHING I NEED.
YOU WANNA SEE A SHOW? WATCH THIS.

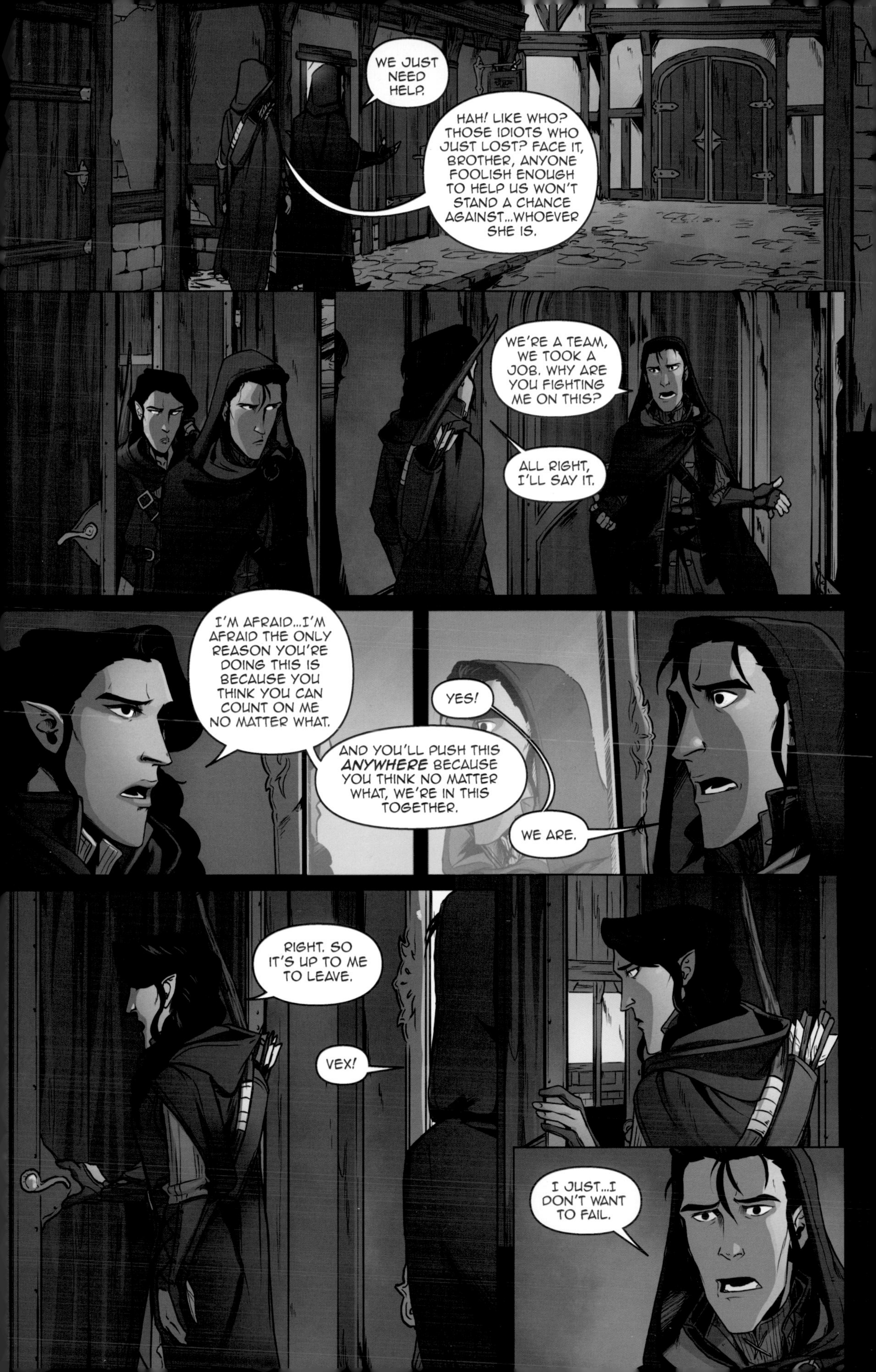
WE JUST NEED HELP.
HAH! LIKE WHO? THOSE IDIOTS WHO JUST LOST? FACE IT, BROTHER, ANYONE FOOLISH ENOUGH TO HELP US WON'T STAND A CHANCE AGAINST...WHOEVER SHE IS.
WE'RE A TEAM, WE TOOK A JOB. WHY ARE YOU FIGHTING ME ON THIS?
ALL RIGHT, I'LL SAY IT.
I'M AFRAID...I'M AFRAID THE ONLY REASON YOU'RE DOING THIS IS BECAUSE YOU THINK YOU CAN COUNT ON ME NO MATTER WHAT.
YES!
AND YOU'LL PUSH THIS ANYWHERE BECAUSE YOU THINK NO MATTER WHAT, WE'RE IN THIS TOGETHER.
WE ARE.
RIGHT. SO IT'S UP TO ME TO LEAVE.
VEX!
I JUST...I DON'T WANT TO FAIL.

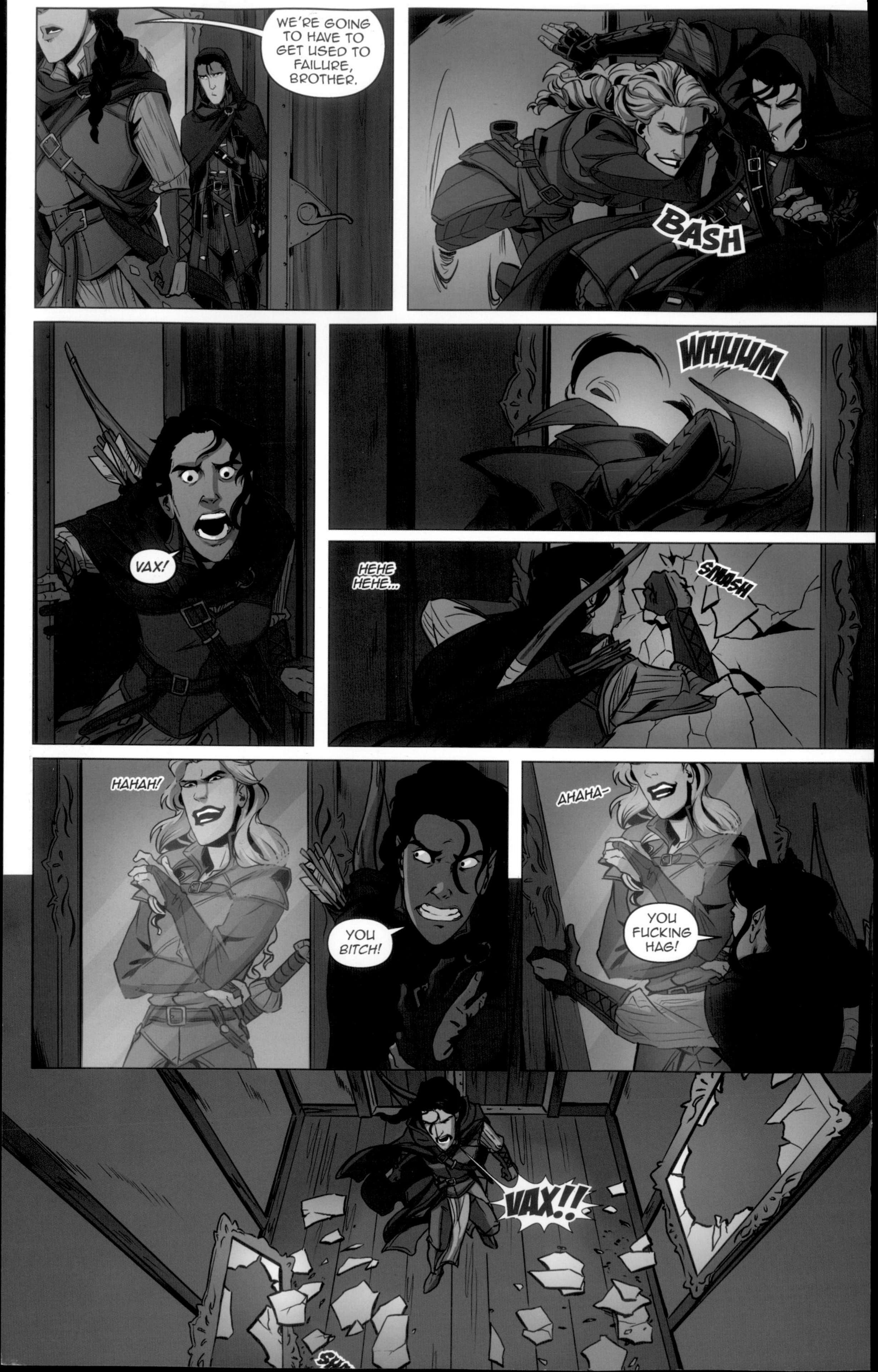
WE'RE GOING TO HAVE TO GET USED TO FAILURE, BROTHER.
BASH
VAX!
WHUUM
HEHE HEHE...
SMASH
HAHAH!
YOU BITCH!
AHAHA-
YOU FUCKING HAG!
VAX!!

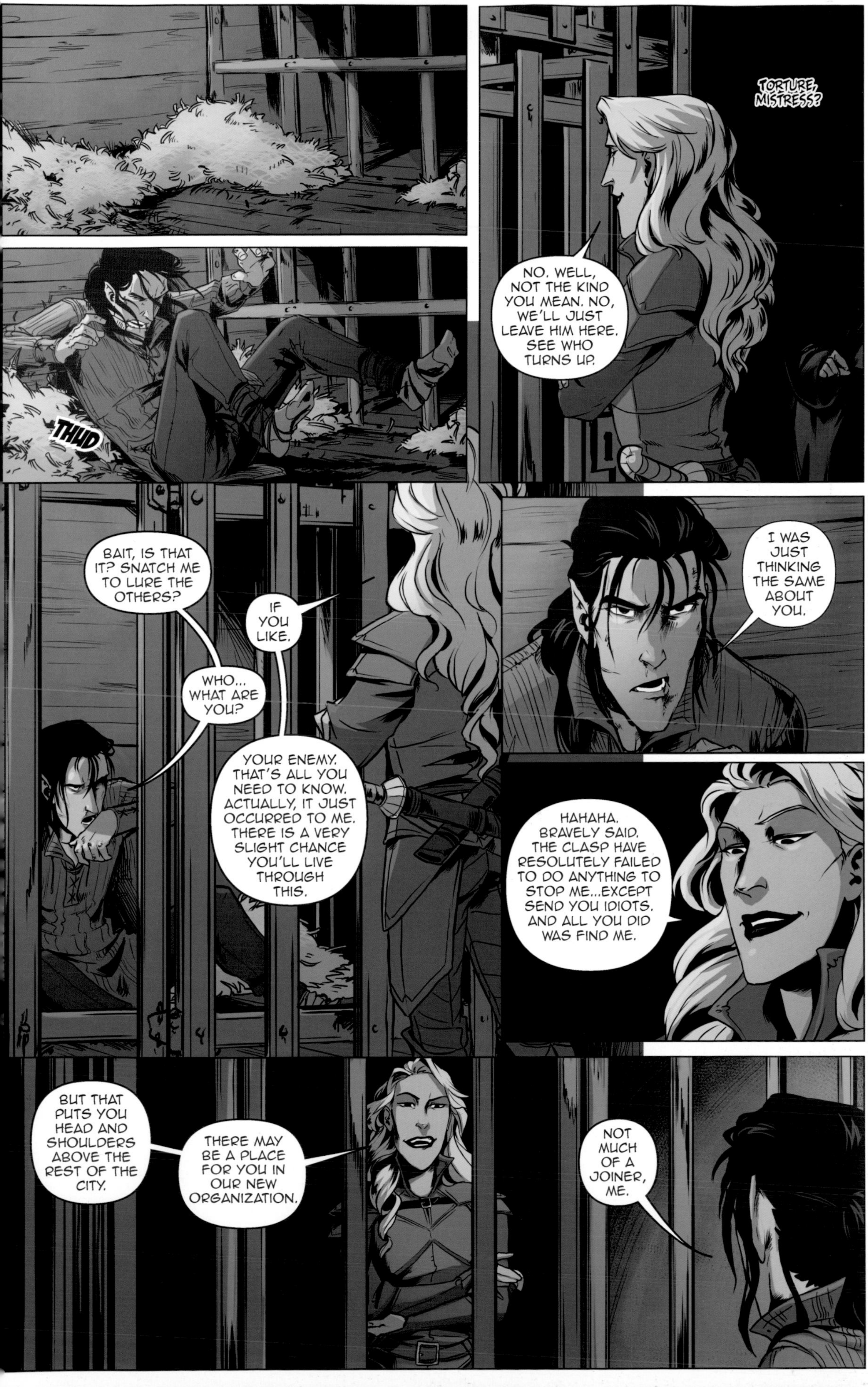
THUD
TORTURE, MISTRESS?
NO. WELL, NOT THE KIND YOU MEAN. NO, WE'LL JUST LEAVE HIM HERE. SEE WHO TURNS UP.
BAIT, IS THAT IT? SNATCH ME TO LURE THE OTHERS?
IF YOU LIKE.
WHO... WHAT ARE YOU?
YOUR ENEMY. THAT'S ALL YOU NEED TO KNOW. ACTUALLY, IT JUST OCCURRED TO ME. THERE IS A VERY SLIGHT CHANCE YOU'LL LIVE THROUGH THIS.
I WAS JUST THINKING THE SAME ABOUT YOU.
HAHAHA. BRAVELY SAID. THE CLASP HAVE RESOLUTELY FAILED TO DO ANYTHING TO STOP ME...EXCEPT SEND YOU IDIOTS. AND ALL YOU DID WAS FIND ME.
BUT THAT PUTS YOU HEAD AND SHOULDERS ABOVE THE REST OF THE CITY.
THERE MAY BE A PLACE FOR YOU IN OUR NEW ORGANIZATION.
NOT MUCH OF A JOINER, ME.

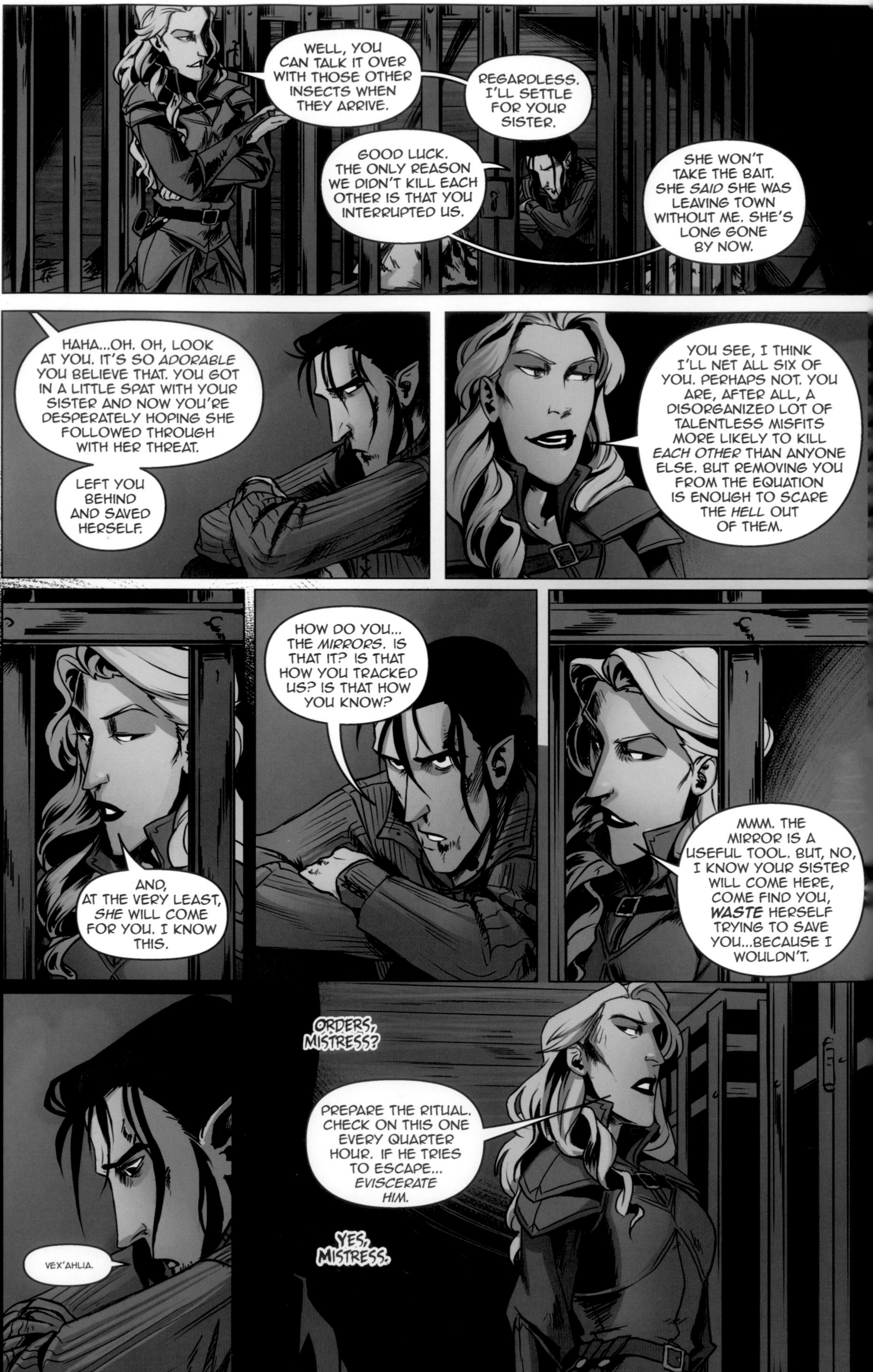
WELL, YOU CAN TALK IT OVER WITH THOSE OTHER INSECTS WHEN THEY ARRIVE.
REGARDLESS. I'LL SETTLE FOR YOUR SISTER.
GOOD LUCK. THE ONLY REASON WE DIDN'T KILL EACH OTHER IS THAT YOU INTERRUPTED US.
SHE WON'T TAKE THE BAIT. SHE *SAID* SHE WAS LEAVING TOWN WITHOUT ME. SHE'S LONG GONE BY NOW.
HAHA...OH. OH, LOOK AT YOU. IT'S SO *ADORABLE* YOU BELIEVE THAT. YOU GOT IN A LITTLE SPAT WITH YOUR SISTER AND NOW YOU'RE DESPERATELY HOPING SHE FOLLOWED THROUGH WITH HER THREAT.
LEFT YOU BEHIND AND SAVED HERSELF.
YOU SEE, I THINK I'LL NET ALL SIX OF YOU. PERHAPS NOT. YOU ARE, AFTER ALL, A DISORGANIZED LOT OF TALENTLESS MISFITS MORE LIKELY TO KILL *EACH OTHER* THAN ANYONE ELSE. BUT REMOVING YOU FROM THE EQUATION IS ENOUGH TO SCARE THE *HELL* OUT OF THEM.
AND, AT THE VERY LEAST, *SHE* WILL COME FOR YOU. I KNOW THIS.
HOW DO YOU... THE *MIRRORS*. IS THAT IT? IS THAT HOW YOU TRACKED US? IS THAT HOW YOU KNOW?
MMM. THE MIRROR IS A USEFUL TOOL. BUT, NO, I KNOW YOUR SISTER WILL COME HERE, COME FIND YOU, ***WASTE*** HERSELF TRYING TO SAVE YOU...BECAUSE I WOULDN'T.
ORDERS, MISTRESS?
PREPARE THE RITUAL. CHECK ON THIS ONE EVERY QUARTER HOUR. IF HE TRIES TO ESCAPE... *EVISCERATE HIM.*
YES, MISTRESS.
VEX'AHLIA.

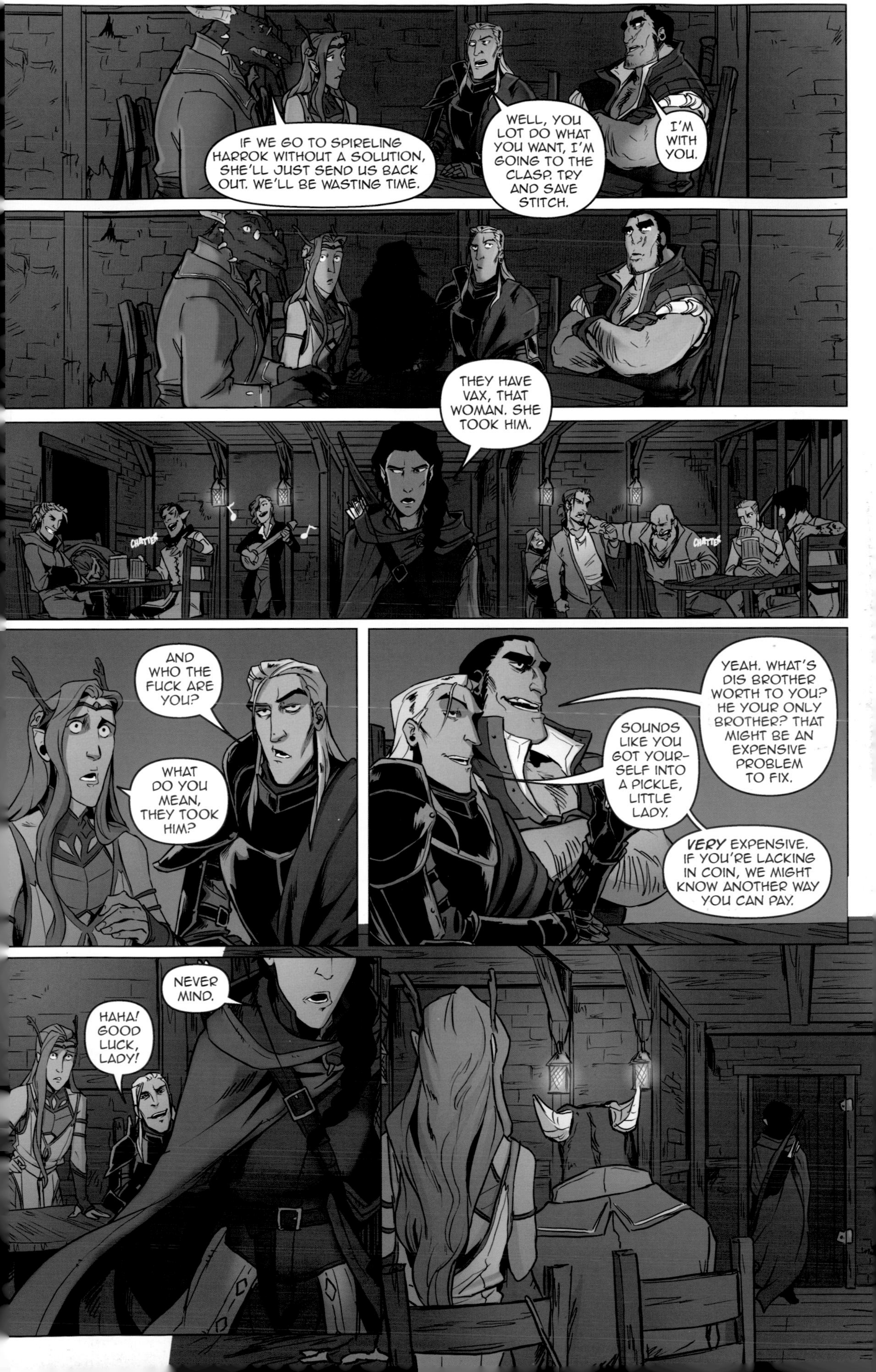
IF WE GO TO SPIRELING HARROK WITHOUT A SOLUTION, SHE'LL JUST SEND US BACK OUT. WE'LL BE WASTING TIME.
WELL, YOU LOT DO WHAT YOU WANT, I'M GOING TO THE CLASP. TRY AND SAVE STITCH.
I'M WITH YOU.
THEY HAVE VAX, THAT WOMAN. SHE TOOK HIM.
CHATTER
CHATTER
AND WHO THE FUCK ARE YOU?
WHAT DO YOU MEAN, THEY TOOK HIM?
YEAH. WHAT'S DIS BROTHER WORTH TO YOU? HE YOUR ONLY BROTHER? THAT MIGHT BE AN EXPENSIVE PROBLEM TO FIX.
SOUNDS LIKE YOU GOT YOURSELF INTO A PICKLE, LITTLE LADY.
VERY EXPENSIVE. IF YOU'RE LACKING IN COIN, WE MIGHT KNOW ANOTHER WAY YOU CAN PAY.
NEVER MIND.
HAHA! GOOD LUCK, LADY!

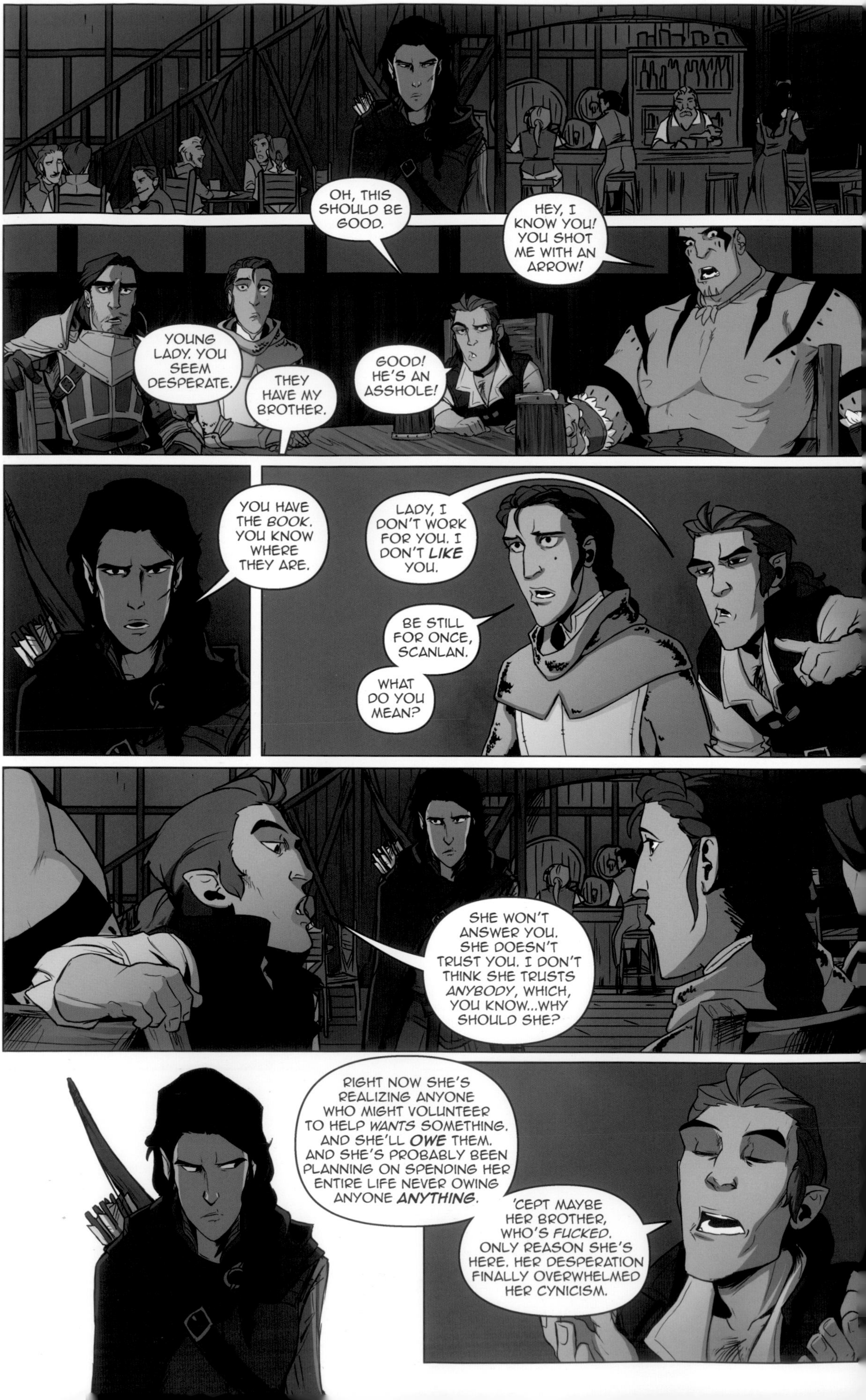
OH, THIS SHOULD BE GOOD.
HEY, I KNOW YOU! YOU SHOT ME WITH AN ARROW!
YOUNG LADY. YOU SEEM DESPERATE.
THEY HAVE MY BROTHER.
GOOD! HE'S AN ASSHOLE!
YOU HAVE THE *BOOK*. YOU KNOW WHERE THEY ARE.
LADY, I DON'T WORK FOR YOU. I DON'T ***LIKE*** YOU.
BE STILL FOR ONCE, SCANLAN.
WHAT DO YOU MEAN?
SHE WON'T ANSWER YOU. SHE DOESN'T TRUST YOU. I DON'T THINK SHE TRUSTS *ANYBODY*, WHICH, YOU KNOW...WHY SHOULD SHE?
RIGHT NOW SHE'S REALIZING ANYONE WHO MIGHT VOLUNTEER TO HELP *WANTS* SOMETHING. AND SHE'LL ***OWE*** THEM. AND SHE'S PROBABLY BEEN PLANNING ON SPENDING HER ENTIRE LIFE NEVER OWING ANYONE ***ANYTHING***.
'CEPT MAYBE HER BROTHER, WHO'S *FUCKED*. ONLY REASON SHE'S HERE. HER DESPERATION FINALLY OVERWHELMED HER CYNICISM.

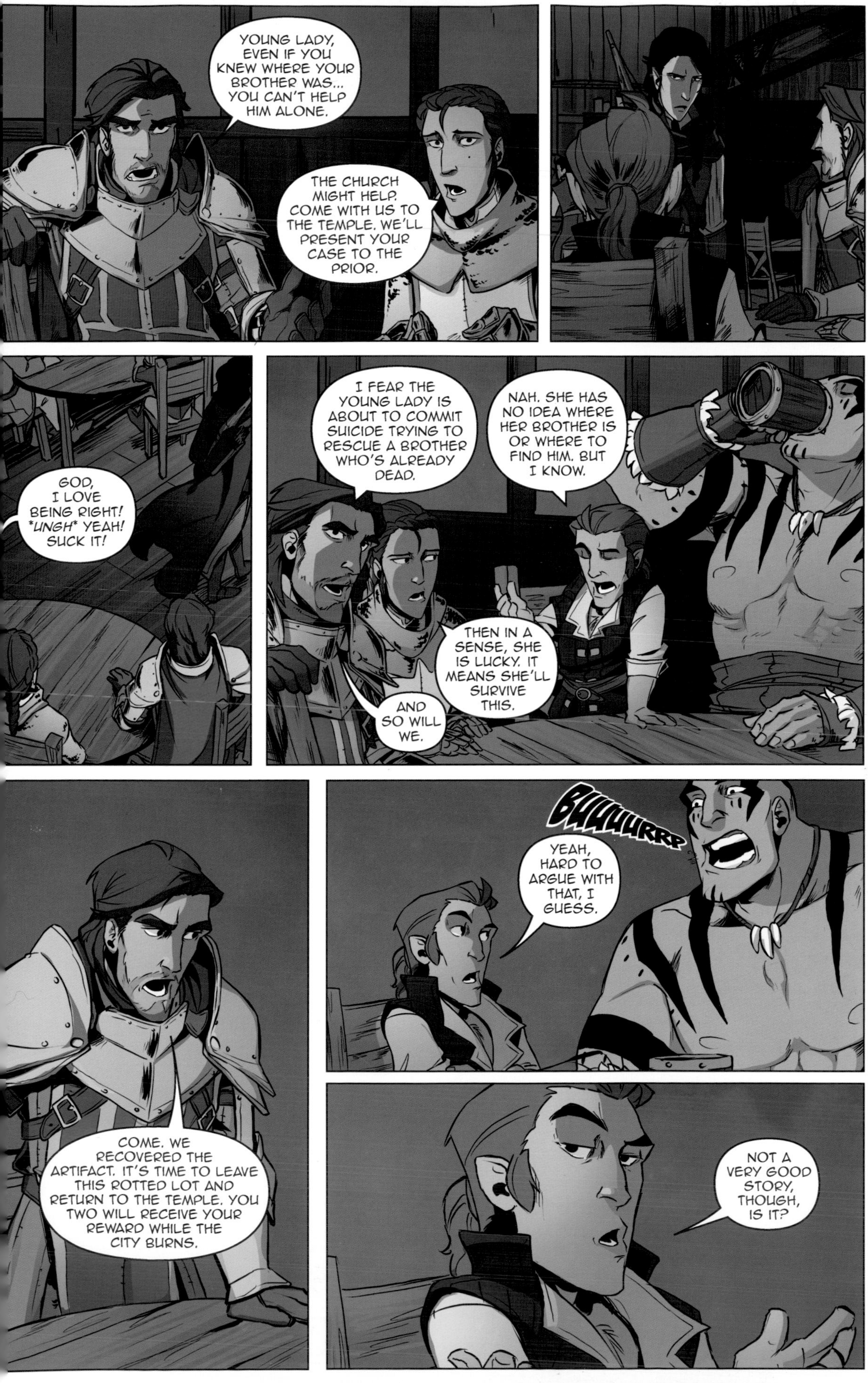
YOUNG LADY, EVEN IF YOU KNEW WHERE YOUR BROTHER WAS... YOU CAN'T HELP HIM ALONE.
THE CHURCH MIGHT HELP. COME WITH US TO THE TEMPLE. WE'LL PRESENT YOUR CASE TO THE PRIOR.
GOD, I LOVE BEING RIGHT! *UNGH* YEAH! SUCK IT!
I FEAR THE YOUNG LADY IS ABOUT TO COMMIT SUICIDE TRYING TO RESCUE A BROTHER WHO'S ALREADY DEAD.
NAH. SHE HAS NO IDEA WHERE HER BROTHER IS OR WHERE TO FIND HIM. BUT I KNOW.
THEN IN A SENSE, SHE IS LUCKY. IT MEANS SHE'LL SURVIVE THIS.
AND SO WILL WE.
COME. WE RECOVERED THE ARTIFACT. IT'S TIME TO LEAVE THIS ROTTED LOT AND RETURN TO THE TEMPLE. YOU TWO WILL RECEIVE YOUR REWARD WHILE THE CITY BURNS.
BUUUURRP
YEAH, HARD TO ARGUE WITH THAT, I GUESS.
NOT A VERY GOOD STORY, THOUGH, IS IT?

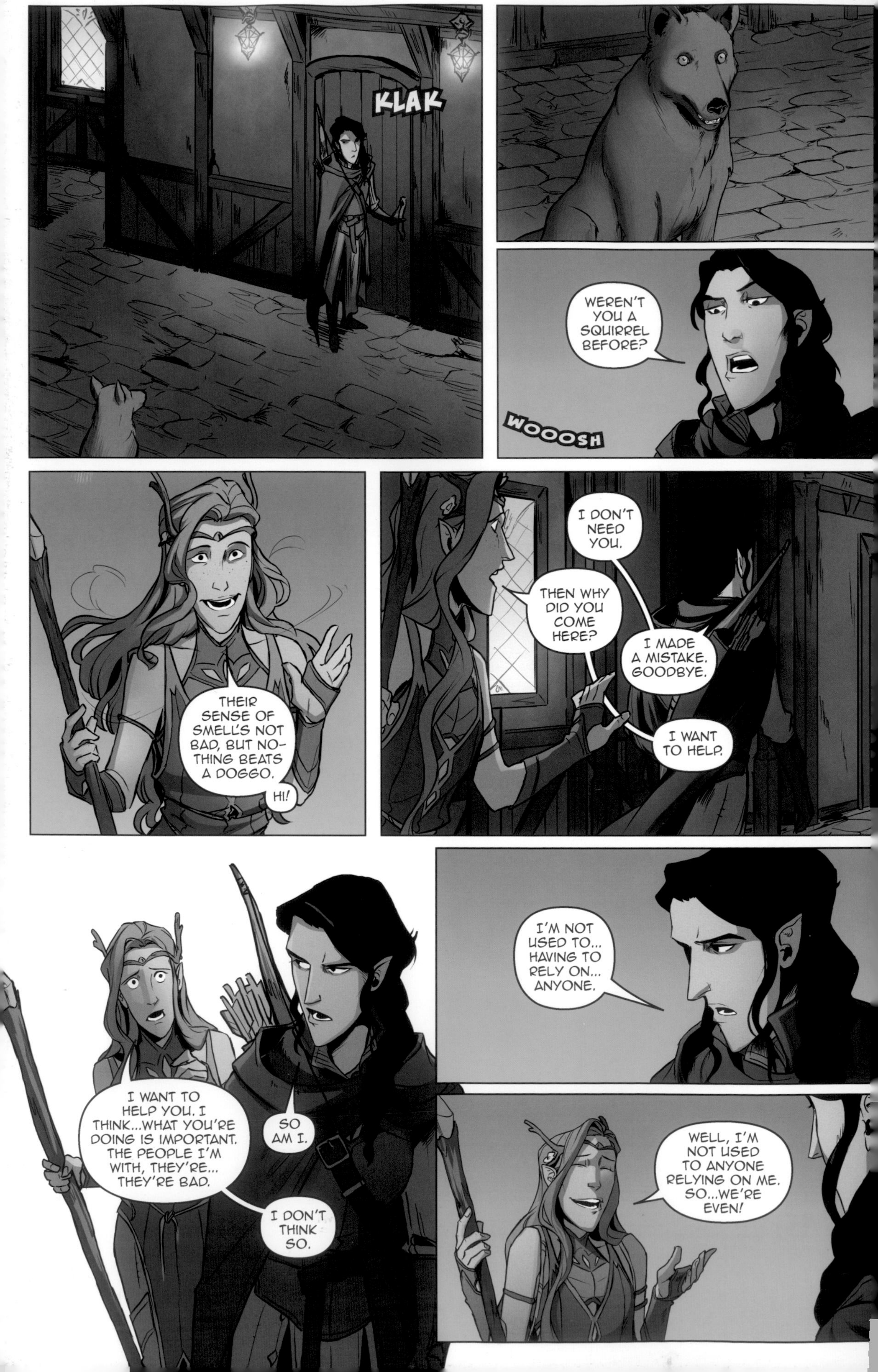
KLAK
WEREN'T YOU A SQUIRREL BEFORE?
WOOOSH
THEIR SENSE OF SMELL'S NOT BAD, BUT NO-THING BEATS A DOGGO.
HI!
I DON'T NEED YOU.
THEN WHY DID YOU COME HERE?
I MADE A MISTAKE. GOODBYE.
I WANT TO HELP.
I WANT TO HELP YOU. I THINK...WHAT YOU'RE DOING IS IMPORTANT. THE PEOPLE I'M WITH, THEY'RE... THEY'RE BAD.
SO AM I.
I DON'T THINK SO.
I'M NOT USED TO... HAVING TO RELY ON... ANYONE.
WELL, I'M NOT USED TO ANYONE RELYING ON ME. SO...WE'RE EVEN!

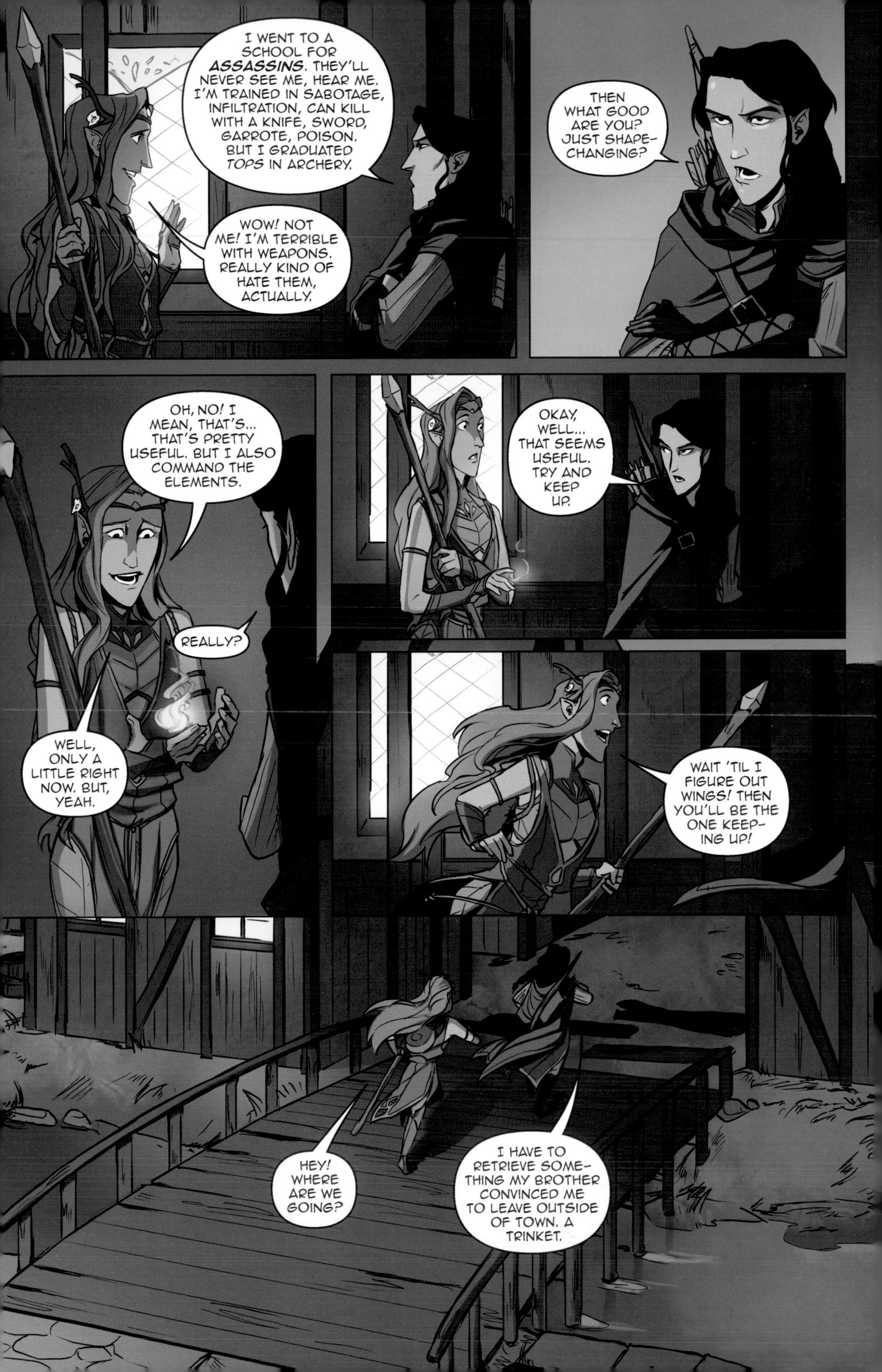
I WENT TO A SCHOOL FOR *ASSASSINS*. THEY'LL NEVER SEE ME, HEAR ME. I'M TRAINED IN SABOTAGE, INFILTRATION, CAN KILL WITH A KNIFE, SWORD, GARROTE, POISON. BUT I GRADUATED *TOPS* IN ARCHERY.
WOW! NOT ME! I'M TERRIBLE WITH WEAPONS. REALLY KIND OF HATE THEM, ACTUALLY.
THEN WHAT GOOD ARE YOU? JUST SHAPE-CHANGING?
OH, NO! I MEAN, THAT'S... THAT'S PRETTY USEFUL. BUT I ALSO COMMAND THE ELEMENTS.
REALLY?
WELL, ONLY A LITTLE RIGHT NOW. BUT, YEAH.
OKAY, WELL... THAT SEEMS USEFUL. TRY AND KEEP UP.
WAIT 'TIL I FIGURE OUT *WINGS!* THEN YOU'LL BE THE ONE KEEPING UP!
HEY! WHERE ARE WE GOING?
I HAVE TO RETRIEVE SOMETHING MY BROTHER CONVINCED ME TO LEAVE OUTSIDE OF TOWN. A TRINKET.

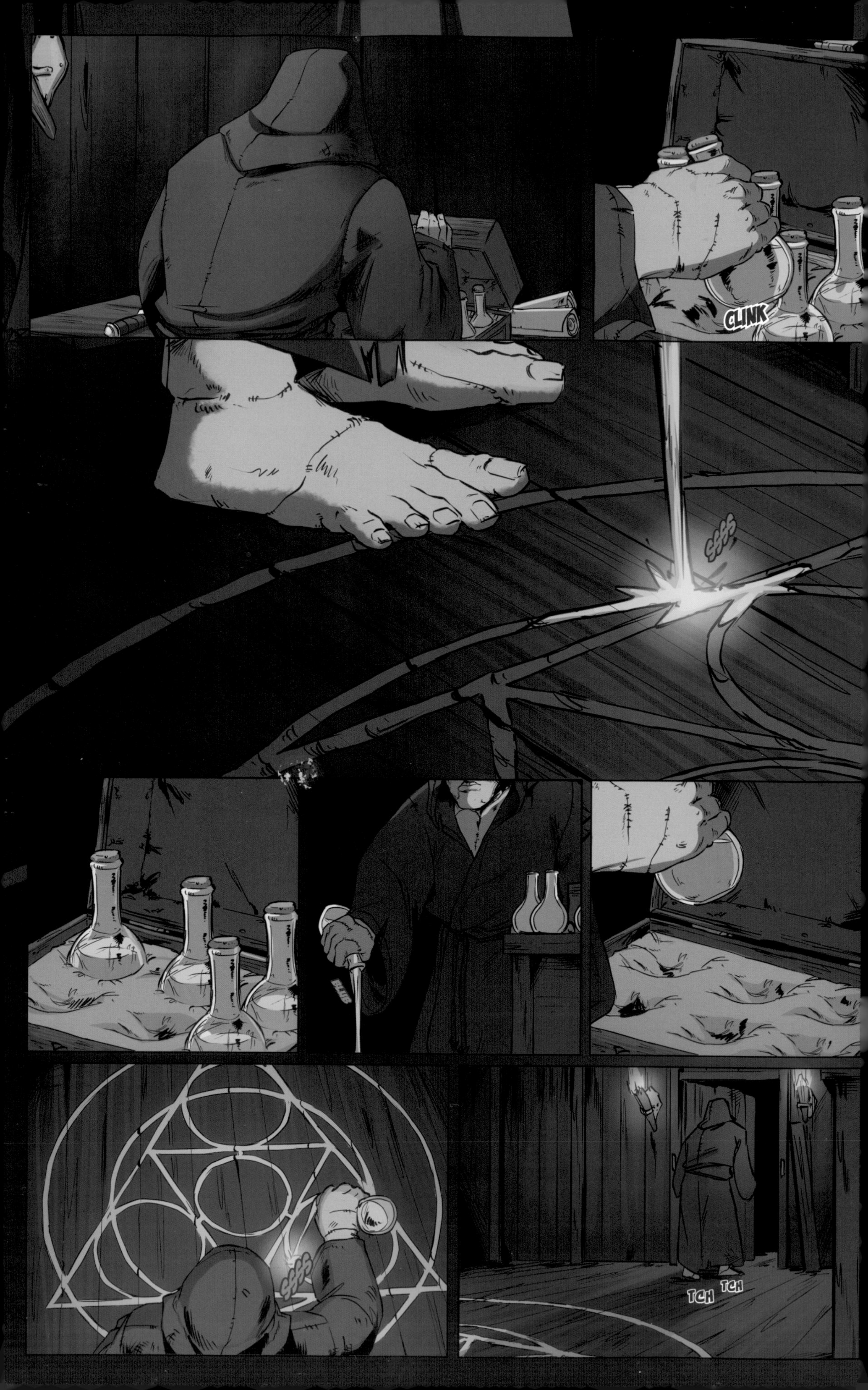
CLINK
SSSS
SSSS
TCH TCH

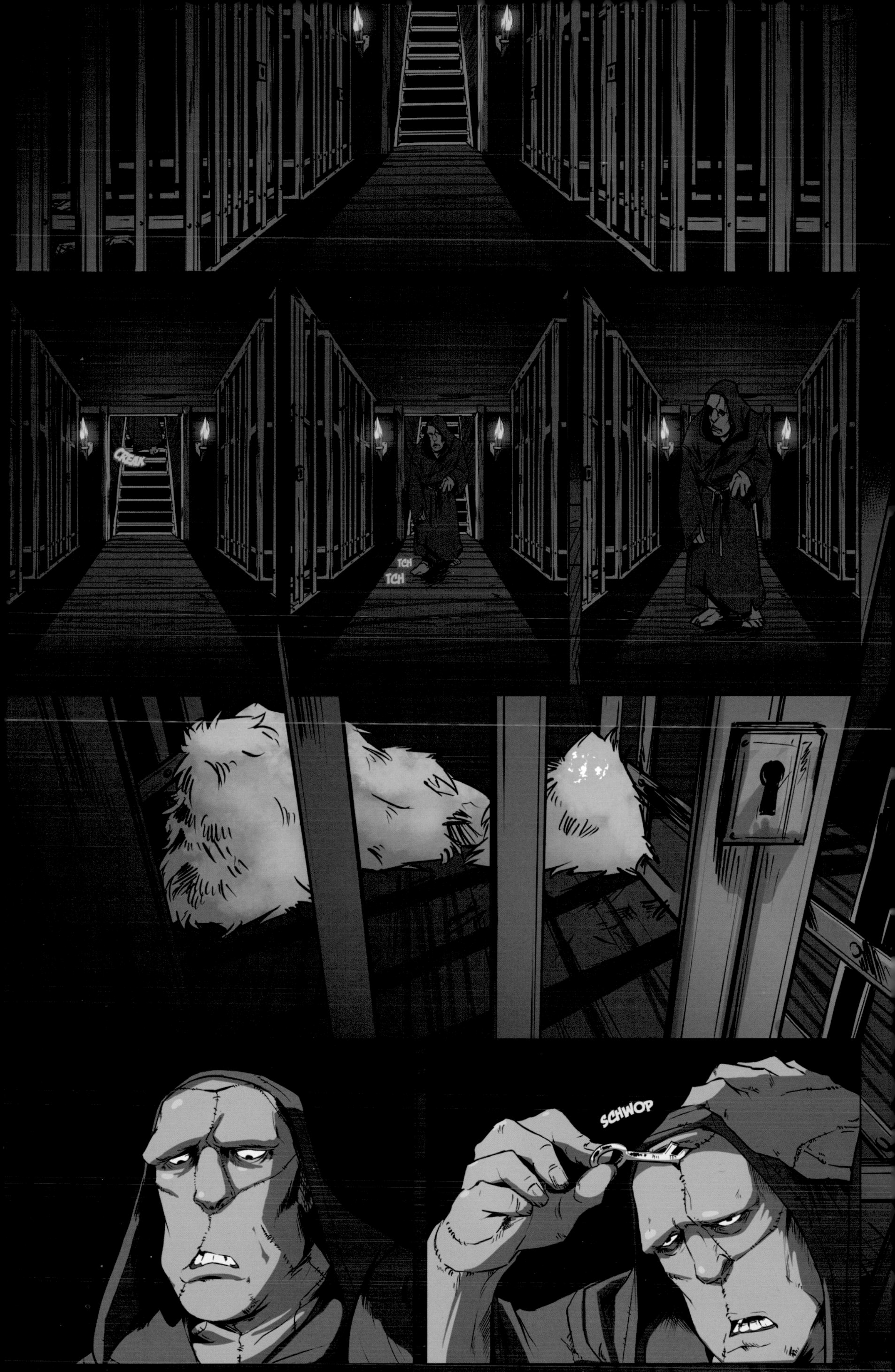
CREAK
TCH
TCH
SCHWOP

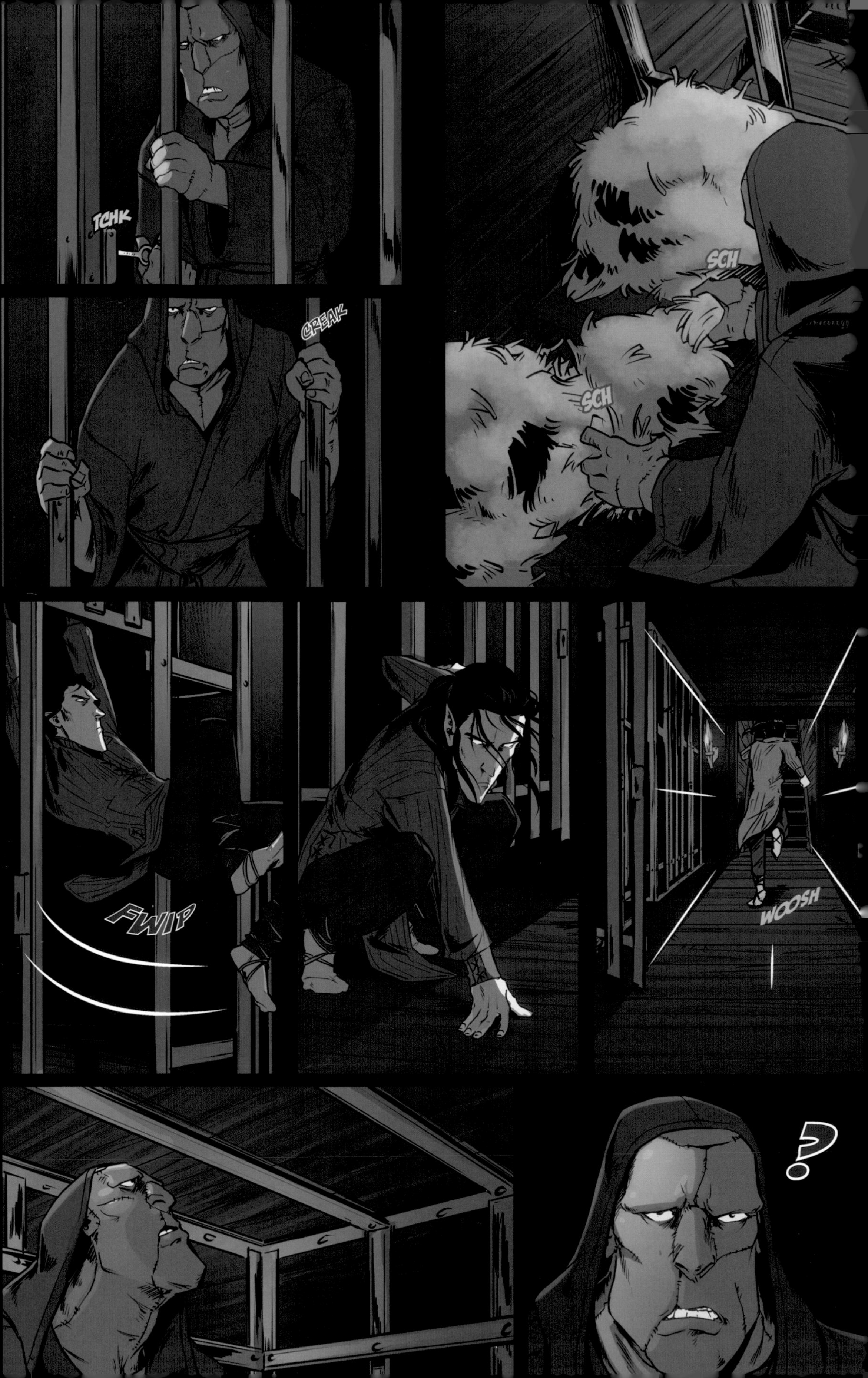
TCHK
CREAK
SCH
SCH
FWIP
WOOSH
?

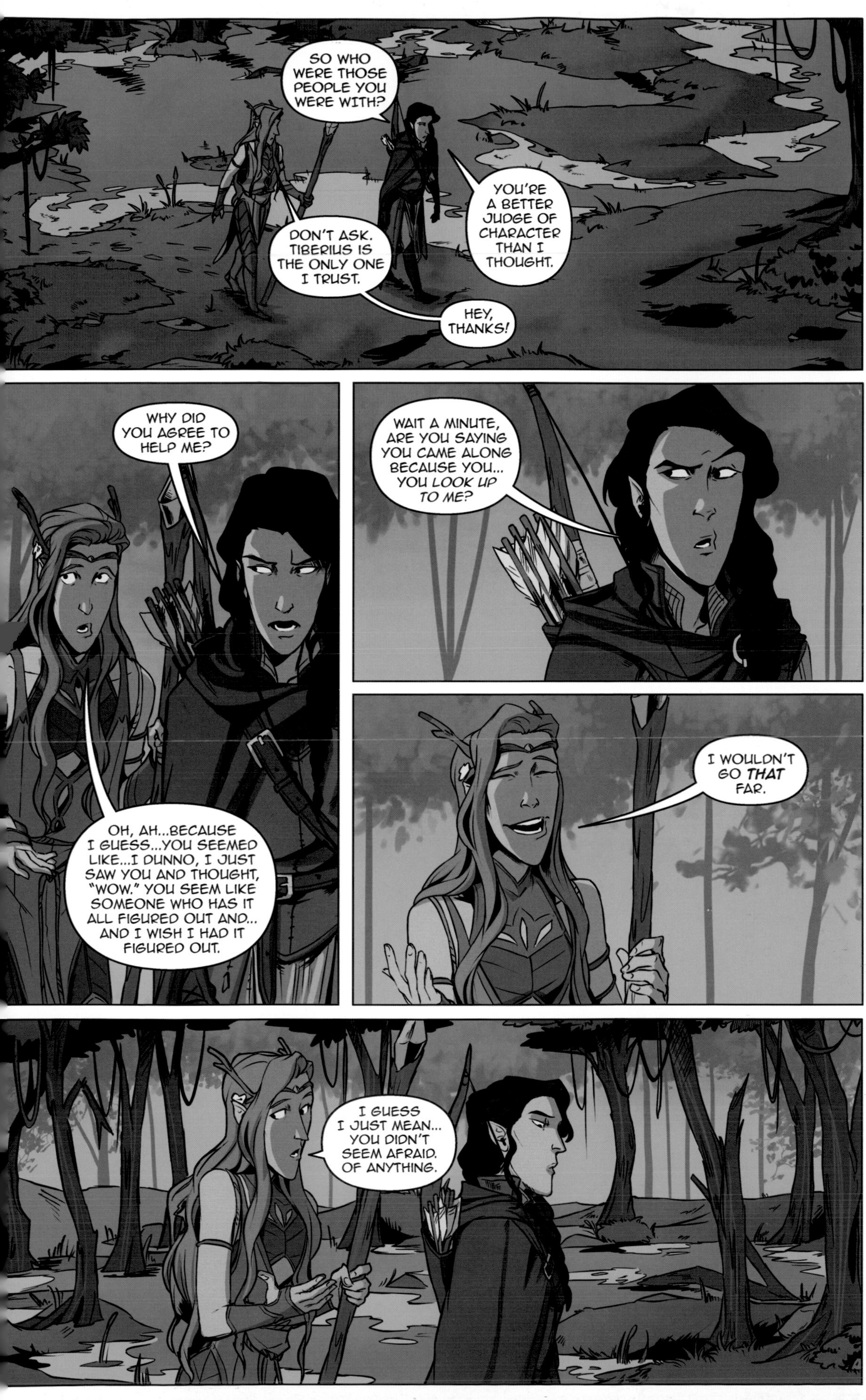
SO WHO WERE THOSE PEOPLE YOU WERE WITH?
YOU'RE A BETTER JUDGE OF CHARACTER THAN I THOUGHT.
DON'T ASK. TIBERIUS IS THE ONLY ONE I TRUST.
HEY, THANKS!
WHY DID YOU AGREE TO HELP ME?
OH, AH...BECAUSE I GUESS...YOU SEEMED LIKE...I DUNNO, I JUST SAW YOU AND THOUGHT, "WOW." YOU SEEM LIKE SOMEONE WHO HAS IT ALL FIGURED OUT AND... AND I WISH I HAD IT FIGURED OUT.
WAIT A MINUTE, ARE YOU SAYING YOU CAME ALONG BECAUSE YOU... YOU *LOOK UP TO ME?*
I WOULDN'T GO ***THAT*** FAR.
I GUESS I JUST MEAN... YOU DIDN'T SEEM AFRAID. OF ANYTHING.

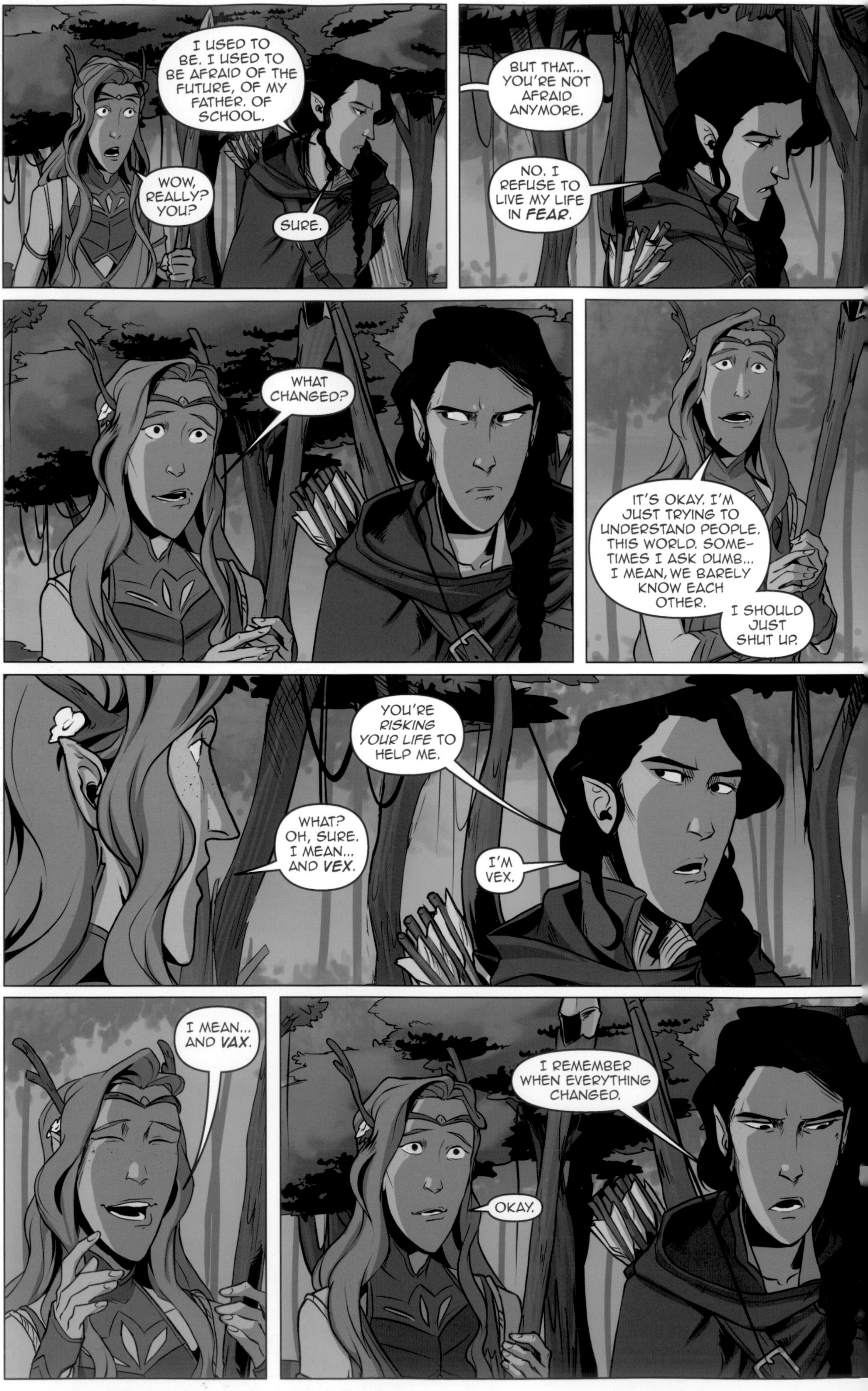
I USED TO BE. I USED TO BE AFRAID OF THE FUTURE, OF MY FATHER. OF SCHOOL.
WOW, REALLY? YOU?
SURE.
BUT THAT... YOU'RE NOT AFRAID ANYMORE.
NO. I REFUSE TO LIVE MY LIFE IN *FEAR*.
WHAT CHANGED?
IT'S OKAY. I'M JUST TRYING TO UNDERSTAND PEOPLE. THIS WORLD. SOME-TIMES I ASK DUMB... I MEAN, WE BARELY KNOW EACH OTHER.
I SHOULD JUST SHUT UP.
YOU'RE *RISKING YOUR LIFE* TO HELP ME.
WHAT? OH, SURE. I MEAN... AND *VEX*.
I'M VEX.
I MEAN... AND *VAX*.
I REMEMBER WHEN EVERYTHING CHANGED.
OKAY.

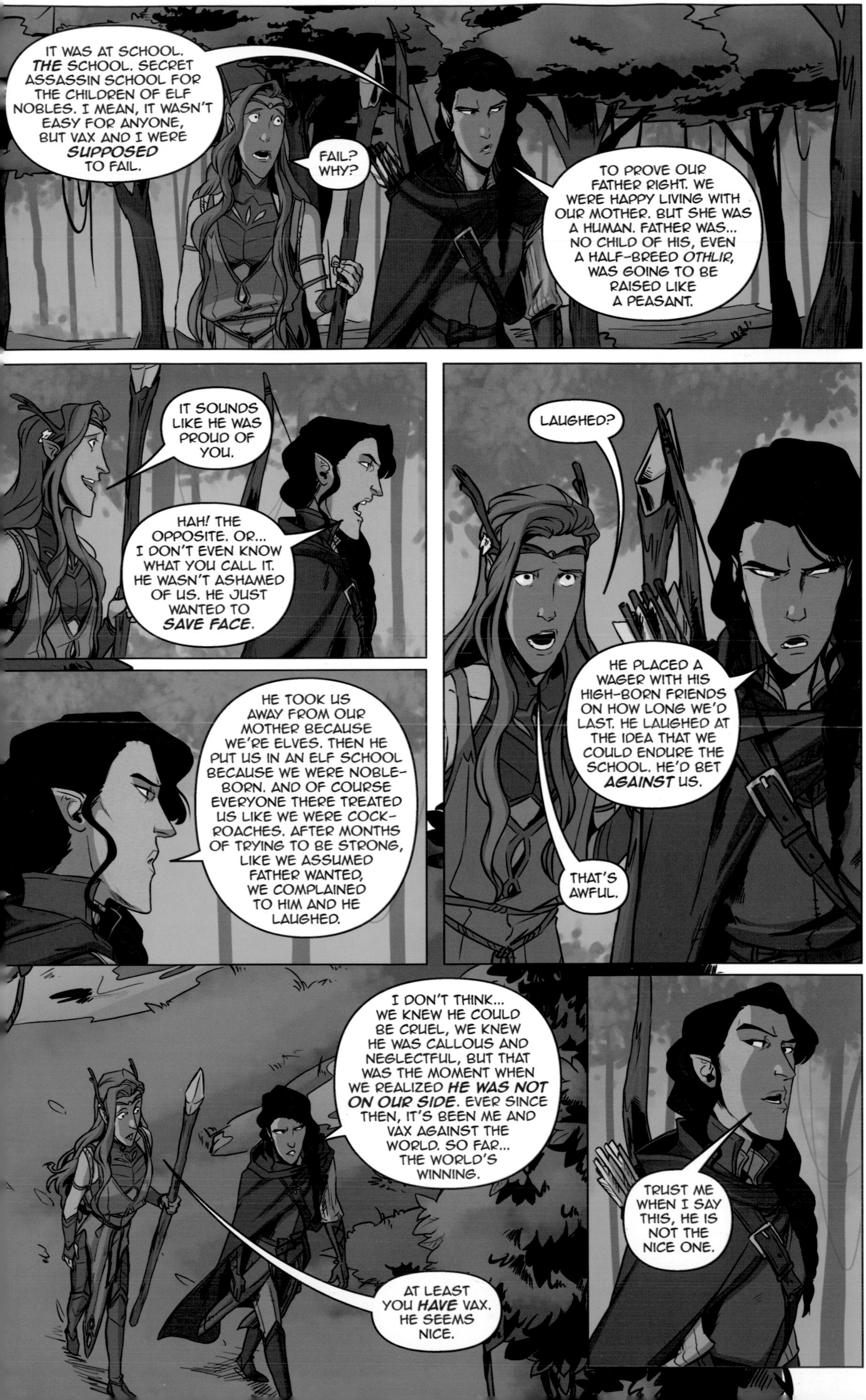
IT WAS AT SCHOOL. THE SCHOOL. SECRET ASSASSIN SCHOOL FOR THE CHILDREN OF ELF NOBLES. I MEAN, IT WASN'T EASY FOR ANYONE, BUT VAX AND I WERE SUPPOSED TO FAIL.
FAIL? WHY?
TO PROVE OUR FATHER RIGHT. WE WERE HAPPY LIVING WITH OUR MOTHER. BUT SHE WAS A HUMAN. FATHER WAS... NO CHILD OF HIS, EVEN A HALF-BREED OTHLIR, WAS GOING TO BE RAISED LIKE A PEASANT.
IT SOUNDS LIKE HE WAS PROUD OF YOU.
HAH! THE OPPOSITE. OR... I DON'T EVEN KNOW WHAT YOU CALL IT. HE WASN'T ASHAMED OF US. HE JUST WANTED TO SAVE FACE.
HE TOOK US AWAY FROM OUR MOTHER BECAUSE WE'RE ELVES. THEN HE PUT US IN AN ELF SCHOOL BECAUSE WE WERE NOBLE-BORN. AND OF COURSE EVERYONE THERE TREATED US LIKE WE WERE COCK-ROACHES. AFTER MONTHS OF TRYING TO BE STRONG, LIKE WE ASSUMED FATHER WANTED, WE COMPLAINED TO HIM AND HE LAUGHED.
LAUGHED?
HE PLACED A WAGER WITH HIS HIGH-BORN FRIENDS ON HOW LONG WE'D LAST. HE LAUGHED AT THE IDEA THAT WE COULD ENDURE THE SCHOOL. HE'D BET AGAINST US.
THAT'S AWFUL.
I DON'T THINK... WE KNEW HE COULD BE CRUEL, WE KNEW HE WAS CALLOUS AND NEGLECTFUL, BUT THAT WAS THE MOMENT WHEN WE REALIZED HE WAS NOT ON OUR SIDE. EVER SINCE THEN, IT'S BEEN ME AND VAX AGAINST THE WORLD. SO FAR... THE WORLD'S WINNING.
AT LEAST YOU HAVE VAX. HE SEEMS NICE.
TRUST ME WHEN I SAY THIS, HE IS NOT THE NICE ONE.

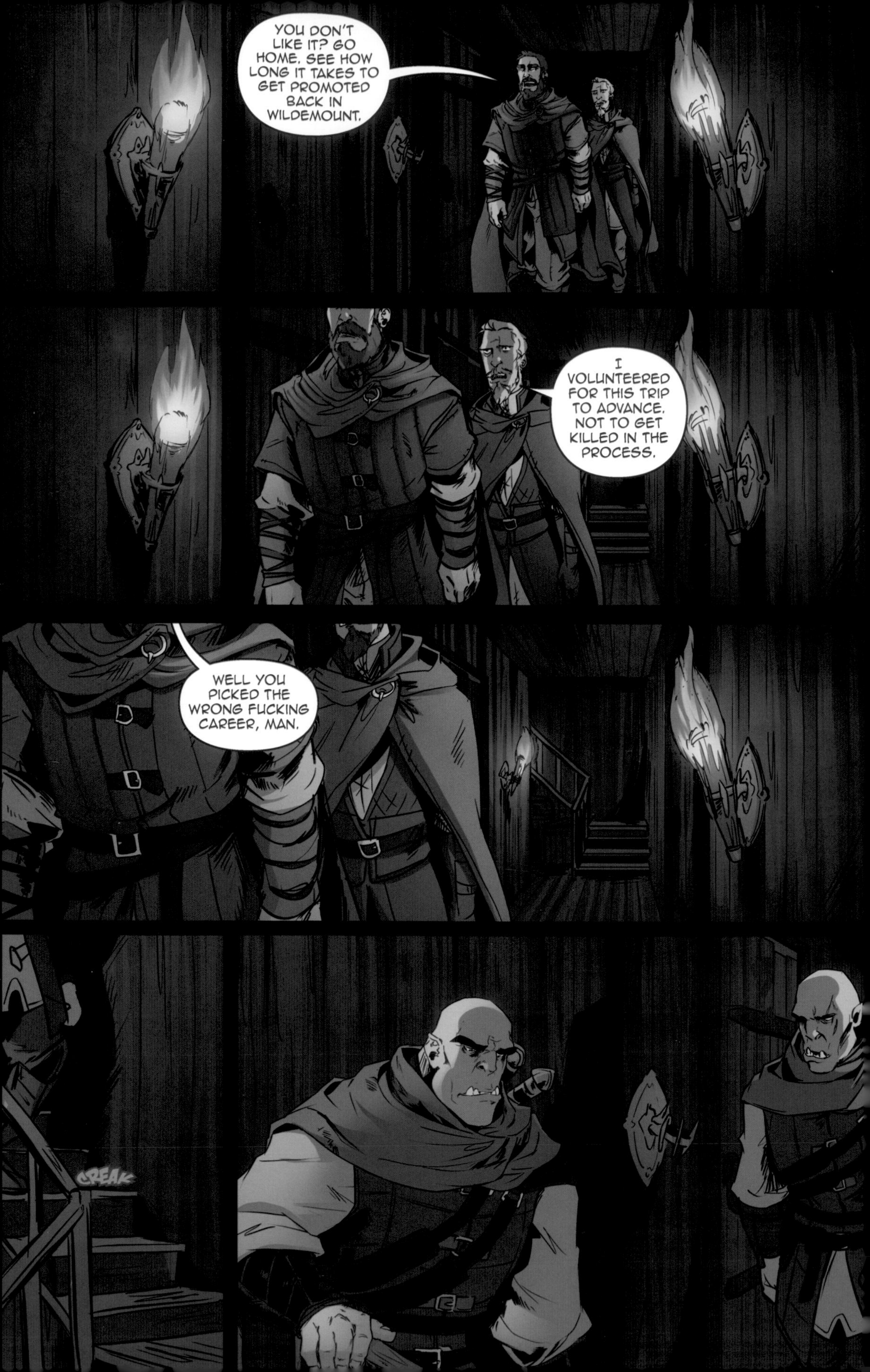
YOU DON'T LIKE IT? GO HOME. SEE HOW LONG IT TAKES TO GET PROMOTED BACK IN WILDEMOUNT.
I VOLUNTEERED FOR THIS TRIP TO ADVANCE. NOT TO GET KILLED IN THE PROCESS.
WELL YOU PICKED THE WRONG FUCKING CAREER, MAN.
CREAK

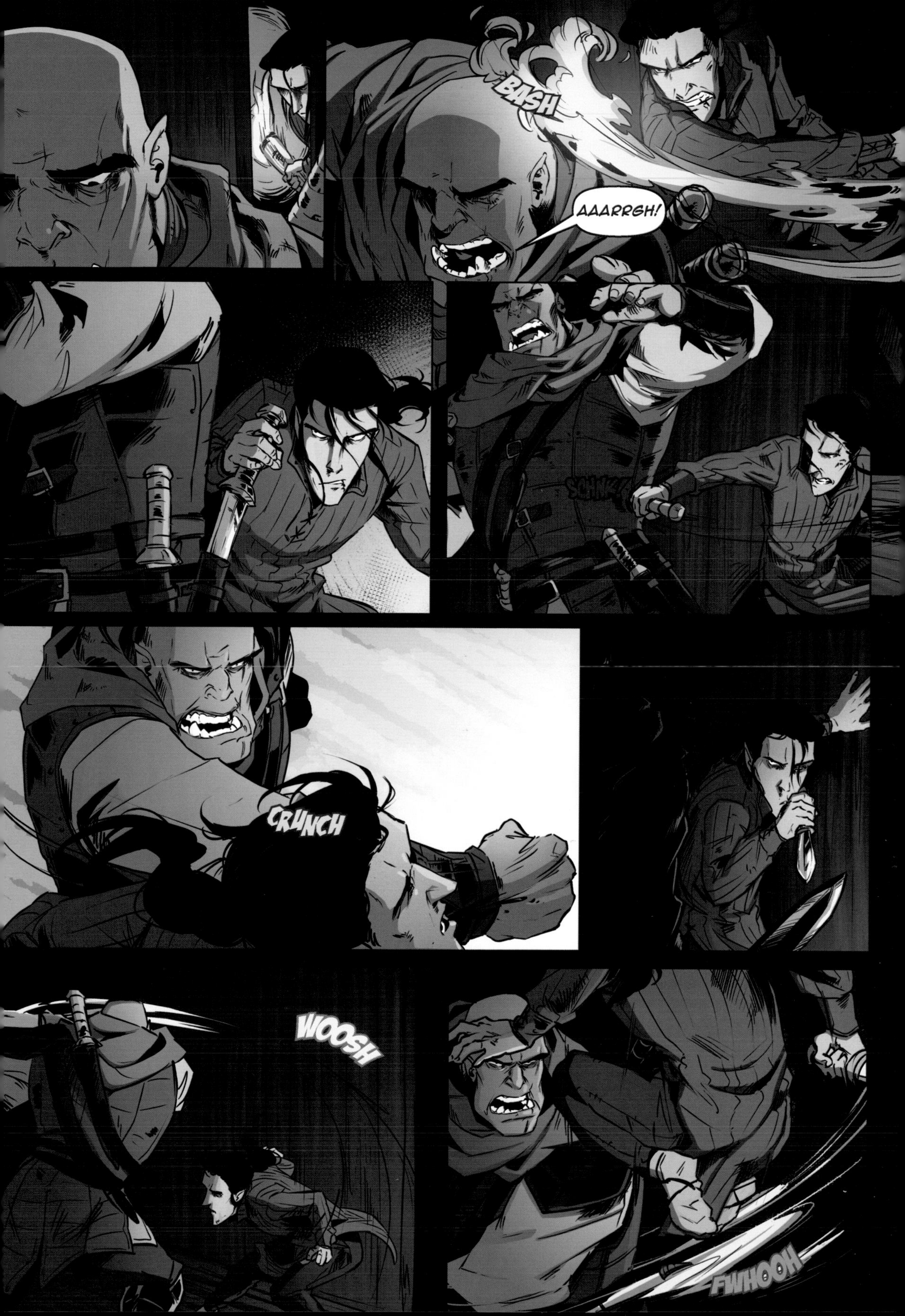
BASH
AAARRGH!
SCHNK
CRUNCH
WOOSH
FWHOOH

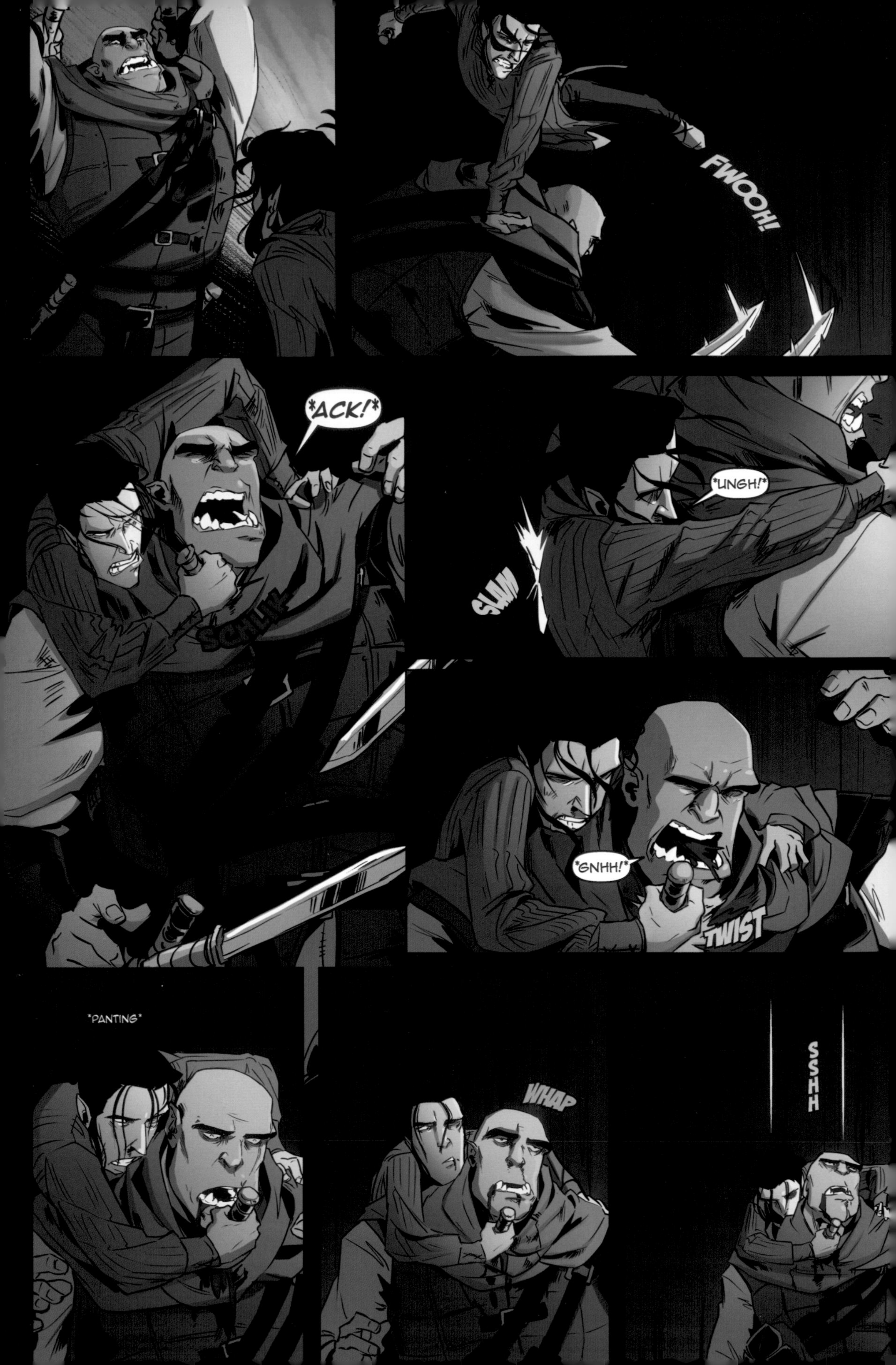
FWOOH!
*ACK!*
SCHLUK
SLAM
*UNGH!*
*GNHH!*
TWIST
*PANTING*
WHAP
SSHH

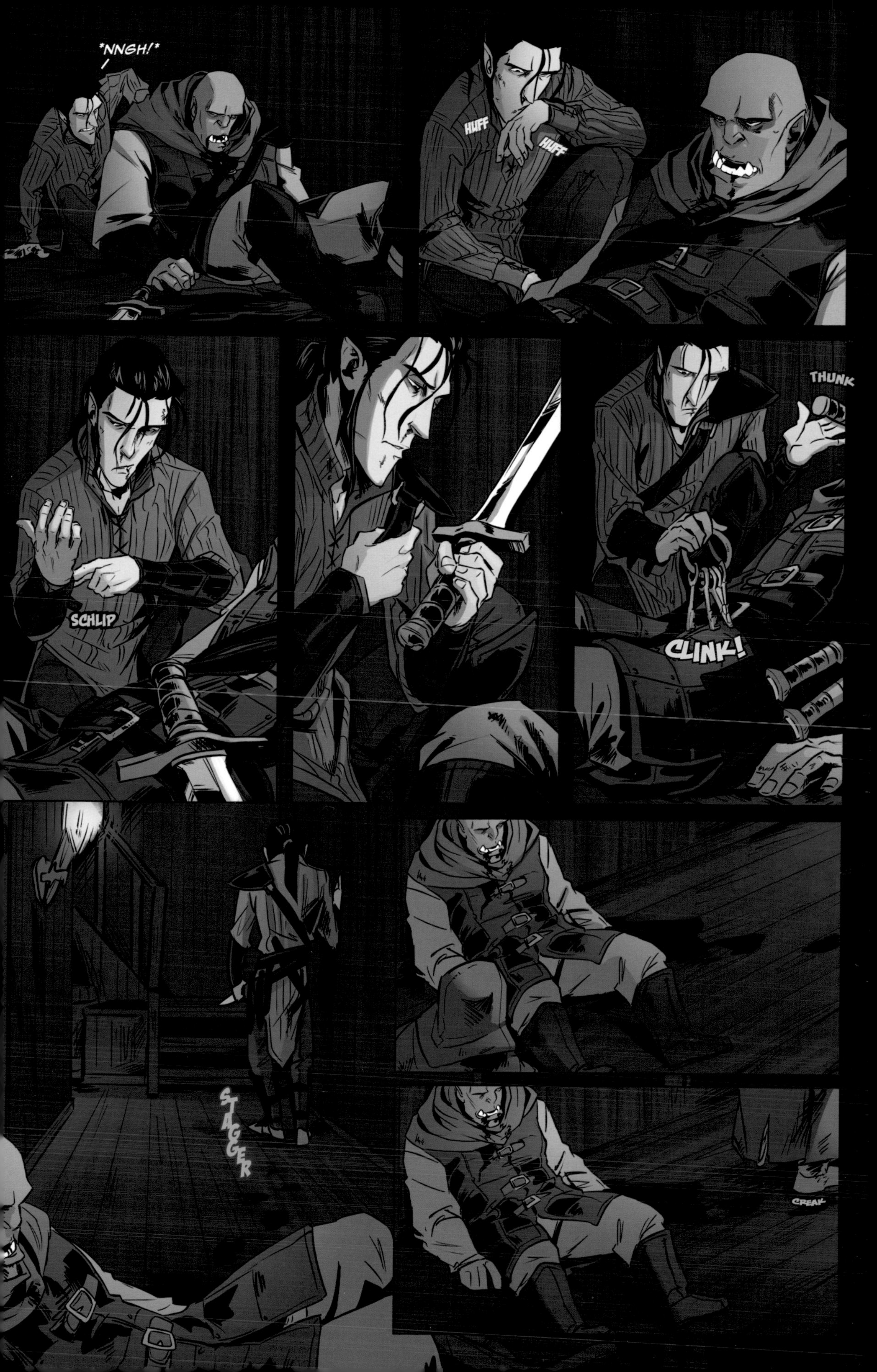
*NNGH!*
HUFF
HUFF
SCHLIP
THUNK
CLINK!
STAGGER
CREAK

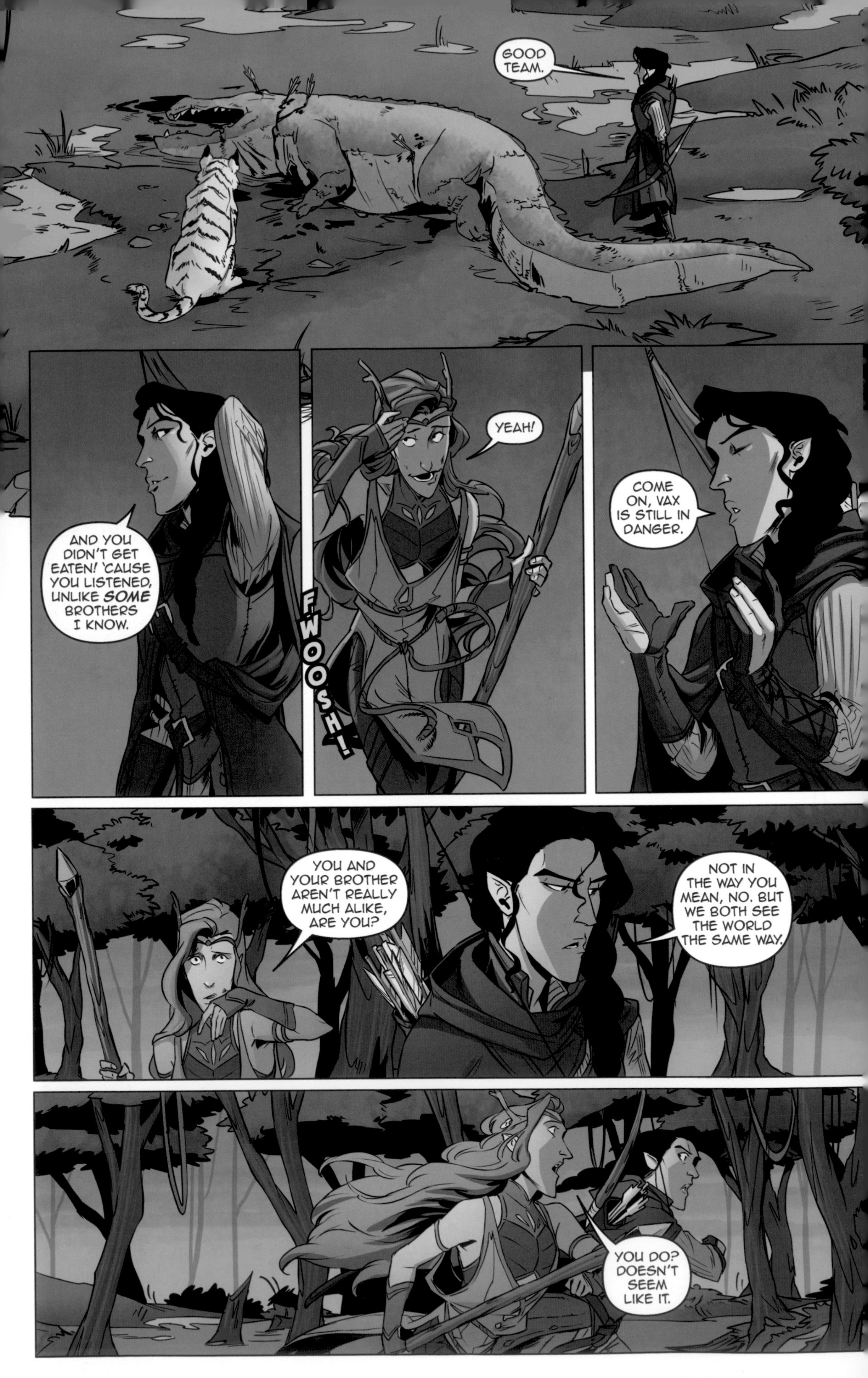
GOOD TEAM.
AND YOU DIDN'T GET EATEN! 'CAUSE YOU LISTENED, UNLIKE *SOME* BROTHERS I KNOW.
YEAH!
FWOOSH!
COME ON, VAX IS STILL IN DANGER.
YOU AND YOUR BROTHER AREN'T REALLY MUCH ALIKE, ARE YOU?
NOT IN THE WAY YOU MEAN, NO. BUT WE BOTH SEE THE WORLD THE SAME WAY.
YOU DO? DOESN'T SEEM LIKE IT.

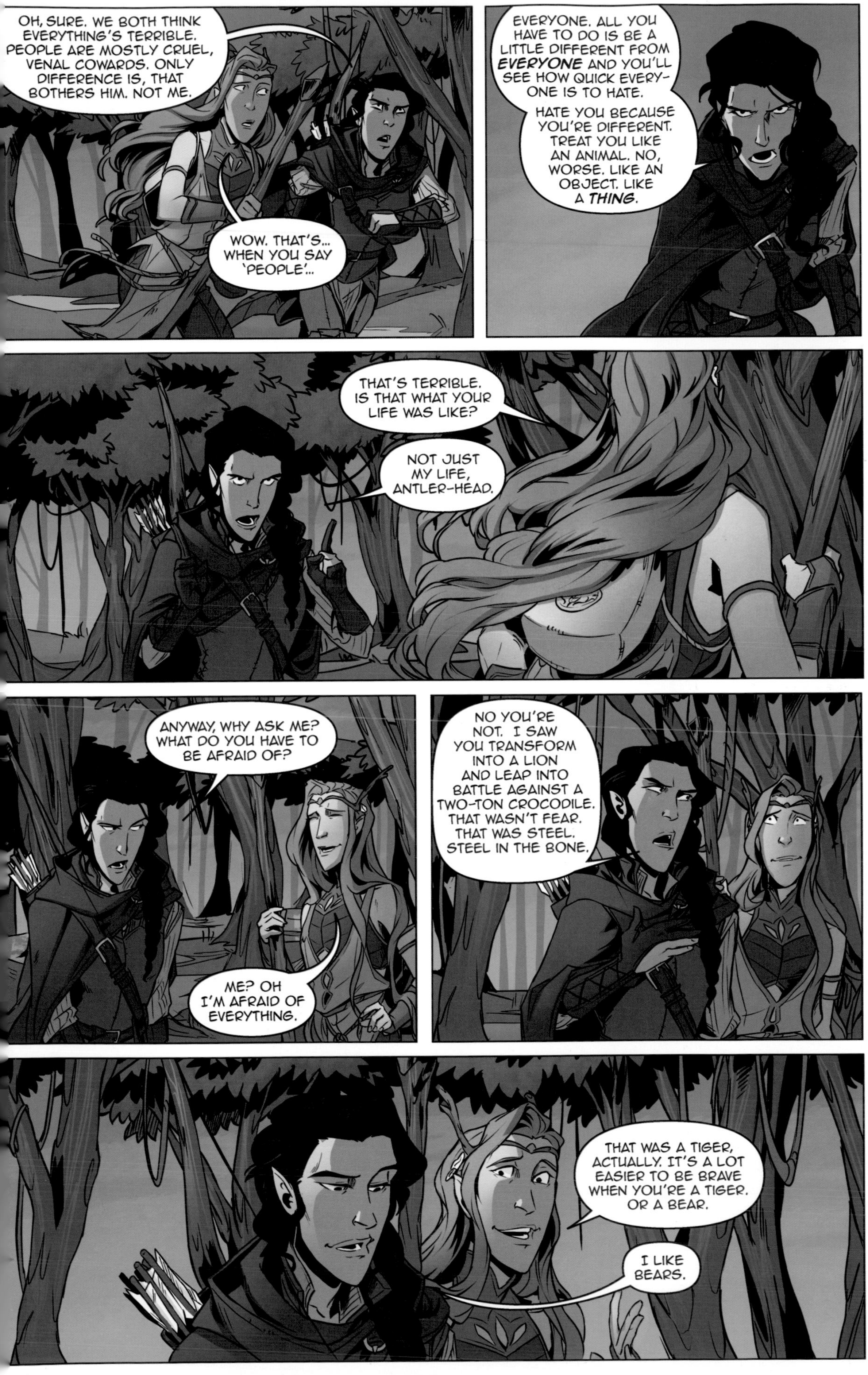
OH, SURE. WE BOTH THINK EVERYTHING'S TERRIBLE. PEOPLE ARE MOSTLY CRUEL, VENAL COWARDS. ONLY DIFFERENCE IS, THAT BOTHERS HIM. NOT ME.
WOW. THAT'S... WHEN YOU SAY 'PEOPLE'...
EVERYONE. ALL YOU HAVE TO DO IS BE A LITTLE DIFFERENT FROM EVERYONE AND YOU'LL SEE HOW QUICK EVERY-ONE IS TO HATE.
HATE YOU BECAUSE YOU'RE DIFFERENT. TREAT YOU LIKE AN ANIMAL. NO, WORSE. LIKE AN OBJECT. LIKE A THING.
THAT'S TERRIBLE. IS THAT WHAT YOUR LIFE WAS LIKE?
NOT JUST MY LIFE, ANTLER-HEAD.
ANYWAY, WHY ASK ME? WHAT DO YOU HAVE TO BE AFRAID OF?
ME? OH I'M AFRAID OF EVERYTHING.
NO YOU'RE NOT. I SAW YOU TRANSFORM INTO A LION AND LEAP INTO BATTLE AGAINST A TWO-TON CROCODILE. THAT WASN'T FEAR. THAT WAS STEEL. STEEL IN THE BONE.
THAT WAS A TIGER, ACTUALLY. IT'S A LOT EASIER TO BE BRAVE WHEN YOU'RE A TIGER. OR A BEAR.
I LIKE BEARS.

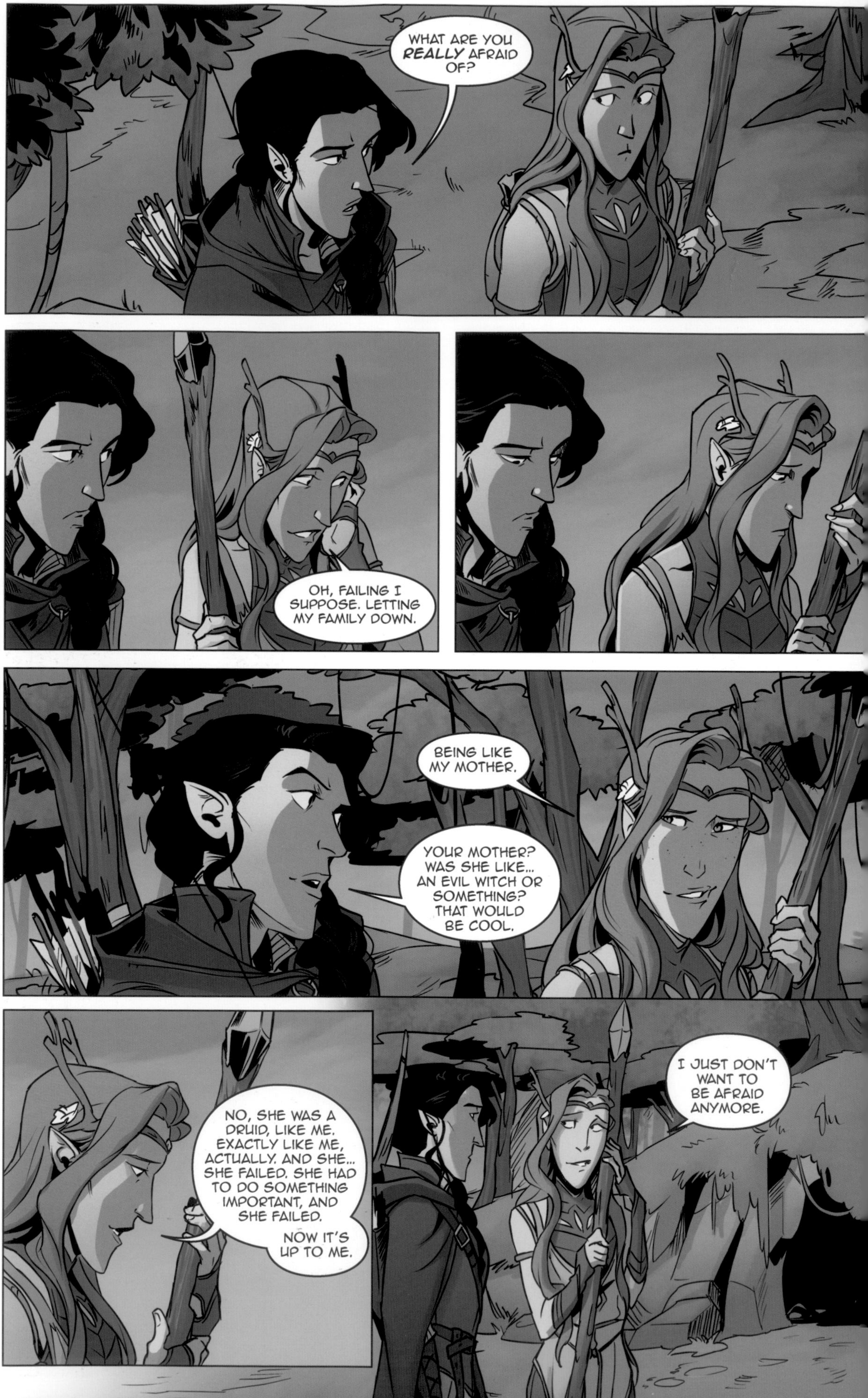
WHAT ARE YOU *REALLY* AFRAID OF?
OH, FAILING I SUPPOSE. LETTING MY FAMILY DOWN.
BEING LIKE MY MOTHER.
YOUR MOTHER? WAS SHE LIKE... AN EVIL WITCH OR SOMETHING? THAT WOULD BE COOL.
NO, SHE WAS A DRUID, LIKE ME. EXACTLY LIKE ME, ACTUALLY. AND SHE... SHE FAILED. SHE HAD TO DO SOMETHING IMPORTANT, AND SHE FAILED.
NOW IT'S UP TO ME.
I JUST DON'T WANT TO BE AFRAID ANYMORE.

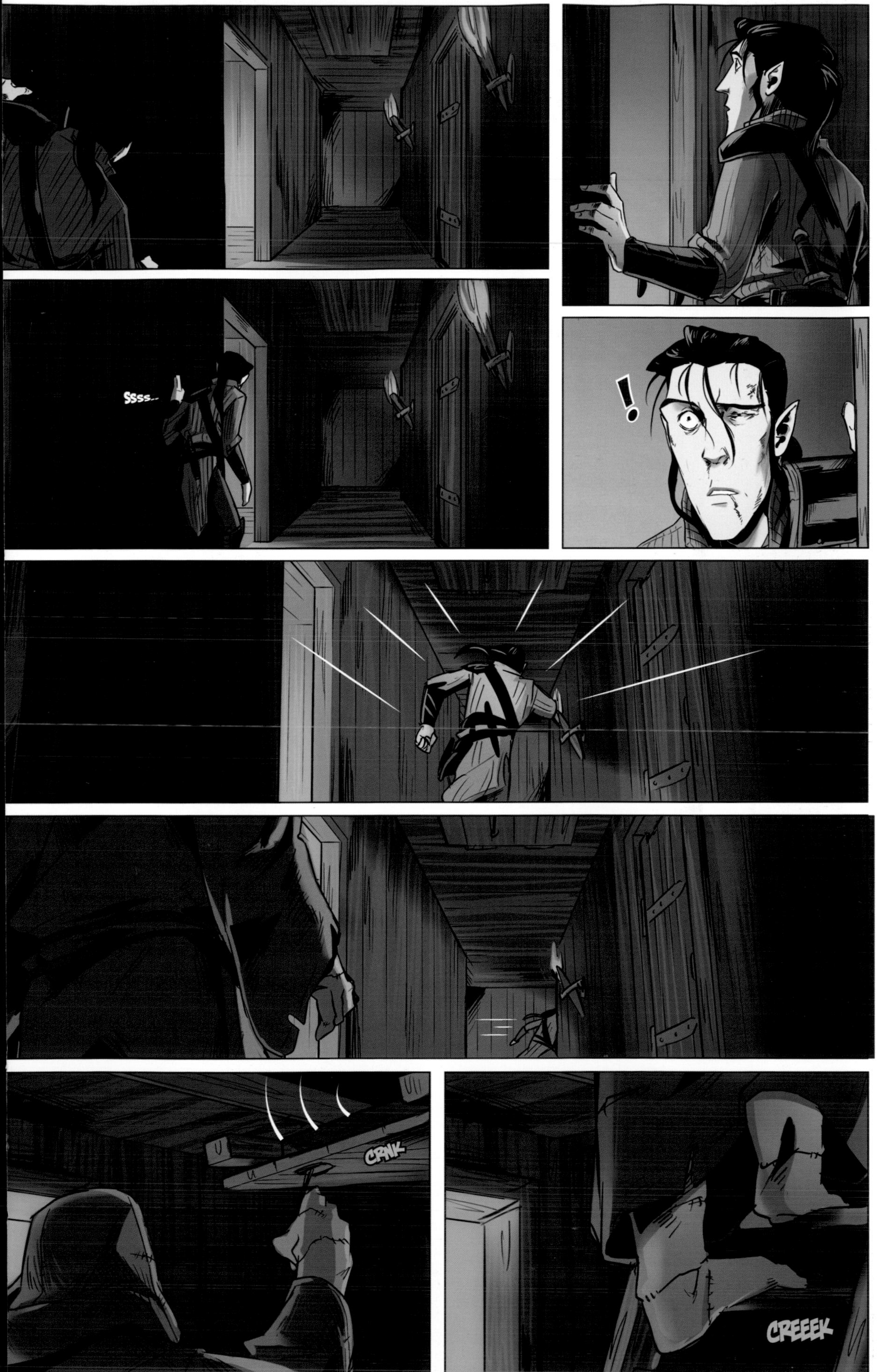

SSSS...
!
CRNK
CREEEK

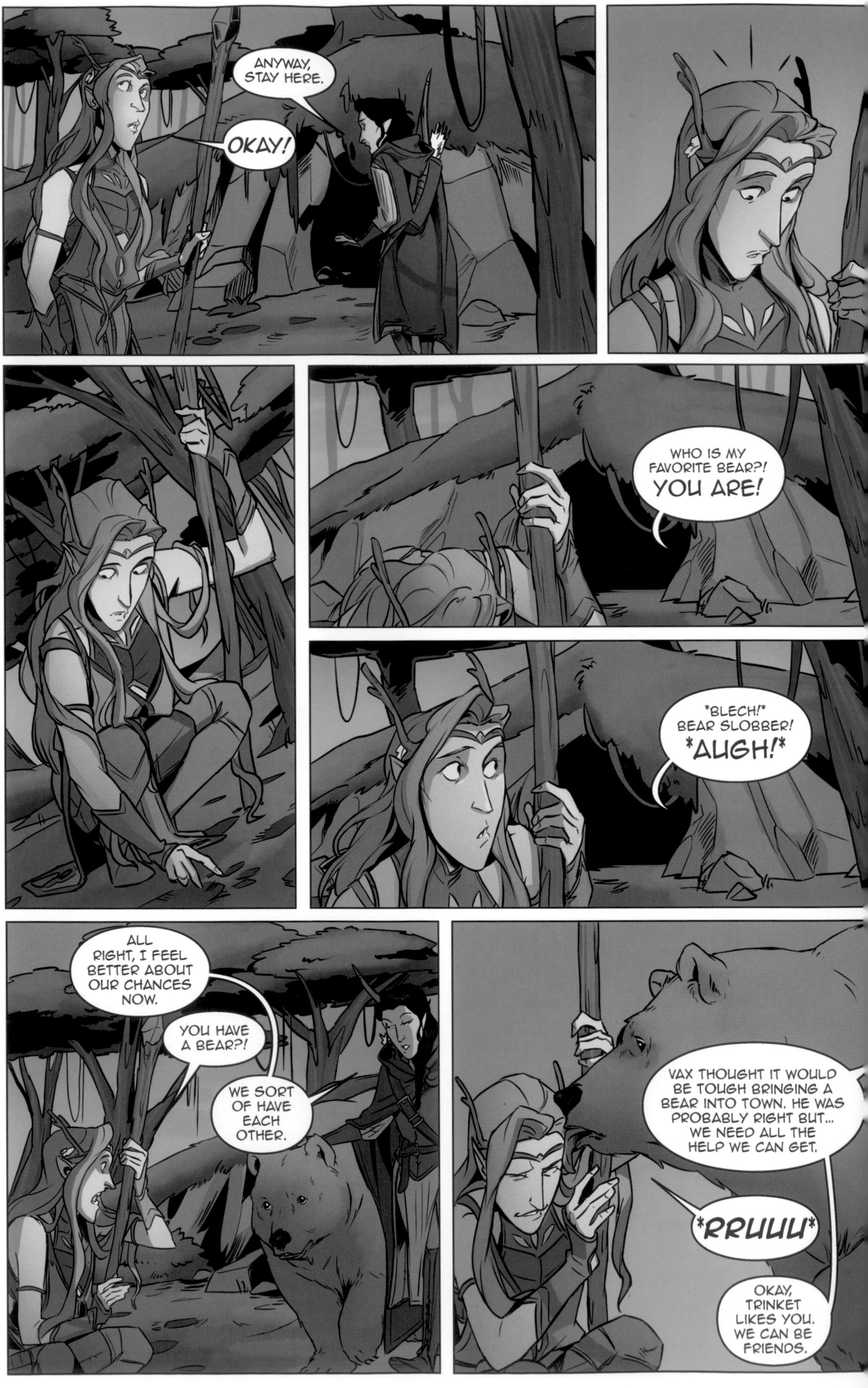

ANYWAY, STAY HERE.
OKAY!
WHO IS MY FAVORITE BEAR?! YOU ARE!
*BLECH!* BEAR SLOBBER! *AUGH!*
ALL RIGHT, I FEEL BETTER ABOUT OUR CHANCES NOW.
YOU HAVE A BEAR?!
WE SORT OF HAVE EACH OTHER.
VAX THOUGHT IT WOULD BE TOUGH BRINGING A BEAR INTO TOWN. HE WAS PROBABLY RIGHT BUT... WE NEED ALL THE HELP WE CAN GET.
*RRUUU*
OKAY, TRINKET LIKES YOU. WE CAN BE FRIENDS.

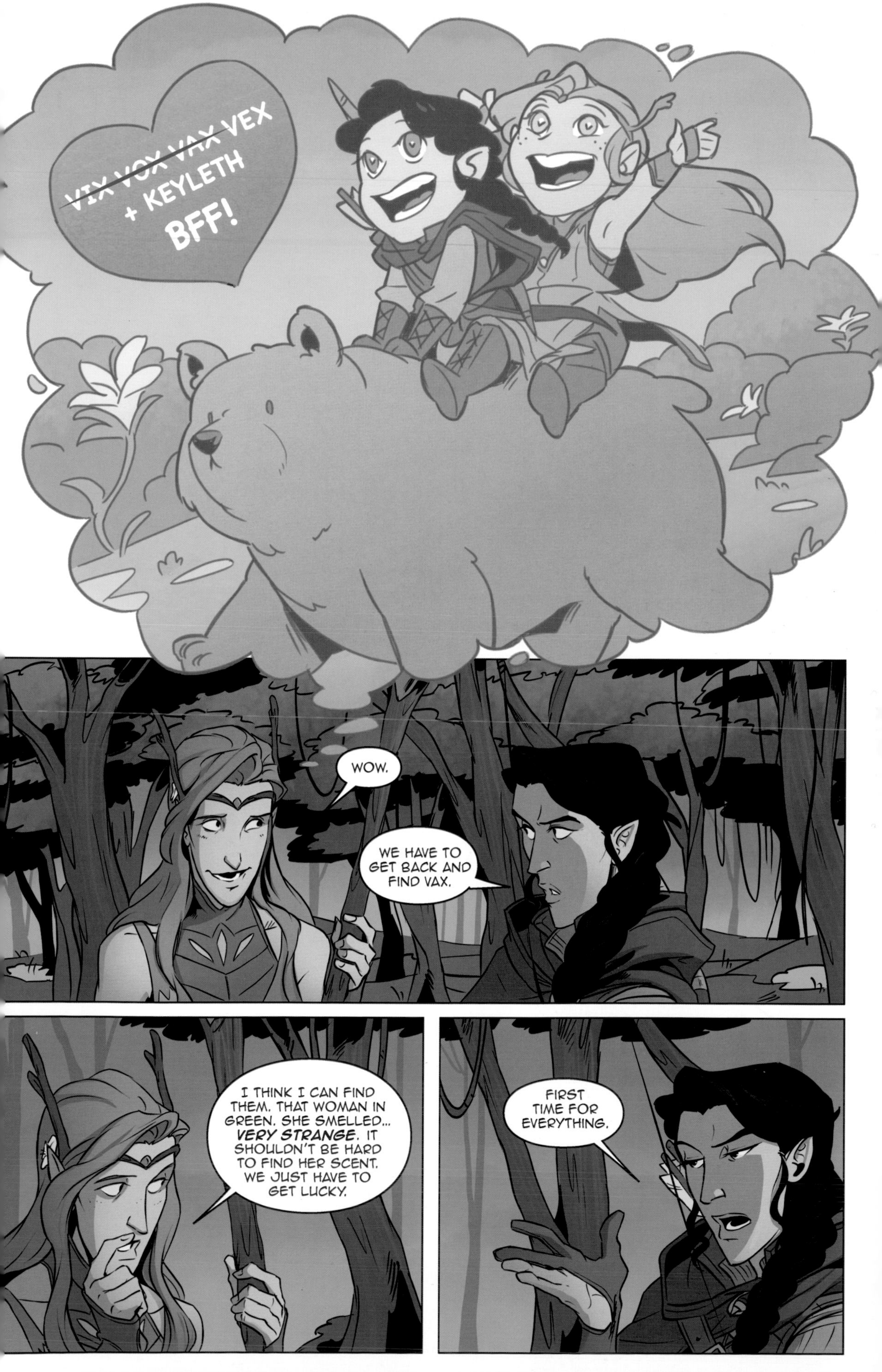
VIX VOX VAX VEX + KEYLETH BFF!
WOW.
WE HAVE TO GET BACK AND FIND VAX.
I THINK I CAN FIND THEM. THAT WOMAN IN GREEN. SHE SMELLED... *VERY STRANGE*. IT SHOULDN'T BE HARD TO FIND HER SCENT. WE JUST HAVE TO GET LUCKY.
FIRST TIME FOR EVERYTHING.

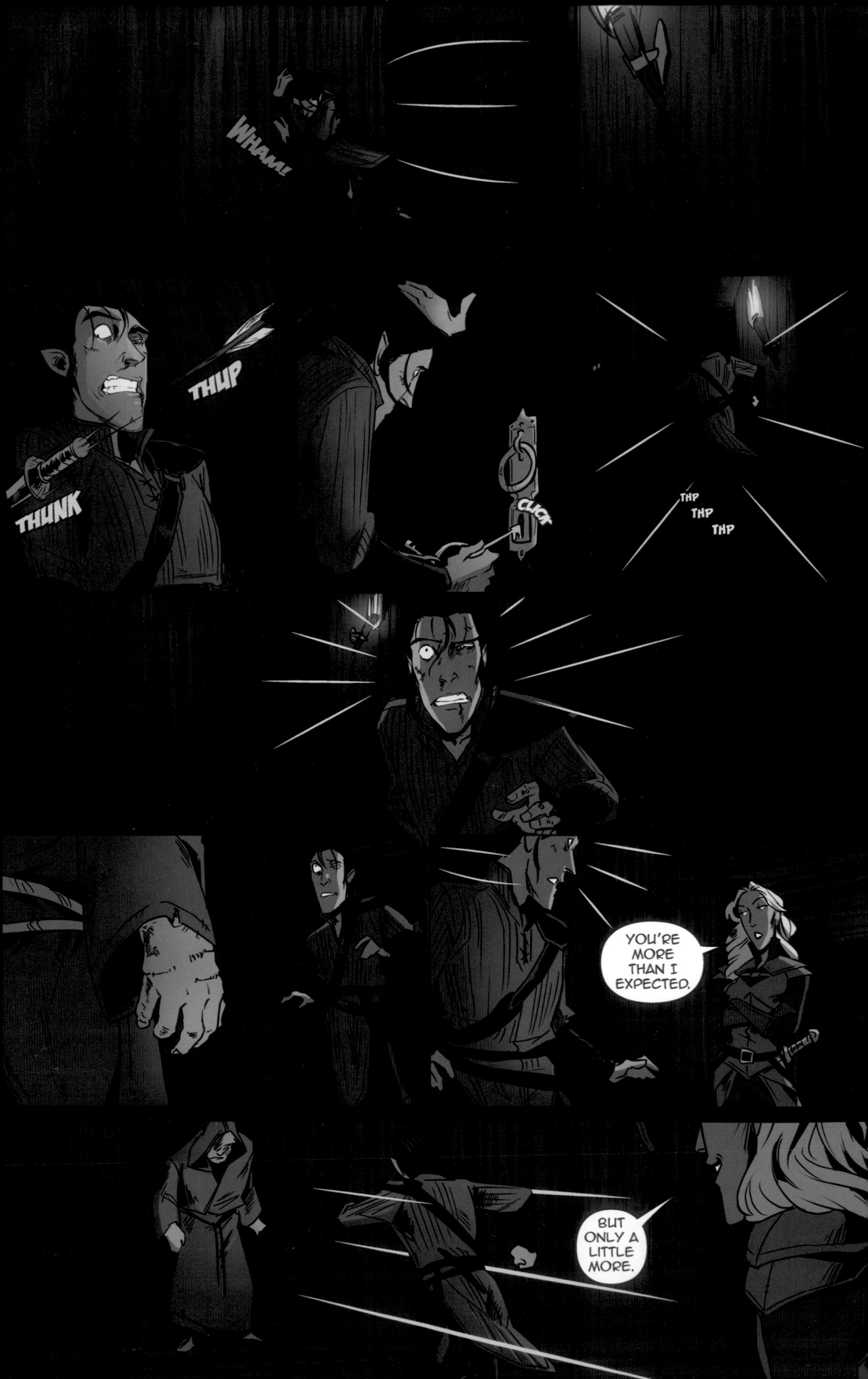
WHAM!
THUP
THUNK
CLICK
THP
THP
THP
YOU'RE MORE THAN I EXPECTED.
BUT ONLY A LITTLE MORE.

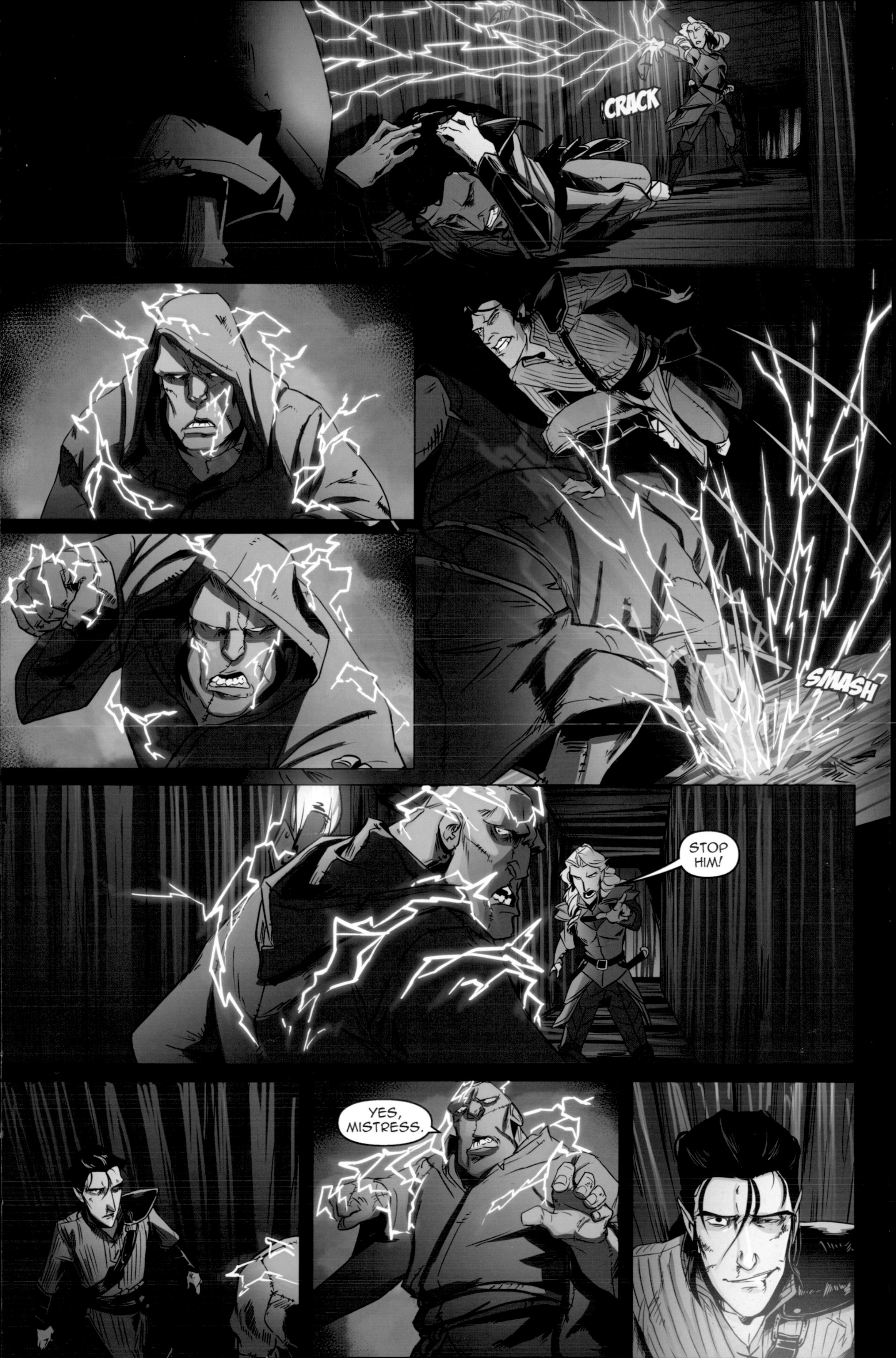
CRACK
SMASH
STOP HIM!
YES, MISTRESS.

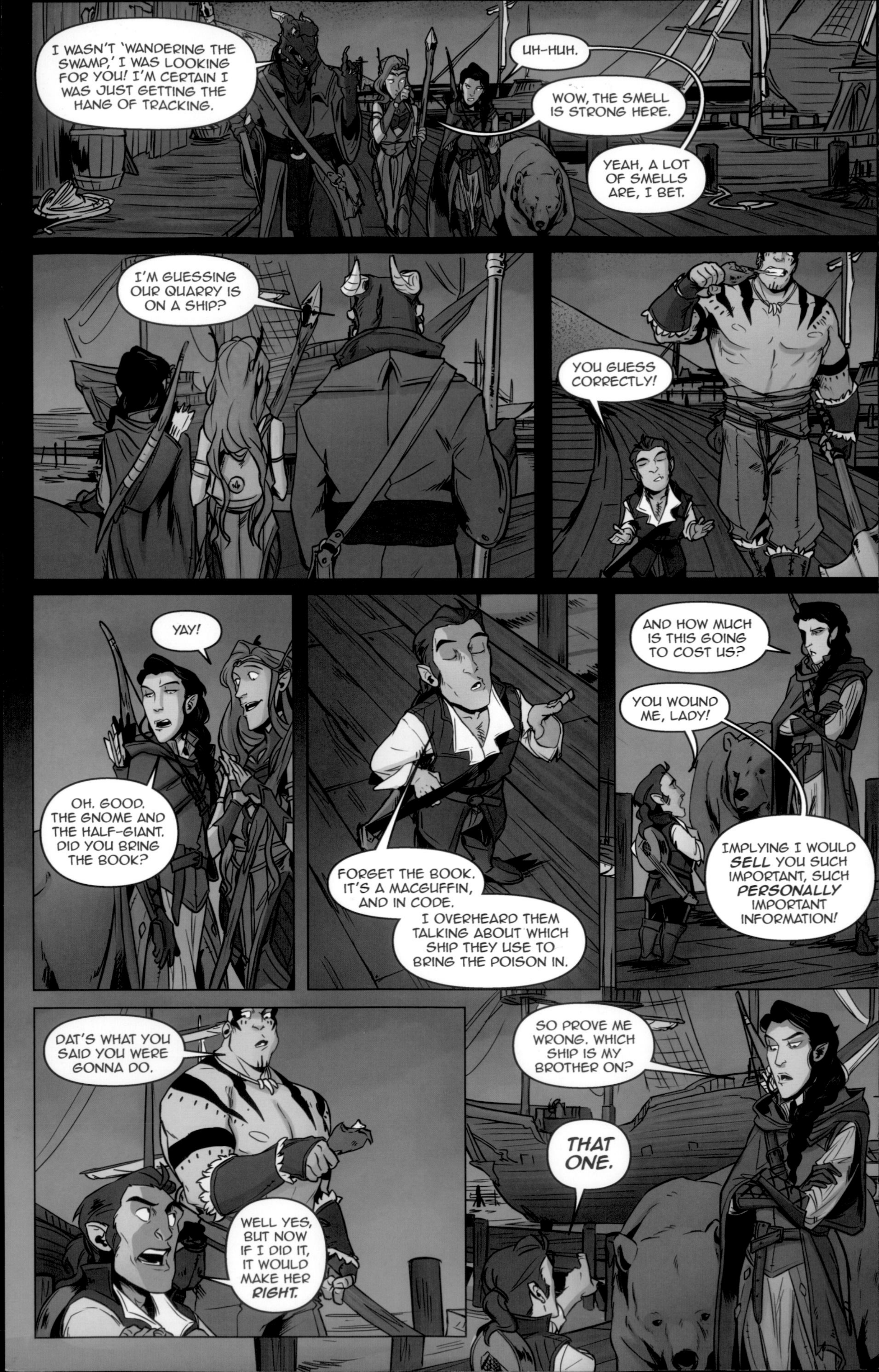
I WASN'T 'WANDERING THE SWAMP,' I WAS LOOKING FOR YOU! I'M CERTAIN I WAS JUST GETTING THE HANG OF TRACKING.
UH-HUH.
WOW, THE SMELL IS STRONG HERE.
YEAH, A LOT OF SMELLS ARE, I BET.
I'M GUESSING OUR QUARRY IS ON A SHIP?
YOU GUESS CORRECTLY!
YAY!
OH, GOOD. THE GNOME AND THE HALF-GIANT. DID YOU BRING THE BOOK?
FORGET THE BOOK. IT'S A MACGUFFIN, AND IN CODE.
I OVERHEARD THEM TALKING ABOUT WHICH SHIP THEY USE TO BRING THE POISON IN.
AND HOW MUCH IS THIS GOING TO COST US?
YOU WOUND ME, LADY!
IMPLYING I WOULD SELL YOU SUCH IMPORTANT, SUCH PERSONALLY IMPORTANT INFORMATION!
DAT'S WHAT YOU SAID YOU WERE GONNA DO.
WELL YES, BUT NOW IF I DID IT, IT WOULD MAKE HER RIGHT.
SO PROVE ME WRONG. WHICH SHIP IS MY BROTHER ON?
THAT ONE.

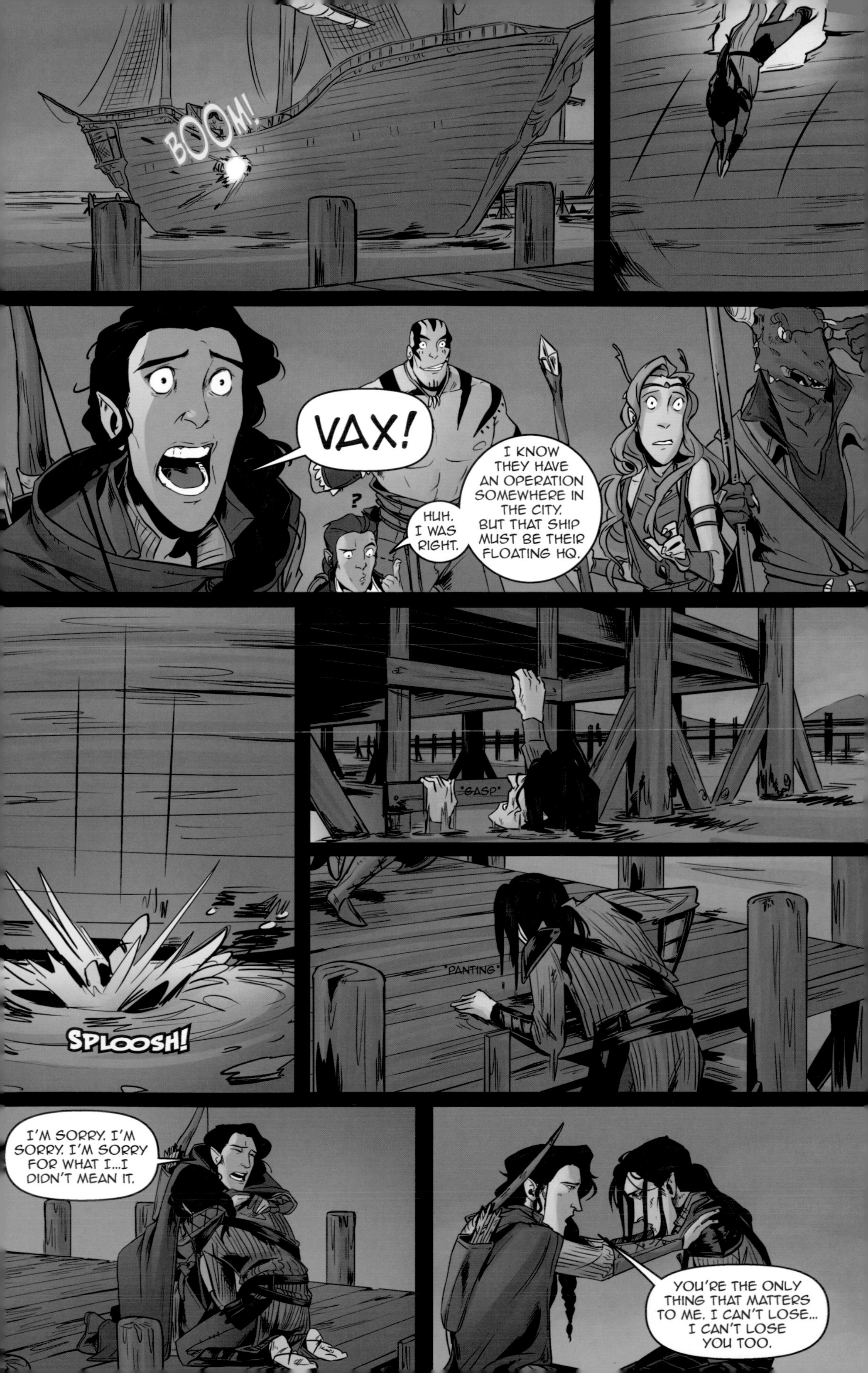
BOOM!
VAX!
?
HUH. I WAS RIGHT.
I KNOW THEY HAVE AN OPERATION SOMEWHERE IN THE CITY. BUT THAT SHIP MUST BE THEIR FLOATING HQ.
SPLOOSH!
*GASP*
*PANTING*
I'M SORRY. I'M SORRY. I'M SORRY FOR WHAT I...I DIDN'T MEAN IT.
YOU'RE THE ONLY THING THAT MATTERS TO ME. I CAN'T LOSE... I CAN'T LOSE YOU TOO.

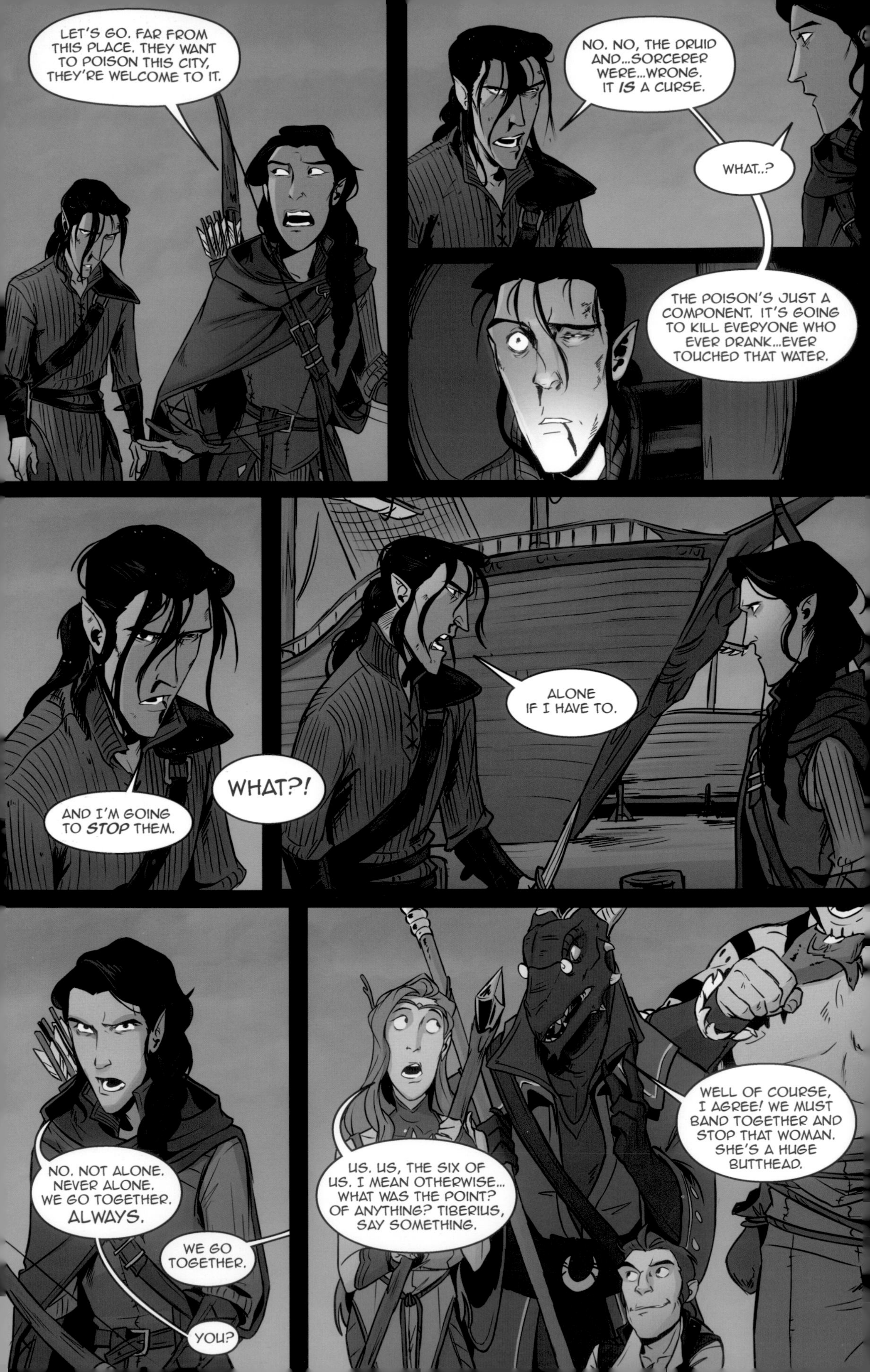
LET'S GO. FAR FROM THIS PLACE. THEY WANT TO POISON THIS CITY, THEY'RE WELCOME TO IT.
NO. NO, THE DRUID AND...SORCERER WERE...WRONG. IT IS A CURSE.
WHAT..?
THE POISON'S JUST A COMPONENT. IT'S GOING TO KILL EVERYONE WHO EVER DRANK...EVER TOUCHED THAT WATER.
AND I'M GOING TO STOP THEM.
WHAT?!
ALONE IF I HAVE TO.
NO. NOT ALONE. NEVER ALONE. WE GO TOGETHER. ALWAYS.
WE GO TOGETHER.
YOU?
US. US, THE SIX OF US. I MEAN OTHERWISE... WHAT WAS THE POINT? OF ANYTHING? TIBERIUS, SAY SOMETHING.
WELL OF COURSE, I AGREE! WE MUST BAND TOGETHER AND STOP THAT WOMAN. SHE'S A HUGE BUTTHEAD.

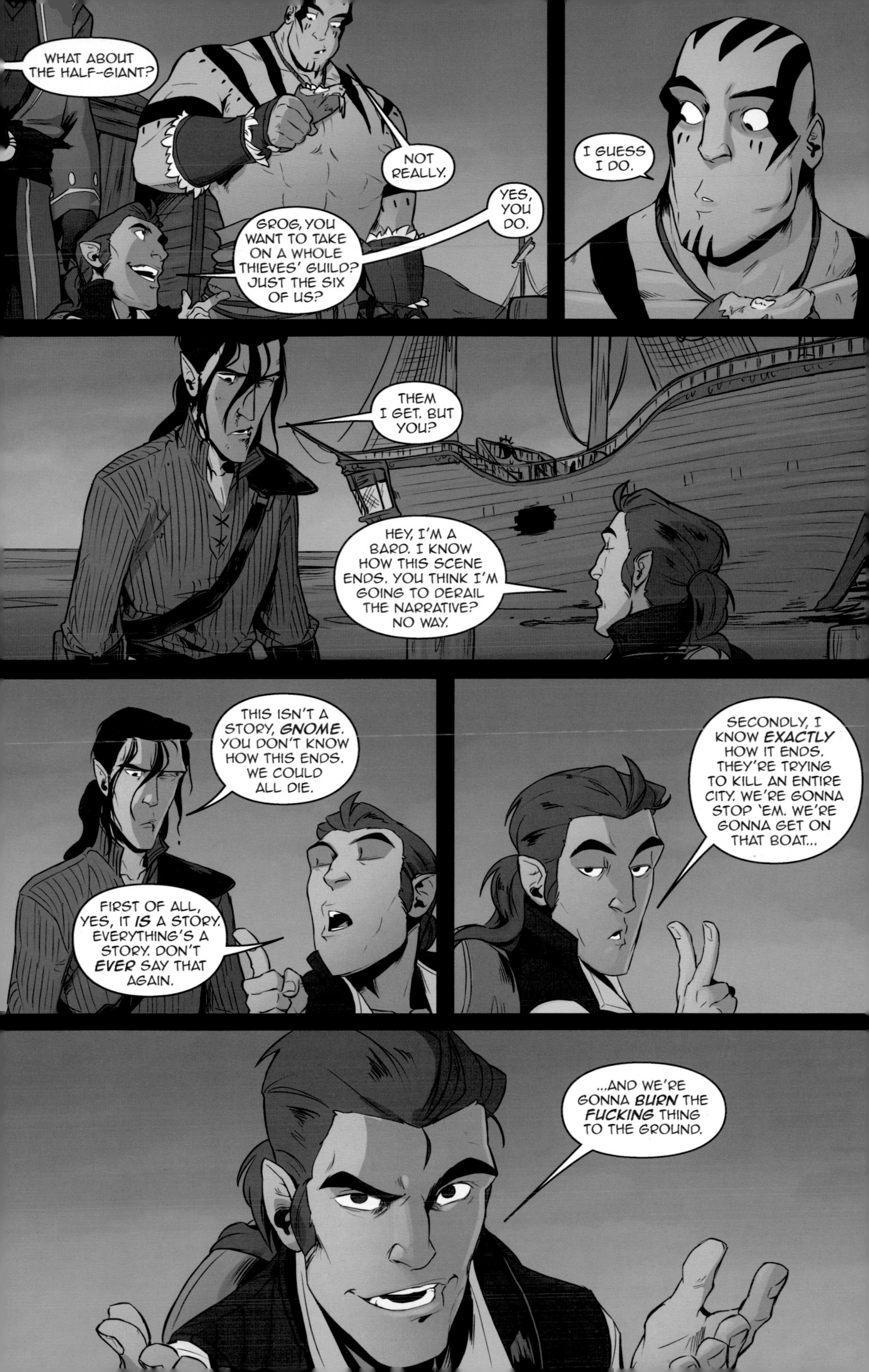
WHAT ABOUT THE HALF-GIANT?
NOT REALLY.
GROG, YOU WANT TO TAKE ON A WHOLE THIEVES' GUILD? JUST THE SIX OF US?
YES, YOU DO.
I GUESS I DO.
THEM I GET. BUT YOU?
HEY, I'M A BARD. I KNOW HOW THIS SCENE ENDS. YOU THINK I'M GOING TO DERAIL THE NARRATIVE? NO WAY.
THIS ISN'T A STORY, **GNOME**. YOU DON'T KNOW HOW THIS ENDS. WE COULD ALL DIE.
FIRST OF ALL, YES, IT ***IS*** A STORY. EVERYTHING'S A STORY. DON'T ***EVER*** SAY THAT AGAIN.
SECONDLY, I KNOW ***EXACTLY*** HOW IT ENDS. THEY'RE TRYING TO KILL AN ENTIRE CITY. WE'RE GONNA STOP 'EM. WE'RE GONNA GET ON THAT BOAT...
...AND WE'RE GONNA ***BURN*** THE ***FUCKING*** THING TO THE GROUND.

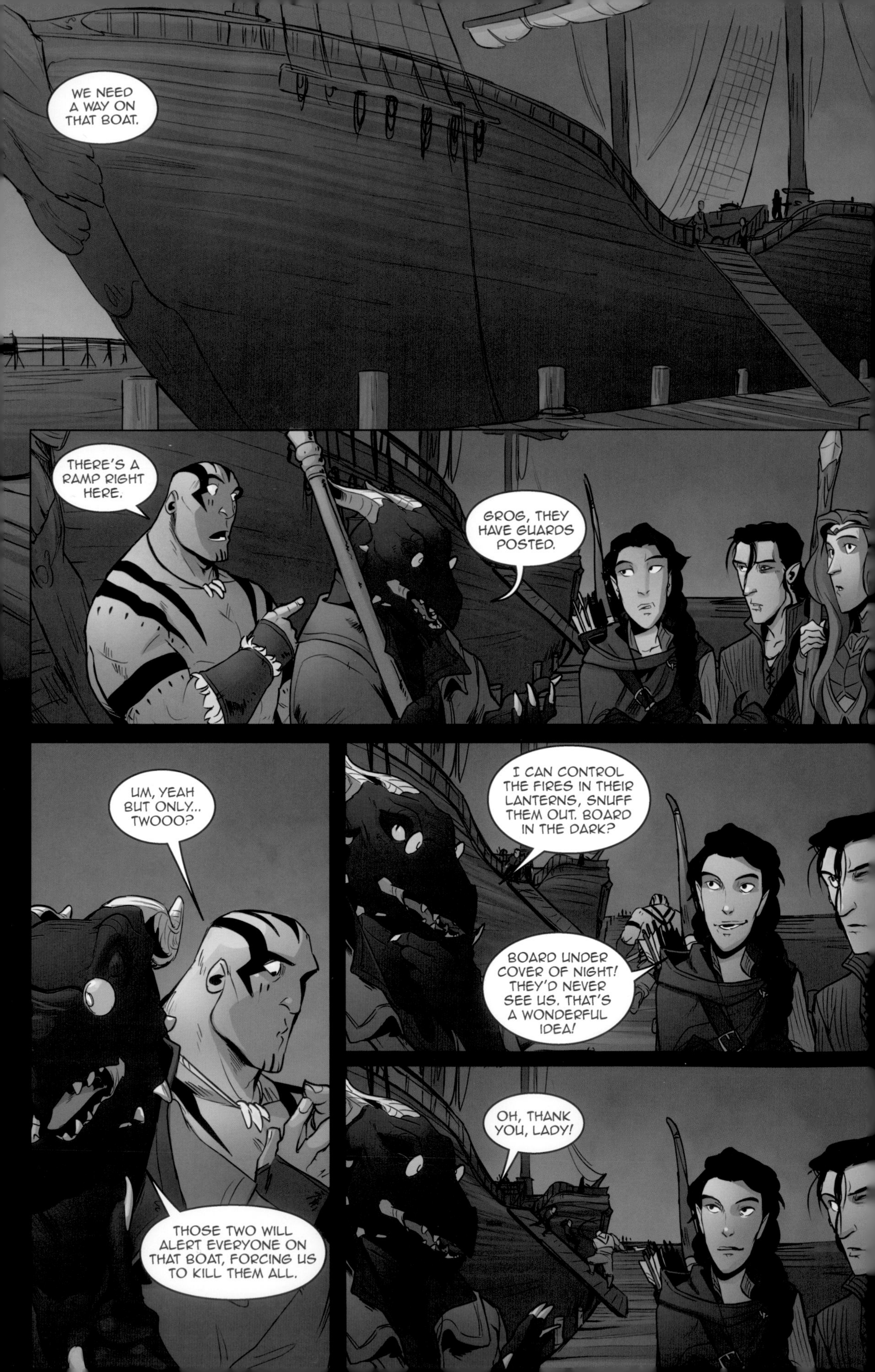
WE NEED A WAY ON THAT BOAT.
THERE'S A RAMP RIGHT HERE.
GROG, THEY HAVE GUARDS POSTED.
UM, YEAH BUT ONLY... TWOOO?
THOSE TWO WILL ALERT EVERYONE ON THAT BOAT, FORCING US TO KILL THEM ALL.
I CAN CONTROL THE FIRES IN THEIR LANTERNS, SNUFF THEM OUT. BOARD IN THE DARK?
BOARD UNDER COVER OF NIGHT! THEY'D NEVER SEE US. THAT'S A WONDERFUL IDEA!
OH, THANK YOU, LADY!

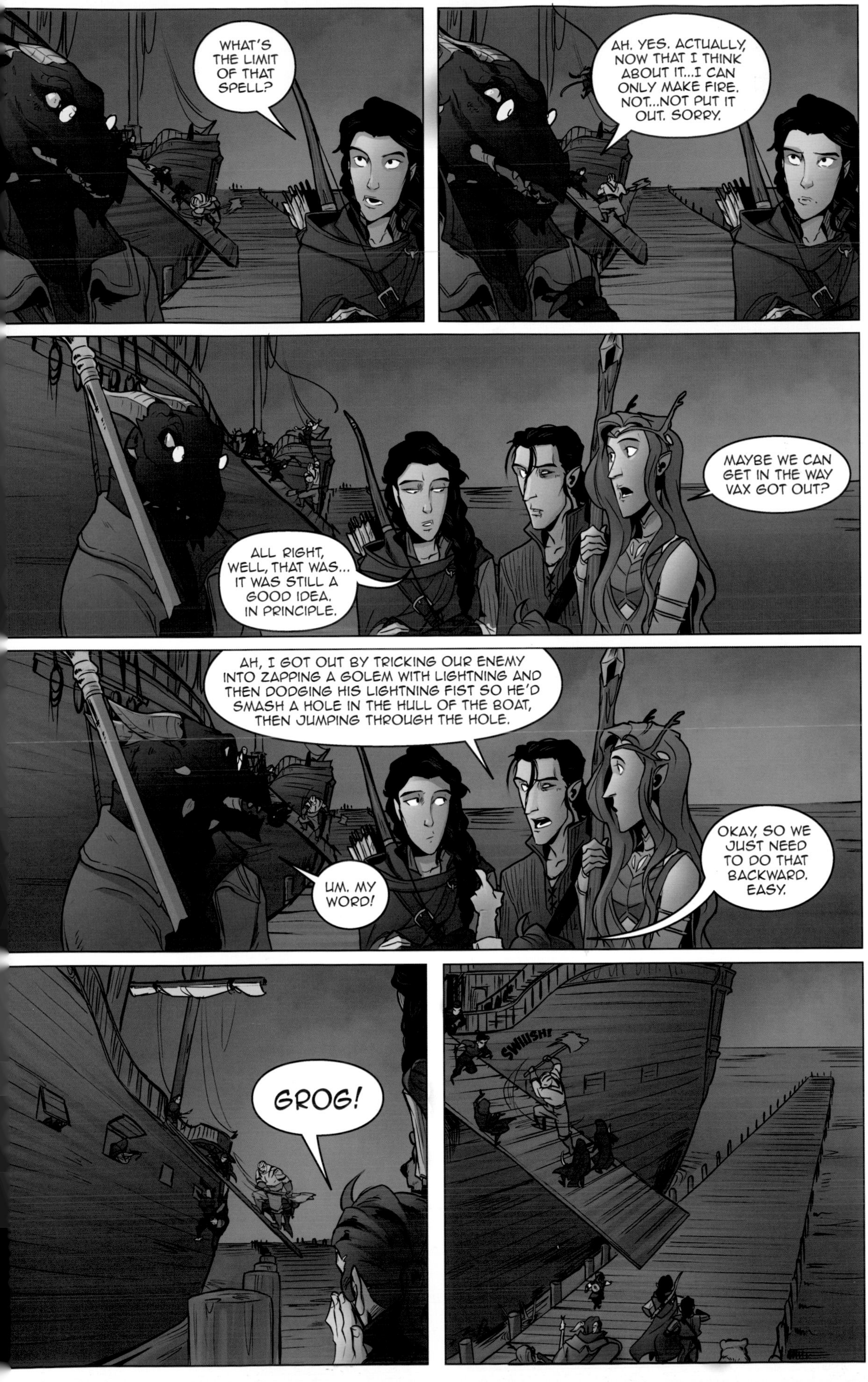
WHAT'S THE LIMIT OF THAT SPELL?
AH. YES. ACTUALLY, NOW THAT I THINK ABOUT IT...I CAN ONLY MAKE FIRE. NOT...NOT PUT IT OUT. SORRY.
MAYBE WE CAN GET IN THE WAY VAX GOT OUT?
ALL RIGHT, WELL, THAT WAS... IT WAS STILL A GOOD IDEA. IN PRINCIPLE.
AH, I GOT OUT BY TRICKING OUR ENEMY INTO ZAPPING A GOLEM WITH LIGHTNING AND THEN DODGING HIS LIGHTNING FIST SO HE'D SMASH A HOLE IN THE HULL OF THE BOAT, THEN JUMPING THROUGH THE HOLE.
UM. MY WORD!
OKAY, SO WE JUST NEED TO DO THAT BACKWARD. EASY.
GROG!
SWIIISH!

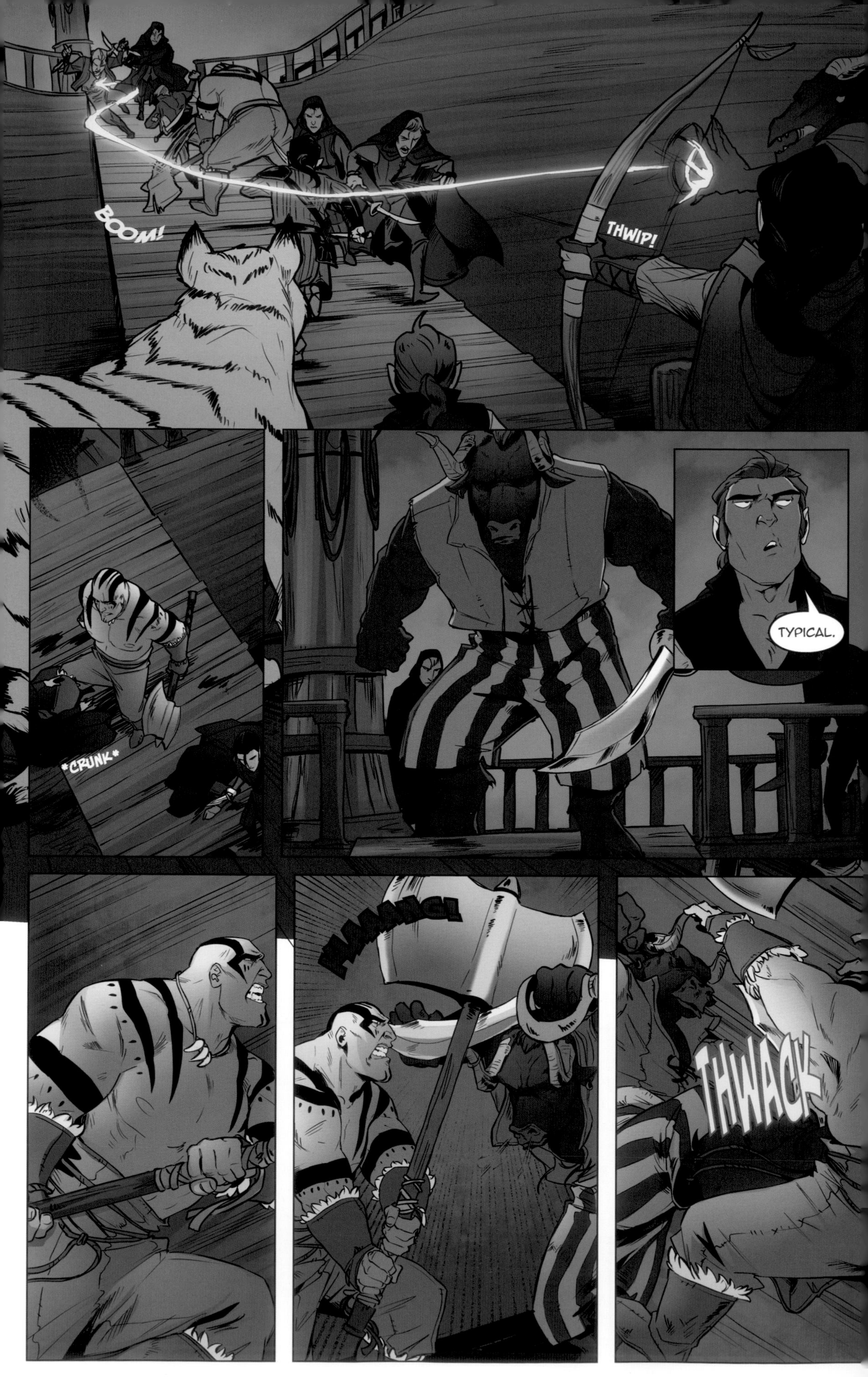
BOOM!
THWIP!
*CRUNK*
TYPICAL.
THWACK

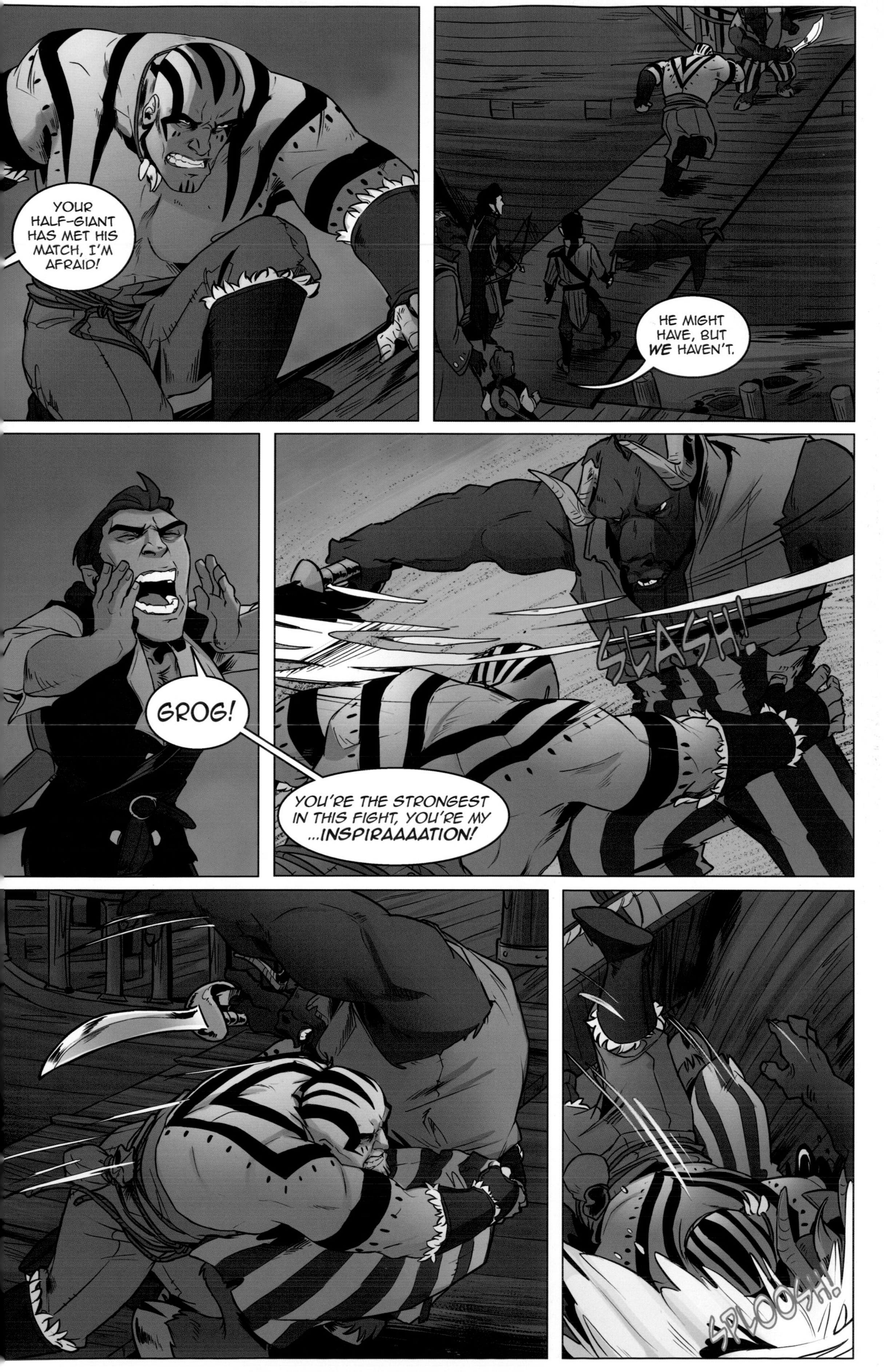
YOUR HALF-GIANT HAS MET HIS MATCH, I'M AFRAID!
HE MIGHT HAVE, BUT WE HAVEN'T.
GROG!
YOU'RE THE STRONGEST IN THIS FIGHT, YOU'RE MY ...INSPIRAAAATION!
SLASH!
SPLOOSH!

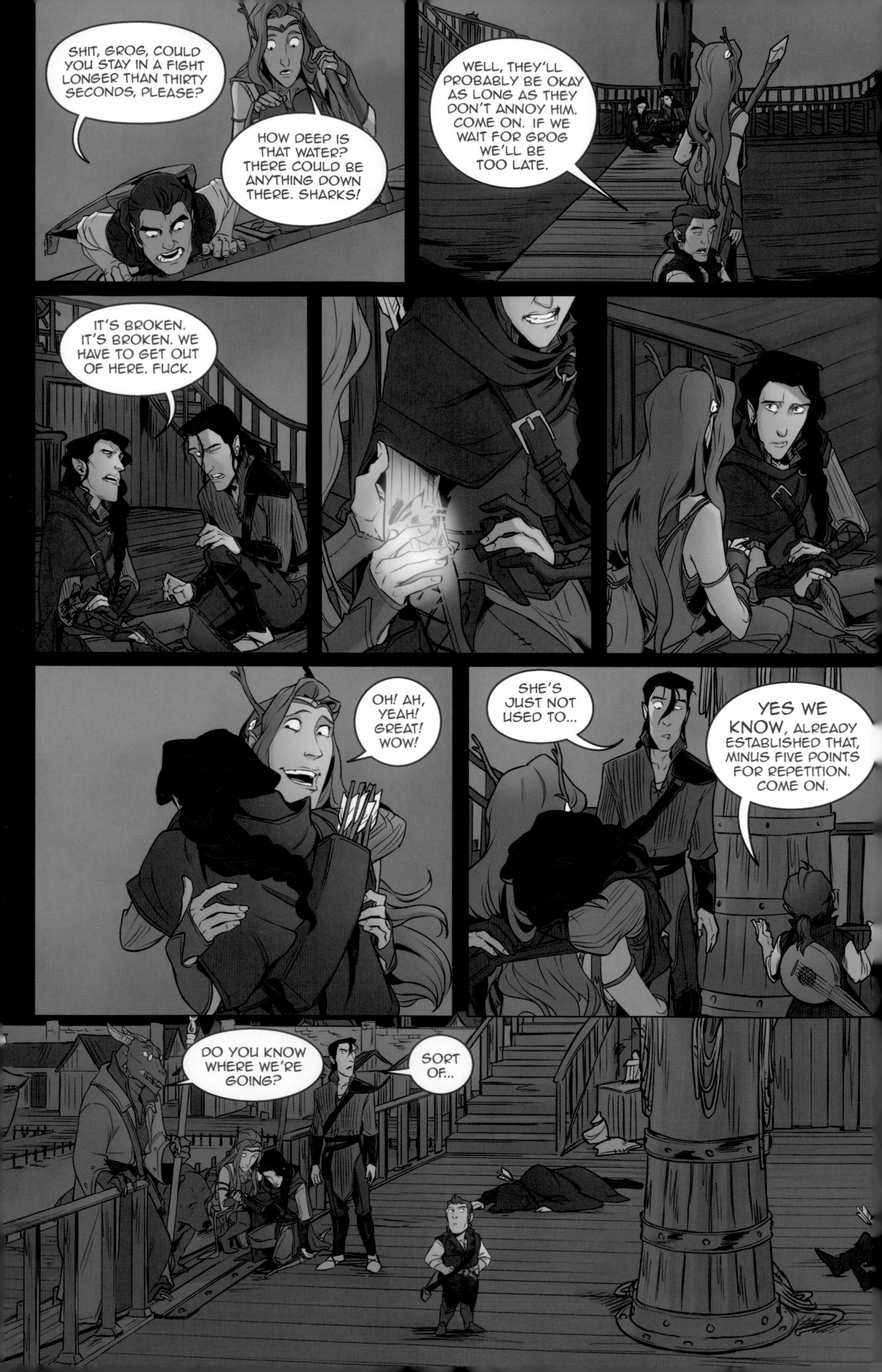
SHIT, GROG, COULD YOU STAY IN A FIGHT LONGER THAN THIRTY SECONDS, PLEASE?
HOW DEEP IS THAT WATER? THERE COULD BE ANYTHING DOWN THERE. SHARKS!
WELL, THEY'LL PROBABLY BE OKAY AS LONG AS THEY DON'T ANNOY HIM. COME ON. IF WE WAIT FOR GROG WE'LL BE TOO LATE.
IT'S BROKEN. IT'S BROKEN. WE HAVE TO GET OUT OF HERE. FUCK.
OH! AH, YEAH! GREAT! WOW!
SHE'S JUST NOT USED TO...
YES WE KNOW, ALREADY ESTABLISHED THAT, MINUS FIVE POINTS FOR REPETITION. COME ON.
DO YOU KNOW WHERE WE'RE GOING?
SORT OF...

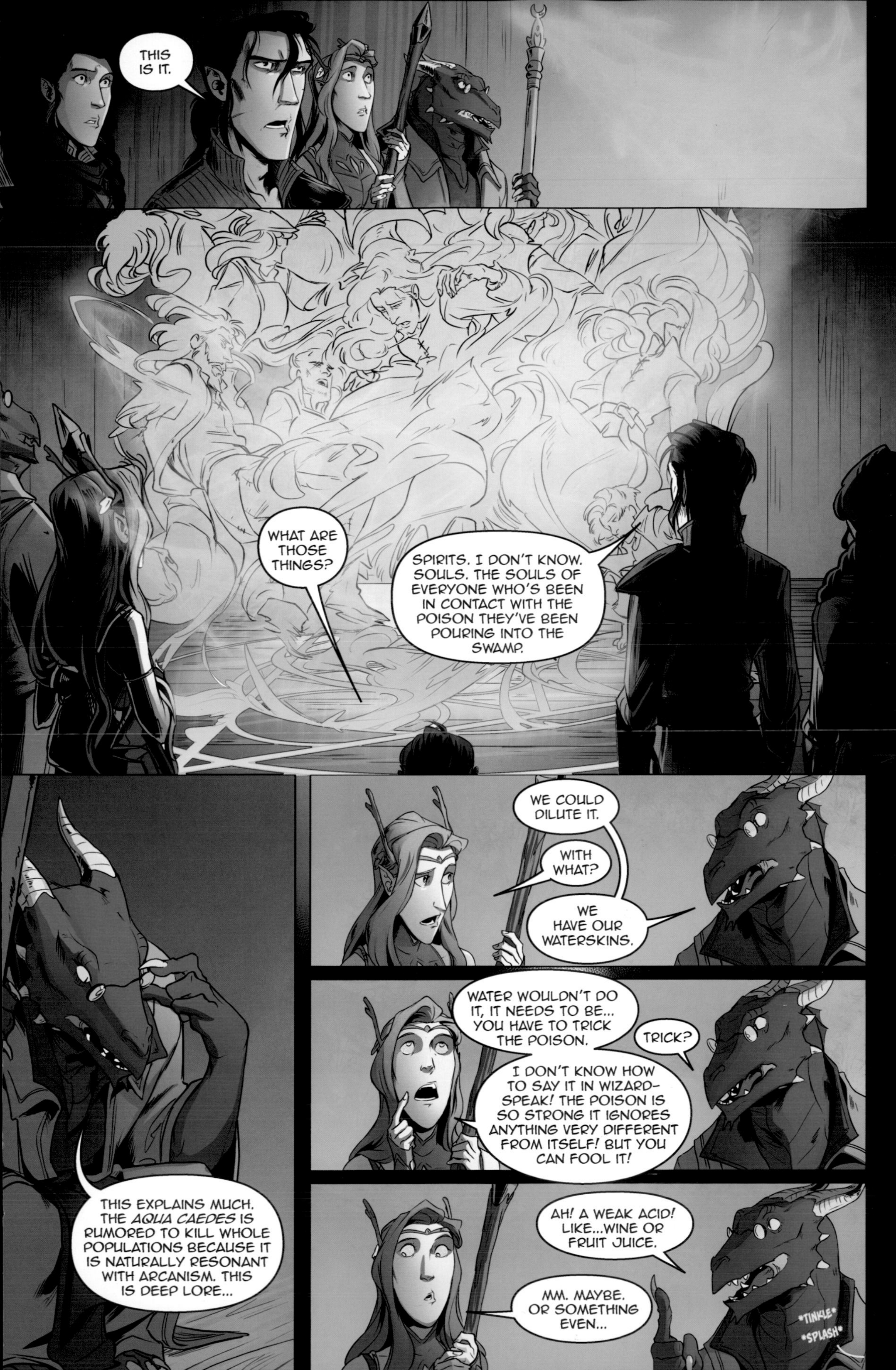
THIS IS IT.
WHAT ARE THOSE THINGS?
SPIRITS. I DON'T KNOW. SOULS. THE SOULS OF EVERYONE WHO'S BEEN IN CONTACT WITH THE POISON THEY'VE BEEN POURING INTO THE SWAMP.
THIS EXPLAINS MUCH. THE *AQUA CAEDES* IS RUMORED TO KILL WHOLE POPULATIONS BECAUSE IT IS NATURALLY RESONANT WITH ARCANISM. THIS IS DEEP LORE...
WE COULD DILUTE IT.
WITH WHAT?
WE HAVE OUR WATERSKINS.
WATER WOULDN'T DO IT, IT NEEDS TO BE... YOU HAVE TO TRICK THE POISON.
TRICK?
I DON'T KNOW HOW TO SAY IT IN WIZARD-SPEAK! THE POISON IS SO STRONG IT IGNORES ANYTHING VERY DIFFERENT FROM ITSELF! BUT YOU CAN FOOL IT!
AH! A WEAK ACID! LIKE...WINE OR FRUIT JUICE.
MM. MAYBE. OR SOMETHING EVEN...
*TINKLE*
*SPLASH*

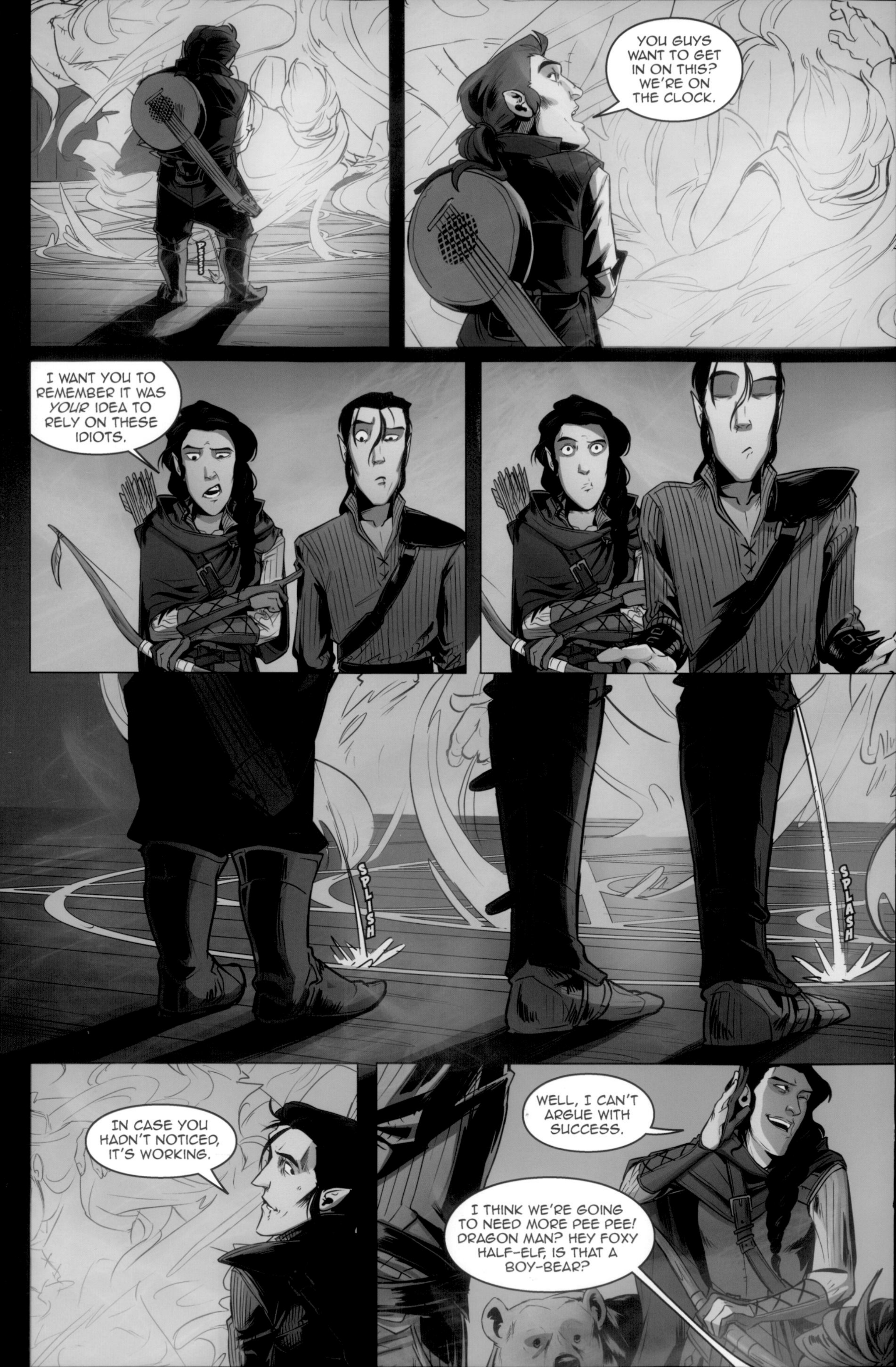
PSSSS
YOU GUYS WANT TO GET IN ON THIS? WE'RE ON THE CLOCK.
I WANT YOU TO REMEMBER IT WAS *YOUR* IDEA TO RELY ON THESE IDIOTS.
SPLISH
SPLASH
IN CASE YOU HADN'T NOTICED, IT'S WORKING.
WELL, I CAN'T ARGUE WITH SUCCESS.
I THINK WE'RE GOING TO NEED MORE PEE PEE! DRAGON MAN? HEY FOXY HALF-ELF, IS THAT A BOY-BEAR?

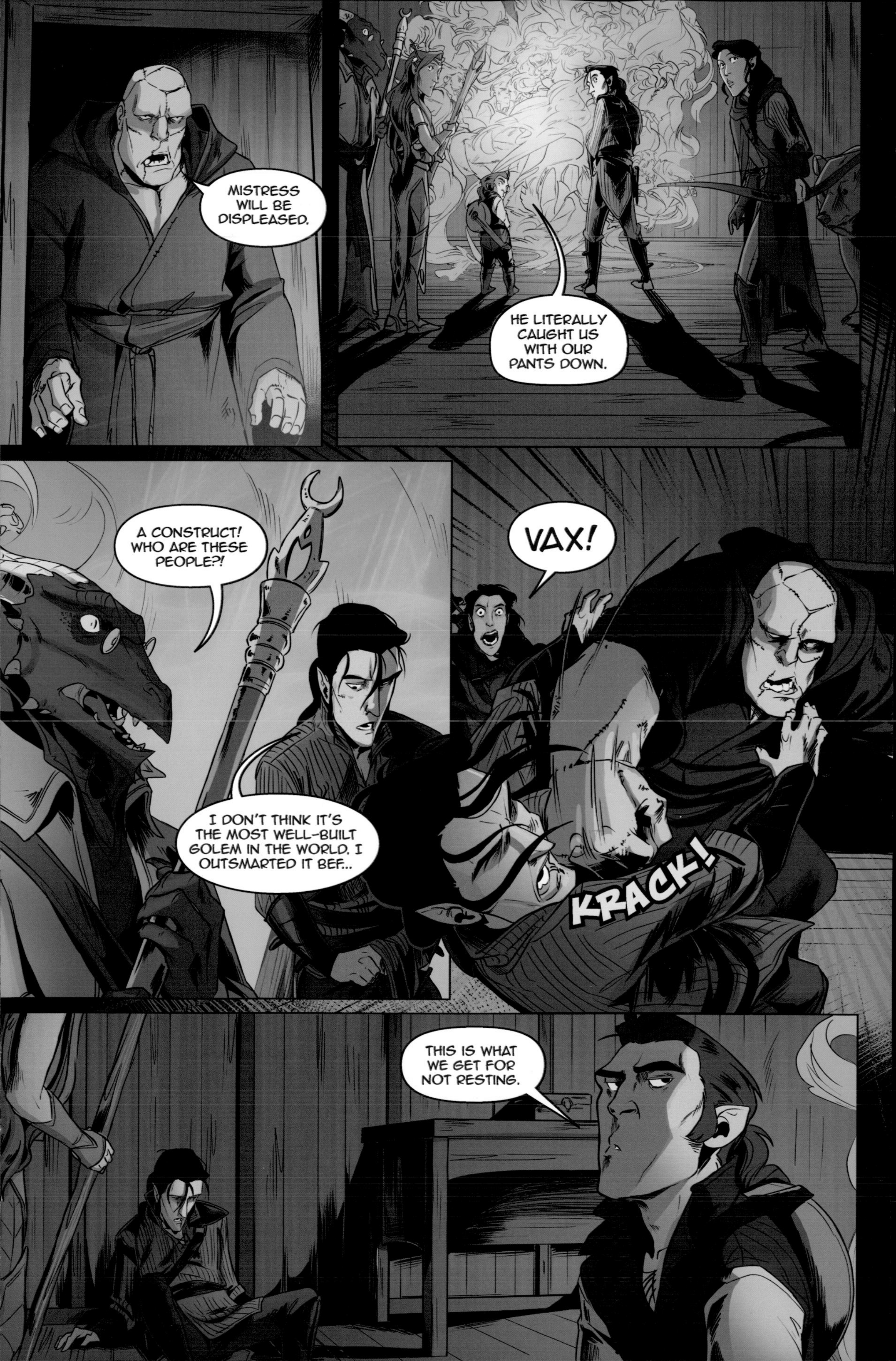
MISTRESS WILL BE DISPLEASED.
HE LITERALLY CAUGHT US WITH OUR PANTS DOWN.
A CONSTRUCT! WHO ARE THESE PEOPLE?!
I DON'T THINK IT'S THE MOST WELL-BUILT GOLEM IN THE WORLD. I OUTSMARTED IT BEF...
VAX!
KRACK!
THIS IS WHAT WE GET FOR NOT RESTING.

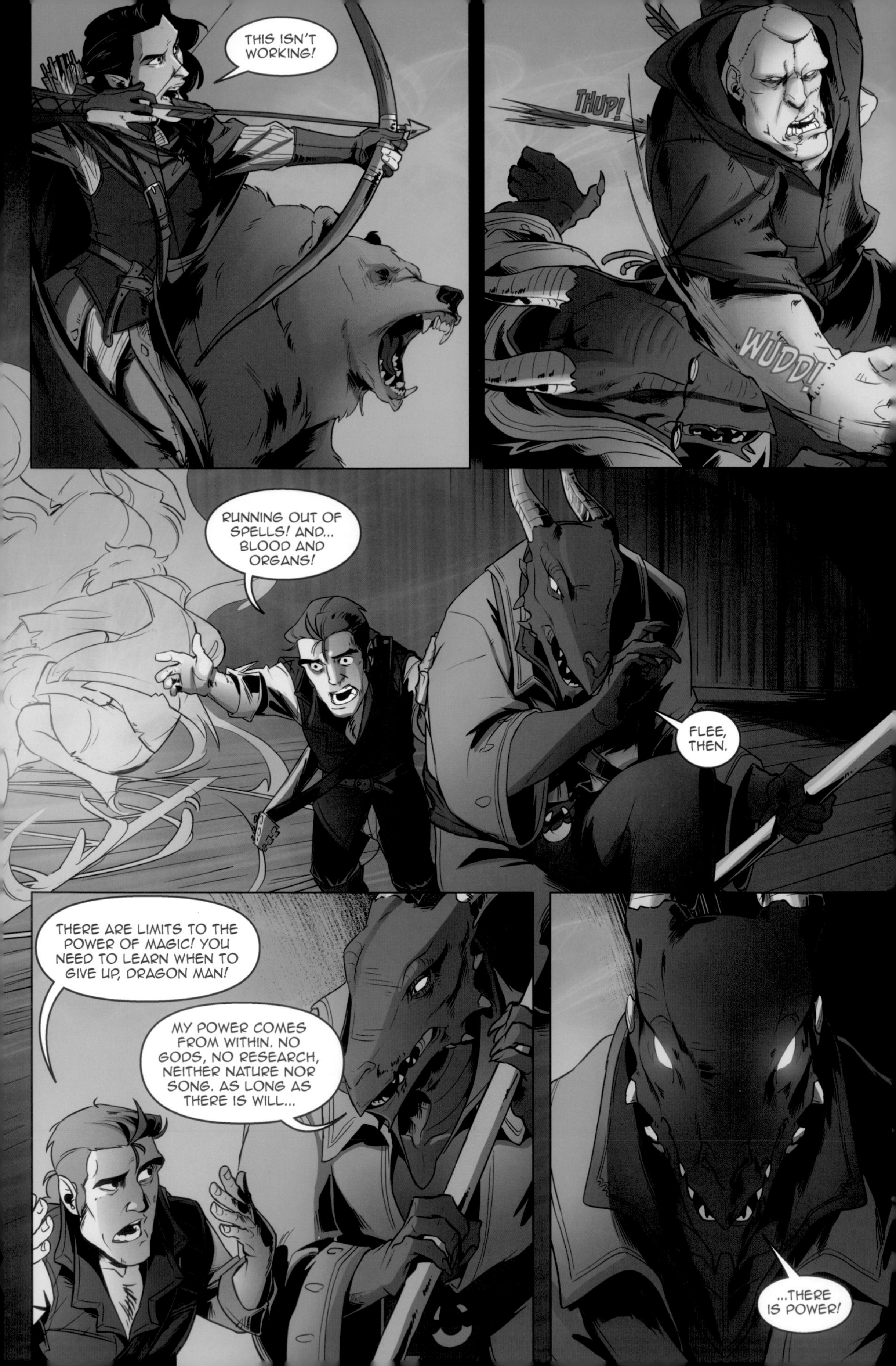
THIS ISN'T WORKING!
THUP!
WUDD!
RUNNING OUT OF SPELLS! AND... BLOOD AND ORGANS!
FLEE, THEN.
THERE ARE LIMITS TO THE POWER OF MAGIC! YOU NEED TO LEARN WHEN TO GIVE UP, DRAGON MAN!
MY POWER COMES FROM WITHIN. NO GODS, NO RESEARCH, NEITHER NATURE NOR SONG. AS LONG AS THERE IS WILL...
...THERE IS POWER!

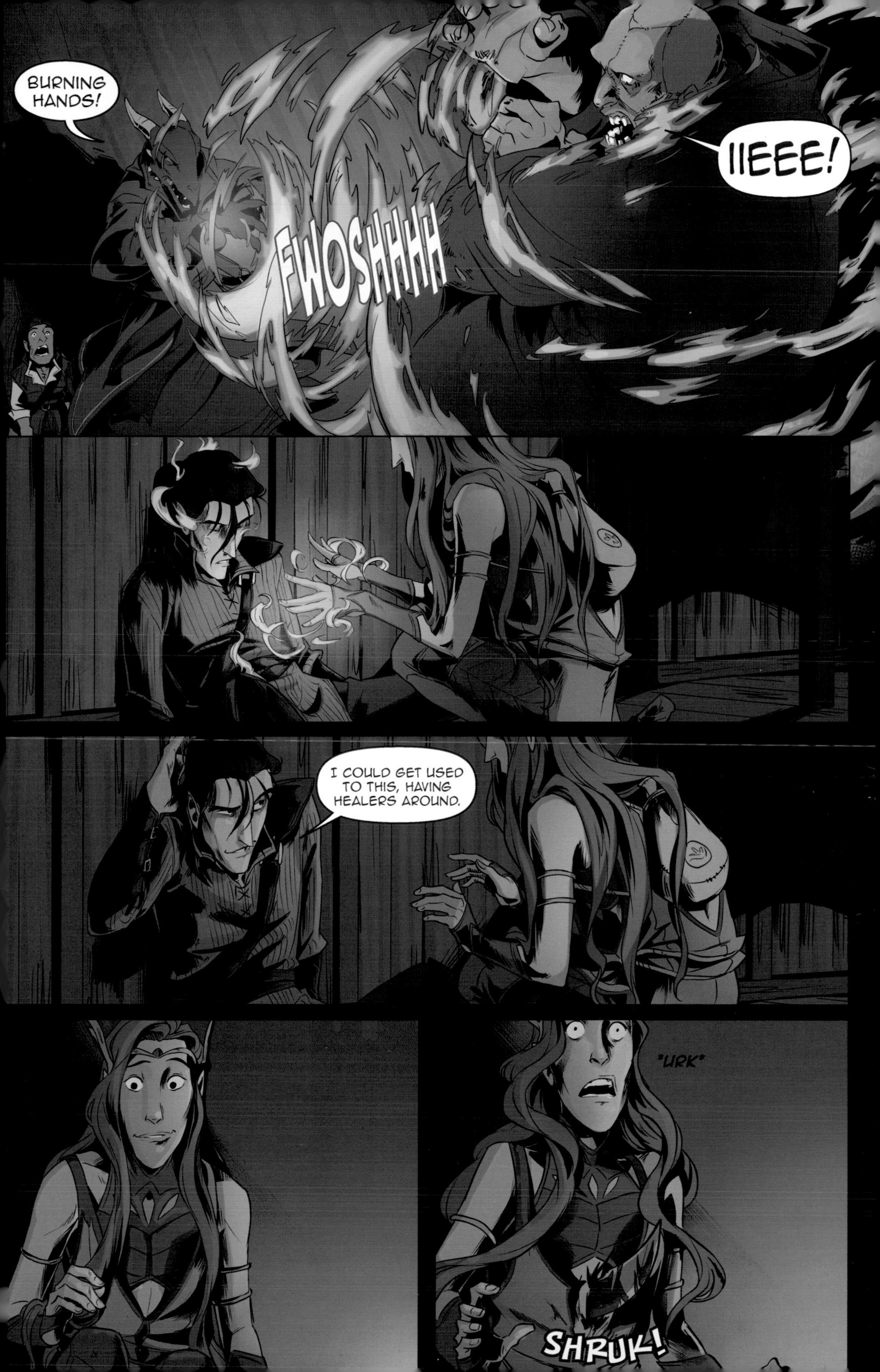
BURNING HANDS!
IIEEE!
FWOSHHHH
I COULD GET USED TO THIS, HAVING HEALERS AROUND.
*URK*
SHRUK!

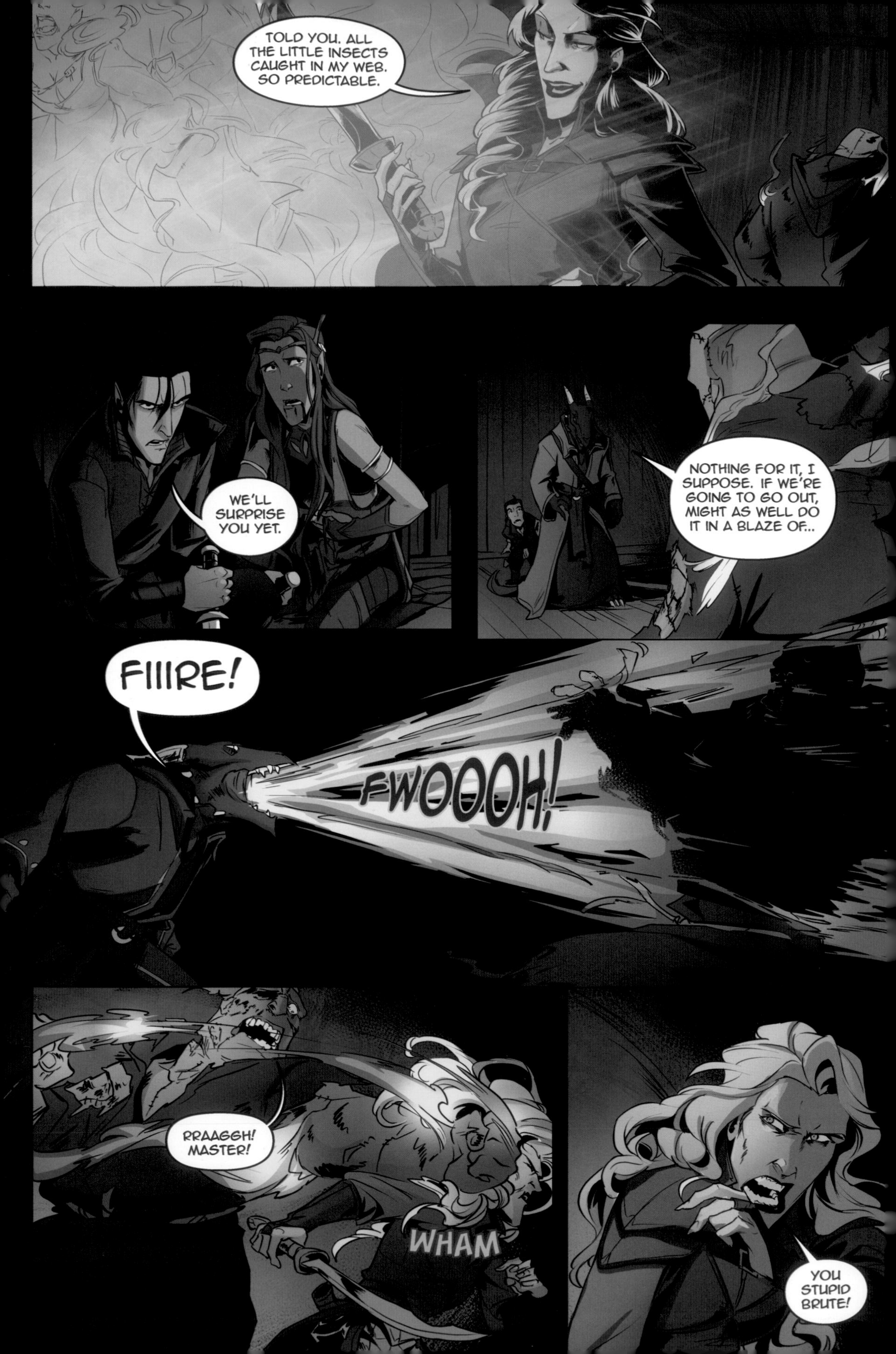
TOLD YOU. ALL THE LITTLE INSECTS CAUGHT IN MY WEB. SO PREDICTABLE.
WE'LL SURPRISE YOU YET.
NOTHING FOR IT, I SUPPOSE. IF WE'RE GOING TO GO OUT, MIGHT AS WELL DO IT IN A BLAZE OF...
FIIIRE!
FWOOOH!
RRAAGGH! MASTER!
WHAM
YOU STUPID BRUTE!

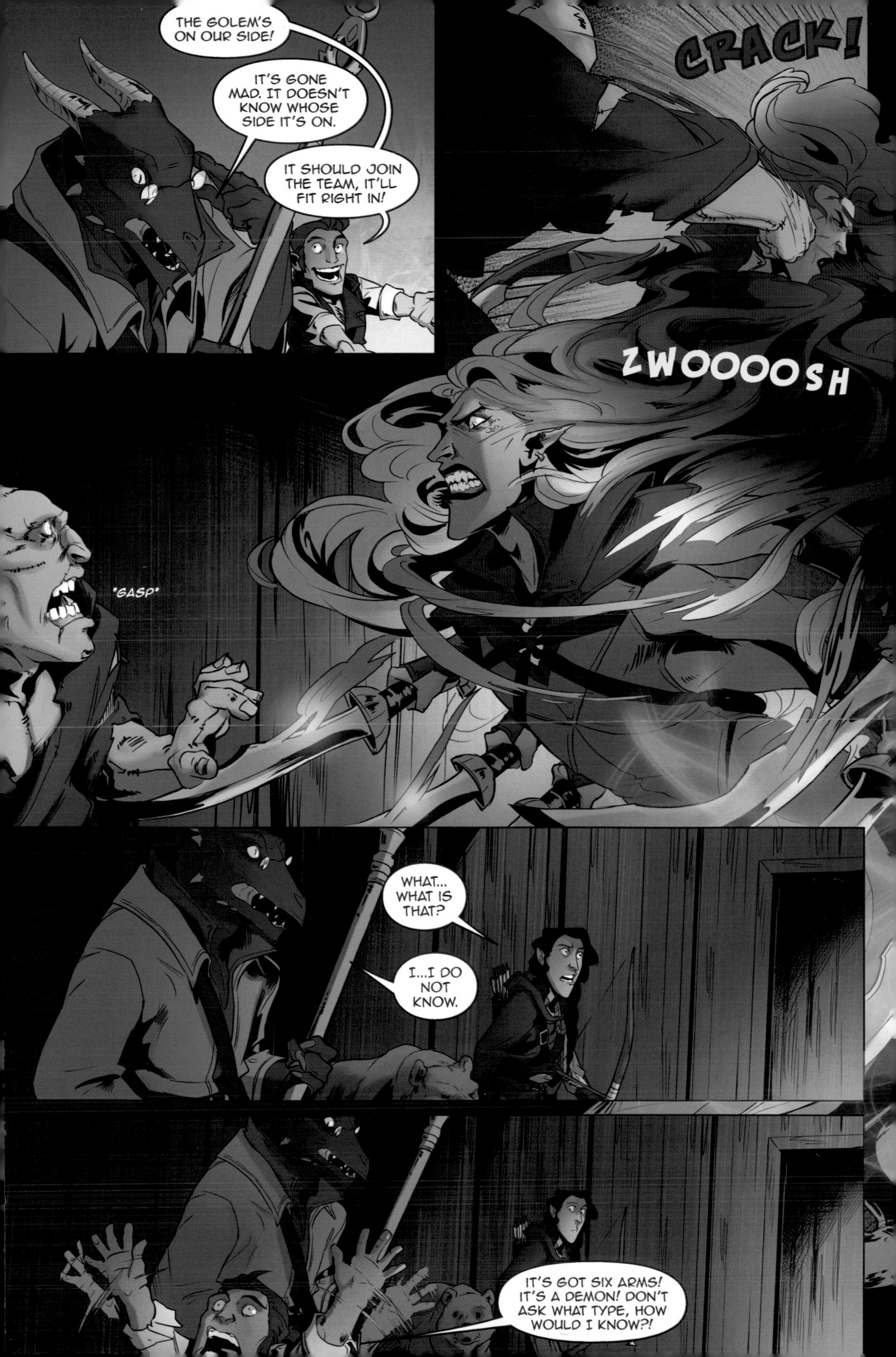
THE GOLEM'S ON OUR SIDE!
IT'S GONE MAD. IT DOESN'T KNOW WHOSE SIDE IT'S ON.
IT SHOULD JOIN THE TEAM, IT'LL FIT RIGHT IN!
CRACK!
ZWOOOOOSH
*GASP*
WHAT... WHAT IS THAT?
I...I DO NOT KNOW.
IT'S GOT SIX ARMS! IT'S A DEMON! DON'T ASK WHAT TYPE, HOW WOULD I KNOW?!

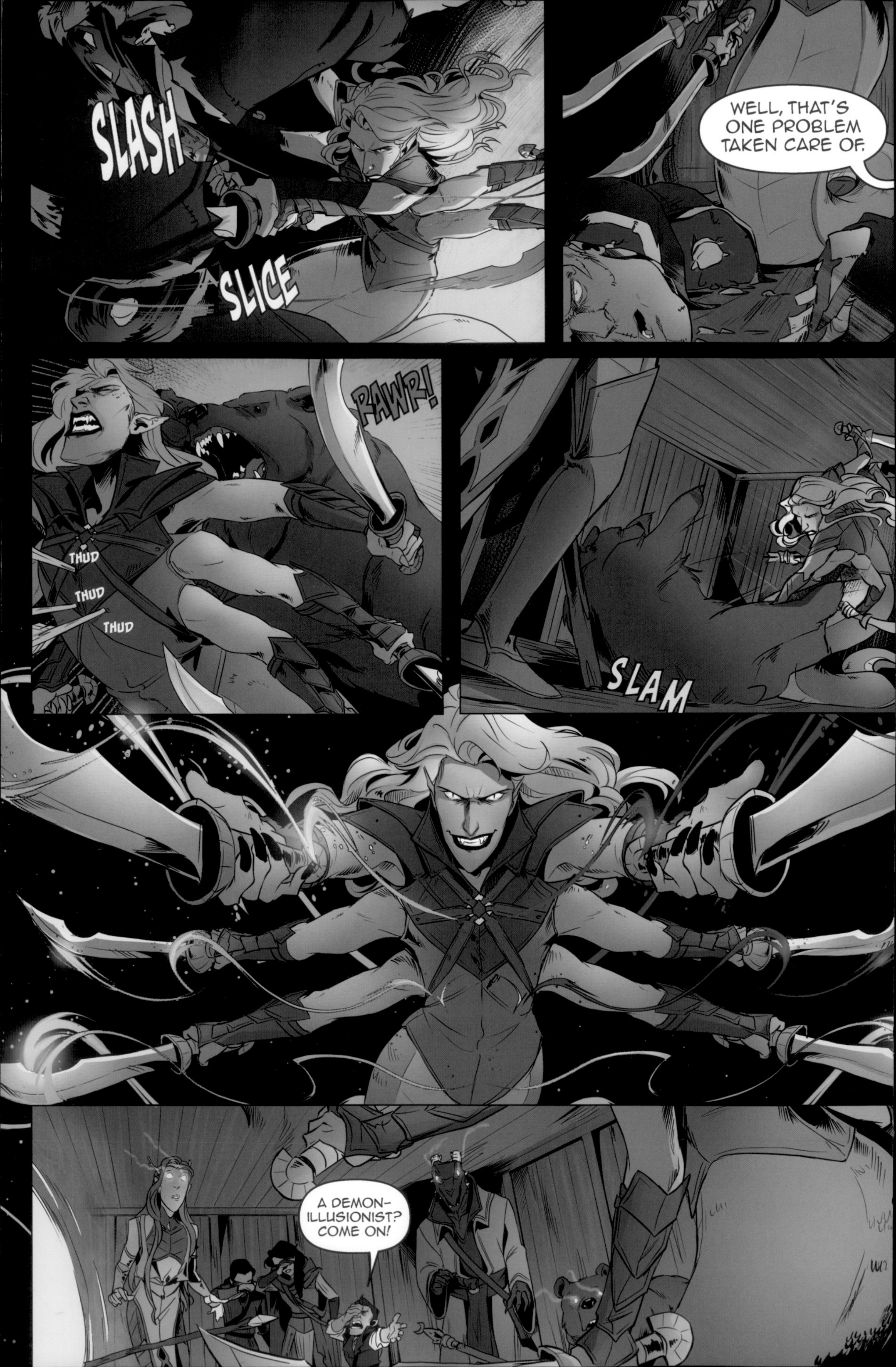
SLASH
SLICE
WELL, THAT'S ONE PROBLEM TAKEN CARE OF.
RAWR!
THUD
THUD
THUD
SLAM
A DEMON-ILLUSIONIST? COME ON!

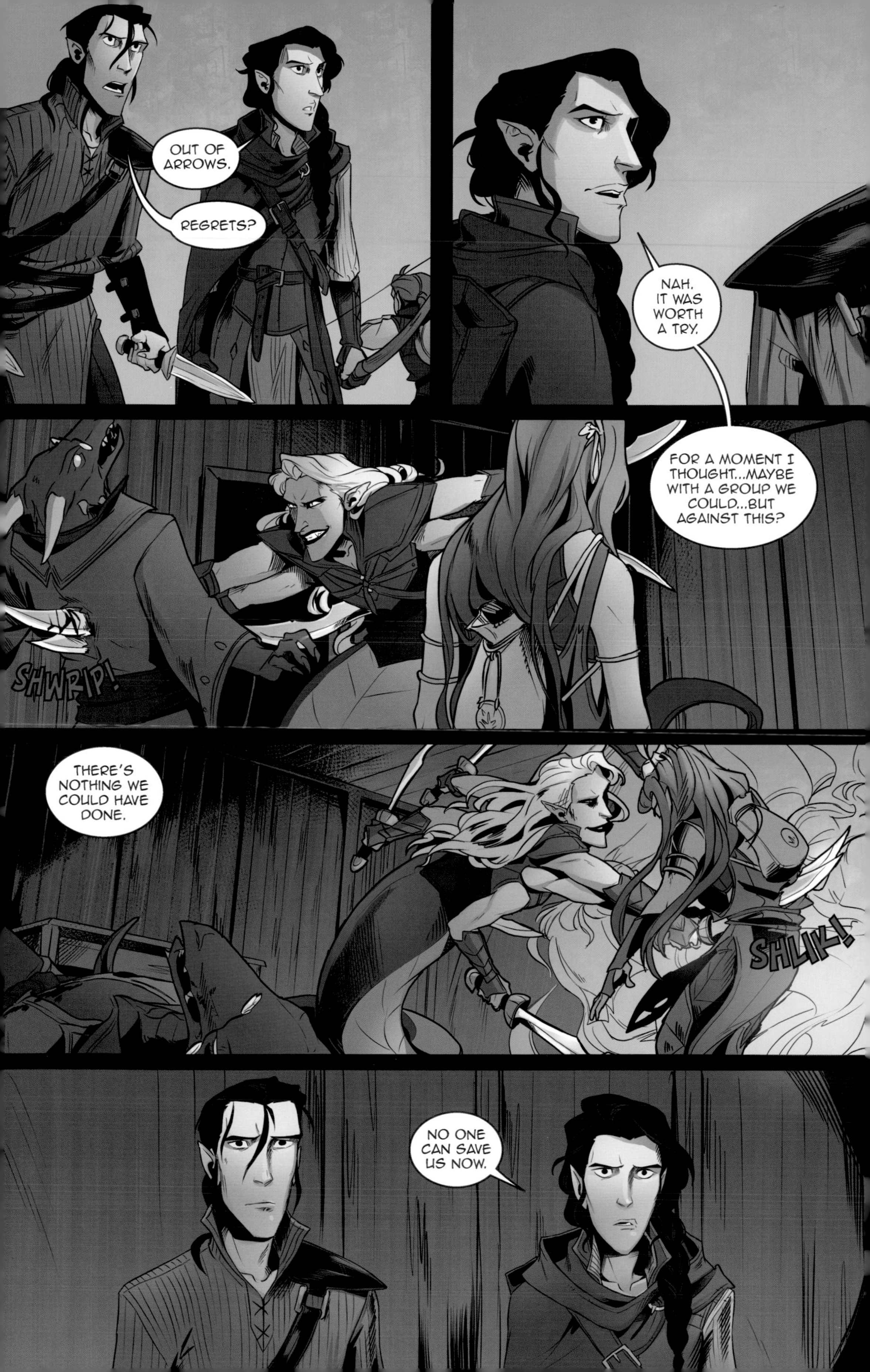
OUT OF ARROWS.
REGRETS?
NAH. IT WAS WORTH A TRY.
FOR A MOMENT I THOUGHT...MAYBE WITH A GROUP WE COULD...BUT AGAINST THIS?
SHWRIP!
THERE'S NOTHING WE COULD HAVE DONE.
SHLIK!
NO ONE CAN SAVE US NOW.

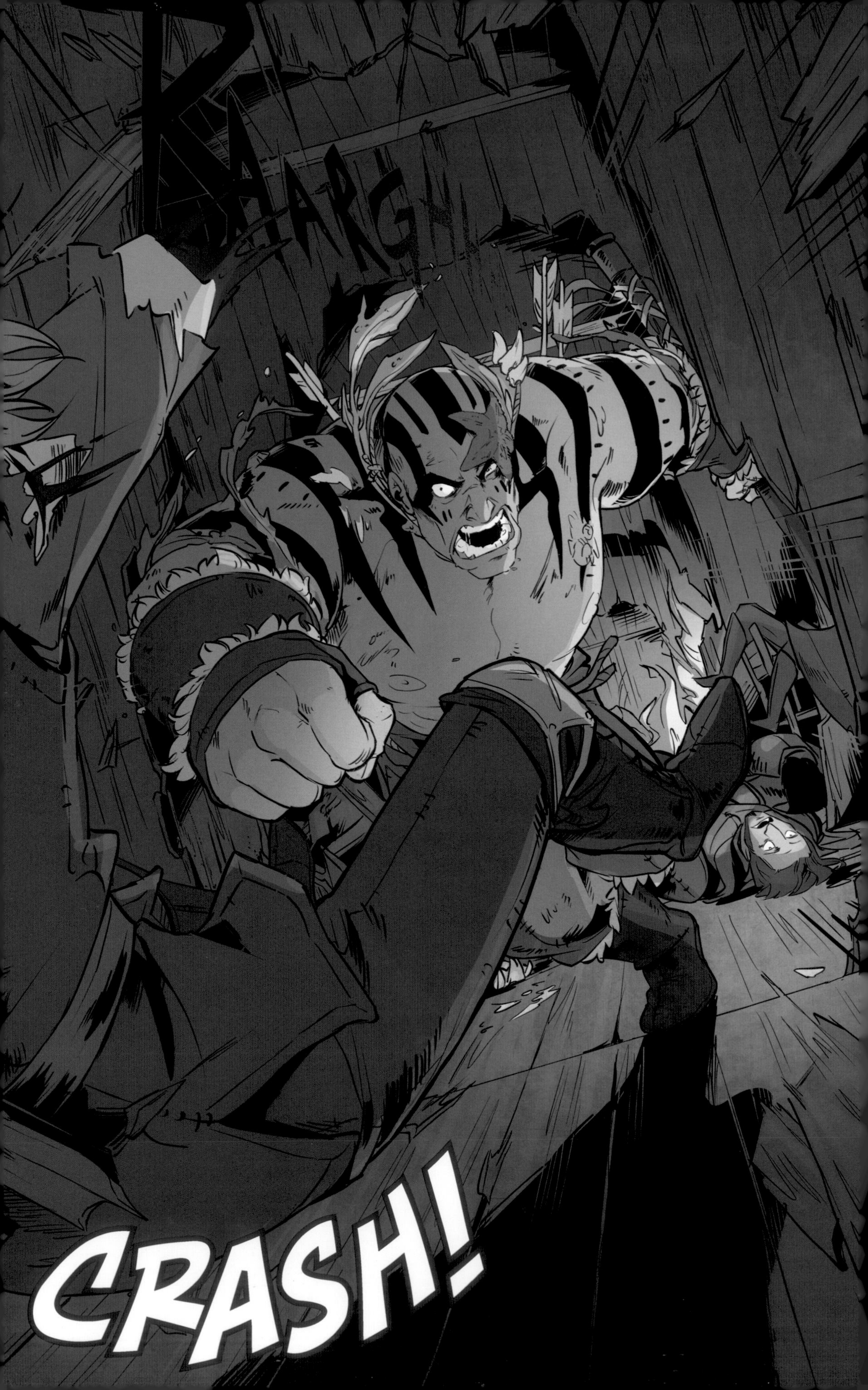
KRAARGH!
CRASH!

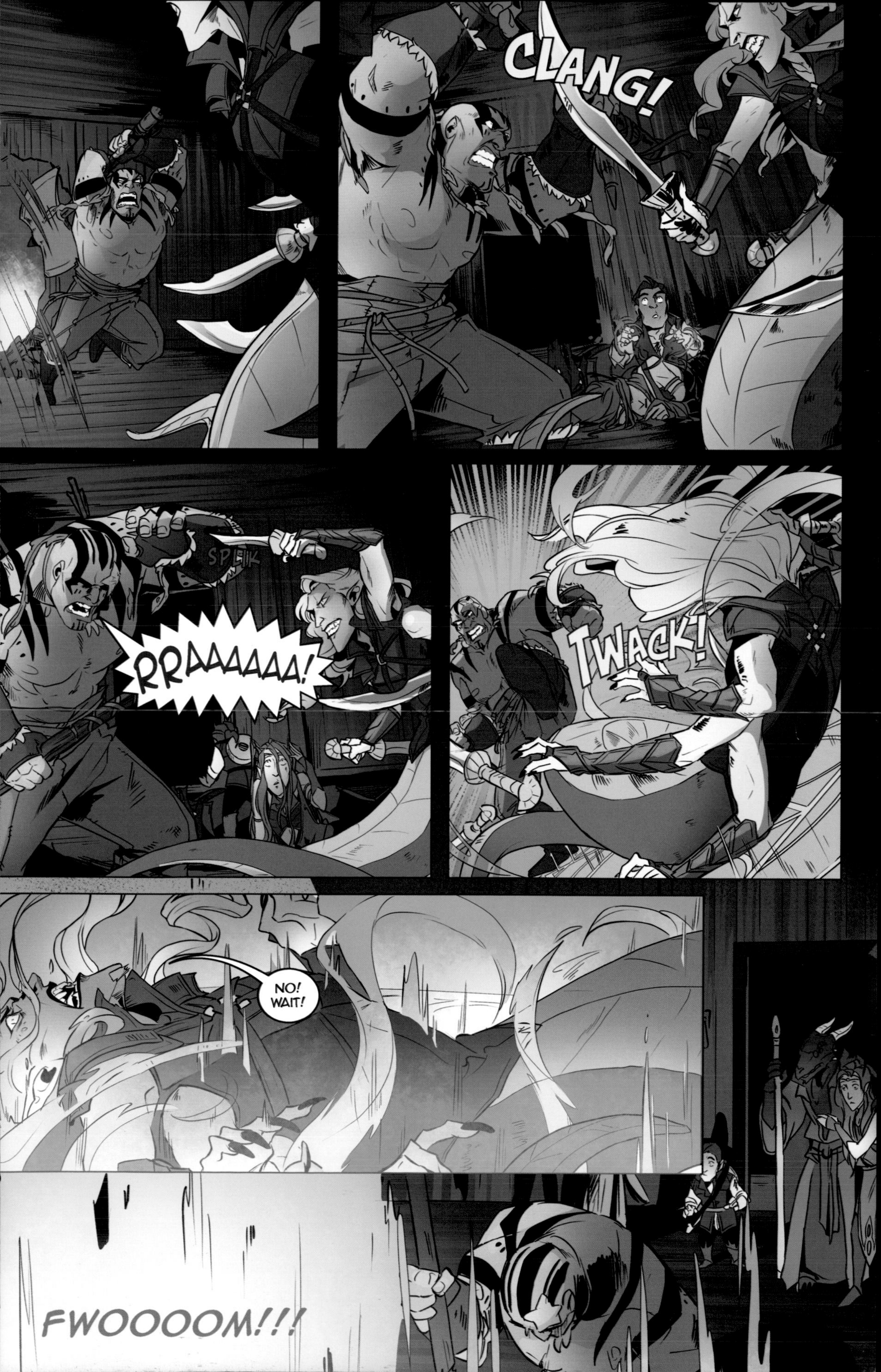
CLANG!
SPLiK
RRAAAAAA!
TWACK!
NO! WAIT!
FWOOOOM!!!

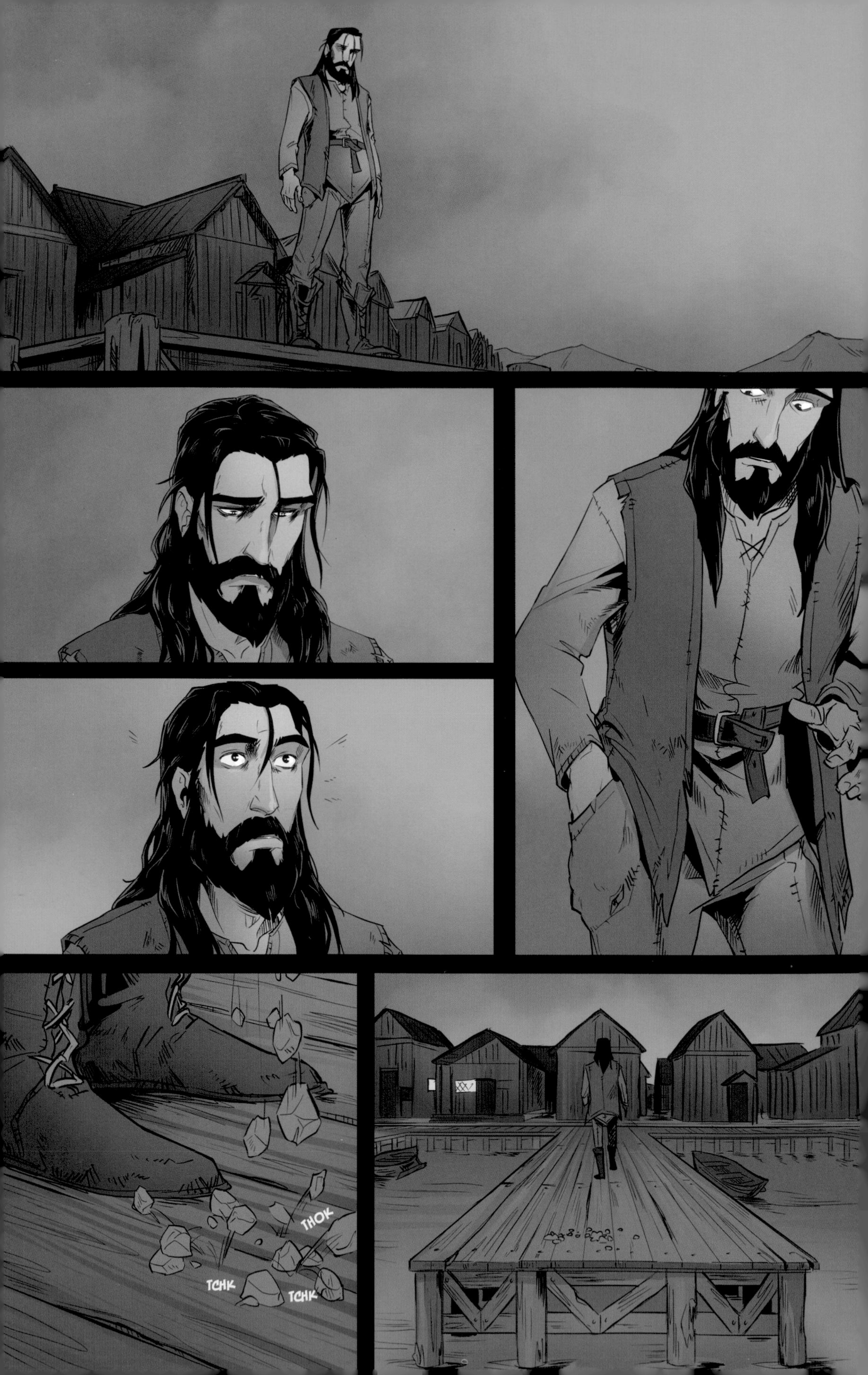
THOK
TCHK
TCHK

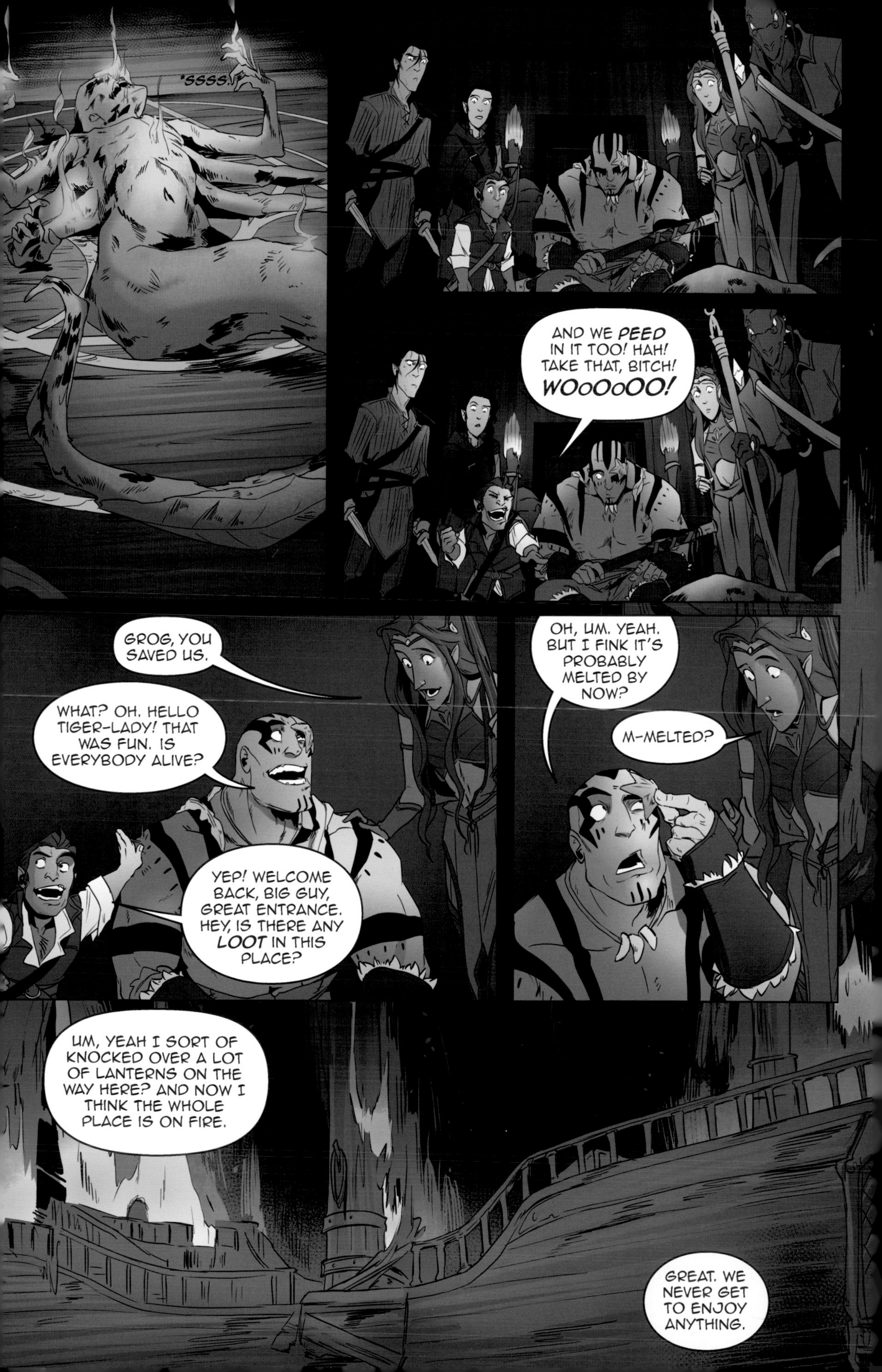
*SSSS*
AND WE PEED IN IT TOO! HAH! TAKE THAT, BITCH! WOoOoOO!
GROG, YOU SAVED US.
WHAT? OH. HELLO TIGER-LADY! THAT WAS FUN. IS EVERYBODY ALIVE?
YEP! WELCOME BACK, BIG GUY, GREAT ENTRANCE. HEY, IS THERE ANY LOOT IN THIS PLACE?
OH, UM. YEAH. BUT I FINK IT'S PROBABLY MELTED BY NOW?
M-MELTED?
UM, YEAH I SORT OF KNOCKED OVER A LOT OF LANTERNS ON THE WAY HERE? AND NOW I THINK THE WHOLE PLACE IS ON FIRE.
GREAT. WE NEVER GET TO ENJOY ANYTHING.

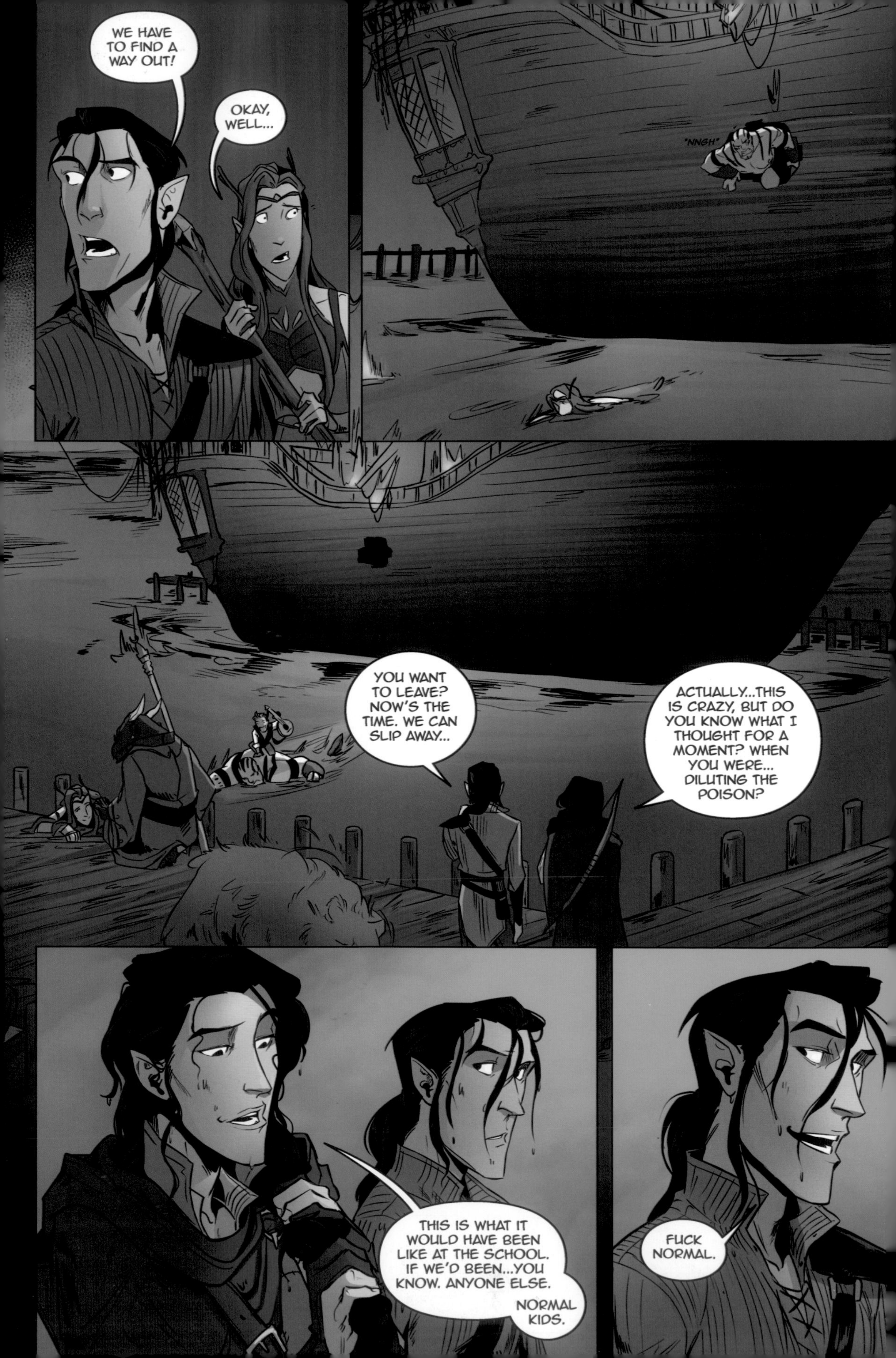

WE HAVE TO FIND A WAY OUT!
OKAY, WELL...
"NNGH"
YOU WANT TO LEAVE? NOW'S THE TIME. WE CAN SLIP AWAY...
ACTUALLY...THIS IS CRAZY, BUT DO YOU KNOW WHAT I THOUGHT FOR A MOMENT? WHEN YOU WERE... DILUTING THE POISON?
THIS IS WHAT IT WOULD HAVE BEEN LIKE AT THE SCHOOL. IF WE'D BEEN...YOU KNOW. ANYONE ELSE.
NORMAL KIDS.
FUCK NORMAL.

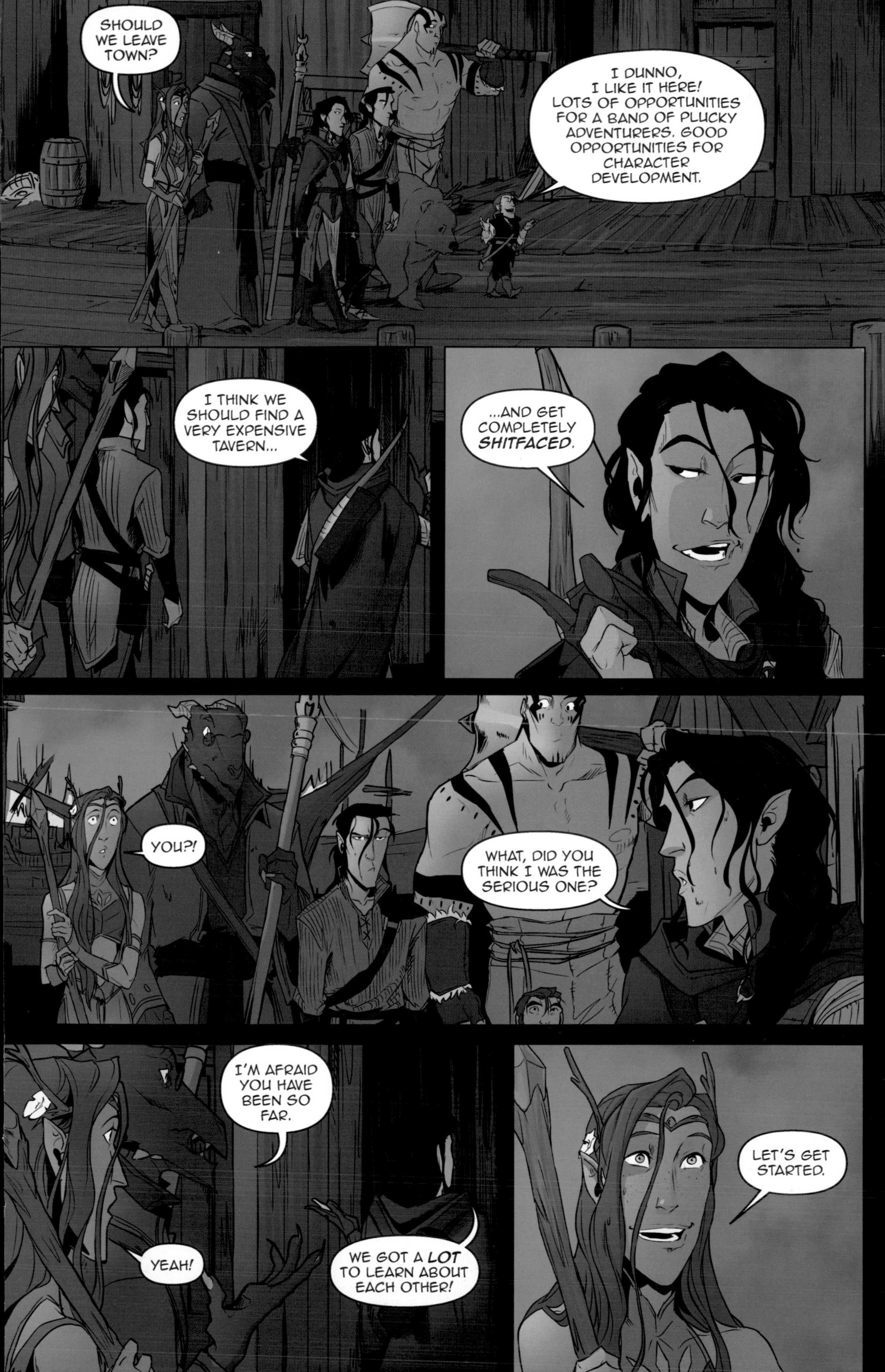
SHOULD WE LEAVE TOWN?
I DUNNO, I LIKE IT HERE! LOTS OF OPPORTUNITIES FOR A BAND OF PLUCKY ADVENTURERS. GOOD OPPORTUNITIES FOR CHARACTER DEVELOPMENT.
I THINK WE SHOULD FIND A VERY EXPENSIVE TAVERN...
...AND GET COMPLETELY SHITFACED.
YOU?!
WHAT, DID YOU THINK I WAS THE SERIOUS ONE?
I'M AFRAID YOU HAVE BEEN SO FAR.
YEAH!
WE GOT A LOT TO LEARN ABOUT EACH OTHER!
LET'S GET STARTED.

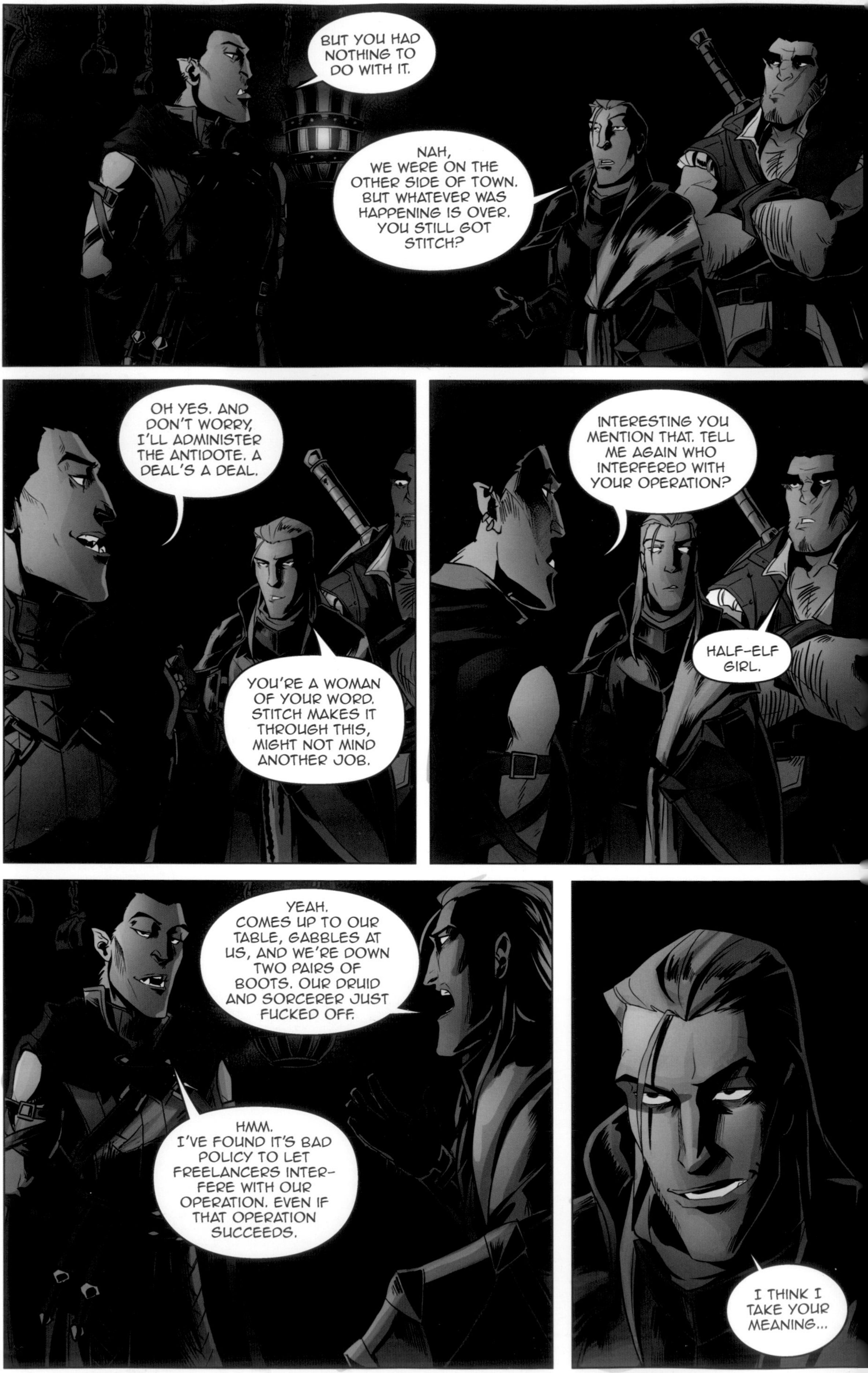
BUT YOU HAD NOTHING TO DO WITH IT.
NAH, WE WERE ON THE OTHER SIDE OF TOWN. BUT WHATEVER WAS HAPPENING IS OVER. YOU STILL GOT STITCH?
OH YES. AND DON'T WORRY, I'LL ADMINISTER THE ANTIDOTE. A DEAL'S A DEAL.
YOU'RE A WOMAN OF YOUR WORD. STITCH MAKES IT THROUGH THIS, MIGHT NOT MIND ANOTHER JOB.
INTERESTING YOU MENTION THAT. TELL ME AGAIN WHO INTERFERED WITH YOUR OPERATION?
HALF-ELF GIRL.
YEAH. COMES UP TO OUR TABLE, GABBLES AT US, AND WE'RE DOWN TWO PAIRS OF BOOTS. OUR DRUID AND SORCERER JUST FUCKED OFF.
HMM. I'VE FOUND IT'S BAD POLICY TO LET FREELANCERS INTERFERE WITH OUR OPERATION. EVEN IF THAT OPERATION SUCCEEDS.
I THINK I TAKE YOUR MEANING...

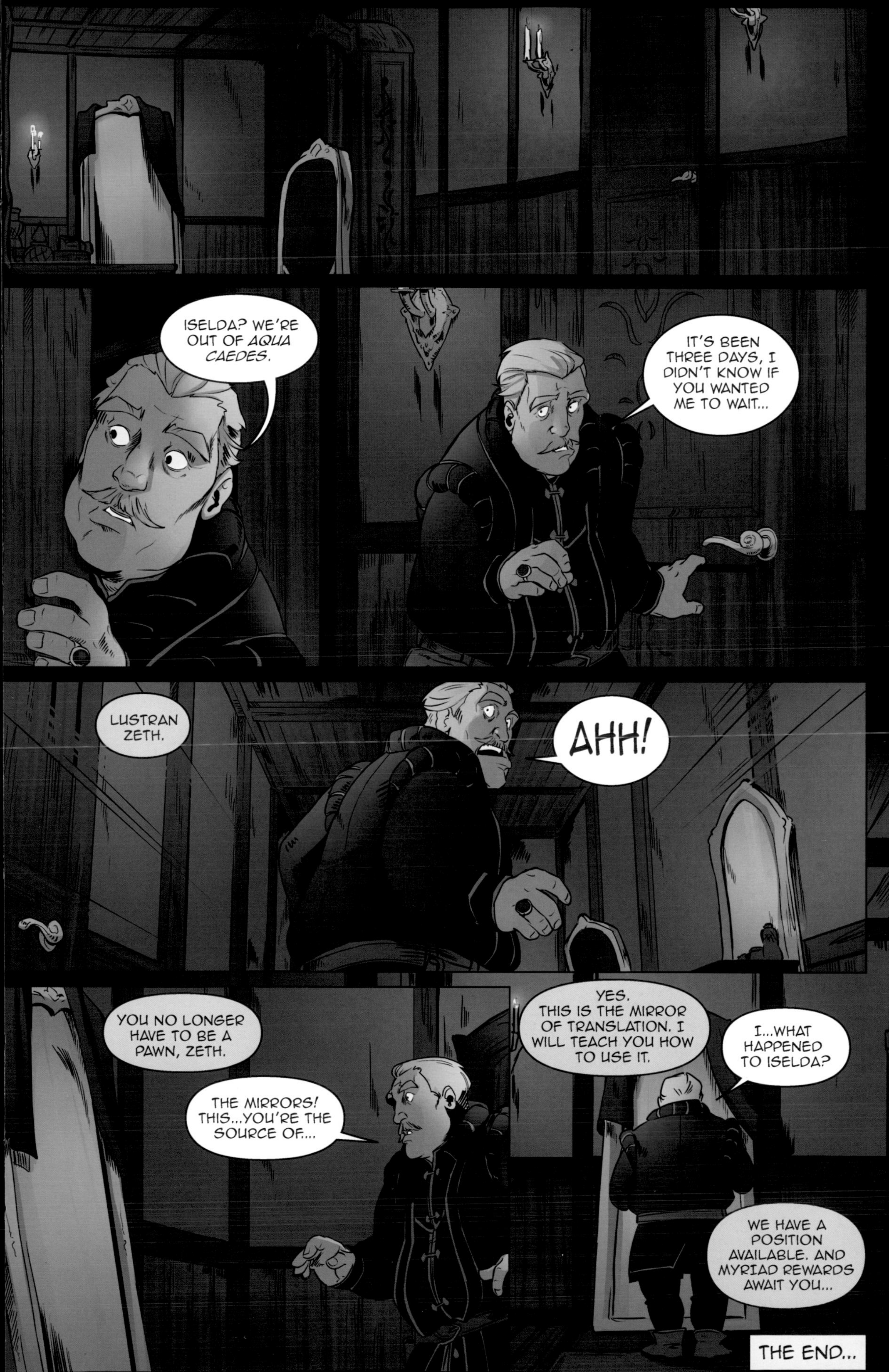
ISELDA? WE'RE OUT OF *AQUA CAEDES*.
IT'S BEEN THREE DAYS, I DIDN'T KNOW IF YOU WANTED ME TO WAIT...
LUSTRAN ZETH.
AHH!
YOU NO LONGER HAVE TO BE A PAWN, ZETH.
THE MIRRORS! THIS...YOU'RE THE SOURCE OF...
YES. THIS IS THE MIRROR OF TRANSLATION. I WILL TEACH YOU HOW TO USE IT.
I...WHAT HAPPENED TO ISELDA?
WE HAVE A POSITION AVAILABLE. AND MYRIAD REWARDS AWAIT YOU...
THE END...

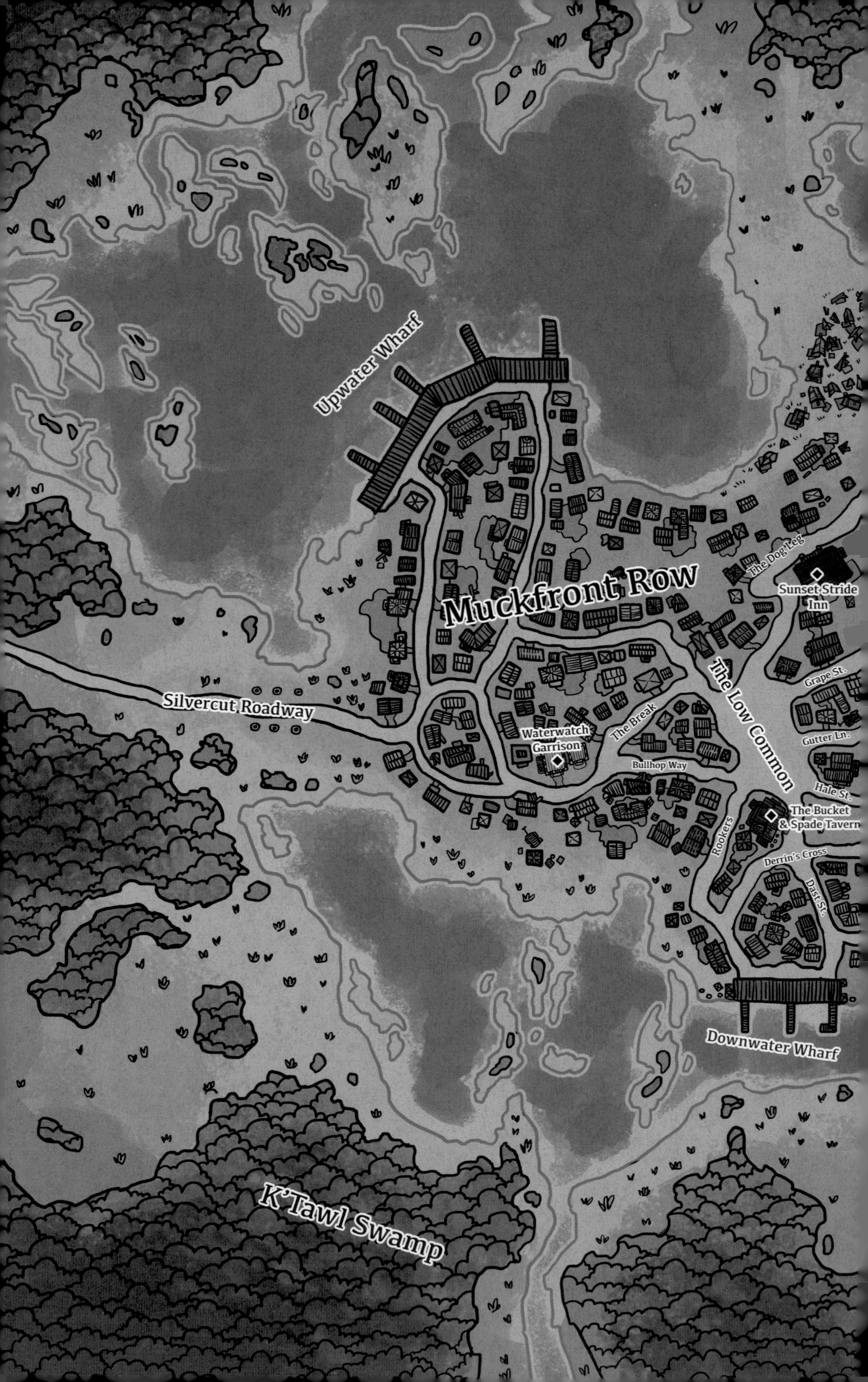
Upwater Wharf
Muckfront Row
The Dog Leg
Sunset Stride Inn
Silvercut Roadway
The Low Common
Grape St.
Gutter Ln.
Waterwatch Garrison
The Break
Bullhop Way
Hale St.
The Bucket & Spade Tavern
Rookers
Derrin's Cross
Dast St.
Downwater Wharf
K'Tawl Swamp

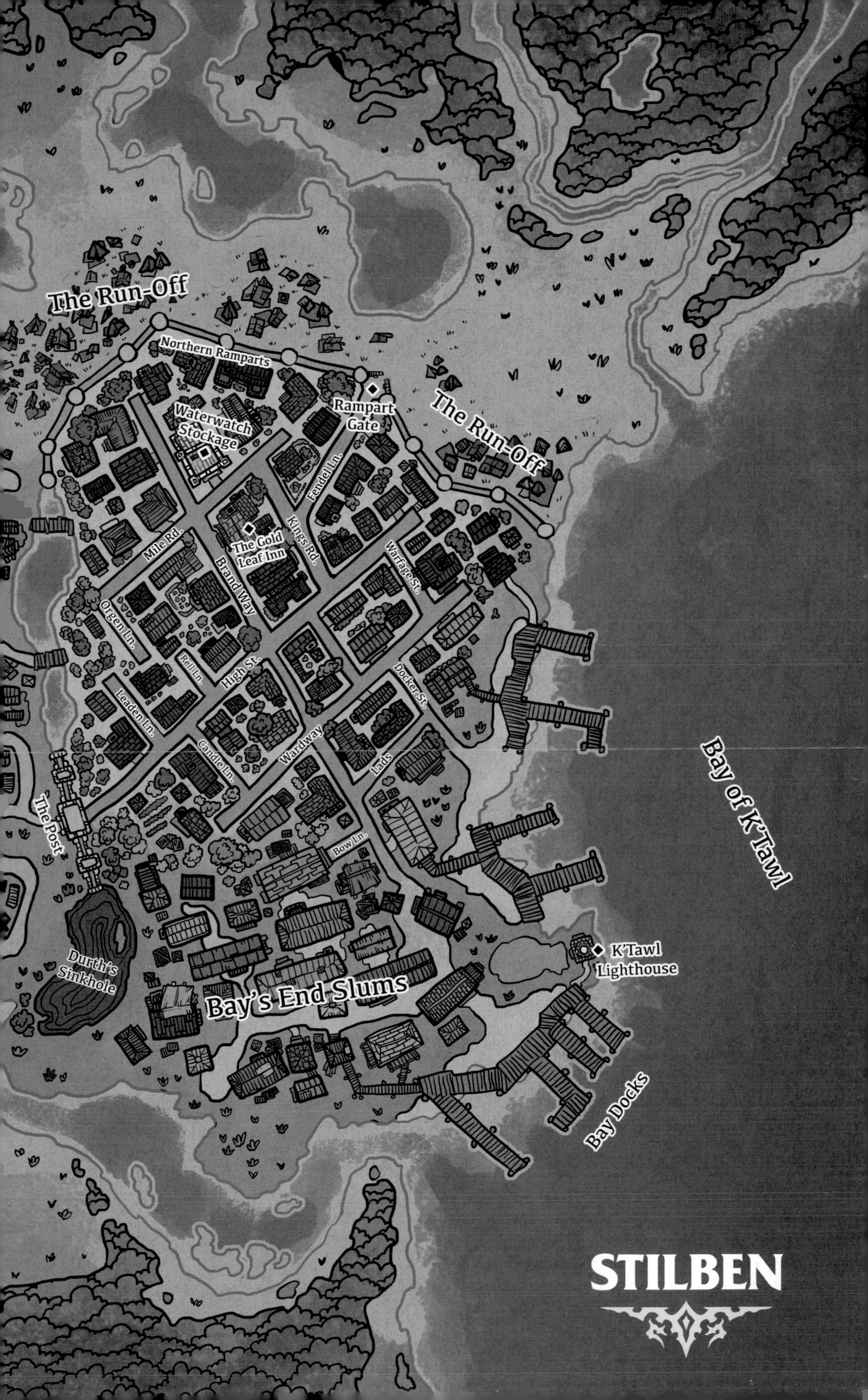
The Run-Off
Northern Ramparts
Waterwatch Stockage
Rampart Gate
The Run-Off
Fendel Ln.
Kings Rd.
The Gold Leaf Inn
Mile Rd.
Brand Way
Warfage St.
Orgen Ln.
Rell Ln.
High St.
Docker St.
Leaden Ln.
Candle Ln.
Wardway
Lads
Bow Ln.
The Post
Bay of K'Tawl
Durth's Sinkhole
K'Tawl Lighthouse
Bay's End Slums
Bay Docks
STILBEN

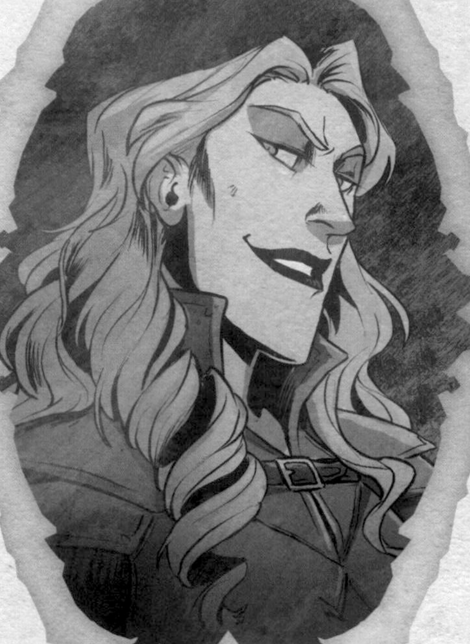

# Iselda

Summoned from her home plane before fulfilling her full allotment of souls, Iselda was trained by the Myriad in illusion. She has all the same ambitions of a demon of her stature, but she has no intention of returning to the Abyss. She finds climbing the ladder in the Myriad far easier than competing for souls. Even if the thing at the top of the ladder is worse than any demon of the Abyss.

## ISELDA, LESSER MARILITH

Medium Fiend (demon), Chaotic Evil

**ARMOR CLASS:** 16 (natural armor)

**HIT POINTS:** 63 (7d10+21)

**STRENGTH:** 16 (+3)

**DEXTERITY:** 15 (+2)

**CONSTITUTION:** 16 (+3)

**INTELLIGENCE:** 16 (+3)

**WISDOM:** 14 (+2)

**CHARISMA:** 17 (+3)

**SAVING THROWS:** Wis +5, Cha +6

**DAMAGE RESISTANCES:** cold, fire, lightning; bludgeoning, piercing, and slashing from nonmagical weapons

**DAMAGE IMMUNITIES:** poison

**CONDITION IMMUNITIES:** poisoned

**SENSES:** passive perception 13

**LANGUAGES:** Abyssal

**CHALLENGE 5 (1,800 XP)**

## TRAITS

**INNATE SPELLCASTING.** Iselda's innate spellcasting ability is Charisma (spell save DC 13). She can innately cast the following spells, requiring no material components:

**AT WILL:** disguise self, fear, hypnotic pattern

## ACTIONS

**MULTIATTACK.** Iselda makes six attacks with her longswords.

**LONGSWORD.** Melee Weapon Attack: +5 to hit, reach 5 ft., One target. Hit: 8 (1d8 + 3) slashing damage.

## REACTIONS

**PARRY.** Iselda adds 5 to her AC against one melee attack that would hit her. To do so, she must see her attacker and be wielding a melee weapon.

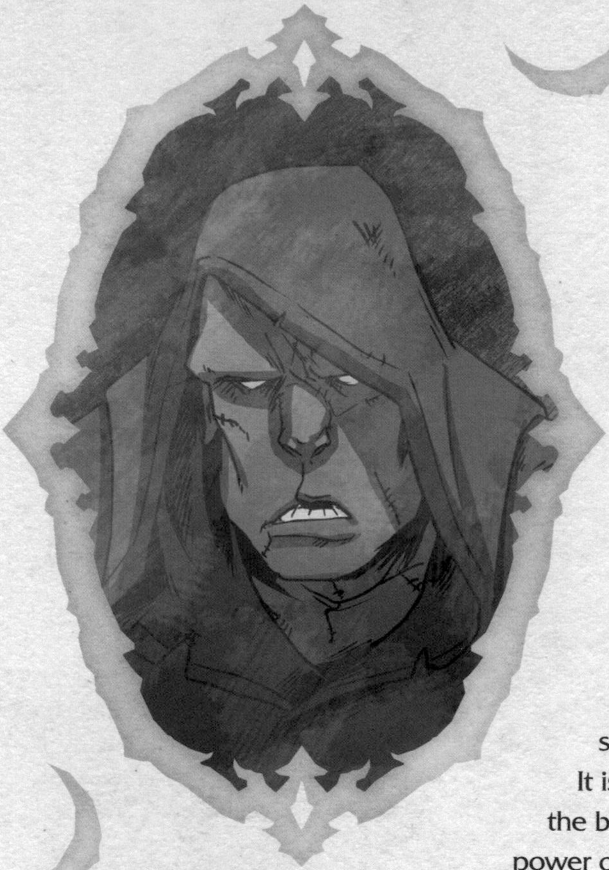

# The Servant, Flesh Golem (Minor)

While the servant obeys Iselda's commands, it's only because it was instructed to by its Master, Iselda's direct supervisor and owner of the Mirror of Translation. In times of great stress, the Servant seeks its master's aid. It is intensely loyal to its original master, the being that made it and granted it the power of speech.

## FLESH GOLEM (MINOR)

Medium construct, neutral

**ARMOR CLASS:** 9

**HIT POINTS:** 58 (6d8 + 18)

**SPEED:** 30 ft.

**STRENGTH:** 18 (+4)

**DEXTERITY:** 9 (-1)

**CONSTITUTION:** 16 (+3)

**INTELLIGENCE:** 6 (-2)

**WISDOM:** 10 (+0)

**CHARISMA:** 5 (-3)

**DAMAGE IMMUNITIES:** lightning, poison; bludgeoning, piercing, and slashing from nonmagical weapons that aren't adamantine.

**CONDITION IMMUNITIES:** charmed, exhaustion, frightened, paralyzed, petrified, poisoned

**SENSES:** darkvision 60 ft., passive Perception 10

**LANGUAGES:** Common, Abyssal

**CHALLENGE 3 (700 XP)**

# TRAITS

**BERSERK.** Whenever the golem starts its turn with 30 hit points or fewer, roll a d6. On a 5 or 6, the golem goes berserk. On each of its turns while berserk, the golem attacks the nearest creature it can see. If no creature is near enough to move to and attack, the golem attacks an object, with preference for an object smaller than itself. Once the golem goes berserk, it continues to do so until it is destroyed or regains all its hit points. The golem's creator, if within 60 feet of the berserk golem, can try to calm it by speaking firmly and persuasively. The golem must be able to hear its creator, who must take an action to make a DC 15 Charisma (Persuasion) check. If the check succeeds, the golem stops berserking. If it takes damage while still at 30 hit points or fewer, the golem might go berserk again.

**AVERSION TO FIRE.** If the golem takes fire damage, it has disadvantage on attack rolls and ability checks until the end of its next turn.

**IMMUTABLE FORM.** The golem is immune to any spell or effect that would alter its form.

**LIGHTNING ABSORPTION.** Whenever the golem is subjected to lightning damage, it takes no damage and instead regains a number of hit points equal to the lightning damage dealt.

**MAGIC RESISTANCE.** The golem has advantage on saving throws against spells and other magical effects.

**MAGIC WEAPONS.** The golem's weapon attacks are magical.

# ACTIONS

**MULTIATTACK.** The golem makes two slam attacks.

**SLAM.** Melee Weapon Attack: +5 to hit, reach 5 ft., one target. Hit: 13 (2d8 + 4) bludgeoning damage.

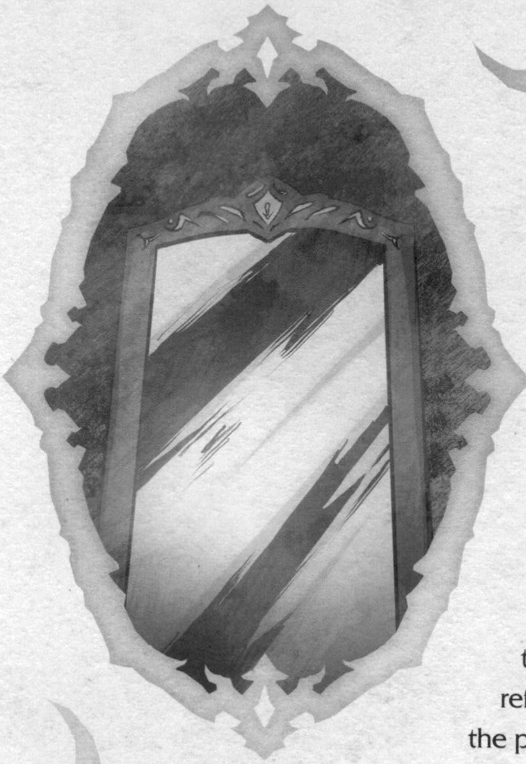

# The Mirror of Translation

**Wondrous Item, very rare**

Loaned to Iselda by the Master of the Myriad, this 5-foot-tall mirror in a gilded frame allows anyone attuned to it to teleport through it and out of any other reflective surface within five miles via the process of focusing.

**ATTUNING:** Attuning to the mirror requires the owner to sacrifice one hit die in a ritual that involves cutting yourself with a ceremonial glass-bladed dagger. Blood from the wound must drip onto the surface of the mirror, which absorbs the blood, leaving no trace. The owner then marks off one hit die, which cannot be restored by rest or healing until someone else attunes to the mirror.

**FOCUSING ON A SUBJECT:** The owner of the mirror can alter the image the mirror displays by focusing its surface on a subject, if that subject is within fifteen feet of a reflective surface, and within five miles of the *Mirror of Translation*. The owner must stand before the mirror, and perform a Charisma check. If the owner of the mirror has never met the subject, the DC is 25. If they have, the DC drops to 20. If they carry a personal possession of the subject of great emotional value, the DC is 15. If they have the blood of the subject, the DC is 10.

The mirror can focus on several reflective surfaces at once, if those surfaces are within 15 feet of each other and all focus on the same subject. While focused, the owner can use any of the available surfaces.

If successful, the mirror acts as a portal between its surface and those reflective surfaces it is focused on, translating the owner through the portal. The portal stays open for one minute, after which the connection closes.

CRITICAL ROLE

# VOX MACHINA™

ORIGINS

## SKETCHBOOK

**Notes by F. Avedon Arcadio Barrera II**

It's always a great pleasure to get to work with talented artists, and we were more than fortunate to find the perfect cover artists in our very own community of Critters.

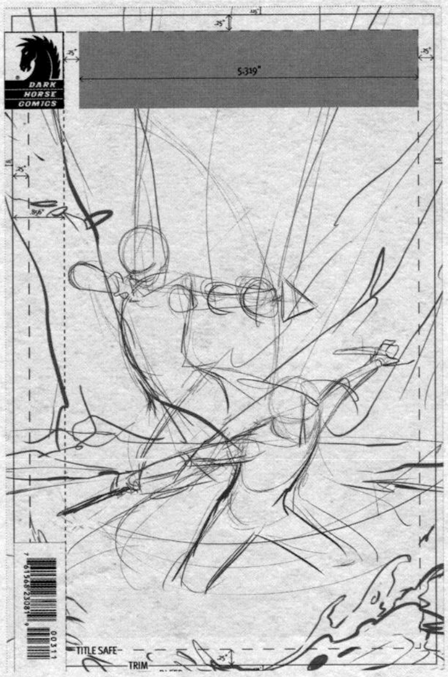
DARK HORSE COMICS
5.319"
TITLE SAFE
TRIM

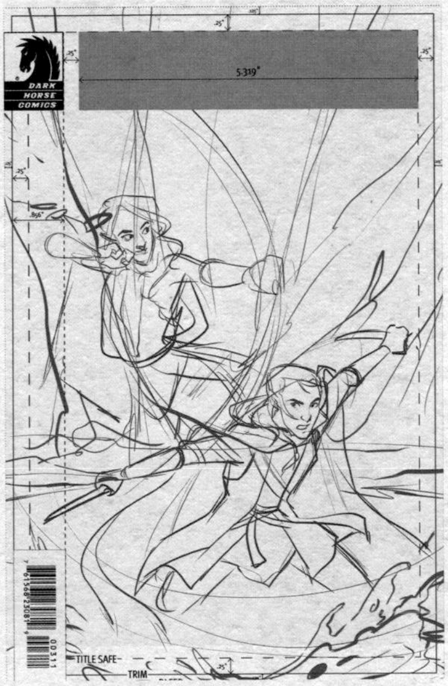
DARK HORSE COMICS
5.319"
TITLE SAFE
TRIM

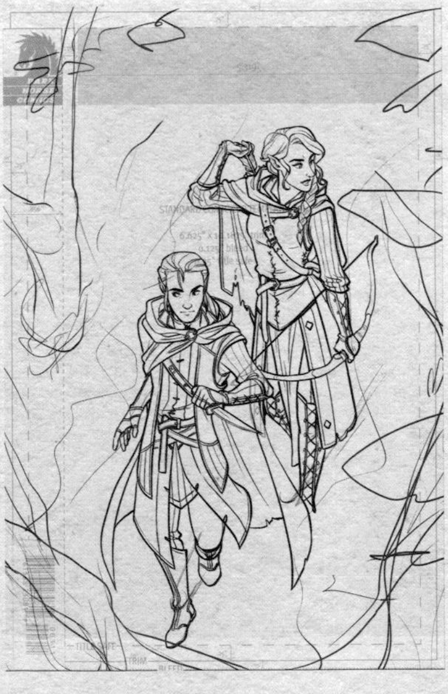

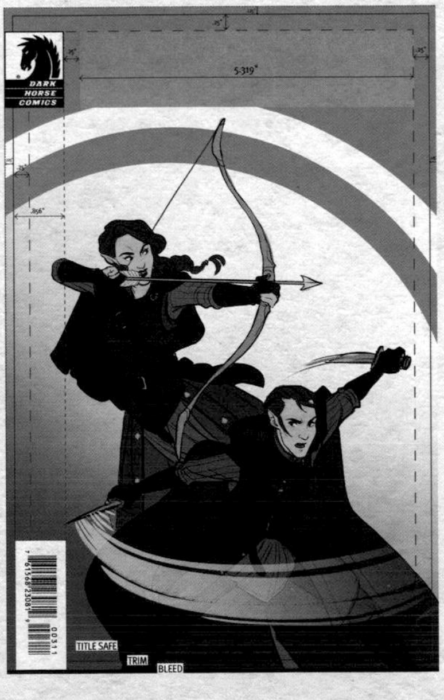
DARK HORSE COMICS
5.319"
TITLE SAFE
TRIM
BLEED

Since the story started with our favorite half-elf twins, Vex'ahlia and Vax'ildan, we had to determine how best to depict them. It was important that we conveyed their personalities through their expressions, so they went from being smiling (*bottom left*) to much more stern (*bottom right*).

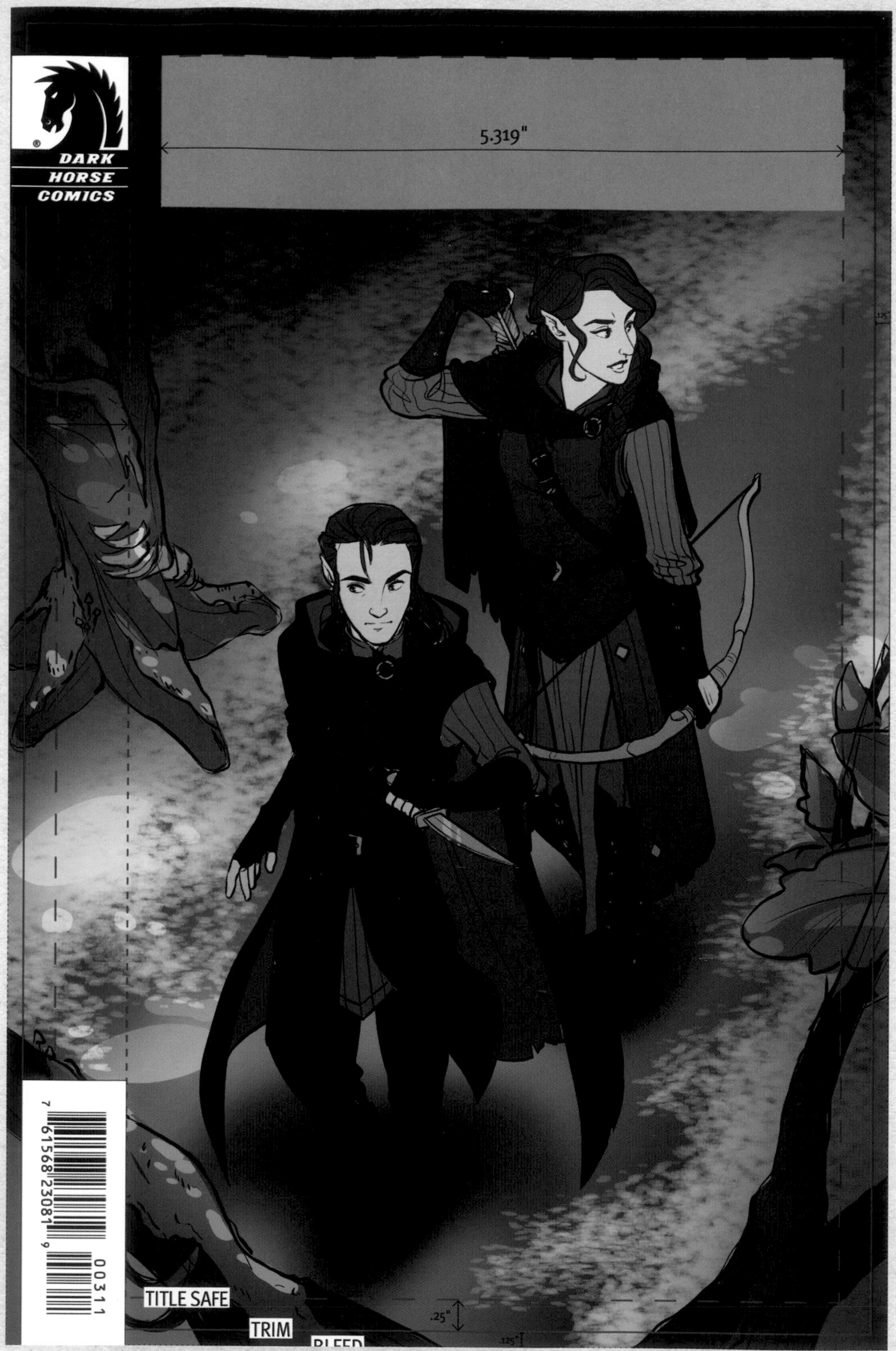
DARK
HORSE
COMICS
5.319"
TITLE SAFE
TRIM

While we ultimately decided to show the twins in an action pose, Deb also sketched out a subtler shot of them wading through the swamps, which also worked very well.

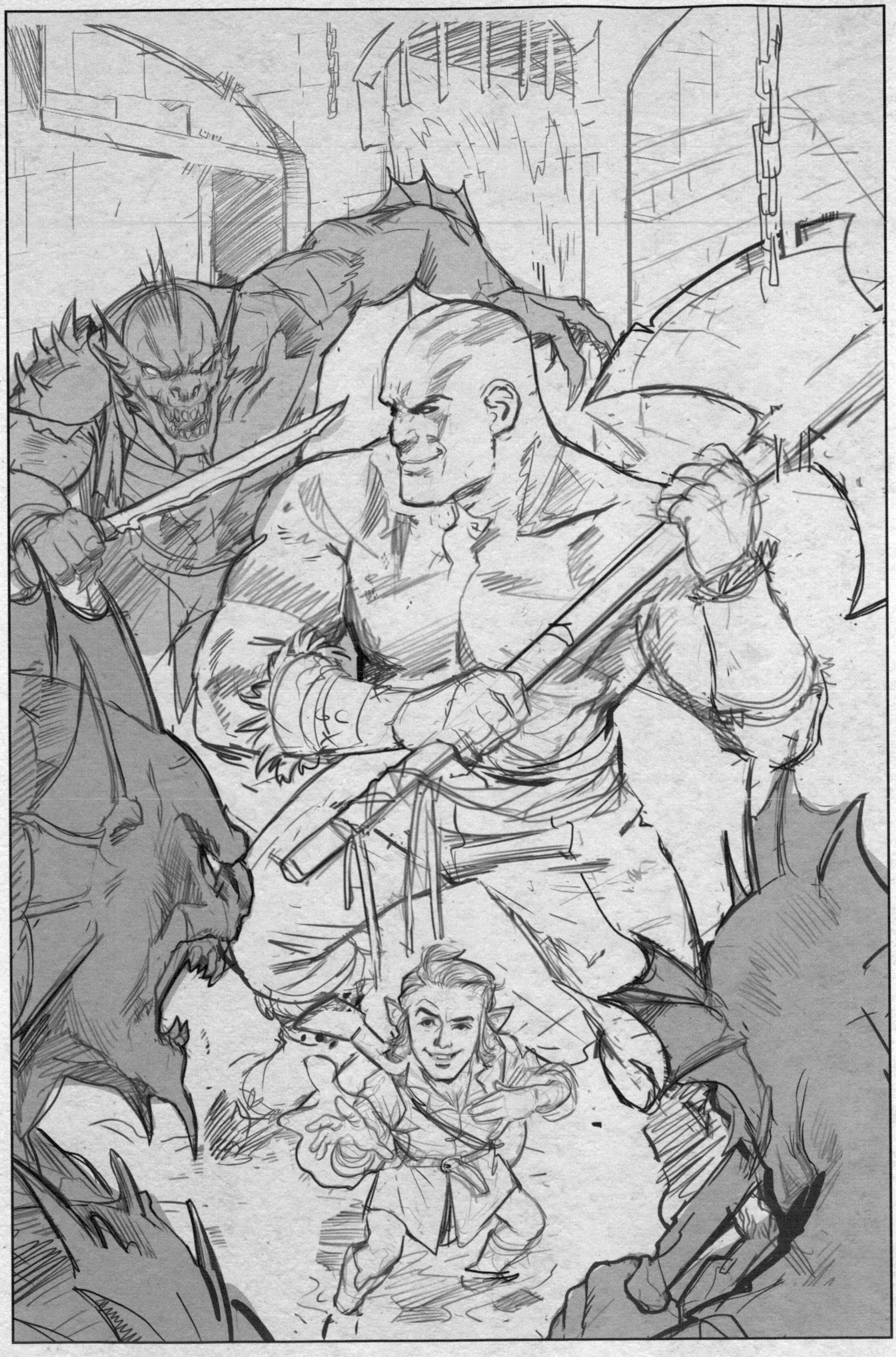

Nick Robles has a knack for evoking that classical fantasy style in his art and I wanted him to channel some *Conan the Barbarian* vibes, which he did perfectly. Juxtaposing a serious warrior with a goof-ball bard could have gone either way, but having someone who understood the characters and their personalities created the perfect distinction between the two.

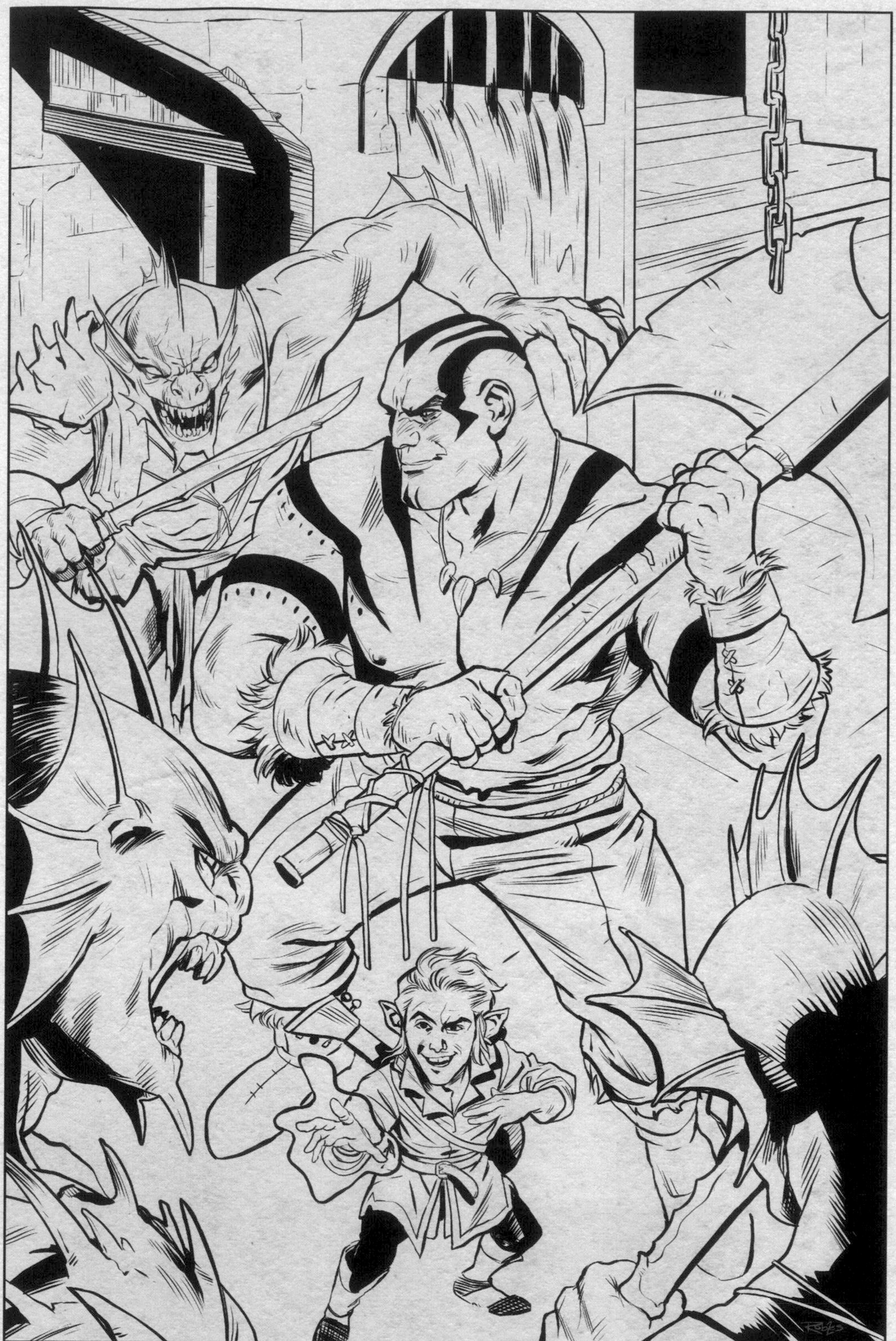

While we would have been happy with his initial designs, the additional tweaks he made for the final inks surpassed all expectations. And as is evident, his linework is fantastic.

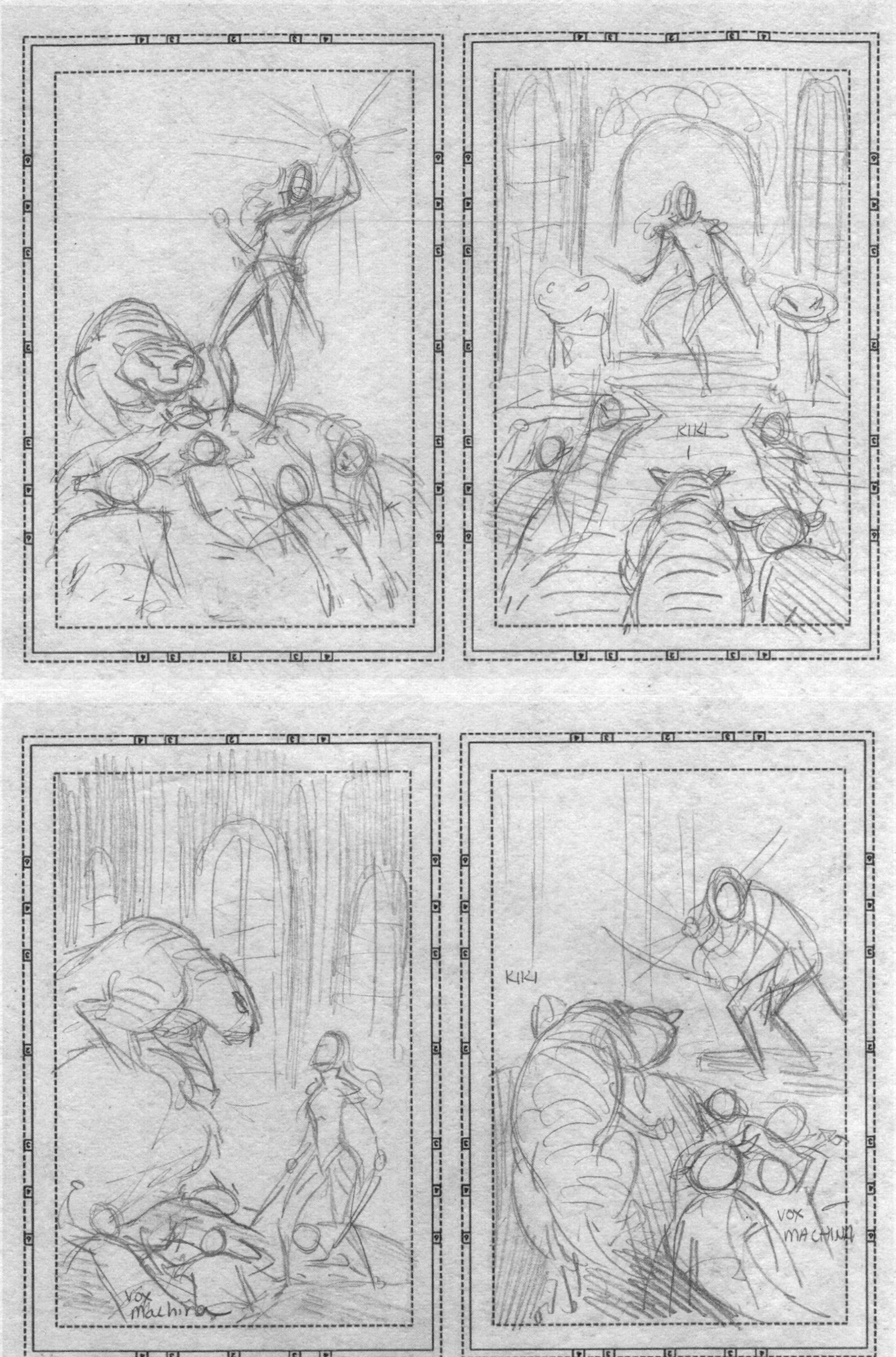
KIKI
Vox Machina
KIKI
VOX MACHINA

Tess Fowler, one of our more well-known Critter artists, was definitely up to the task of creating a dynamic scene featuring Iselda taking on Vox Machina. We went through a variety of comps before we settled on a showdown between Keytiger and Iselda. I think all of them were really great, but ultimately, we had to choose one.

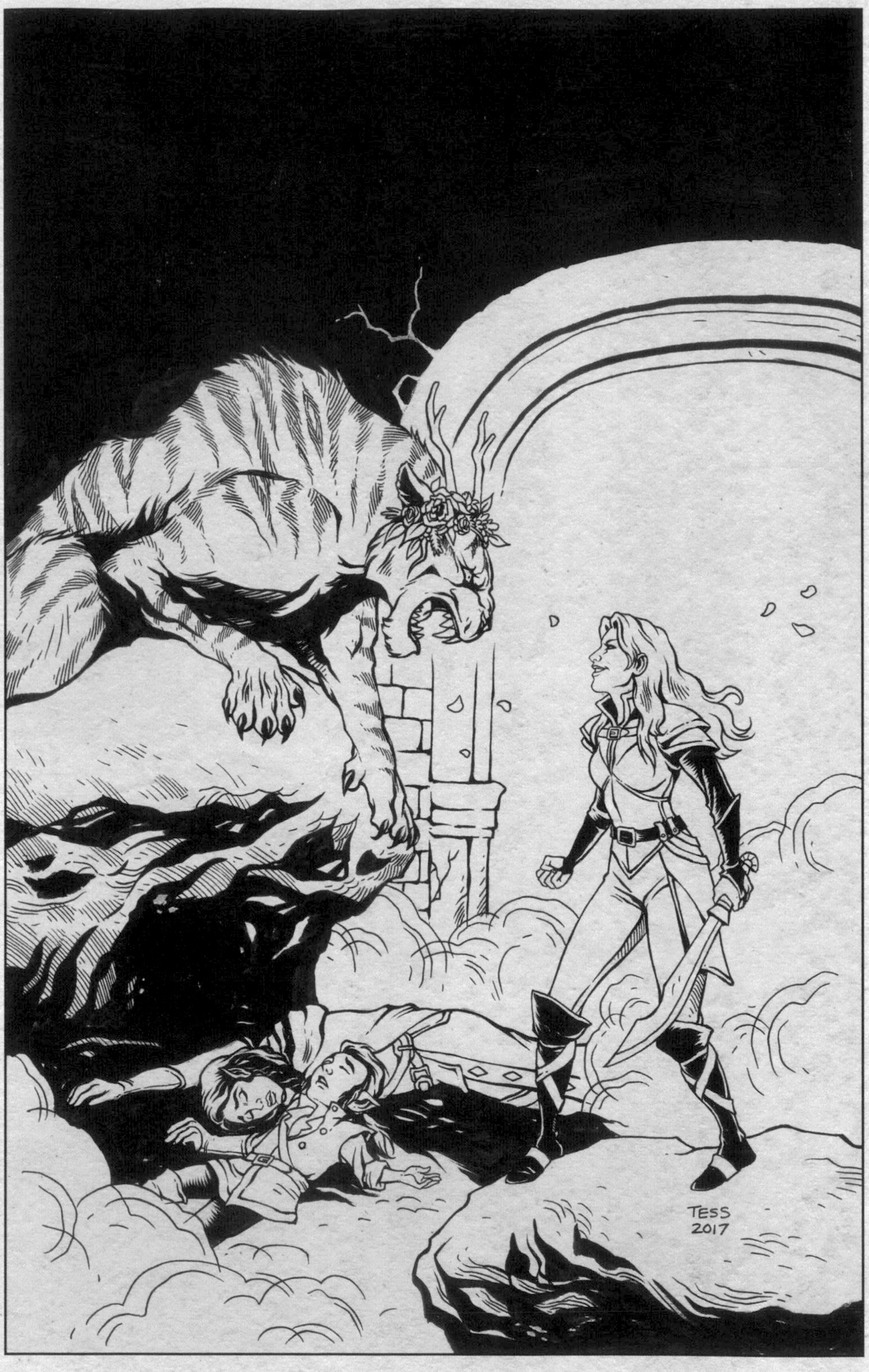
TESS
2017

Right before we had settled on the final concept, we had a version of the cover in which Keytiger was still wearing her tiara. For consistency's sake in the book, we opted not to use it, though it made for a funny image of a ferocious tiger with a pretty little floral crown, about to eviscerate the enemy.

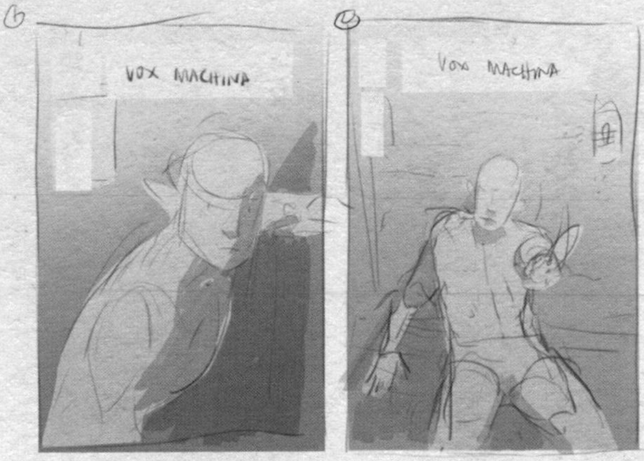
VOX MACHINA
VOX MACHINA

Selina Espiritu is a fantastic artist who understood immediately what we were asking for, which was basically Vax stranded, beaten, and cornered in the enemy's stronghold. Some of the early comps had him a bit more vulnerable or ready for a fight.

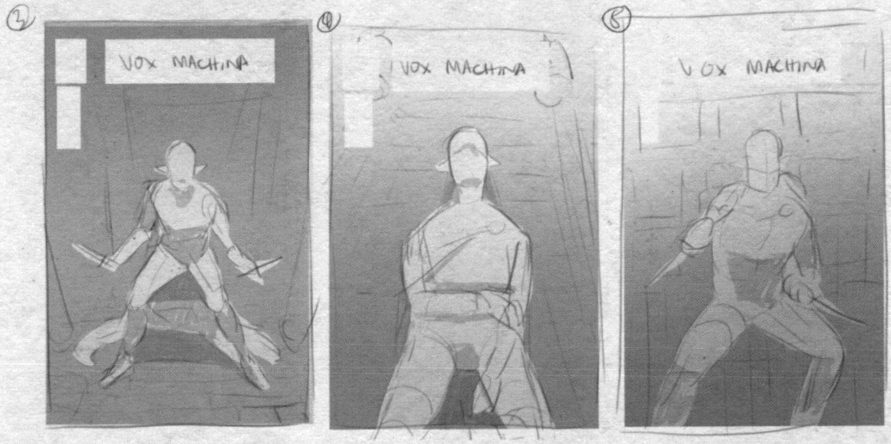
VOX MACHINA
VOX MACHINA
VOX MACHINA

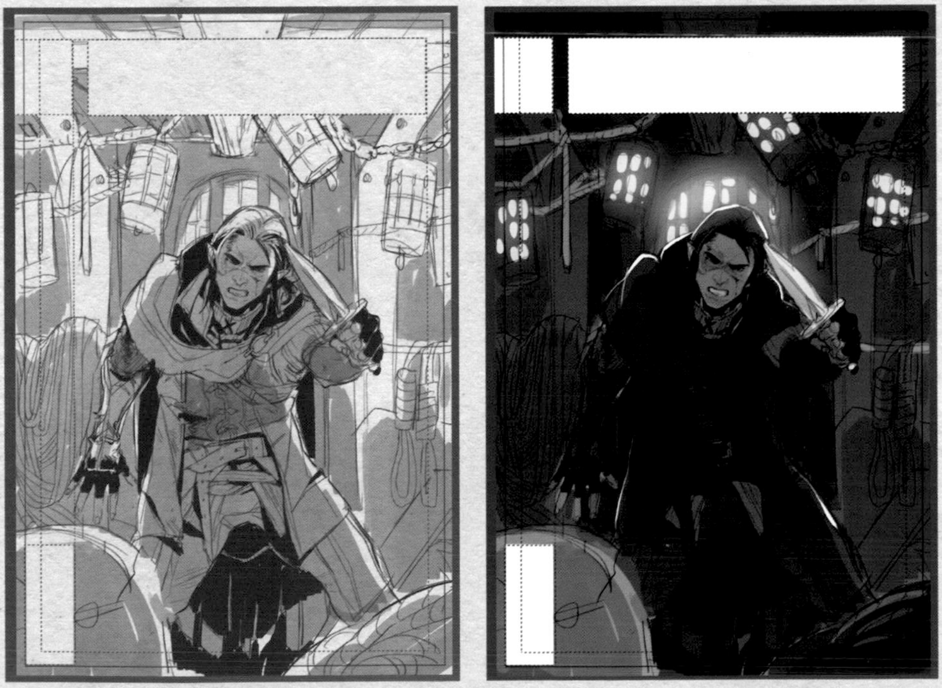

We found that perfect balance in the final version, where beaten, but not broken, Vax was not going to go down without a fight. The additional accoutrements in the background really sold it as being within the hold of a ship.

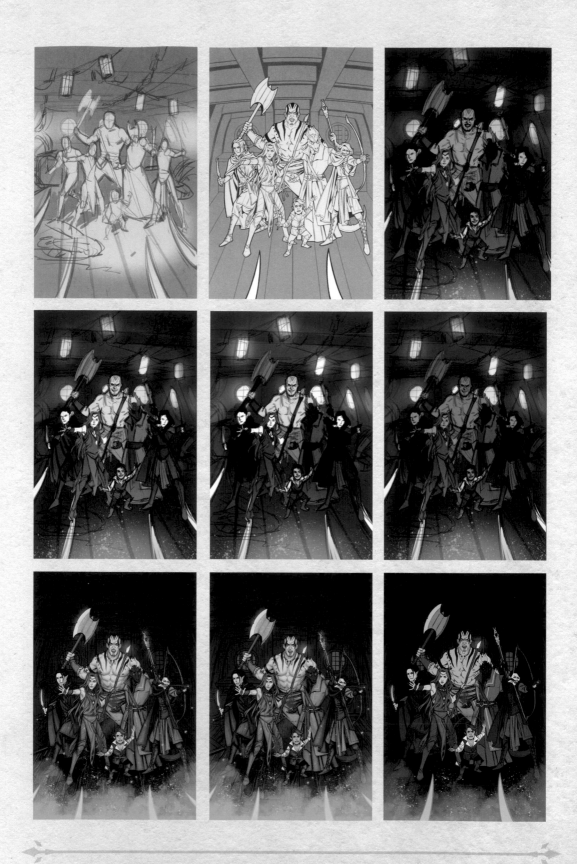

Many Critters will recognize Ariana Orner's name—she was the artist that introduced the second campaign's new cast. It made perfect sense to have her contribute cover art. We had the concept pretty dead-on from the beginning but went through a variety of color palettes to choose the right tone and emphasize how unique each character is.

Olivia's early take on the characters was a bit more subdued, which then transitioned to a more expressive style.

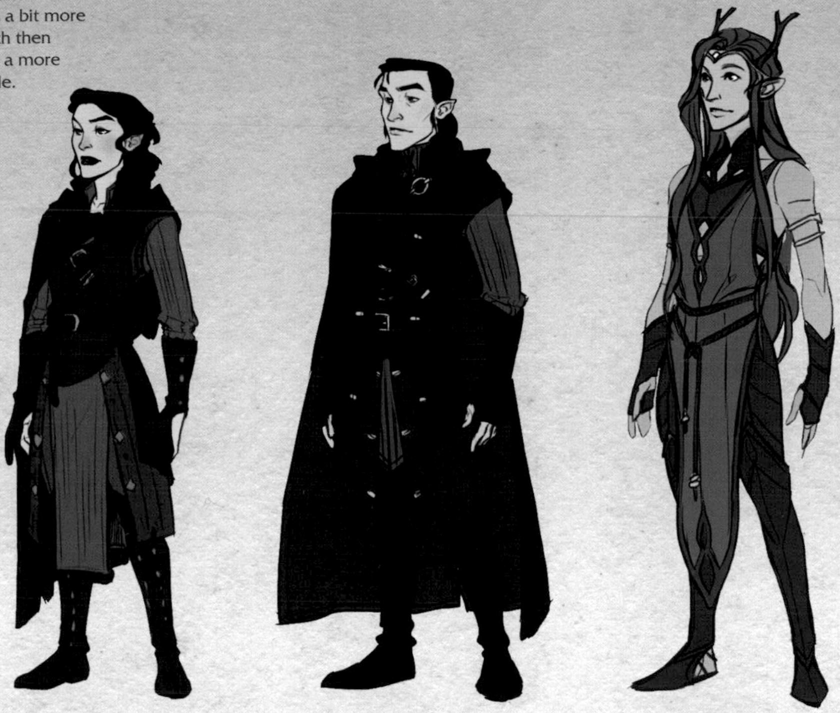

VEX'AHLIA

VAX'ILDAN

KEYLETH

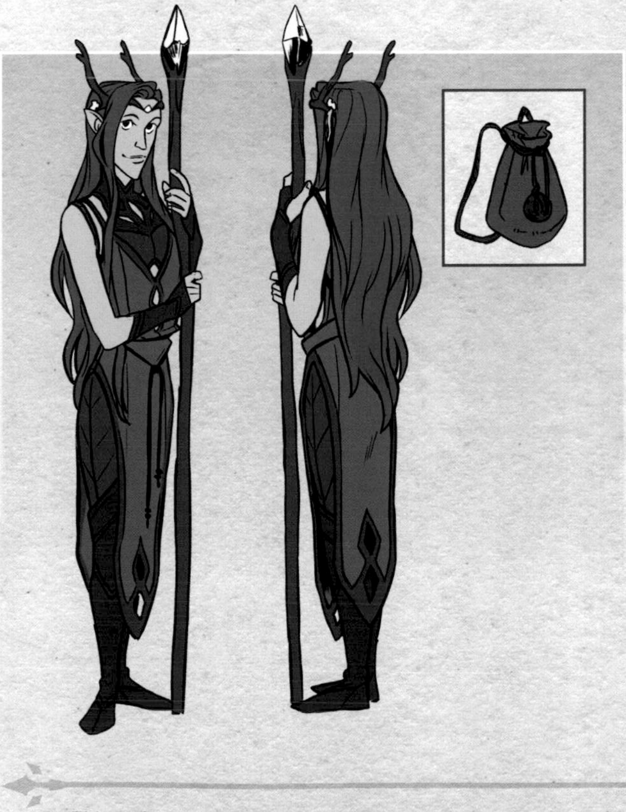

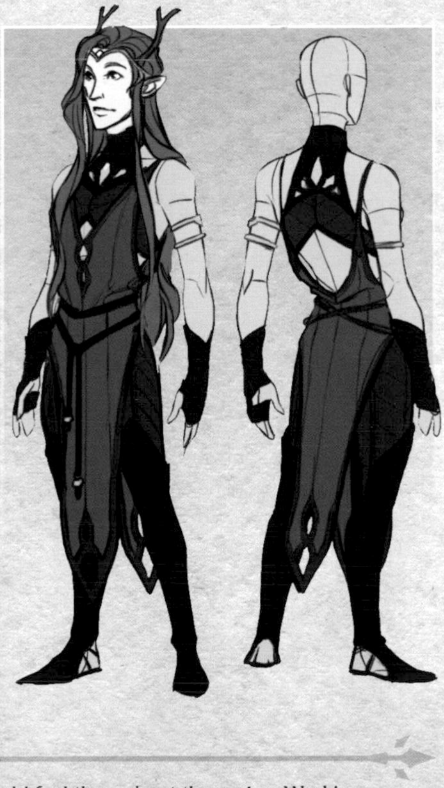

This style would help convey the emotions each character would feel throughout the series. Working closely with the cast and writers, we made sure that the outfits were something each character would actually wear. While we wanted to reference what fans had already seen from years of fan art, we also wanted to create something brand new.

It was interesting to see the characters in a way that almost felt like younger versions of each one, yet still carried a palette that would represent them now, at the end of their campaign. In a way, each character showed a degree of naiveté.

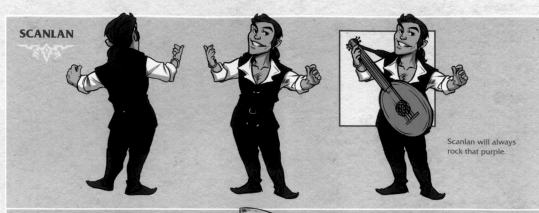

## SCANLAN

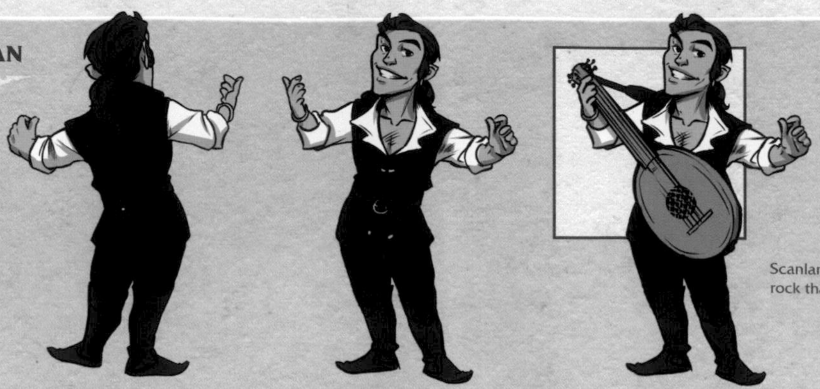

Scanlan will always rock that purple.

## GROG

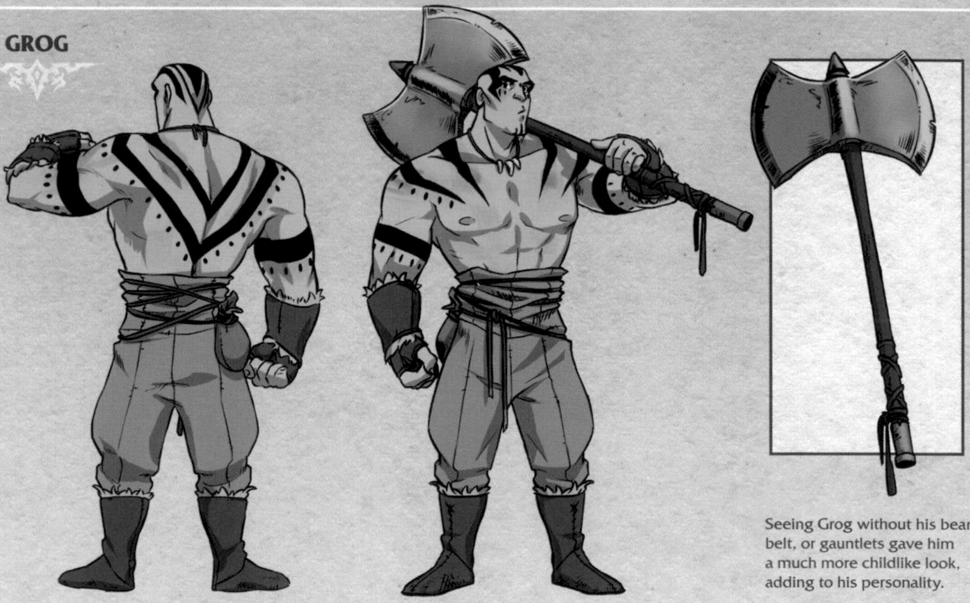

Seeing Grog without his beard, belt, or gauntlets gave him a much more childlike look, adding to his personality.

## TIBERIUS

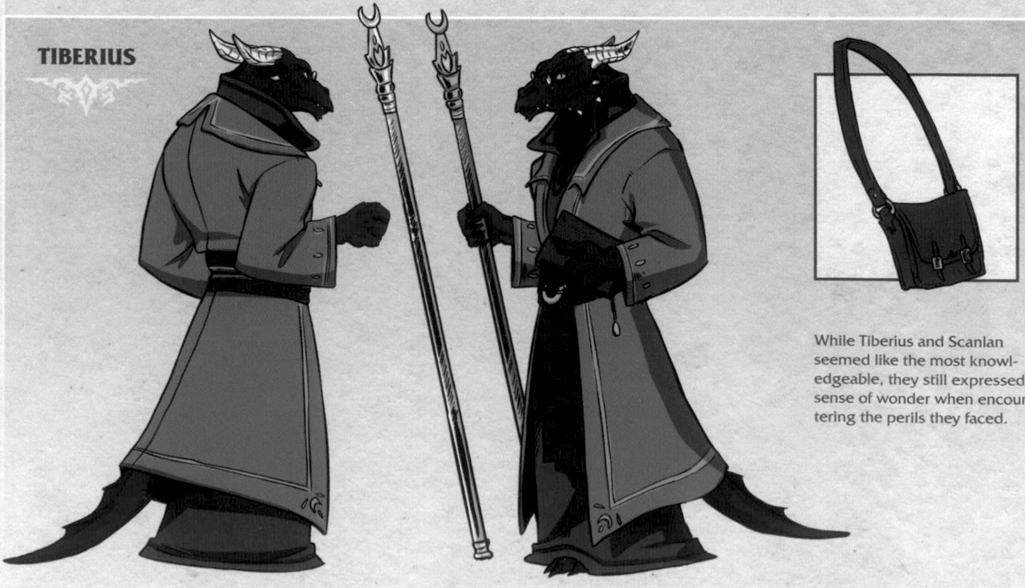

While Tiberius and Scanlan seemed like the most knowledgeable, they still expressed a sense of wonder when encountering the perils they faced.

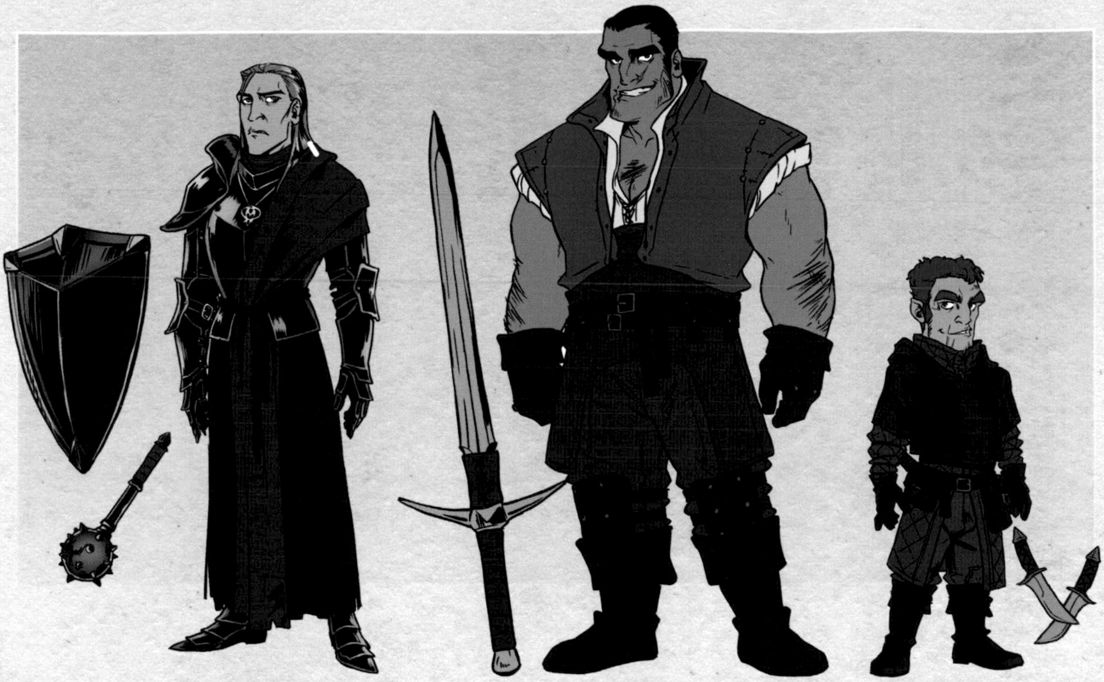

**HELICAX** **BRUL** **STITCH**

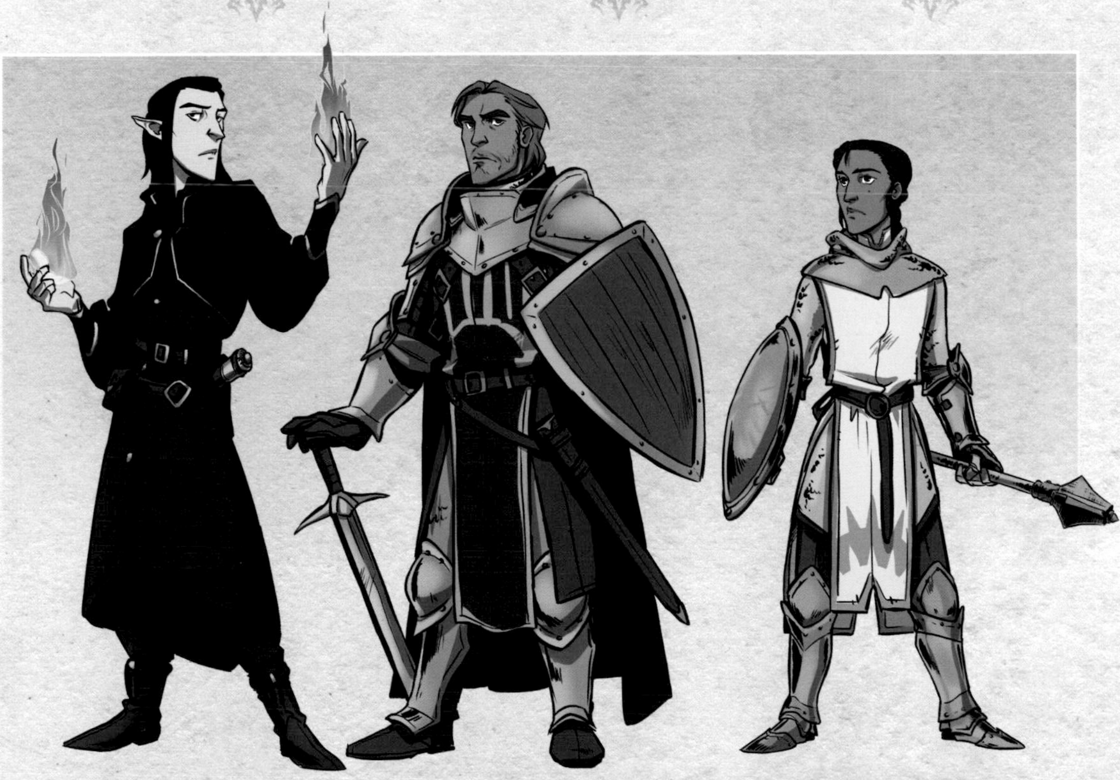

**VASH** **ARNICOR** **THURISTA**

With an origin series, designing brand new characters to interact with our party was a must. Olivia showed her artistic range wonderfully with the variety of new characters written into the story. Each one was unique, as they were, after all, different adventuring parties crossing paths, but you could see them having their own adventures out in the world.

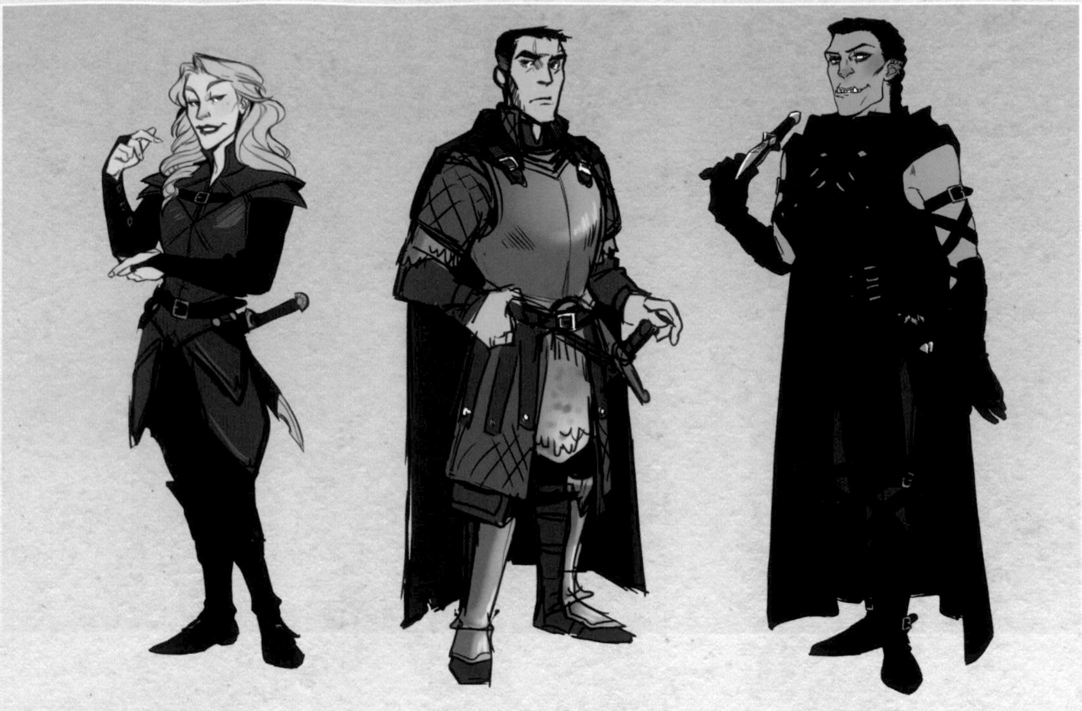

**ISELDA** **THE WATCHMAN** **SPIRELING HARROCK**

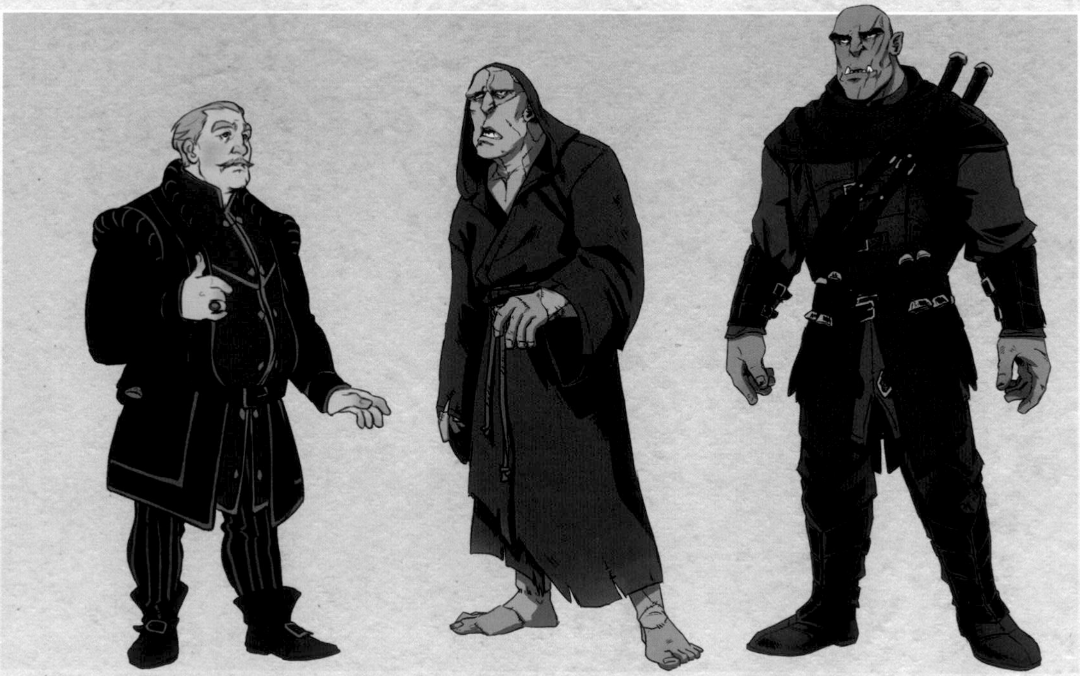

**THE ALCHEMIST** **GOLEM** **ORC**

The enemies had to be just as interesting as our heroes, and even more fearsome. We also had to make it obvious that the Four from Foramere weren't the nicest group to be hanging around with. When it came time to reveal Iselda as a demonic Marilith, Olivia notes, "I just made a cooler version of Iselda."

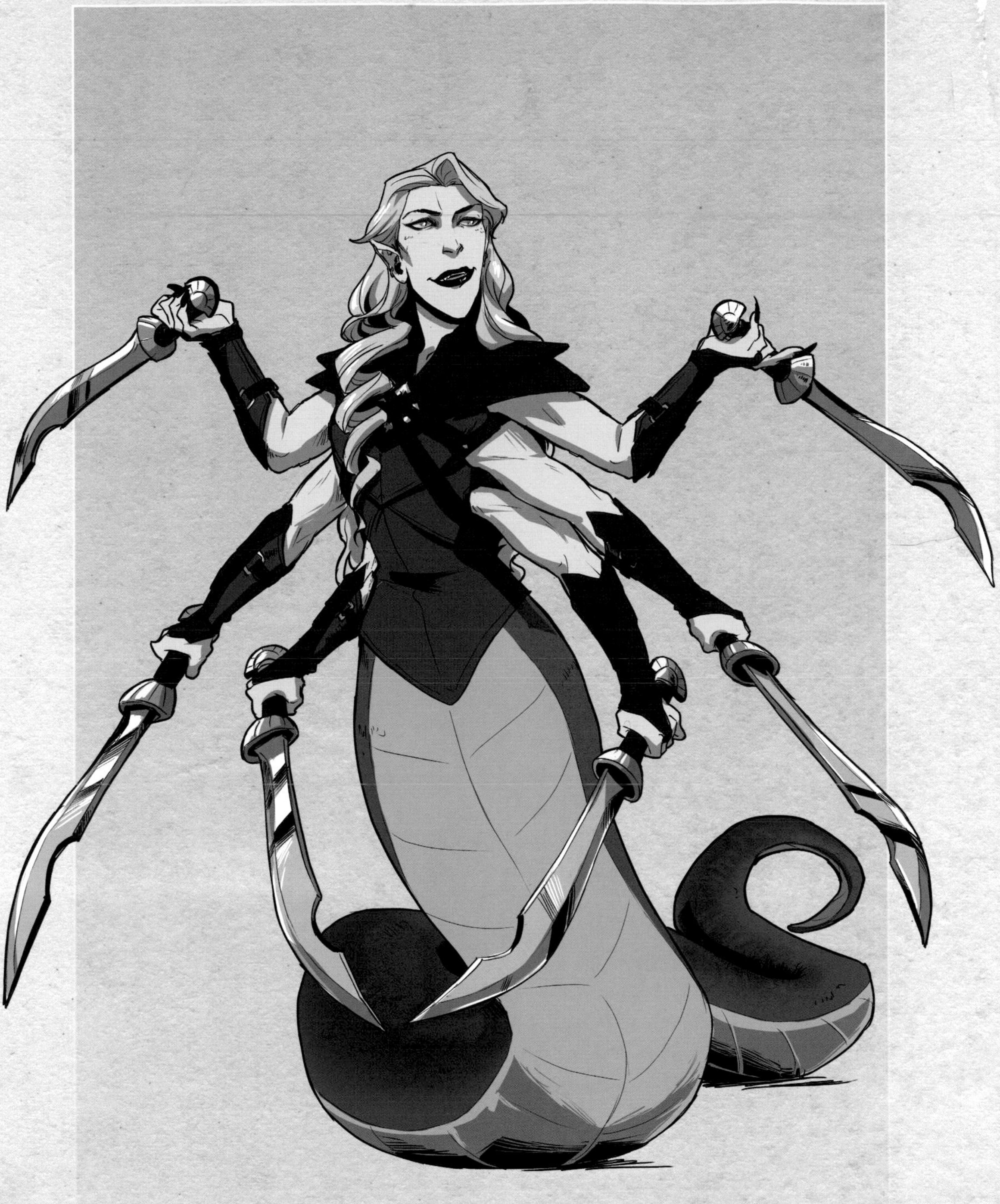

ULTIMATE ISELDA